Writings 1973–1983 on Works 1969–1979

Michael Asher

Writings 1973—1983 on Works 1969—1979

Written in collaboration with Benjamin H.D. Buchloh

Edited by Benjamin H.D. Buchloh

Primary Information

The Nova Scotia Series
Source Materials of the Contemporary Arts

Editor: Benjamin H. D. Buchloh

Bernhard Leitner	*The Architecture of Ludwig Wittgenstein*
Claes Oldenburg	*Raw Notes*
Yvonne Rainer	*Work 1961-1973*
Simone Forti	*Handbook in Motion*
Steve Reich	*Writings About Music*
Hans Haacke	*Framing and Being Framed*
Donald Judd	*Complete Writings 1959-1975*
Michael Snow	*Cover to Cover*
Paul—Emile Borduas	*Ecrits/Writings 1942-1958*
Dan Graham	*Video-Architecture-Television*
Carl Andre/Hollis Frampton	*12 Dialogues 1962-1963*
Daniel Buren	*Les Couleurs: sculptures Les Formes: peintures*
Leslie Shedden	*Mining Photographs and other Pictures 1948-1968*
Serge Guilbaut (ed.)	*Modernism and Modernity—The Vanvouver Conference Papers*

Volumes 1-8 were edited by Kasper Koenig

CONTENTS

Editor's Note

This volume—the fifteenth in the Nova Scotia Series —presents the work by Michael Asher from 1969 to 1979 and the descriptions and commentaries on this work that were written by Michael Asher for this book from 1973 (with my collaboration from 1978) to 1983. It is an attempt on the side of the author and the editor to make accessible to readers and viewers the documents of an artistic practice that one could characterize as being both extremely ephemeral and transient and that is—in the view of the editor—at the same time among the most concrete and materialist aesthetic productions of the Sixties and Seventies.

Asher's work committed itself to the development of a practice of situational aesthetics that insisted on a critical refusal to provide an existing apparatus with legitimizing aesthetic information, while at the same time revealing, if not changing, the existing conditions of the apparatus. More than any other artist of his generation that I am aware of did he maintain that stance once it had been defined after the shortcomings and compromises of Minimal art had become apparent in the late Sixties and Conceptual art had revealed its idealist fallacies.

When notions such as site specificity or dematerialization and the denial to commodify the work had already become myths that were used by the institutions to rejuvenate their legitimation at a historical moment when their liberal humanist public image had come under scrutiny by philosophers and artists alike, Asher's work increased the specificity of its critical analysis of the conditions of aesthetic production and reception with every work that he inscribed into the institutional framework. It is as a result of the radicality of that specific analysis (its emphasis on institutional and spatial contiguity, and a sense of temporality that is operational) that Asher's work —with the exception of one work in a public collection and another work that was commissioned by a private collector—has ceased to exist without any vestige whatsoever. In that respect alone it differs already from most other work of the conceptual period that objectified itself after all in the photo—

document, the written definition or the archive (as art object).

The book's paradoxical function—to document as discourse what operated as practice at one time (or, to be more accurate, as both, practice and discourse)—results partially from the fact that the work seems to have generated the same resistance on the side of the institutions (and the historians and critics and collectors) that it performed itself with respect to the notion of visual culture that they represent. Or, what is more appropriate historically, the definition of aesthetic production as it is inherent in Asher's work could not be accomodated culturally (as the work of most artists in the twentieth century who profoundly affected, if not outrightly dismantled the modernist framework). Quite to the opposite, as soon as the legitimation crisis of the institutions that contain the discourse of visual culture seemed to be overcome—not by a resolution of their increasingly apparent contradictions and conflicts of interest, of course, but by a rigid socio-political reconstitution of traditional hierarchies and the aesthetic myths that adorn them, the radical practice of artists of Asher's generation could be marginalized to the extent that the work was made to appear historical before it had even properly entered the culture. I hope it will be one of the functions of this volume to publicly contradict that tendency and to denegate the falsification of history that goes along with it.

If it is one of the paradoxes of this book to transfer from practice to discourse what was defined as a temporally and spatially specific and efficient operation, another one is its attempt to reconstruct the material data of the work as accurately as possible when in fact the work's strategies required a systematic abstention from a quantifiable enduring construct. In fact, one of the ambitions of the author and one of the most difficult and time-consuming tasks in the formation of the manuscript for this publication was the rendering and reconstruction of the actual data (architectural size, dimensions of areas affected by the particular work, placement, location, etc.) which indicate the problems of that transformation that the book tries to perform.

It might well turn out to be the most cumbersome aspect of the writings and on first glance the least attractive for readers working their way through the accumulation of minutely specified data and measurements of each individual installation. If this condition reflects certainly the author's concern to maintain the material element of his practice even within its transformation into discourse (and it might indicate his relative disregard for the latter), I would all the more emphasize that it is in this rigorous devotion to the materiality of his deconstructive practice that Asher's position might best be understood.

I might go further and say that among the many rewarding experiences that working with Michael Asher on this project implied, the most important has been the recognition to what extent of material detail the contemplation and analysis of history and ideology can be (and have to be) developed in order to generate knowledge through the construction of perceptual models. To put it simply: if the tradition of sculptural production upon which Asher has obviously founded the development of his work could have a meaningful continuation and evolution (and that mode of production could claim authenticity and validity) it would be in that devotion to *all* the material conditions within which an aesthetic construct is produced and perceived.

I would like to thank Michael Asher for having offered me the experience to work with him on this book and to have confronted me with those attitudes in his work and during the preparation of the manuscript. Among the many individuals who have been involved at some stage of the planning, preparation and production of this volume (their names are acknowledged separately) I would like to thank especially Lawrence Kenny, the architect who has produced most of the drawings and plans for the documentation with a clear understanding and a commitment to the project, and, resulting from that with excellence that not many contemporary architects would be willing to provide in their ambition to compete with, if not replace, the artist.

Furthermore, this volume of the Nova Scotia Series, probably more than any other before it, in the time and means that the production of the manuscript and the book required, has put considerable demands on Garry N. Kennedy, the president of the Nova Scotia College of Art & Design. For his continued support, and for his generous patience with and interest in a long and complicated project, I would like to express my sincere thanks.

Finally I would like to thank Gerald Pryor who has designed the book in collaboration with Michael Asher.

Benjamin H. D. Buchloh
New York, July 1983

Author's Introduction

Late in 1973 Kasper Koenig, then editor of the Press of the Nova Scotia College of Art and Design, proposed that I should publish a documentation of my work for the Nova Scotia Series. The projected volume should comprise writings and detailed documentation (photographs and architectural drawings) on each individual work that I had completed by the time of publication. I accepted the conditions set forth by this proposal since the book would provide me with an opportunity to document and problematize my production and it would offer a coherent reading of my work that would have remained otherwise isolated and dispersed.

From 1973–1976 I developed the first written drafts while I was teaching and while I continued to produce work. In 1976 Kasper Koenig left the Press of the Nova Scotia College to commit himself to different projects, and in 1978 Benjamin H.D. Buchloh was appointed as the new editor of the Press. Prior to his appointment, Benjamin Buchloh and I had corresponded on a contribution for the journal that he was editing at that time. We first met in 1976 at the Venice Biennale and we agreed that he would write an essay for the catalogue of my forthcoming exhibition at the Stedelijk van Abbe Museum in Eindhoven. In 1978 Benjamin Buchloh proposed the continuation of the book project, suggesting that the few initial writings and all future writings should be developed beyond their limits of material description and that they should include elements of a perceptual and theoretical analysis of my work.

I agreed to this proposal in spite of the risk inherent in such an approach. Because of the change in approaching the project, the editor had to invest a significant amount of time in the development of the writings. This book is therefore the result of a close collaboration between author and editor; the writings are often the result of a joint authorship. Nevertheless the reader should know that all proposals for description and analysis that were contributed by the editor, were examined carefully until I opted to include or exclude those proposals.

Although the reader might expect otherwise, this technique of writing in collaboration is most likely the slowest process, but both author and editor considered it to be the method that would guarantee as precise a documentation as currently possible.

In retrospect I can say that the nature of our working relationship was partly defined by Benjamin Buchloh's critical and historical interest in my practice. His contributions to the formation of this text affected the outcome of the project considerably. In my experience I do not know of any publication where an artist and a critic have shared authorship to this degree. Our collaboration has been essential for the analysis of the individual works as well as for an understanding of the general historical context. Yet I hope that the fusion of the two approaches has not resulted in a seamless text, but rather reveals the parallelism that exists within the two enterprises of art production and criticism that are generally considered separate if not oppositional.

As this manuscript was being proofread, Benjamin Buchloh and I were still discussing whether to add or subtract writings. Also, due to the circumstances of jointly writing the texts for this book, we had to agree to an artificial cut-off date for the writing and the documentation of my production. It would have meant to delay the publication of this volume endlessly if we had attempted to include every new work that I produced while the documentation was established for this publication. The date that we chose was 1979.

Even though the more recent work since 1979 seems less removed in time and more accessible, I would very much hope to publish at a later date a second volume. In the meantime the reader is encouraged to view the operation of my present work and compare it to the work in this documentation and its texts.

This book as a finished product will have a material permanence that contradicts the actual impermanence of the art-work, yet paradoxically functions as a testimony to that impermanence of my production.

Only those works were included in the documentation that were actually installed at some time in an

institutional context of a museum, commercial gallery or exhibition. All proposals or projects that I
might have submitted or considered and that turned
out to be unfeasible or were refused by the institution
for other reasons, are not considered to be work and
have therefore been excluded from the documentation.

Each chapter tries to assemble as accurately as
possible the documentation of the individual work (or
those aspects of it that can be represented in one
form or another): text, photographs, drawings and
architectural plans. Even though this will at best
approximate certain aspects of the actual work, I
hope the reader will be able to develop a critical
examination of the work on the grounds of this material.

I am indebted to Benjamin Buchloh for his
advice, the insight that he has invested into this
book project, of the time he spent assisting me with
writing and for his editing of the book.

I would also like to thank Kasper Koenig for the
commitment and guidance during the initial phase of
this project. Equally, my thanks should go to Garry N.
Kennedy, the president of the Nova Scotia College of
Art and Design, who has supported this project with
generosity and patience for an extended period of
time. I wish to thank also the various persons who
were on the staff of the Press of the Nova Scotia
College during the years of the preparation of this book
for their dedicated attention to the different stages of
its manuscript preparation and production.

Michael Asher
Los Angeles, March 1983

The author and editor would like to thank the following for having assisted in various ways in the preparation of the manuscript of this book:

Anna Astner
Daniel Buren
Dorit Cypis
Courtney Donnell
Thierry de Duve
Gerald Ferguson
Gretchen Glicksman
Marge Goldwater
Dan Graham
Ian Hazlitt
Kim Hubbard
Than Hyun
Gary Kibbins
John Knight

Connie Lewallen
Jennifer Licht
Sarah Pugh
Steve Prina
Thomas Repensek
Anne Rorimer
Cora Rosevear
Allan Scarth
Mark Stahl
Barbara Taylor
John Vinci
Bob Wilkie
Chris Williams

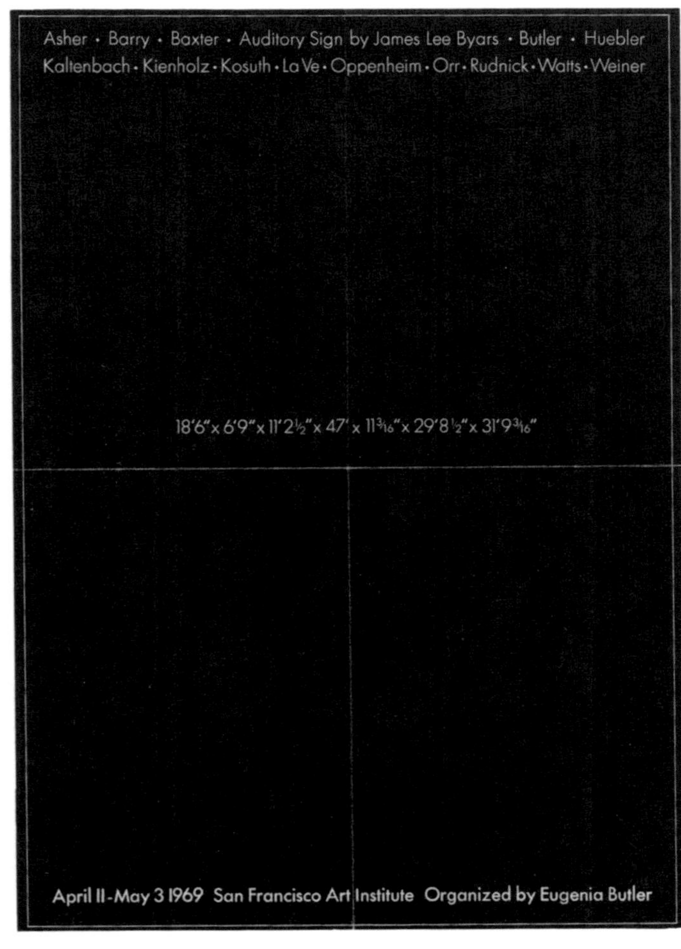

Poster and announcement for the exhibition "18′6″ X 6′9″ X 11′2½″ X 47′ X 11 3/16″ X 29′8½″ X 31′9 3/16″" at the San Francisco Art Institute, 1969.

The work at the San Francisco Art Institute was defined exclusively by the gallery's preexisting architectural elements and visible equipment. Givens were considered to be those elements that were not prefabricated or produced and not inserted from outside into the existing institution for the production of the work.

The given elements were: the whole real gallery space, whose aggregate wall dimensions were 41 feet-2 inches by 29 feet 8½ inches, with a maximum ceiling height of 36 feet. The gallery had three doors—one used for entry/exit, the second leading to an office, and the third one blocked off. Natural ambient light was diffused mainly from a skylight that bisected the length of the gallery, and from four windows, 20 feet off the floor; in addition, shielded fluorescent lights lined the perimeter of the gallery 10 feet from the floor.

The actual constituent elements of the work were interlocking modular wall panels. Nine of the panels (each 10 feet high by 4 feet wide) were attached together to form a 36-foot partition which was abutted against the 29 foot-8½ inch south structural wall. Installed 10 feet from the entry, the partition extended the length of the 41 foot-2 inch wall, forming a passageway to the larger area 5 feet 2 inches wide. Two thirds of the gallery were light and airy, but had no real exit; one-third was essentially a hallway, slightly darker, inviting the visitor to walk around the partition into the more open area.

Installation took less than half a day and was accomplished with the assistance of students from the art school. Once the panels were joined together, the vertical seams were finished with tape and painted to create a continuous wall, similar to the preexisting exhibition walls. The structural walls were 26 feet higher than the partition walls.

Modular walls are designed to function as a backdrop for the presentation of paintings and objects using real space. They are successfully employed in exhibition institutions to vary interior architectural design and to increase the existing amount of wall surface. They are support and decoration for the work as opposed to being part of the work. Modular walls involve

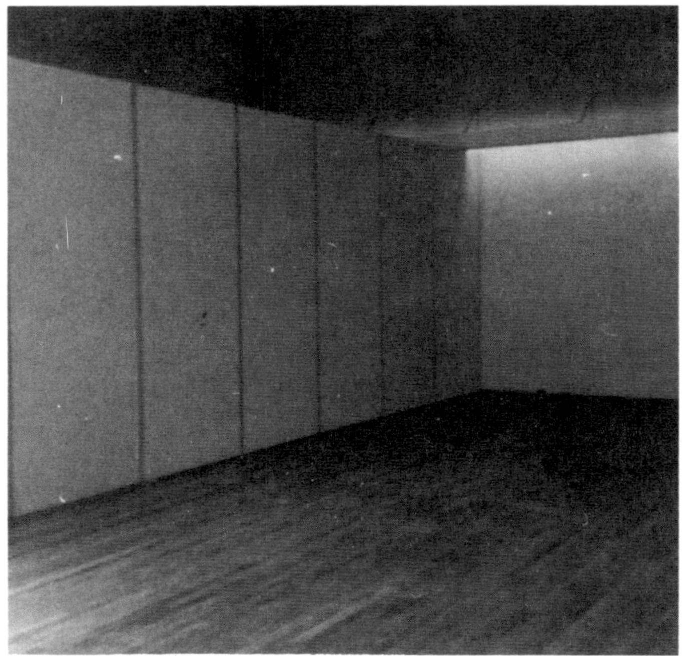

South wall during the construction of partition wall. Photographs by Michael Asher.

South wall with open entry/exit of gallery space and smaller bisected area on the left with partition wall installation during construction.

North wall with end of partition wall installation during construction. Closed curtains behind the north wall cover mural by Diego Rivera.

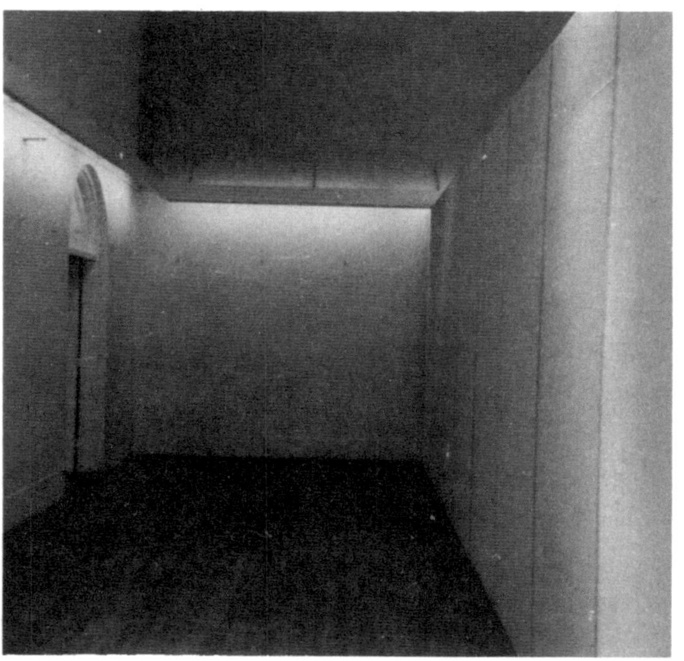

a structural ambiguity: they constitute a static structure, whereas, in fact, they are movable; they appear to be architectural surfaces when they are really planar objects.

The decision to use existing elements as determinants for the work—as opposed to prefabricated materials—was based on the assumption that the viewer will most likely be familiar with certain pre-existing characteristics of the institutional context. The work related, therefore, more directly to the viewer's prior experience of that context, making it less likely to be read as an arbitrary abstraction.

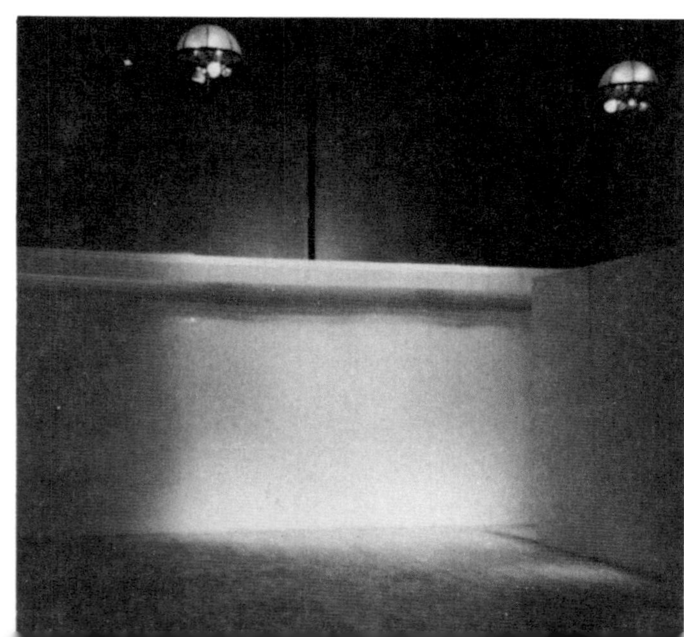

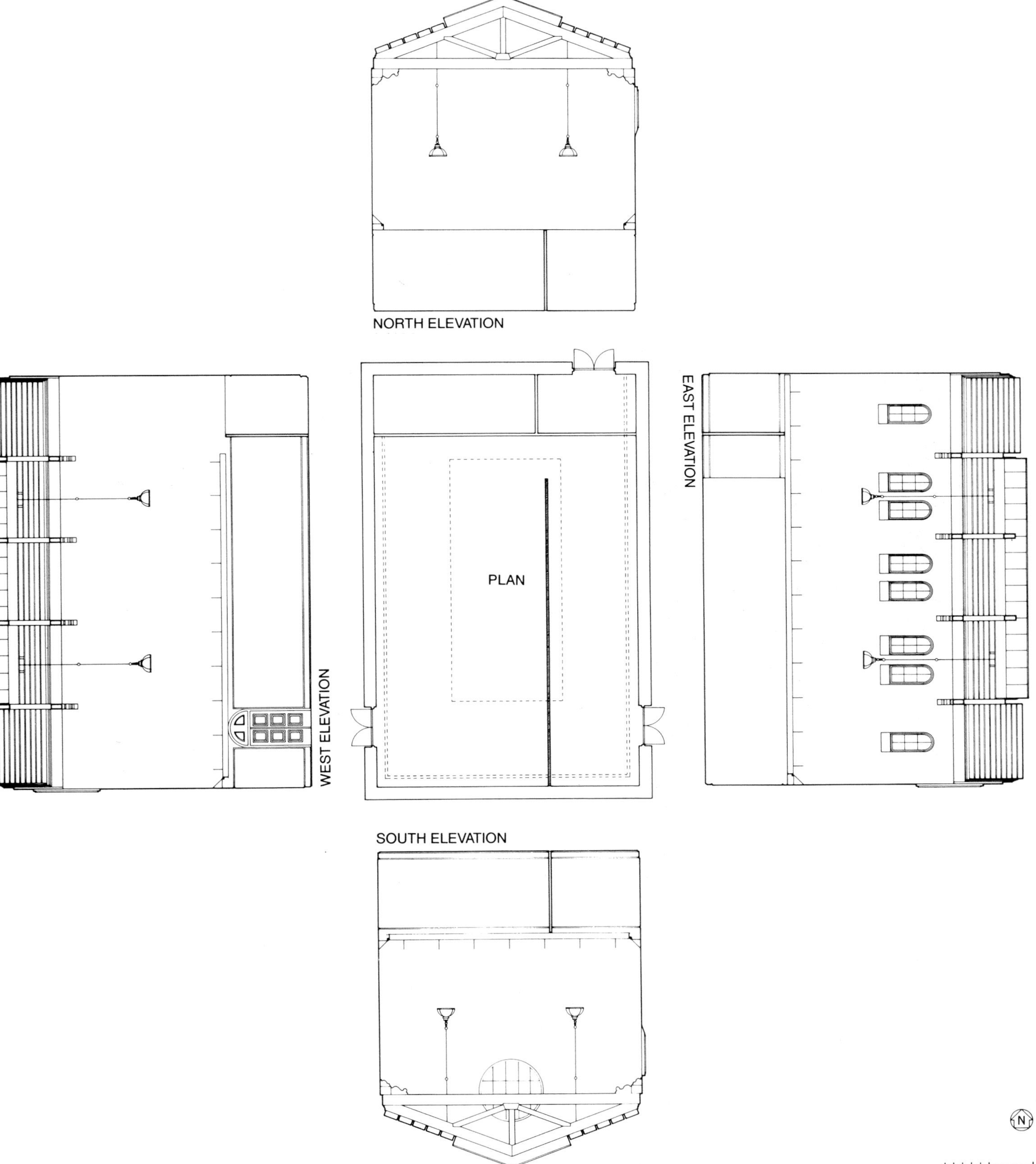

Ground plan and elevations of the installation in the Diego Rivera
Gallery. Drawing by Lawrence Kenny.

Completed partition wall installation photographed from the passageway between the entry/ exit zone area on the left and the open area on the right. Photograph by Phil Linhares.

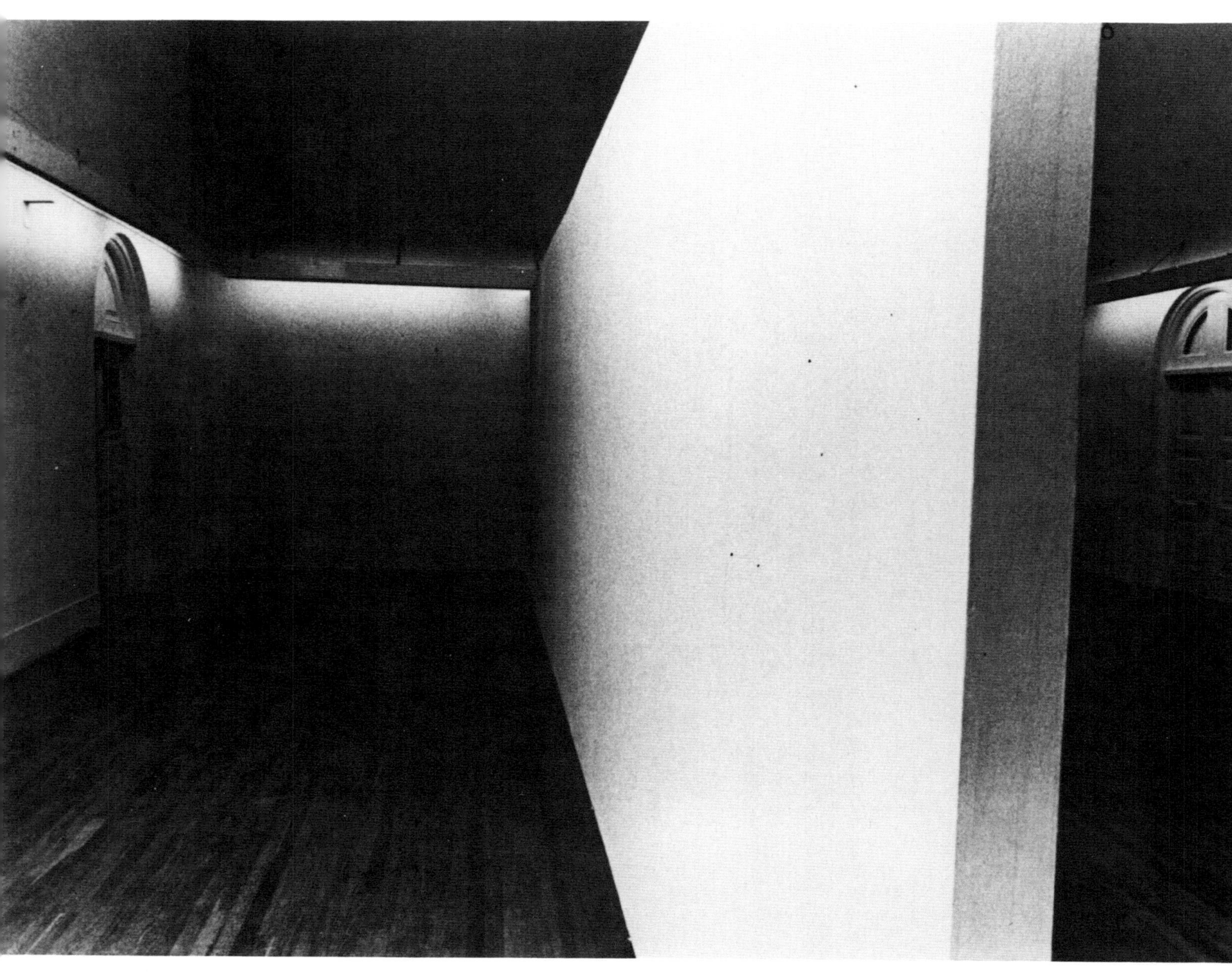

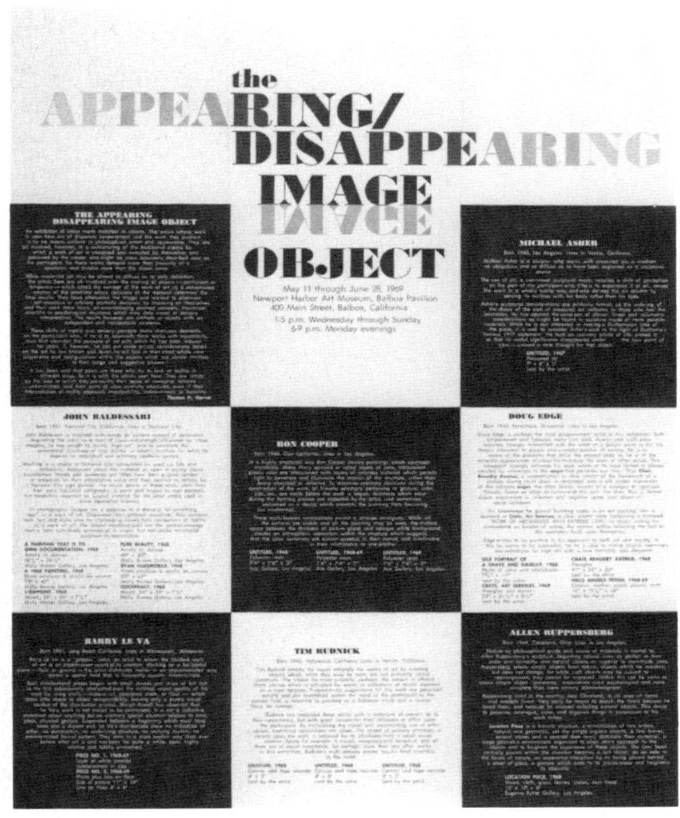

Poster/Announcement for the exhibition "The Appearing/
Disappearing Image/Object" at the Newport Harbor Art Museum,
1969.

In response to Joe Goode's window paintings of the mid-sixties, and wondering why he would not use the actual windows as he claimed to be interested in the window phenomenon, I decided to open my own window and sit beside it, and feel the air as it passed through. This was the first step that eventually led to the air works.

Next I opened various windows in the apartment in east-west directions and observed the air as it condensed and accelerated in corridorlike zones of the apartment (Venturi effect). Finally, I bought a standard fan from Sears and placed it on the floor.

In the airworks I attempted to avoid specific, formally ordered art-object materiality. Most of the air works were ready for public exhibition by the end of 1967. A group of pressured air works had already been installed in 1967 in a garage adjacent to my apartment. The production of these works is documented in the sales receipts for materials bought for their construction. On August 2, 1967, I purchased a simple fixed fan from Sears.

On August 4 I returned the fixed fan and purchased two oscillating floor-model fans. On August 8 I bought a Dayton airblower to see what it would do in combination with the oscillating floor fans. I decided that I wanted the air-generating units concealed, so on August 27 I purchased from L & M Lumber some two-by-fours to frame-in the ceiling, and, a little later, enough drywall to finish the garage walls and construct four-by-four movable panels to be placed above the ceiling frame. The air blower was installed above the ceiling to generate a vertical column of accelerated air from ceiling to floor. The diameter of the ceiling outlet was approximately 4 inches, the column diameter gradually increasing toward the floor. The air units were moved around to different ceiling outlets to produce linear, ambient, and planar bodies of air for a more efficient and versatile air-delivery system. On October 31 of the same year I purchased two large air-conditioning blowers and mounted them on adjustable platforms suspended above the ceiling. I constructed a plenum chamber to equalize the air generated by the blowers. Ducting attached to the blowers made it possible to create a continuous planar body of air and to insert it like a wall across the full width of the garage from floor to ceiling.

Subsequently I extended the ducting so that it delivered air simultaneously to four outlets approximately 4 inches in diameter, located in all four corners, which directed air at an angle to converge at the center of the garage floor. Finally, I installed the two oscillating fans above the ceiling at opposite ends on the same side to generate randomly phased light air currents throughout the space. A fine mesh screen fit over the ceiling outlet to diffuse the air.

All the hardware was given away or sold in the summer of 1968, except the Dayton blower with its flexible tubing. Further development in the areas of noise reduction and columniation based on greater technical know-how and improved equipment resulted in the exhibition "The Appearing/Disappearing Image/Object", and later, at the Whitney Museum of American Art, New York, in the exhibition "Anti-Illusion: Procedures/Materials."

In the Newport Harbor installation, a planar body of air was located just inside the main passageway to the inner gallery of the museum. The pressured air extended across the entranceway so that visitors encountered it on entering or leaving the museum. At point of origin the plane was 3 feet wide (parallel to the doorway) and 3 feet ⅜ inches thick, and dispersed gradually in both dimensions until it reached the floor and spread into ambient air.

The planar air body was generated by a self-contained blower unit (rented from Curtainaire of California). The blower was centered—with approximately 1 foot on either side—between the joists of a suspended ceiling (4 feet by 7 feet), which had been constructed and attached to the existing west wall at the height of the doorheader, 6 feet 7 inches from the floor. The length of the constructed ceiling concealed the blower unit from view.

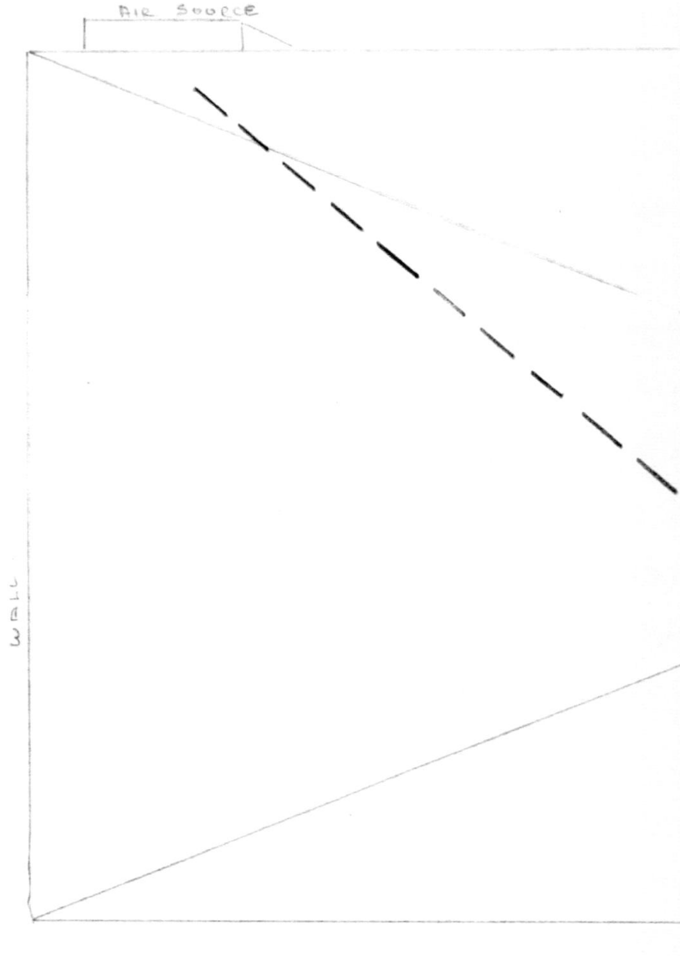

Diagram for a series of air works 1965-1966. This is one of
four air works which were installed in Michael Asher's garage
in 1965-1966. Drawing by Michael Asher.

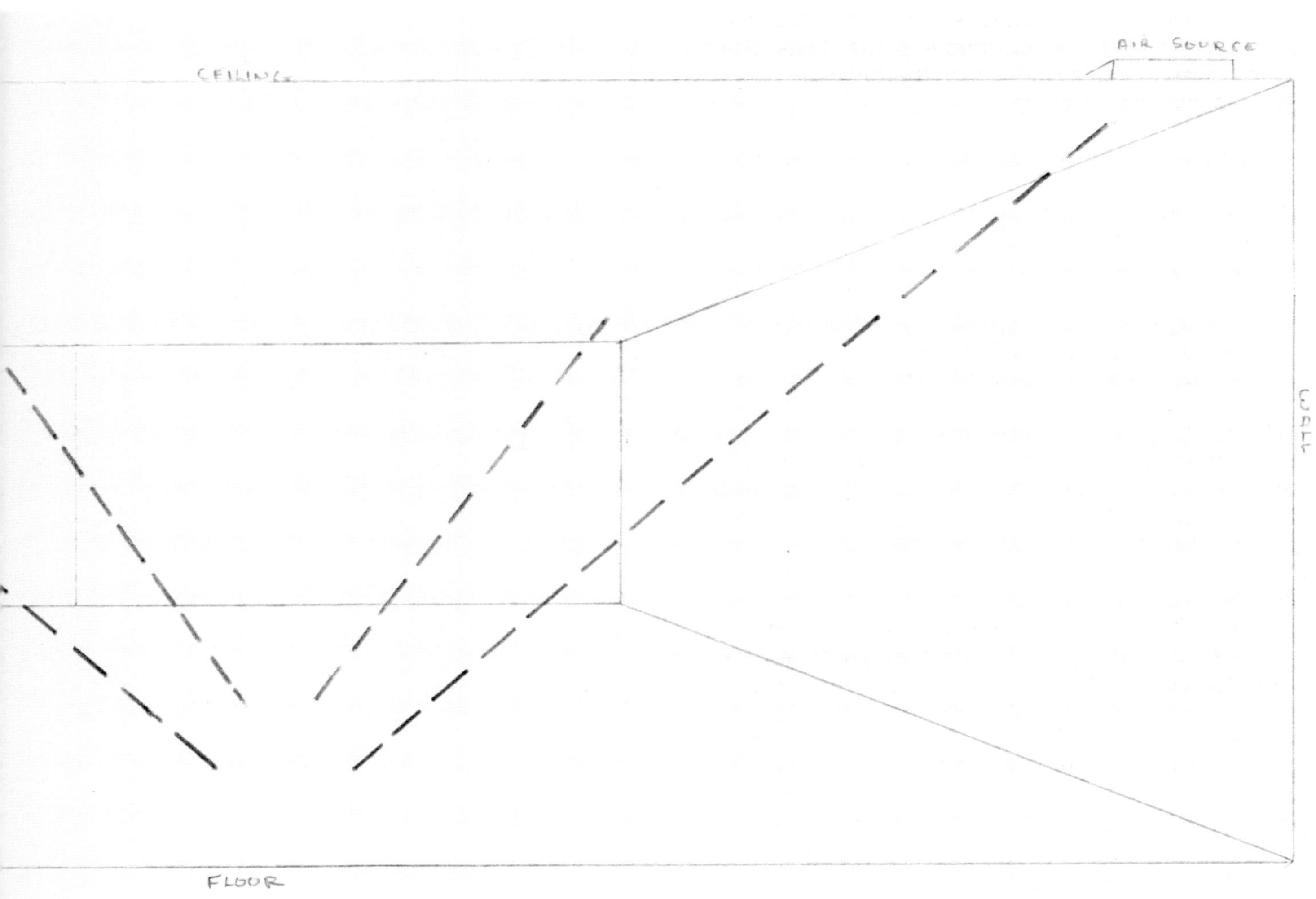

A planar body of pressured air, 8 feet high and 5 feet long, extended across an existing 8-foot wide passageway between the large gallery of the fourth floor and Gallery 401. The air body was produced by a self-contained blower and plenum-chamber unit with velocity control, custom engineered by and rented from Air Economy Corporation.

A container for the air-blowing unit was constructed and mounted at doorhead level flush with a preexisting architectural recess, thereby lowering the existing doorframe by approximately 2 feet. The housing contained the bracing, the unit itself, and sound-insulating material; a narrow air-intake opening was provided along the ceiling of the small gallery as well as an air-outlet grill in the constructed doorheader. The enclosure corresponded to the architectural detail in structure and finish and appeared from both sides of the doorway as if it were part of the wall. The velocity of the airstream was reduced to a minimum. The blower maintained a consistent level of air pressure along the grill and the laminar airflow gradually expanded from ceiling to floor, leaving unaccelerated air to the left side of the passage, so that the airflow could be bypassed unnoticed.

The noise level of the blower was also kept to a minimum so that it was hardly noticeable over the noise level of the room.

In this work I was dealing with air as an elementary material of unlimited presence and availability, as opposed to visually determined elements. I intervened therefore to structure this material, given in the exhibition container itself, and to reintegrate it into the exhibition area.

It was necessary to enclose the generating device and integrate the enclosure with its architectural context in order to focus the viewer's attention on an ordered body of air, juxtaposed to and continuous with the ambient air that was defined by the exhibition container.

The works in this group show ranged from such expressively solid sculptural pieces as Richard Serra's *House of Cards* to the extreme subtlety of my laminar airflow. Understanding the potential for comparative analysis of different works and their possible interrelationship within an exhibition, I decided to reduce the velocity of the airflow to a minimum.

Considering the terms of this exhibition ("Anti-Illusion: Procedures/Materials") and the works it contained, I felt that reducing the airflow would strengthen its conceptual dimension.

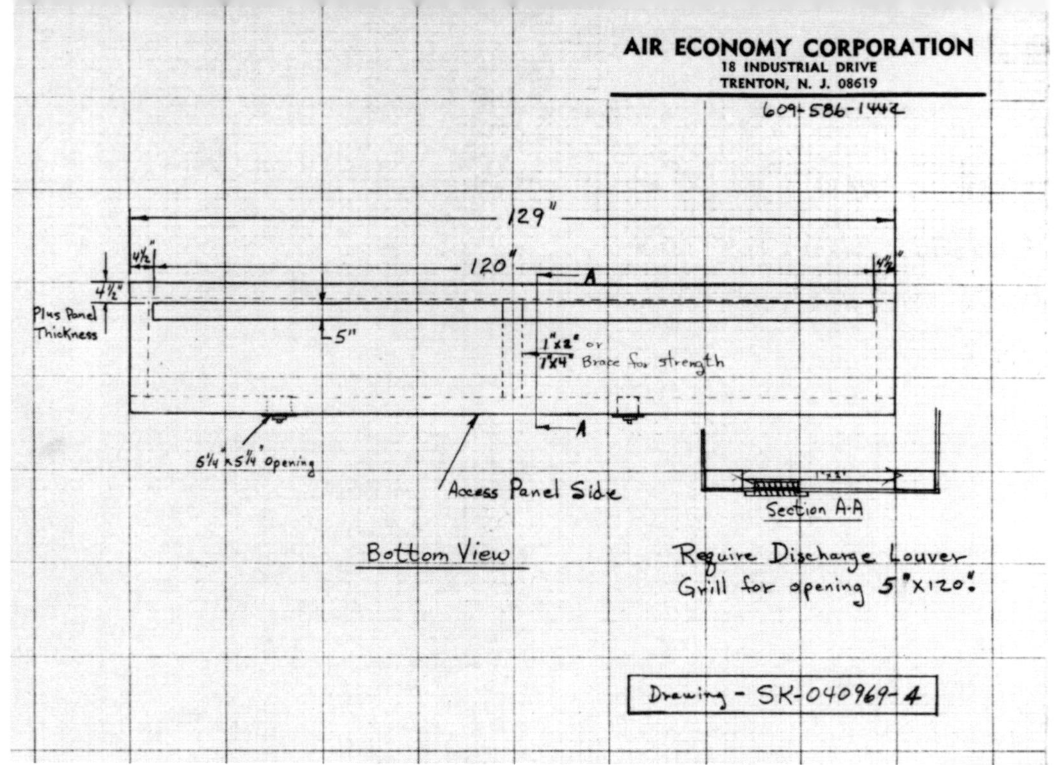

Bottom View

Section of installation

End View

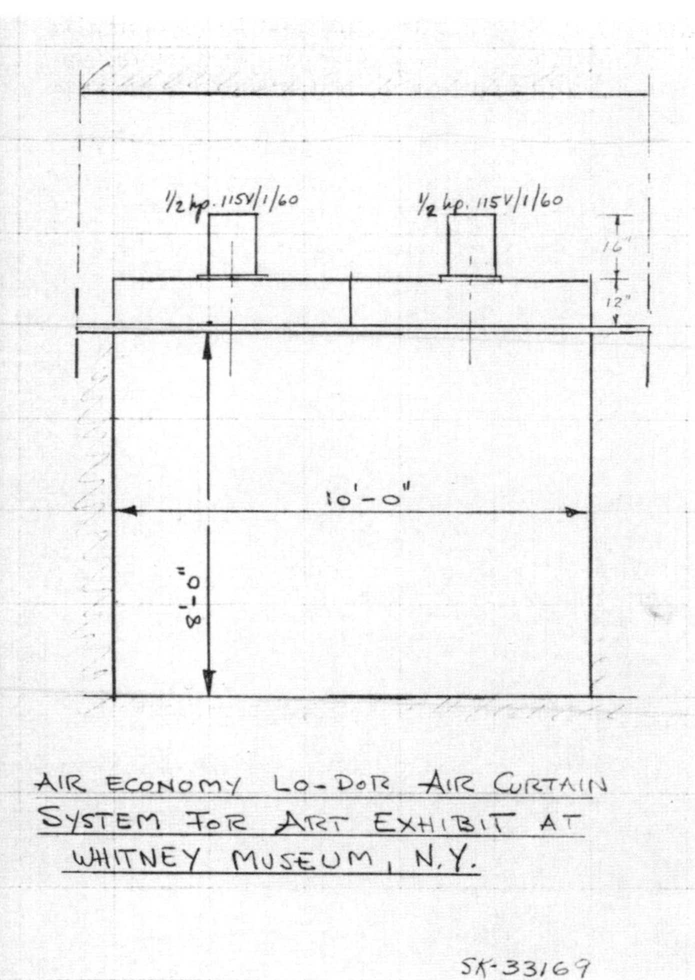

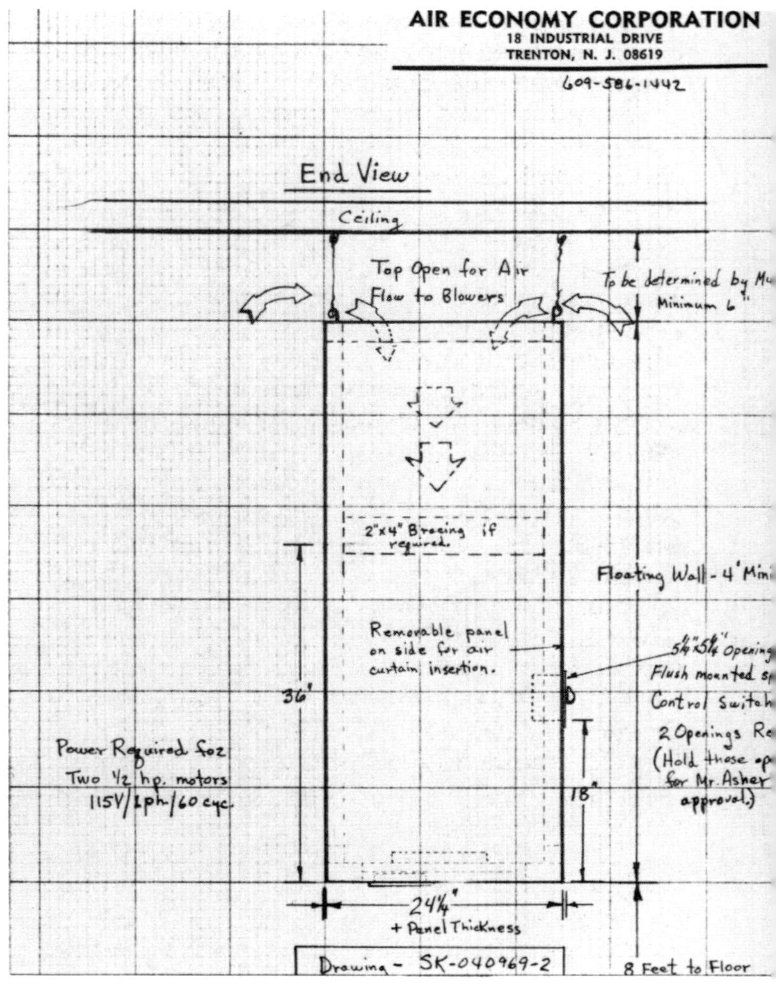

Preliminary construction plans for the air-curtain installation
by Michael Asher, designed by Air Economy Corporation.

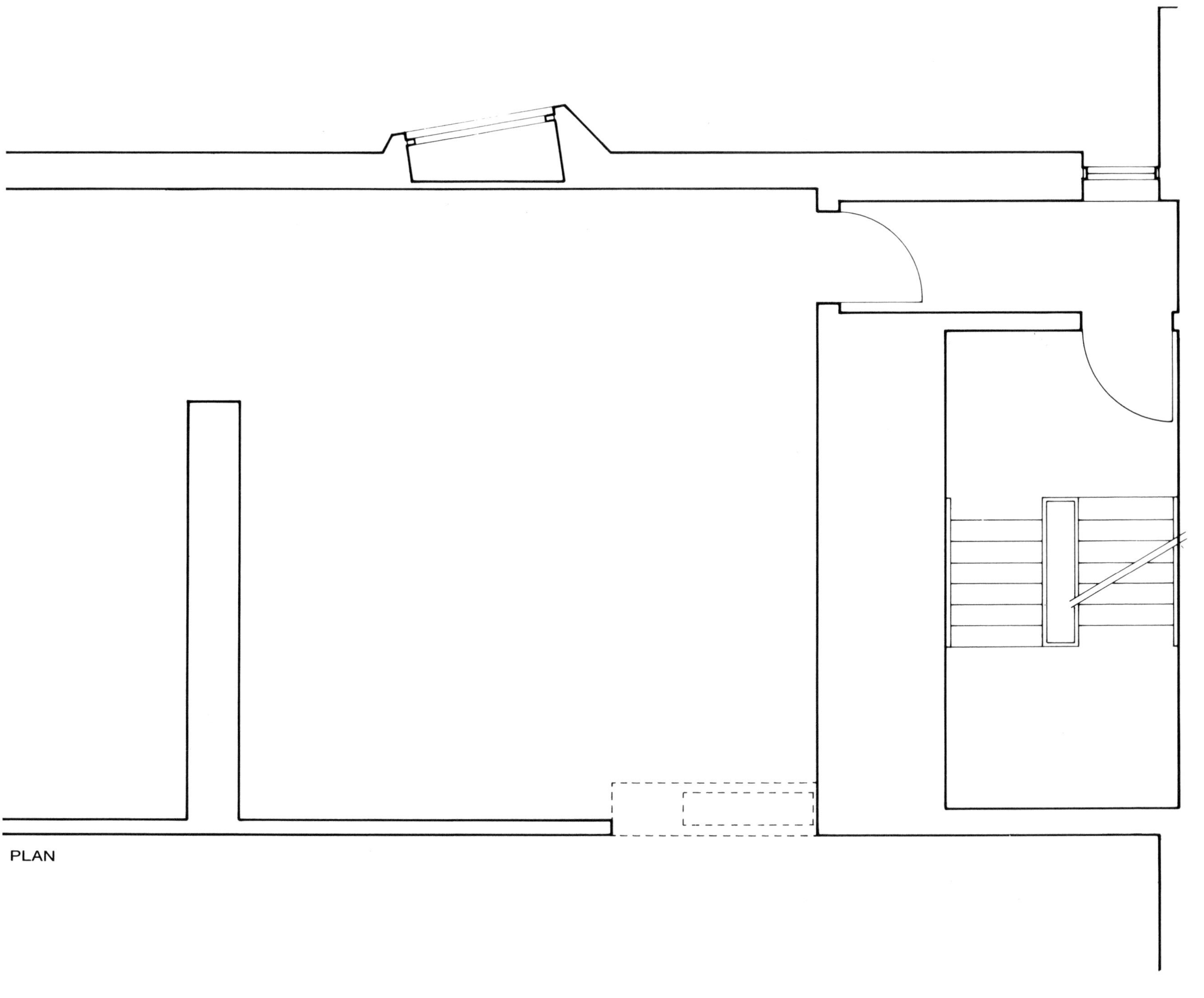

PLAN

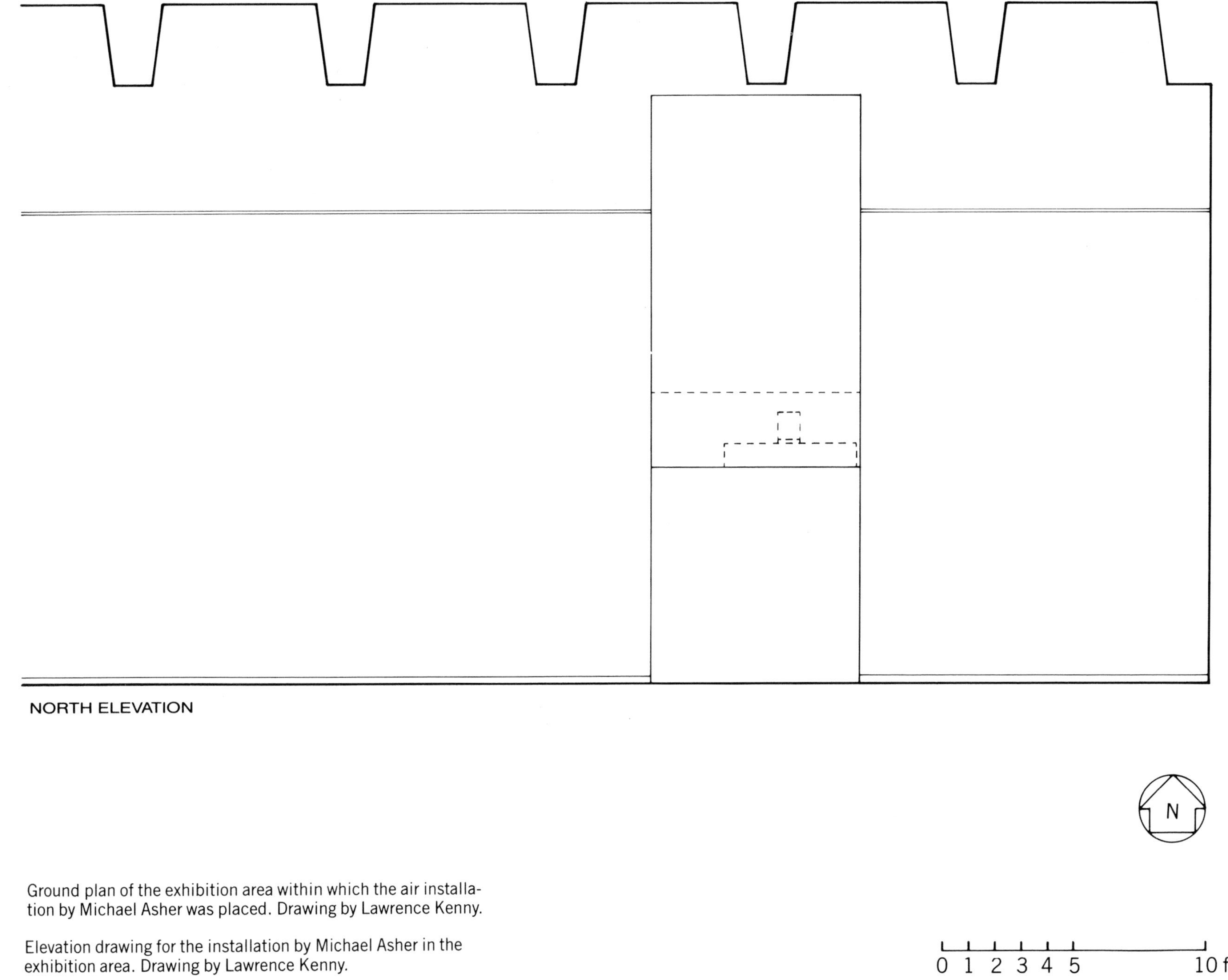

Ground plan of the exhibition area within which the air installation by Michael Asher was placed. Drawing by Lawrence Kenny.

Elevation drawing for the installation by Michael Asher in the exhibition area. Drawing by Lawrence Kenny.

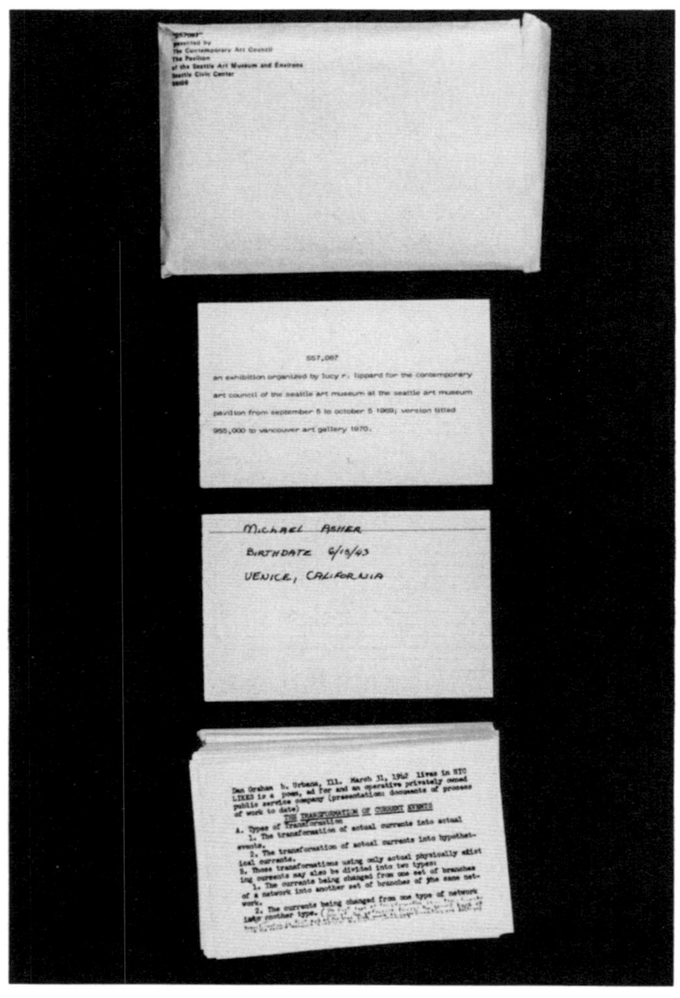

Index cards and envelope functioning as catalogue of the exhibition "557087" at the Seattle Art Museum Pavilion.

Until now I had not attempted to investigate the function of a space in its own terms. In all instances, my work—like that of most contemporary artists that I knew of—was involved with adding an element into a given architectural context. Even though the work at the San Francisco Art Institute had reduced this practice of adding objects to a given space to the use of objects already found within the given space, the Seattle installation was the first time the actual entire space was incorporated in the work.

After accepting an invitation to participate in a group exhibition at the Seattle Art Museum Pavilion, my original proposal turned out to be unrealizable. I submitted no further proposal on arrival, and was given a place in the exhibition area and five days to do the work.

Throughout the museum the ceiling height was 15 feet; in the area allocated for my work, which measured 18 feet by 30 feet, the ceiling was 9 feet high. The viewer could reach the area from the main entrance of the pavilion by crossing the adjacent large exhibition space, where numerous works by other artists were on display. This exhibition space was illuminated primarily by natural light entering from the south facade's glass curtain wall.

I partitioned the space with two movable walls (9 feet by 9 feet) to bisect its width and to reduce its size to approximately a squarelike format. The area's 14-foot width was formed by two parallel preexisting walls. The preexisting wall adjacent to the large gallery was 11 feet long, thus leaving an 8-foot access to the area. Parallel to this wall I placed a third movable wall (8 feet by 9 feet) in front of the accessway, 2½ feet into the large gallery.

The third movable wall also functioned as a light baffle for the large gallery's glass curtain wall. It served simultaneously as a screen for artificial light from the interior of the partially enclosed area, where two 150-watt blue spotlights were installed in preexisting ceiling sockets that were directed toward the screen. The rest of the fluorescent and incandescent light fixtures of the enclosed space were not used.

Drawing by Michael Asher, documenting the elements
and their placement in the installation for the
Seattle Art Museum Pavilion, September 1969.

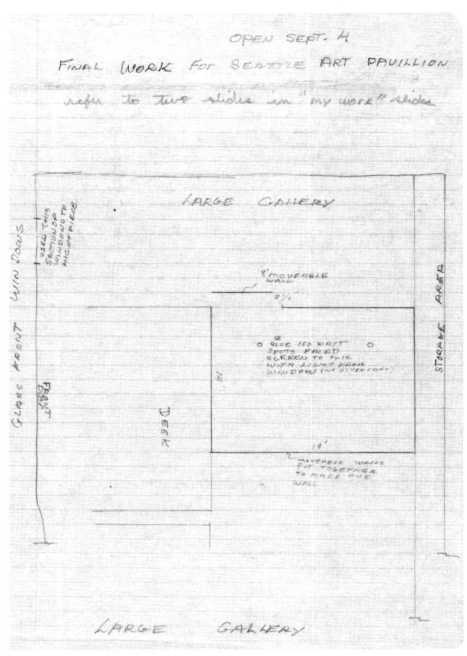

The natural light converged at the baffle and merged with the artificial light in the partially enclosed area. The artificial light did not pass through the screen.

The surface of the structural walls of the enclosed space and the movable walls were all covered in the same light burlap. Both static and movable walls were framed by anodized aluminum angles. The movable walls were weighted at the bottom so that they could stand without being secured to the floor. The color of the floor was approximately the same as the color of the walls. Where the movable walls were joined and where they joined the structural walls in the partially enclosed room, I fabricated three wooden blocks which were inserted into the walls at their bases. The vertical seam between the two movable walls was covered with masking tape to make a continuous wall similar to the continuity of the permanent walls.

The three wooden blocks, the masking tape, and the two blue light bulbs were the only objects added to the 14 foot-by-18 foot area. The two movable walls as objects created the partially enclosed space. The condition of the third movable wall was clearly defined: it served as a partition for entry/exit; connected to the ceiling, it was visible from both sides. Each part of the enclosed area could be seen in terms of its prior or temporary function.

Can space itself become an object of perception? I would have created an enclosure in a given enclosure because that was the only way to adapt the proposition to the given conditions of the group show.

It is very clear that I was creating a space in relation to all these objects. If you create an enclosure in an enclosure, it is considered a more intimate space.

Either everybody in the show objectified his work or the artists closed their works off.

I had always asked myself: "Why put stuff on the wall, why put stuff on the floor?" And then I ended up facing the fact that what I was doing was probably an object. Looking at blue light, I wanted people to see that they were looking at blue light.

What is the difference between making a room with nothing in it and inserting an object into a room?

What is a room with nothing in it? After all, it was made out of a lot of stuff, but people treated it as though it was an empty, leftover room of the museum that had not been filled, with blue lights in it. There was still the question: "Why place anything at all in a room, in a space, in an area?"

The work emerged historically at precisely the moment when Minimal sculpture developed into Conceptual art. The work tried to come to terms with both, without being part of either. At the time of the Seattle show I still thought of the artist as being an innovator. So I asked: "Why are all these artists continuing to produce objects?" I wasn't aware of what I was doing: I was doing objects. Real space for me was defined as the space between the object and the viewer.

The work is accepting the concrete materiality of preexisting givens, or responding to the aesthetic practice of the moment; which is to say, that the work is essentially an inquiry into aesthetic practice.

Traditional practice had been to insert something into a space rather than to comment on that insertion. A space with an object in it is dominated by the object, rather than by itself.

So the idea in this work was to use the partially enclosed area as the object.

The work could be analyzed in terms of its specific situation, or its entire cultural context. It wasn't the walls that were objectified, for they were treated as secondary objects. Nor could they be conceived of as a support system, since I used them for something else. Any analysis assumed either a sculptural or architectural determinant. Yet a sculptural approach would have defeated the purpose.

The walls were still part of the building for me: I wanted to incorporate their *use* into my work; once incorporated into the work, they would be read differently, as long as they did not have anything on them. Their use is a cultural definition, so once again I was responding to a cultural definition.

By concretizing the work you automatically have *some* material analysis, and a theoretical analysis at the same time. Why would an analysis always have to

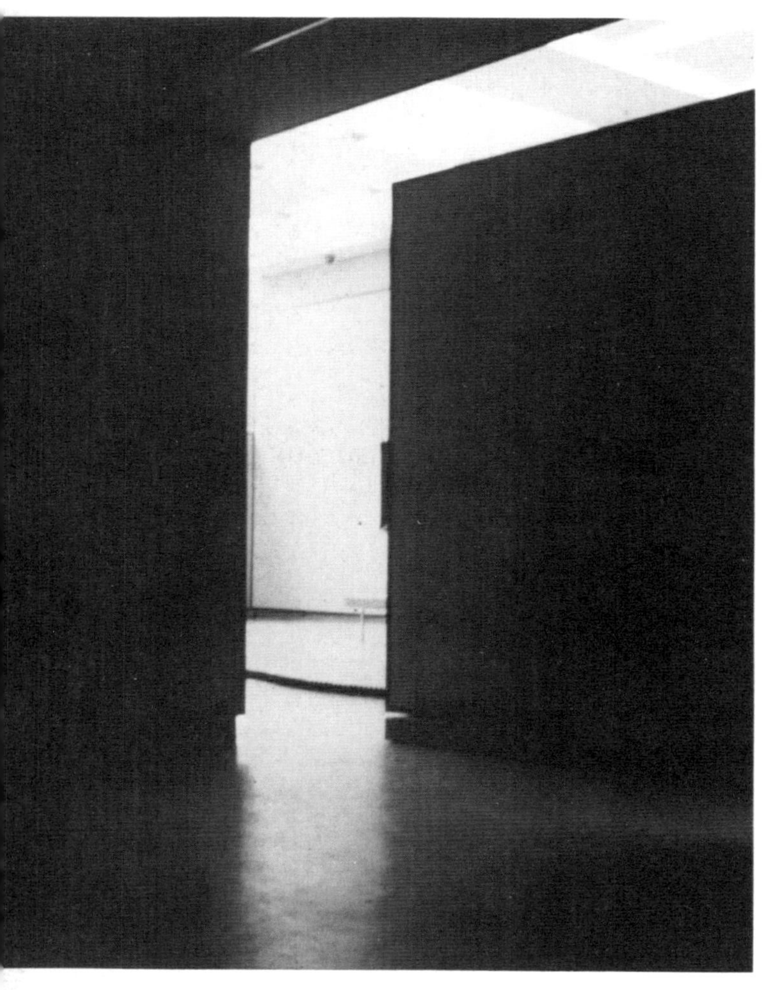

precede the fact? I first felt that an analysis partly precedes, and partly comes after the fact. My feeling is now that one could pose the analysis oneself, but it would be a very self-conscious act. One might say that the fact that the work relates to other works directly makes it a response.

Detail view of the installation showing passageway and partition wall (camera viewing northeast direction).

Detail view into the installation from passageway (camera viewing southwest).

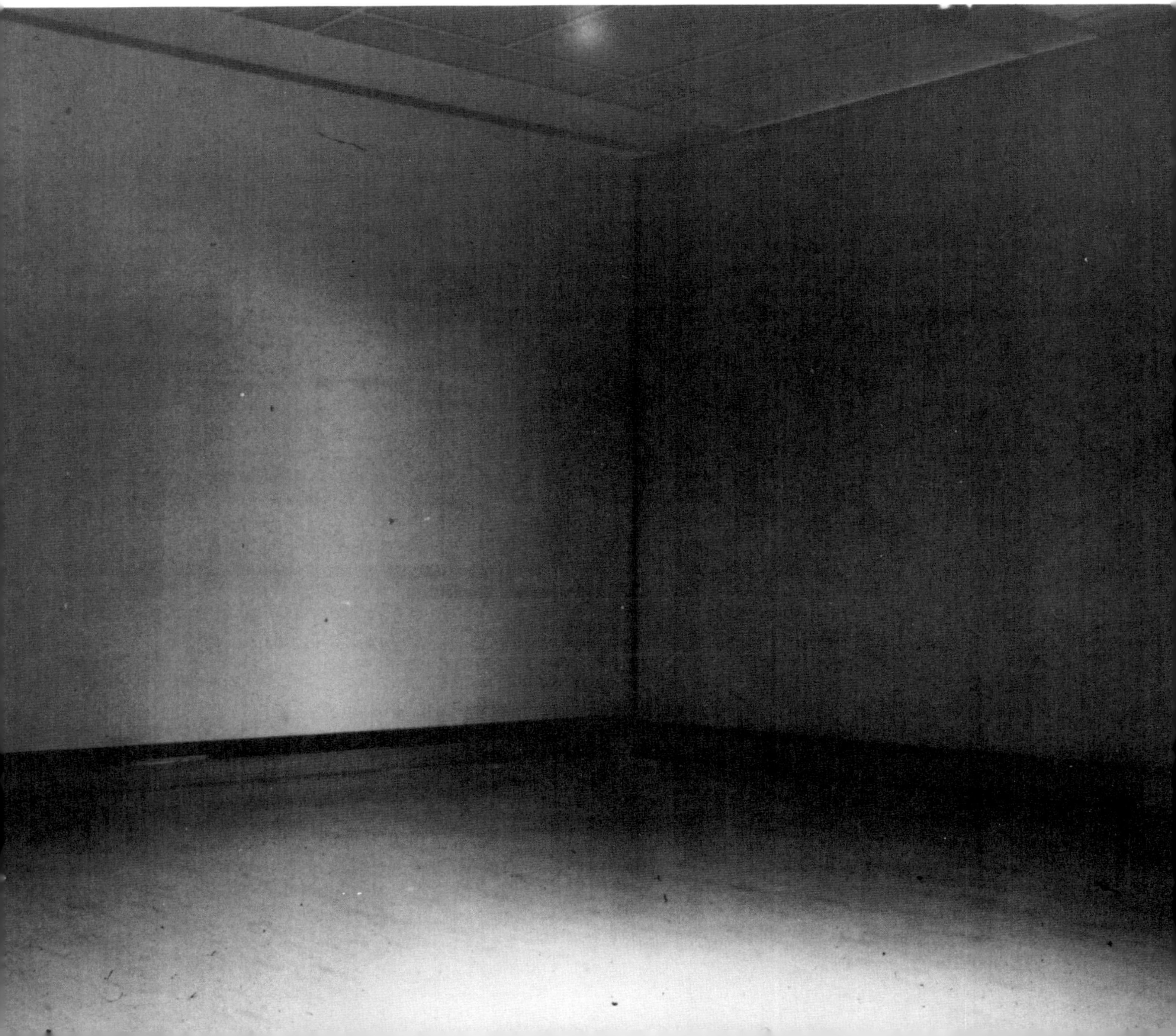

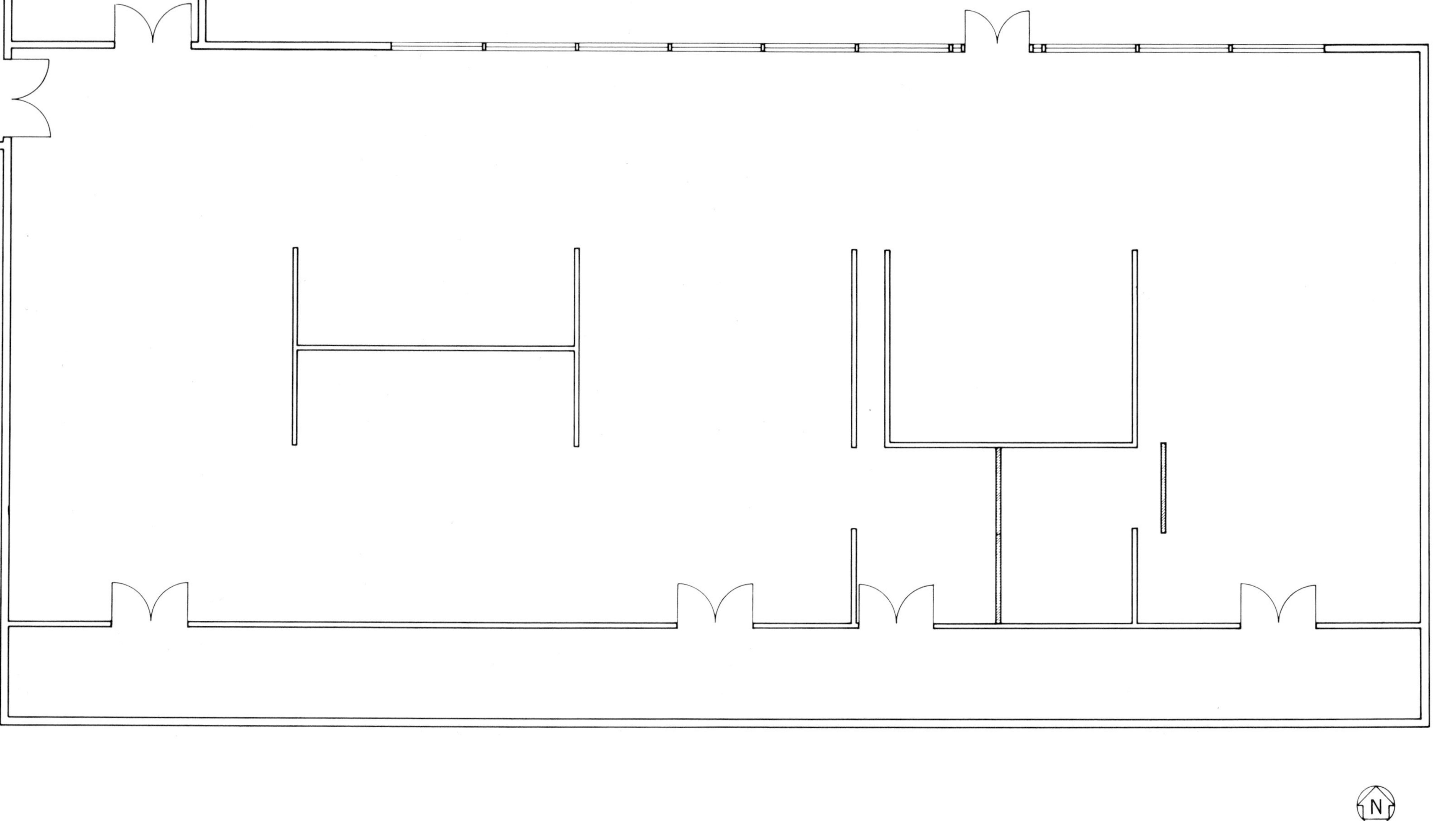

Seattle Art Museum Pavilion, Ground plan. Drawing by Lawrence Kenny.

Seattle Art Museum Pavilion, Interior Elevation. Drawing by
Lawrence Kenny.

WEST ELEVATION FROM GALLERY

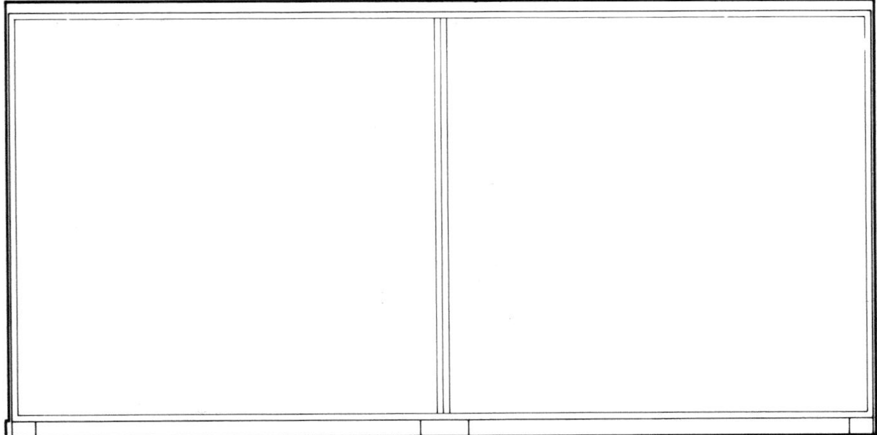

WEST ELEVATION OF INSTALLATION

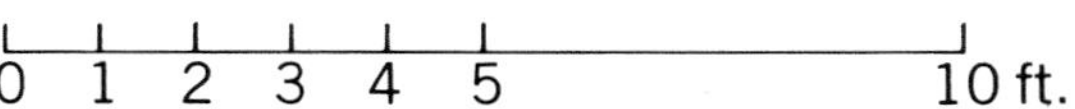

Early in 1969, Lawrence Urrutia, then Curator at the La Jolla Museum of Art in California, invited me to do a one-person exhibition which was to be open to the public from November 7 to December 31, 1969.

The Meyer Gallery, where the exhibition was located, was a room in a private house designed by Irving Gill in 1915, which had been modified by Mosher and Drew in 1948, and again modified in 1960 to serve as a museum. The actual dimensions of the room were 37 feet 8 inches on the north-south axis and 23 feet on the east-west axis.

The ceiling was 8 feet 11 inches high, recessed all around 4 inches deep and 35 inches wide. Above the perimeter of the lower ceiling, incandescent lights were installed and covered with glass at a 45-degree angle. At the centers of the east and south walls were two passageways, each 5 feet wide: the south-wall passageway was 6 feet 10 inches high and the east-wall passageway, which led into a small room that since then has been closed off, was approximately the same height.

For the purposes of this exhibition a complete floor-to-ceiling wall was constructed 3 feet 6 inches in from, and parallel to, the passageway of the south wall, stopping short of the west wall by 3 feet. This resulted in an entrance partition and an 11 feet hallway between the constructed space and the existing space. The area within the gallery when completed measured 23 feet by 29 feet 2¼ inches.

A third and fourth wall were butted at 90-degree angles to the east side of the south-wall entry-passage: one closing off the 3½-foot-wide hallway in order to direct the viewer to the entry/exit passage; and the other extending 52 inches into the outside corridor, to function as a baffle against noise and light filtering into the room.

A speaker was installed into the east-wall entry-passage and this entry was surrounded by a drywall construction, closing it flush with the gallery wall. Also, flush with the white surface of the drywall, a matching white cloth was attached to cover the open speaker elements.

Two fabricated aluminum shields each 48 inches long were attached to the functioning perimeter lights at the center point 14 feet 6⅛ inches of the north-south axis.

Behind the glass face of the perimeter fixtures, blue gels, diffusers, and polarizers were attached to produce a low level of tinted light.

All other incandescent lights within the perimeter fixtures were disconnected. Therefore the light shields directed light towards the center of the floor where the light dispersed evenly across the gallery. The intensity of the light gradually decreased from the center to the wall surfaces.

The walls appeared as though they were evenly generating light, creating an illusion, on first observation, of changing spatial depth.

Existing and newly constructed wall surfaces were made of drywall and finished with white paint. The original white sound-dampening finish of the ceiling surface was left untouched. The floor was covered for this exhibition with a white wall-to-wall carpet so that both of the horizontal surfaces in the room had a sound-dampening quality. I also attempted in this way to establish a visual conformity between the walls, floor, and ceiling of the gallery.

The sound equipment consisted of an audio oscillator, an amplifier, and a speaker. This equipment generated a constant tone at a very low frequency (approximately 85 cps) which was amplified only enough to be audible. The vertical surfaces responded to the sound frequency, which caused them to resonate as if they were tuned, while the horizontal surfaces, due to their sound-dampening effect, reduced the frequency. The cancellation of the sound waves occurred when these frequencies coincided. The sound waves cancelled each other out at a point exactly in the center of the gallery and, on a diagonal axis, on the right hand side of each corner. Up to each point of sound wave cancellation, the sound increased gradually in intensity; whereas at the exact cancellation point none of the generated sound was heard.

The work which I had done just previous to this

First-floor ground plan of the La Jolla Museum of Art.

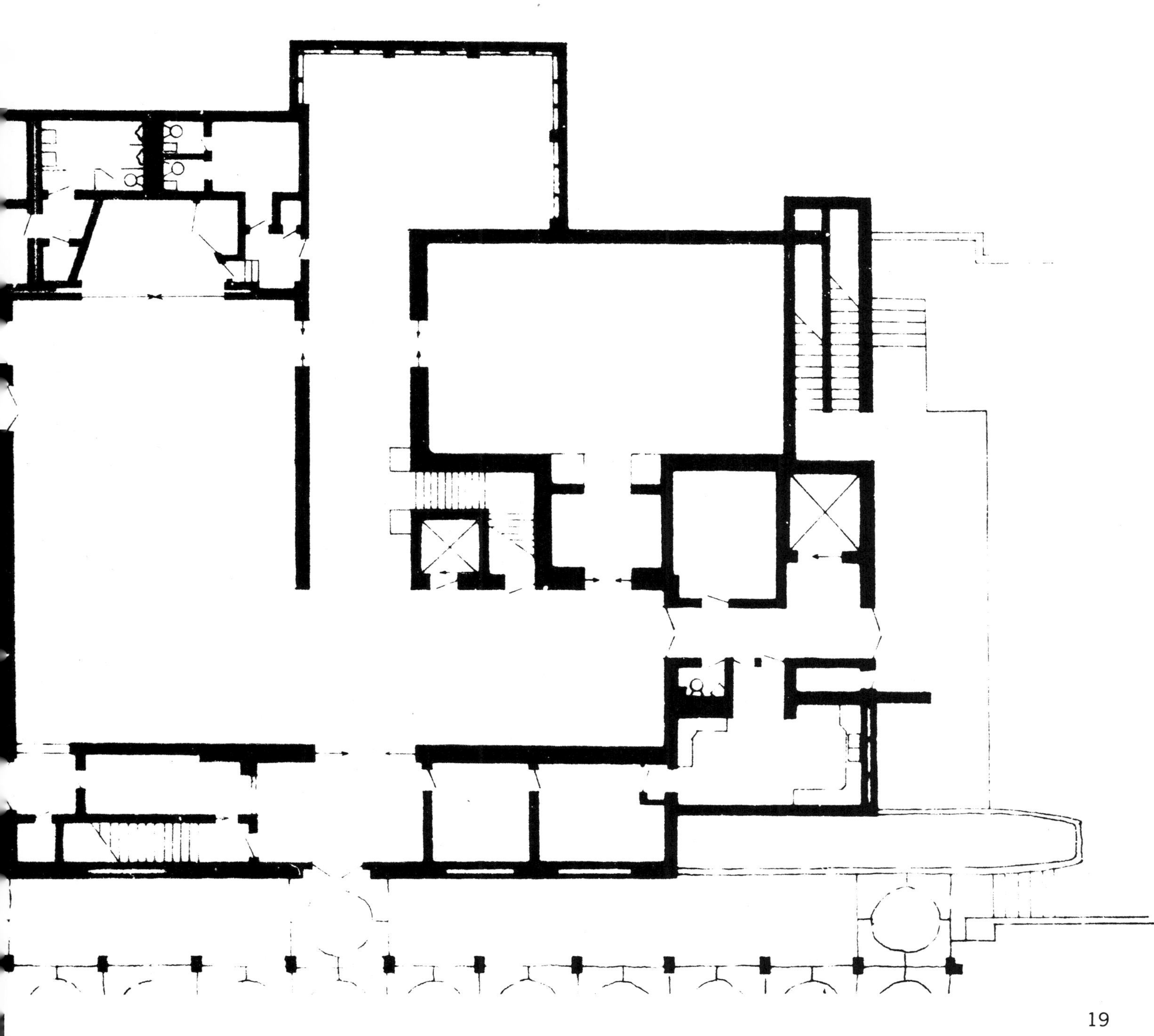

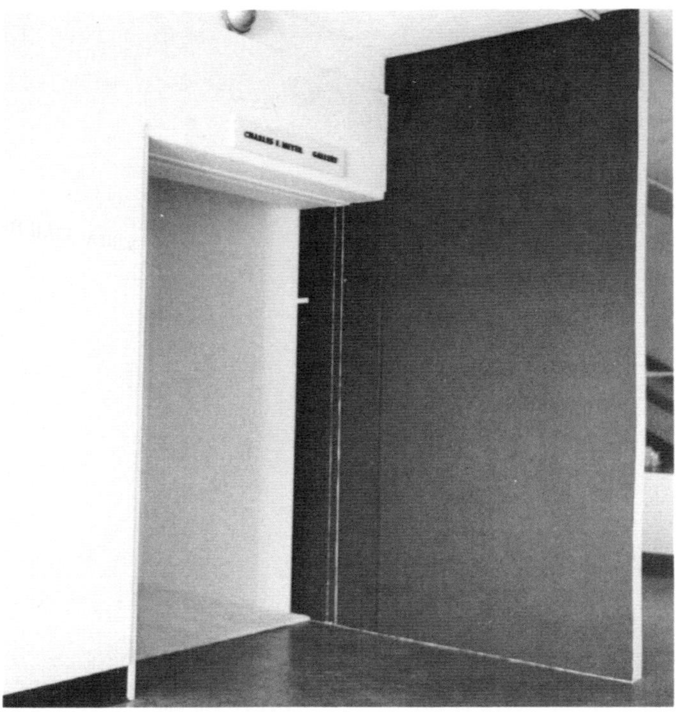

Viewing northeast: entry/exit of installation and constructed light and sound baffle.

Viewing east down the constructed hallway and toward entry/exit.

at the Seattle Art Museum could be considered an outline for the La Jolla work, which differed from it in the labor and materials that were needed to achieve a visual and spatial continuity.

As with light, the use of sound had the capacity to confront the viewer's understanding of space as static, tactile, and formally structured (a dominant trend in art during this period in Southern California), with the notion of its temporality and dynamics.

Regional conditions were exemplified in the "disc-paintings" of Robert Irwin whose exhibition had previously been in the same gallery. This work's presence as a highly finished object seemed to deny its interdependence on general external conditions. While being interdependent and pretending to be disconnected, it set up a ritualized event which could only be perceived from one position on a bench in front of the presentation, thereby making the presentation more important than the person viewing it. The symmetry of presentation and object were idealized and abstracted from the viewer's perception. In response to works such as this, my work employed a formally comparable point of departure, but was manifested in real space and time. The materials and the structure prevented the work from being perceived in exclusively visual and objectified terms. The constructed space functioned as a container for perceptual phenomena leading beyond the usual wall and floor references in the placement of works of art in a gallery.

The light in this installation, rather than highlighting any one point of the display walls of the container, was directed away from them and dispersed over the floor into the room. All of the elements—the spread of tinted light, the walls, and the equipment generating the light—were equally visible and accessible and existed on the same spatial level as the viewer. This was in contradistinction to installation work where colored light emanated from specific objects and materials, and where the light source was contained in objects or concealed in constructions.

It becomes apparent to me in retrospect that the experience of the work was based on a contradiction

Northwest corner of constructed wall and existing wall.

View of north wall on east-west axis showing detail of constructed light baffle (aluminum shields).

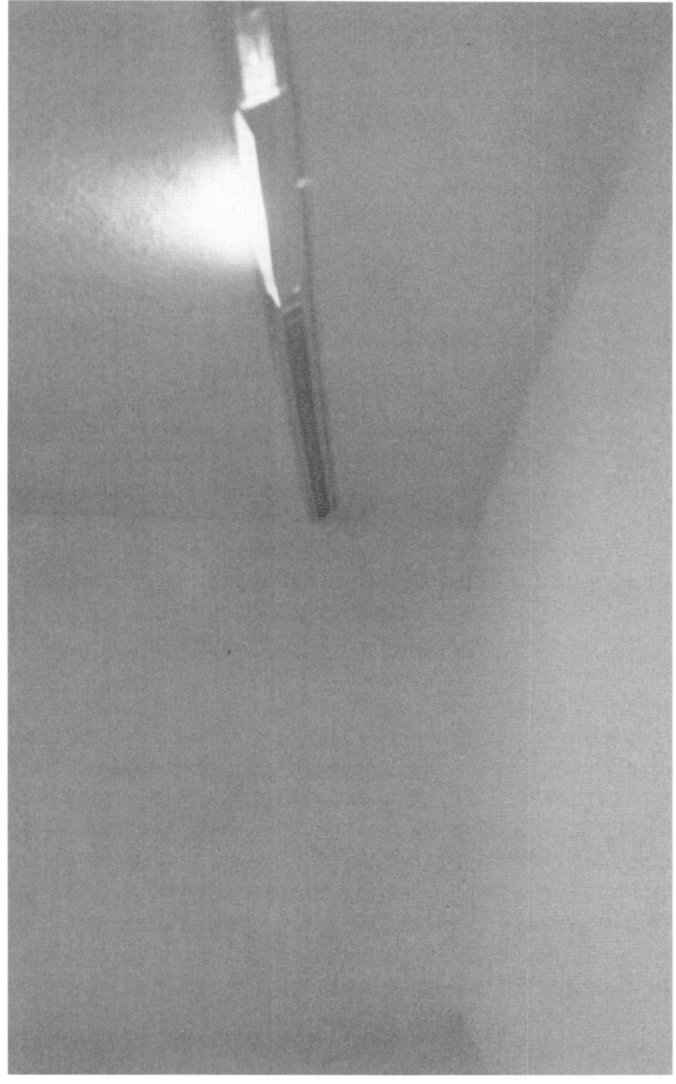

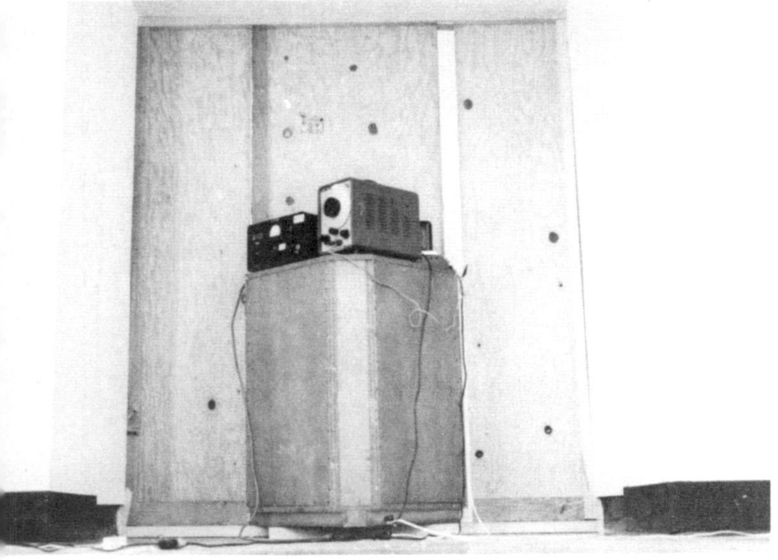

Sound equipment for installation in the adjacent room on the east side.

of principles: nonvisual material had been treated and organized according to principles that had been derived from formal-visual aesthetics. The work served to aestheticize those contradictions. At the same time the work became problematic: instead of the work's being developed from and contingent upon existing material conditions, it was based on, and developed by the use of preselected materials and principles.

Ground plan and elevations of the Charles E. Meyer Gallery illustrating the installation of the light baffles and the sound-generating equipment. Drawing by Lawrence Kenny.

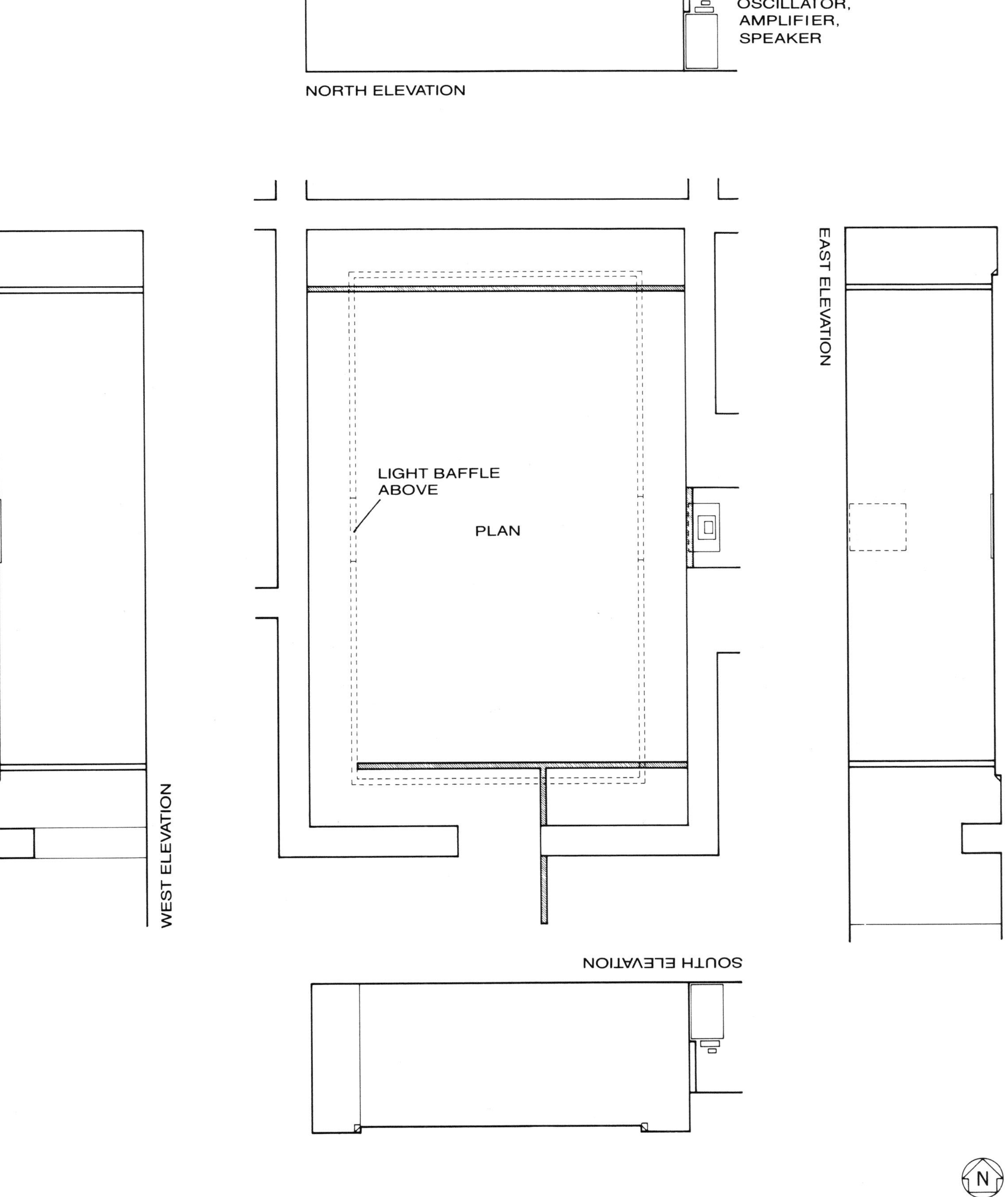

OSCILLATOR, AMPLIFIER, SPEAKER
NORTH ELEVATION
WEST ELEVATION
EAST ELEVATION
LIGHT BAFFLE ABOVE
PLAN
SOUTH ELEVATION
N
0   5   10 ft.

December 30, 1969–March 1, 1970
Spaces
Museum of Modern Art
New York, New York

In the late summer of 1969, I was invited to participate in a group exhibition curated by Jennifer Licht at the Museum of Modern Art entitled "Spaces." The exhibition area allocated for my work—located in the southeast part of the Garden Wing of the museum —measured 20½ feet by 23½ feet. Corridors 6 feet wide extended along the north-south and east-west axes, while the north and west sides were defined by two floor-to-ceiling walls which had been previously constructed for the installation of work by other participating artists.

I had two walls constructed: one on the north-south axis (22 feet long) and the other on the east-west axis (18½ feet long), from the floor to the ceiling (14 feet high). These were positioned in the corridor, reducing it to a width of 4 feet 10 inches. Both walls stopped 3 feet short of the two preexisting walls to leave an entry/exit opening. All of the walls were of standard-grade wood-frame construction.

Then, a wood-joist ceiling was constructed below the 14 foot ceiling at a height of 8 feet, spanning the entire 20½ foot-by-23½ foot area. All ceiling and wall surfaces were covered with drywall.

To make the area highly sound absorbent, I had two additional layers of wall added to the interior surfaces of all four walls. The existing walls had been filled with fiberglass insulating material. The two additional wall layers were separated by a one-inch area which functioned as an acoustical plenum. The first layer was adjacent to the existing wall surface, and consisted of a wood-frame construction filled with fiberglass insulation and covered with drywall. The second layer, set adjacent to the air plenum, was a wood-frame construction filled with fiberglass insulation and covered with textured fiberglass acoustical paneling.

These sound absorption layers extended from the floor to the height of the 8-foot ceiling and the length of the existing walls.

This resulted in final interior area dimensions of 22 feet 10 inches (north-south) by 19 feet 10 inches (east-west).

Once finished, the composite thickness of the wall and plenum on the west side was 1 foot 4 inches, while the composite thickness of the three other walls was 1 foot 3 inches. The open edges of the constructed wall layers were covered with drywall at the point of entry/exit.

Each of the completed wall sections stood on a rubber pad to isolate them from subsonic sounds caused by vibrations affecting the building. Fiberglass acoustical insulation material 2 inches thick was placed above the constructed ceiling.

Finally, two layers of textured acoustical paneling were installed to cover the ceiling and floor completely. This reduced the ceiling height to 7 feet 10 inches.

The finished work *absorbed* sound, as opposed to the previous work at the La Jolla Museum which *reflected* it.

Ambient sound from the exterior, such as street traffic, the interior, such as movement and voices of people in the corridor of the museum, as well as mechanical noises, such as the air delivery-and-return system of the Garden Wing, all merged and condensed on a diagonal axis at the two entry/exit openings. Because of the increased absorption on the entry/exit axis, the sound reached its lowest level toward the center of the installation. On the opposite diagonal axis sound steadily decreased, gradually approaching complete absorption where the walls met in the corners of the installation.

Two lights illuminated the north-south corridor, serving also as a light source for the installation. The east-west corridor was illuminated by incandescent light and, in addition, by the fluorescent light of Dan Flavin's contribution to the exhibition. After passing through the two entry/exits, the light spread out across the textured surfaces of the installation, causing a progressively lower light level toward the center and corners. The areas where sound was almost totally absorbed were also the areas with the least amount of light.

The highly secluded installation space was juxta-

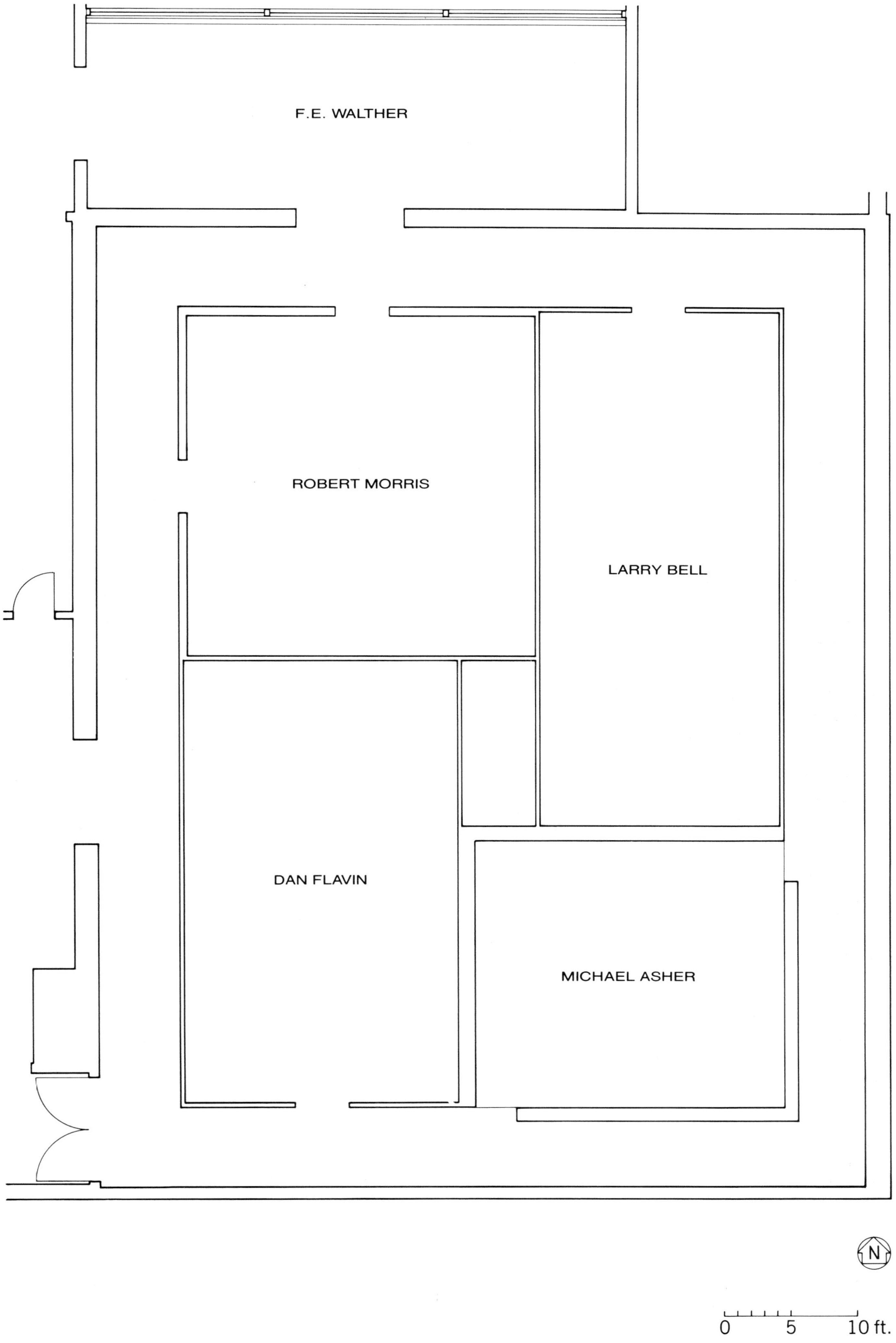

Ground plan of the garden wing of the Museum of Modern Art, N.Y. and layout of exhibition areas for the "Spaces" exhibition. Drawing by Lawrence Kenny.

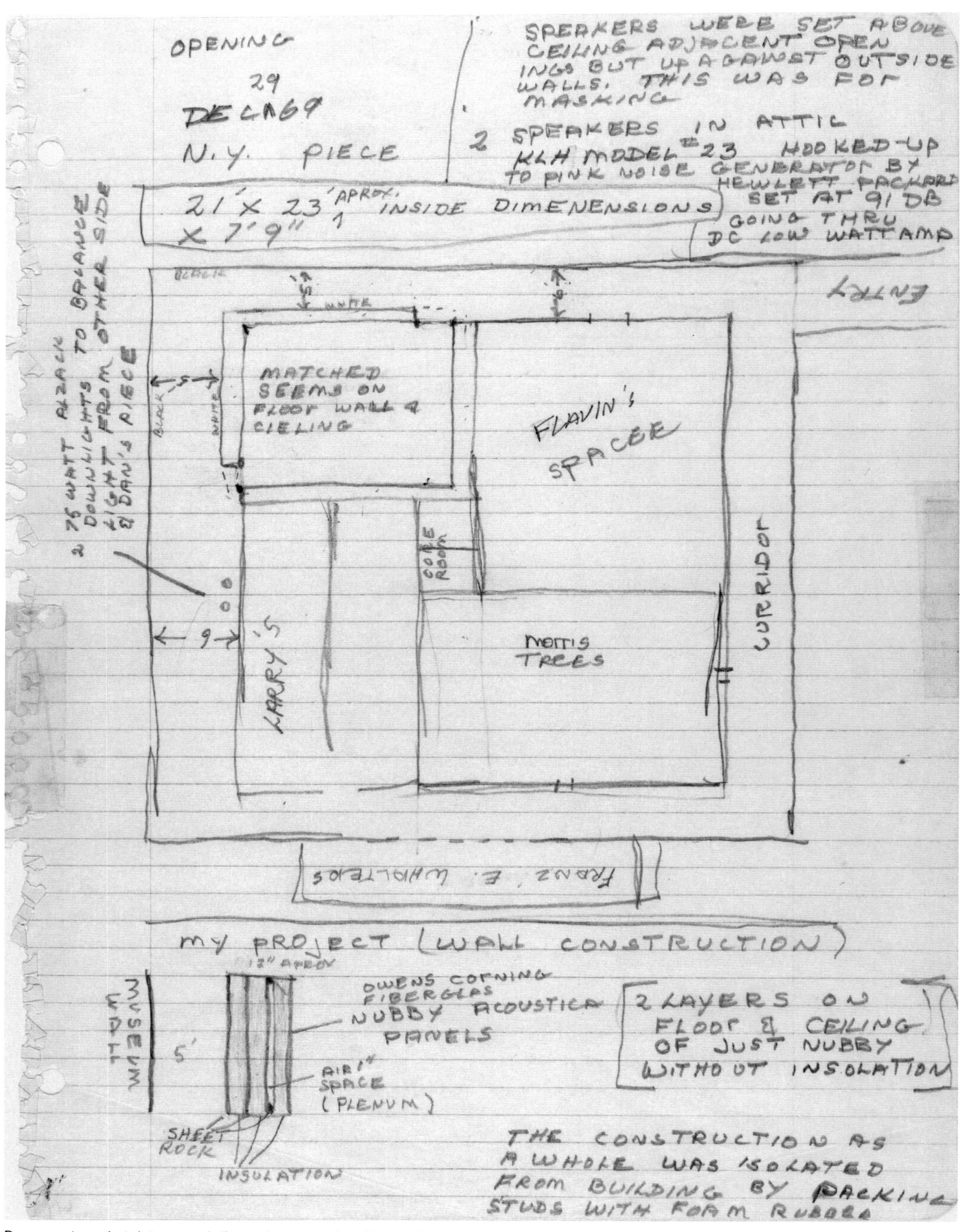

Documentary sketch to record dimensions, construction and location of completed installation. Drawing by Michael Asher.

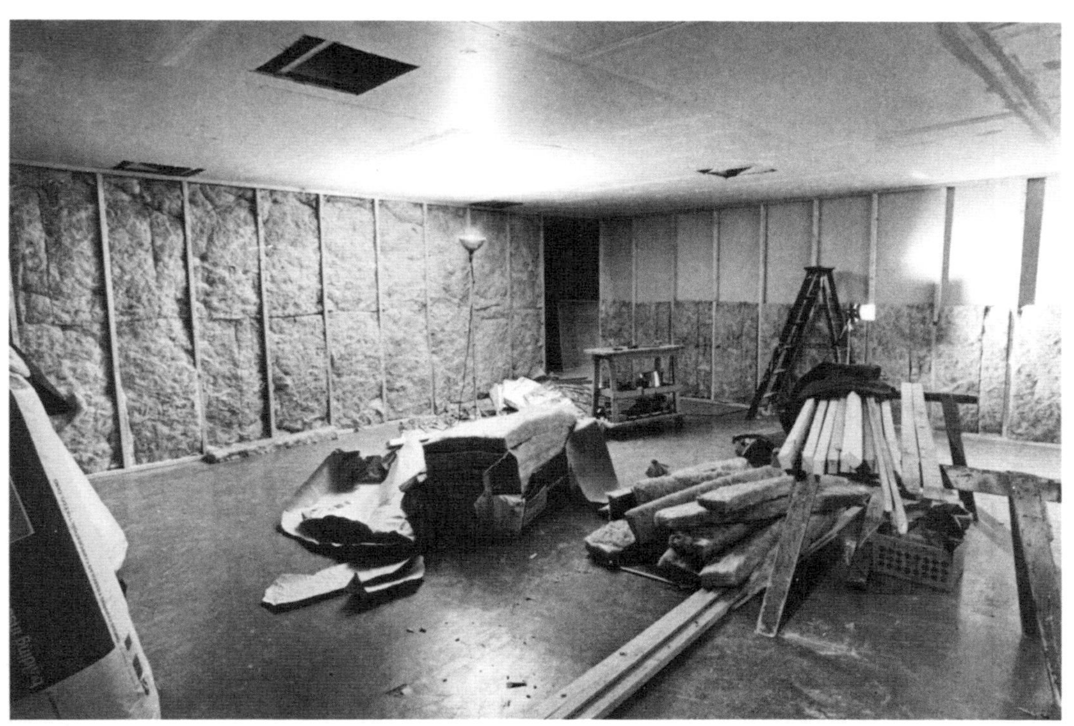

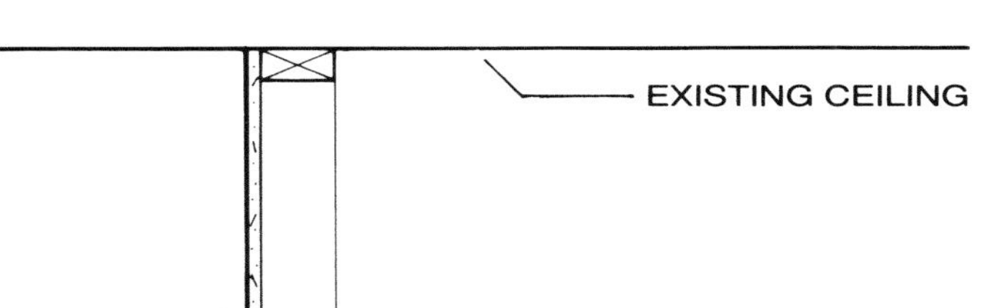

Section of acoustic wall construction (Detail). Drawing by Lawrence Kenny.

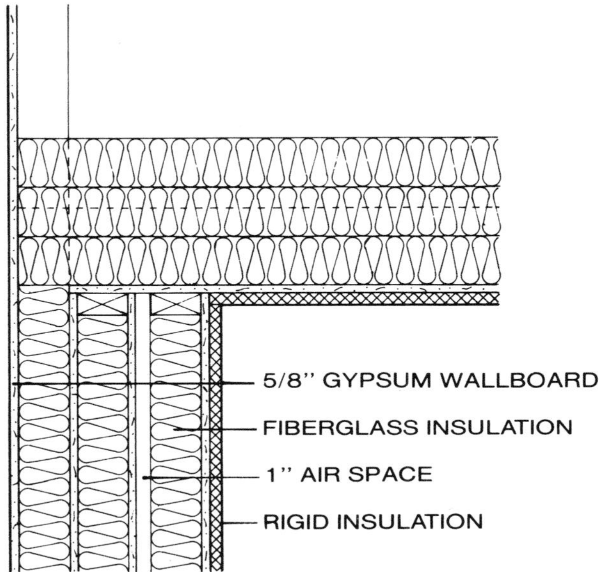

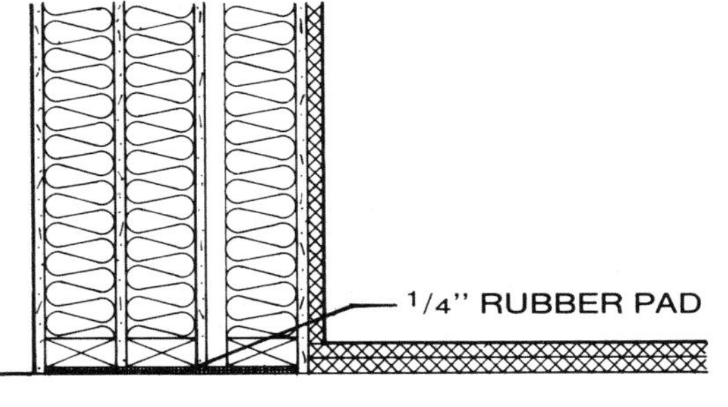

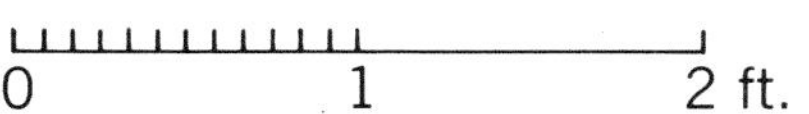

View of the installation and the northeast entry/ exit. Photograph by Claude Picasso.

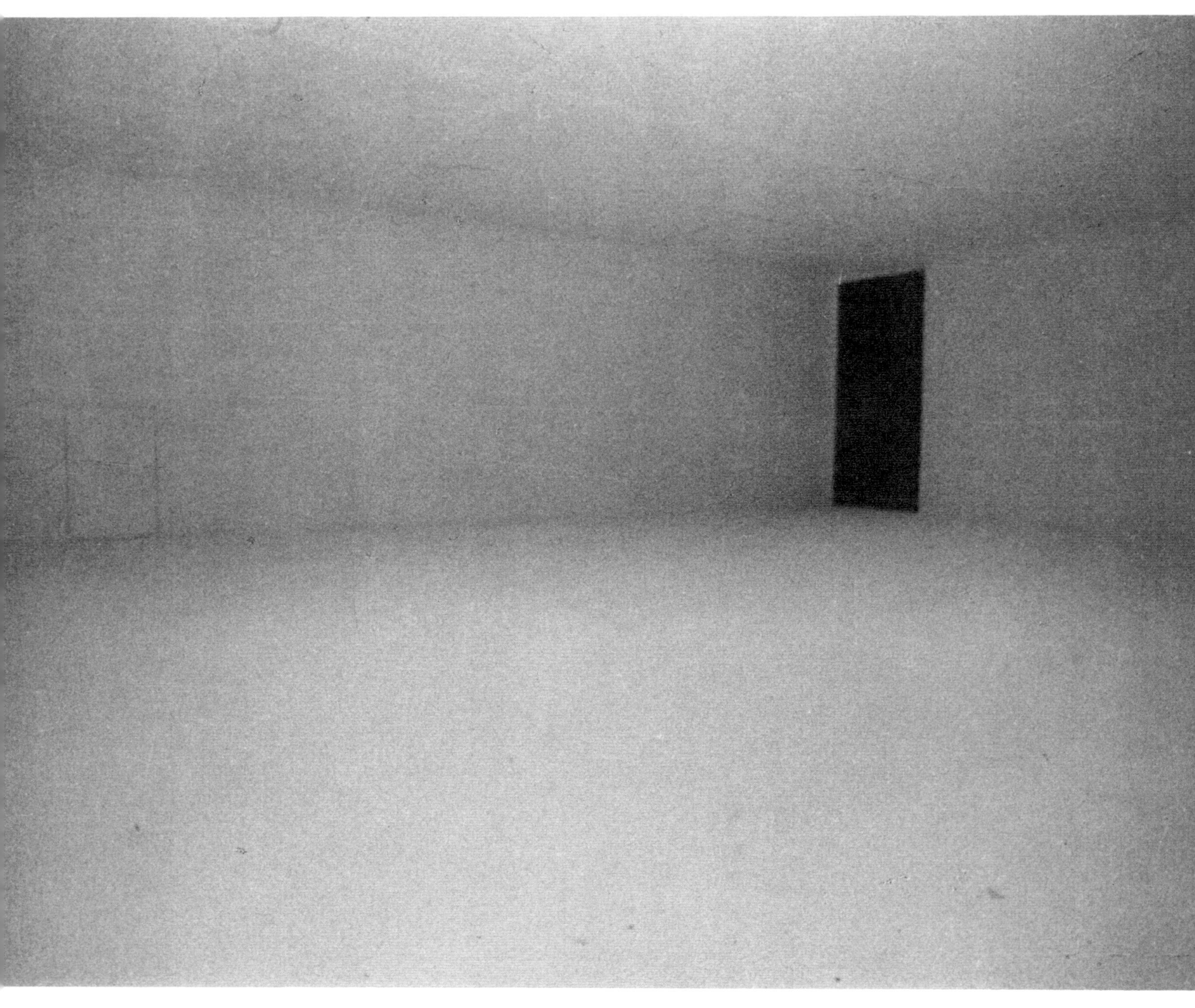

Alternate view of the installation and the northeast entry/
exit. Photograph by Claude Picasso.

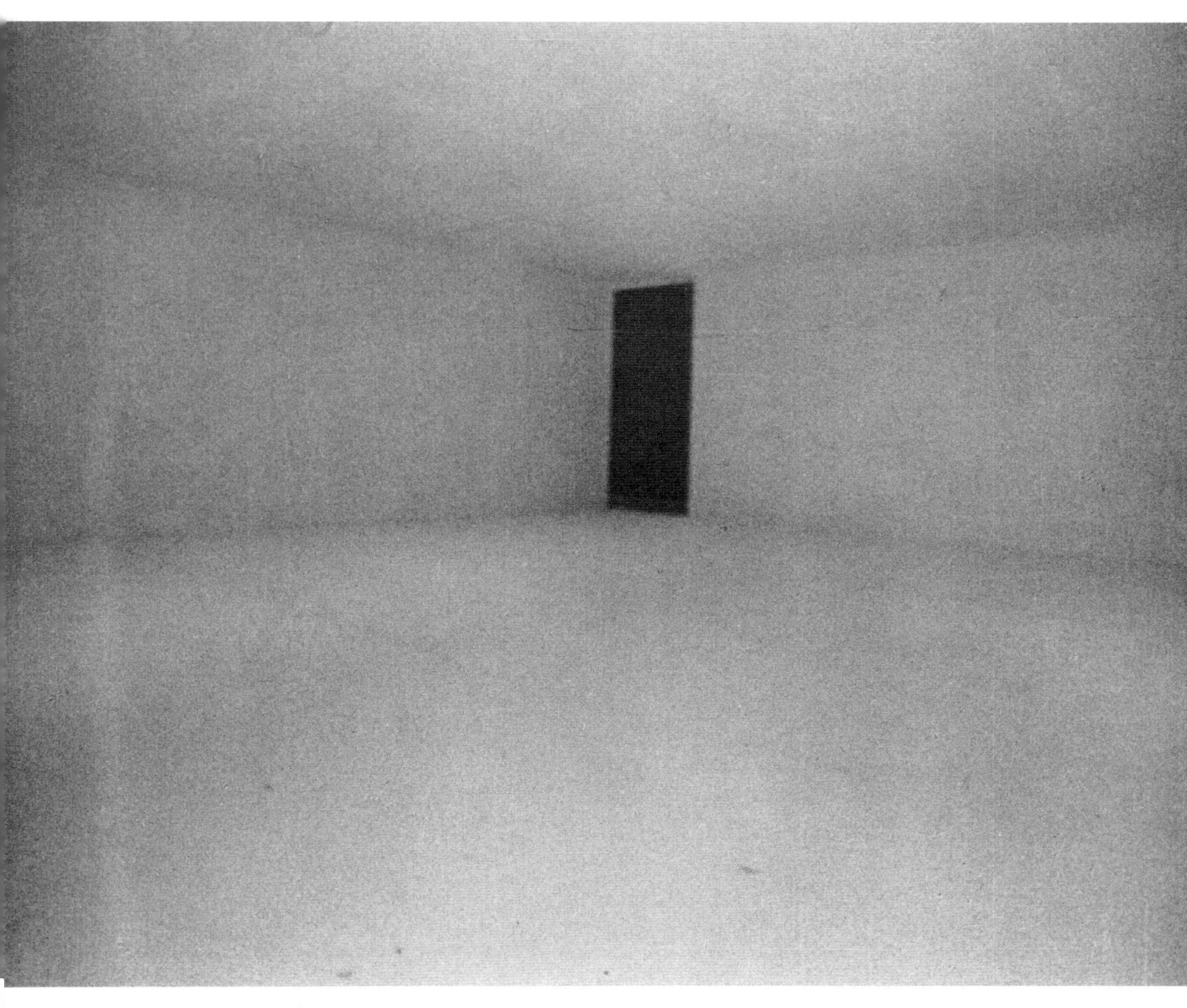

posed with the open hallway, continually receiving and directing all sounds and light in its vicinity. The work was itself isolated from the museum, yet functioned by simultaneously integrating the sound and light produced within the museum. Once these sounds had entered the work, they were structured on a diagonal axis and were ultimately dissolved within the confines of the installation.

As a rectangular container with all of its surfaces treated in the same way, the work created a continuity with no singular point of perceptual objectification, unlike phenomenologically determined works which attempted to fabricate a highly controlled area of visual perception. The various constituent elements and functions of the space were made accessible to the viewer's experience. This was in contradistinction to an installation that would insert a predetermined object between the viewers and their perception of the space, while, at the same time, attempt to control the viewers' perception, eventually creating a hierarchy between the object and the viewers where the viewers subsequently became subservient to the object.[1]

---

[1]Contrary to information in the "Spaces" catalogue, edited by Jennifer Licht, Museum of Modern Art, New York, 1969, the plan to use sound-generating equipment in the work (speakers, noise generator, oscillator) was eventually dropped. The dead space allocated for the installation of the sound equipment, which is depicted in the catalogue, was therefore not used. Furthermore, no lighting system was installed within the constructed area. Finally, the perspective diagram reproduced in the catalogue is upside down.

MICHAEL ASHER'S PROJECT

at Pomona College Art Gallery

is now completed and will be open

day and night until March 8, 1970.

In 1969, Hal Glicksman, the curator of the Gladys K. Montgomery Art Center at Pomona College, offered me the opportunity to stage a work in the center's large exhibition gallery. After visiting and inspecting the center, I considered using a location in the building that was outside of the area normally allocated for exhibition purposes.

Only after I had taken up residence in a dormitory at the college to plan and install the work, did I decide to use the large exhibition gallery, the lobby, and the main entrance from the street.

The art center is situated at one end of the campus. There is an intersection of public streets on its south and west sides. The main entrance is on the west side of the gallery. On the northeast side, the gallery is open to a patio which is surrounded by other college buildings.

A portico at the front entrance leads into the gallery lobby which is flanked on the south by an enclosed office space. The lobby is 27 feet square with an 11 foot-8 inch ceiling. At the southeast corner of the lobby a corridor 6 feet wide opens into the large exhibition space. The dimensions of the space are 41 feet 3 inches in length and 25 feet 9 inches in width with a ceiling height identical to that of the lobby.

For this exhibition, three walls were constructed, one in the large gallery and two in the lobby. The wall in the large gallery, a three-part construction incorporating two already existing walls, delineated a triangular area. One wall was adjacent to the west edge of the passageway and extended 43 feet 4 inches across the gallery to its southeast corner. The other two already existing walls measured 28 feet 5 inches on the north side and 25 feet 9 inches on the east side.

A second constructed wall, adjacent to the east edge of the passageway, ran parallel to the first wall and extended 27 feet into the lobby. I had a third wall constructed adjacent and perpendicular to the existing north wall of the main entrance. It ran parallel to the gallery's west wall and extended 8 feet 9 inches, joining the end of the second constructed wall at an acute angle.

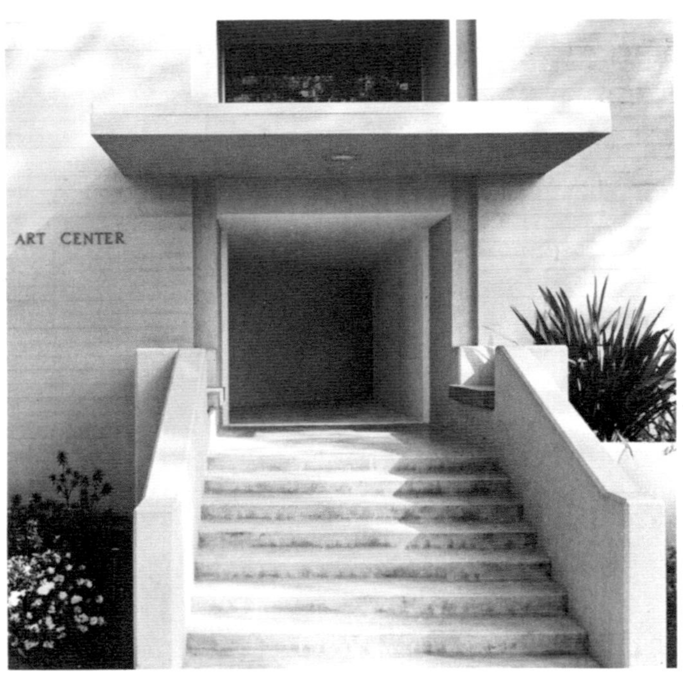

Gladys K. Montgomery Art Center Gallery; main entry/exit viewed from street during exhibition. Photo taken with daylight.

Detail of entry/exit and view into constructed triangular area. Photo taken with daylight.

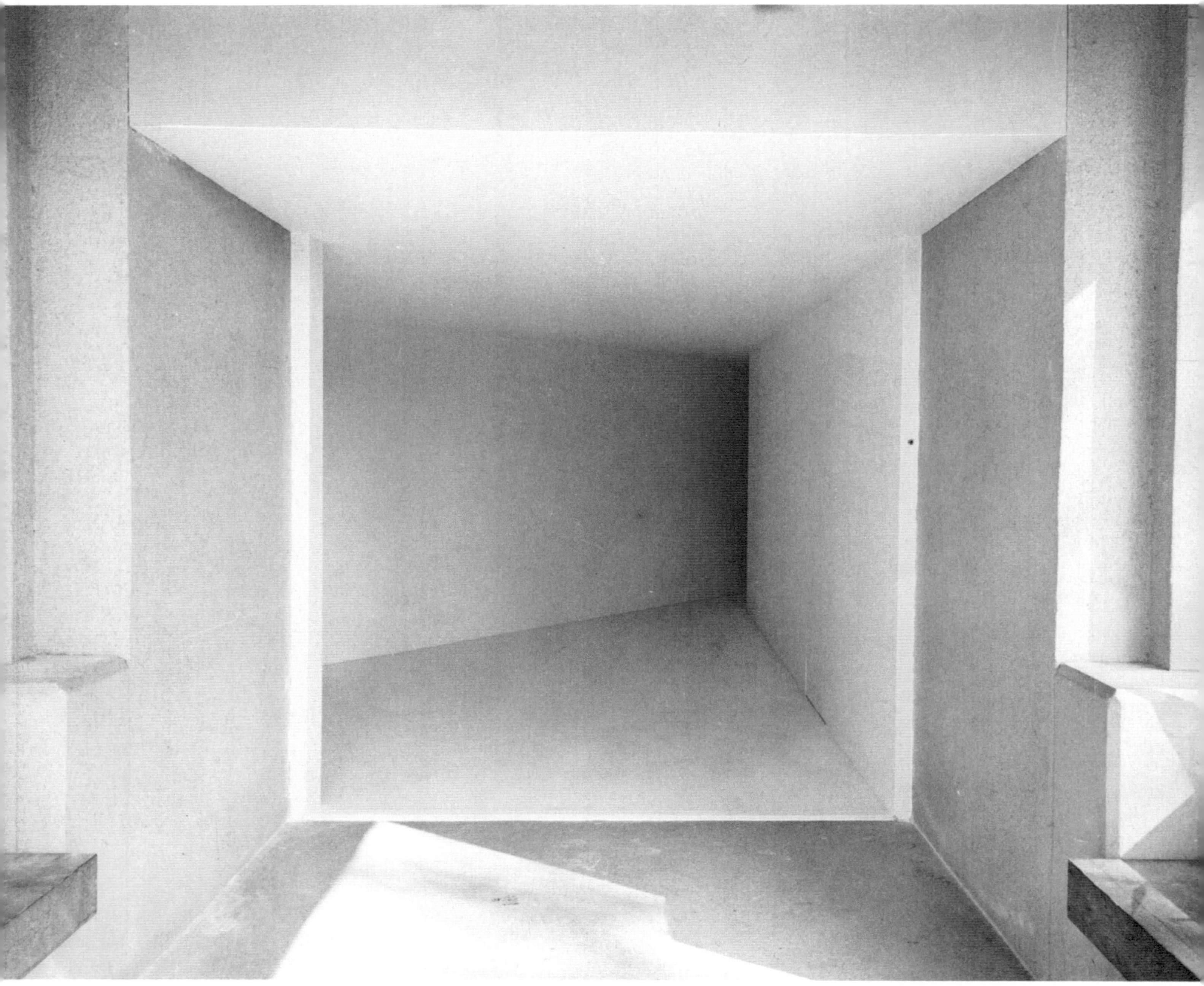

Viewing out of gallery toward street from small triangular area.
Photo taken with daylight. Photographs by Frank Thomas.

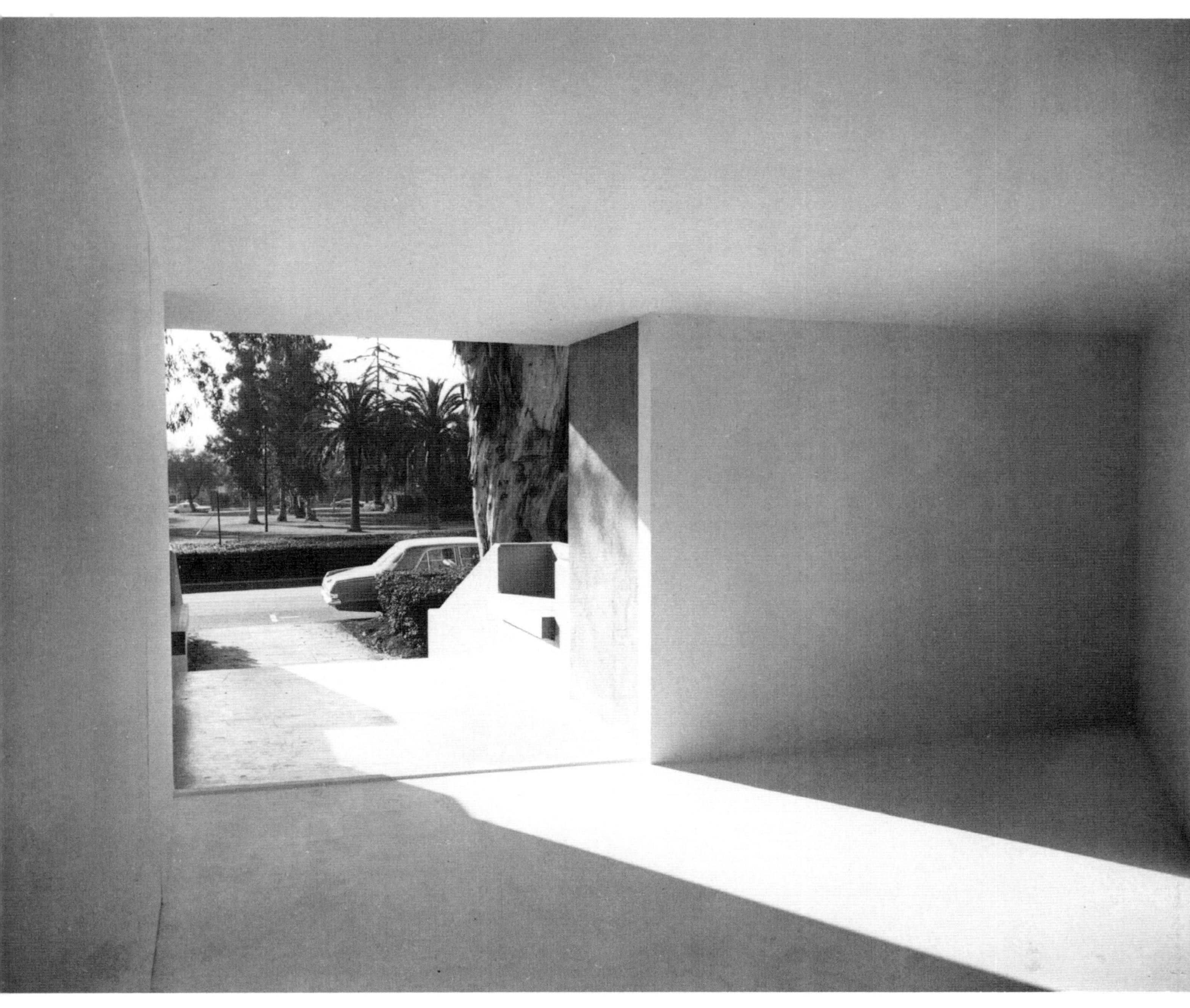

Together with the two constructed walls, another existing wall measuring 21 feet 4 inches on the south side of the lobby and main entrance, completed a smaller triangular area. A flush door construction was added to the office door of the existing wall for a smooth, unbroken wall surface.

The two glass doors that normally partitioned the main entryway and lobby, and which were hinged to the north and south walls at a point 5 feet 2 inches from the outer wall, were removed for the duration of the exhibition, leaving an open entry/exit 6 feet 4 inches in width. The doorjamb and hardware were covered.

A 6 foot-10-inch-high ceiling was constructed that totally covered the two triangular areas, and turned the 6 foot-4-inch-wide entry into a perfect square. It extended through the main entry passage and ended outside, flush with the exterior front wall of the gallery where the gap was boxed in with a drywall panel. The constructed ceiling and walls were drywall mounted on wood framing. All drywall surfaces were finished with off-white paint. The linoleum floor, which had been covered with a protective tape, was painted the same off-white color.

The ceiling, lowered to a height of 6 feet 10 inches, became as integral a part of the work's spatial continuity as the walls and the floor. As such, the ceiling directed the viewer's awareness to standard architectural usage within an exhibition space, similar to the way in which the constructed walls altered perception of the standard rectilinear areas.

As the ground plan indicates, each triangular area was positioned in reverse of the other. Each side of one triangular area had a corresponding parallel wall in the other. Therefore, both triangular areas had a right angle and two identical acute angles. Finally, the parallel hypotenuses of each triangular area overlapped for a distance of 5 feet, resulting in a corridor 2 feet in width.

The interior of the architectural container, housing the office and additional gallery space, could be reached from a courtyard behind the gallery building. From this area the viewer could see the construction and the support of the smaller triangular space, including structural details (i.e., the two-by-four framing, the sandbag props that were used to stabilize the walls, the joists holding the ceiling and walls together, and the back of the drywall panels (see photos p. 40–41).

While in the office/gallery space, viewers could observe the backside of the construction, and at the same time the frontside and the outdoor elements in their formalized context.

In this case, as in many others, the architectural site did not exclusively determine how the work was structured or perceived. However, it did give the viewer an opportunity to see what could be accommodated within the parameters of a museum's architectural structure.

With the two glass doors removed, the installation was open to anyone twenty-four hours a day. Exterior light, sound, and air became a permanent part of the exhibition. Daylight saturated all the surfaces of the first small triangular area. It condensed in the corridor and gradually dispersed over all the surfaces of the large triangular area. Only the back wall facing the corridor was fairly evenly lit by the projected daylight from the corridor. Light intensity, color, and shadows varied, depending on the sun's position in the sky. Reflected light had a yellow tint due to the off-white color of the interior.

Nighttime light entered from streetlights which cast a low, tinted blue light into the installation. Also a 75-watt bulb in the lobby ceiling, which was covered with a clear blue Plexiglass sheet and several layers of fiberglass diffusers in order to match the color of the streetlights, cast a dim, tinted blue light into the triangular areas, producing an extent and degree of illumination similar to that of daylight.

Sound was generated from such sources as street traffic, people walking past the gallery, and people within the installation. Exterior and interior sounds were collected and amplified in the smaller triangular space and transmitted through the corridor. Channeled and intensified in the corridor, sound was further am-

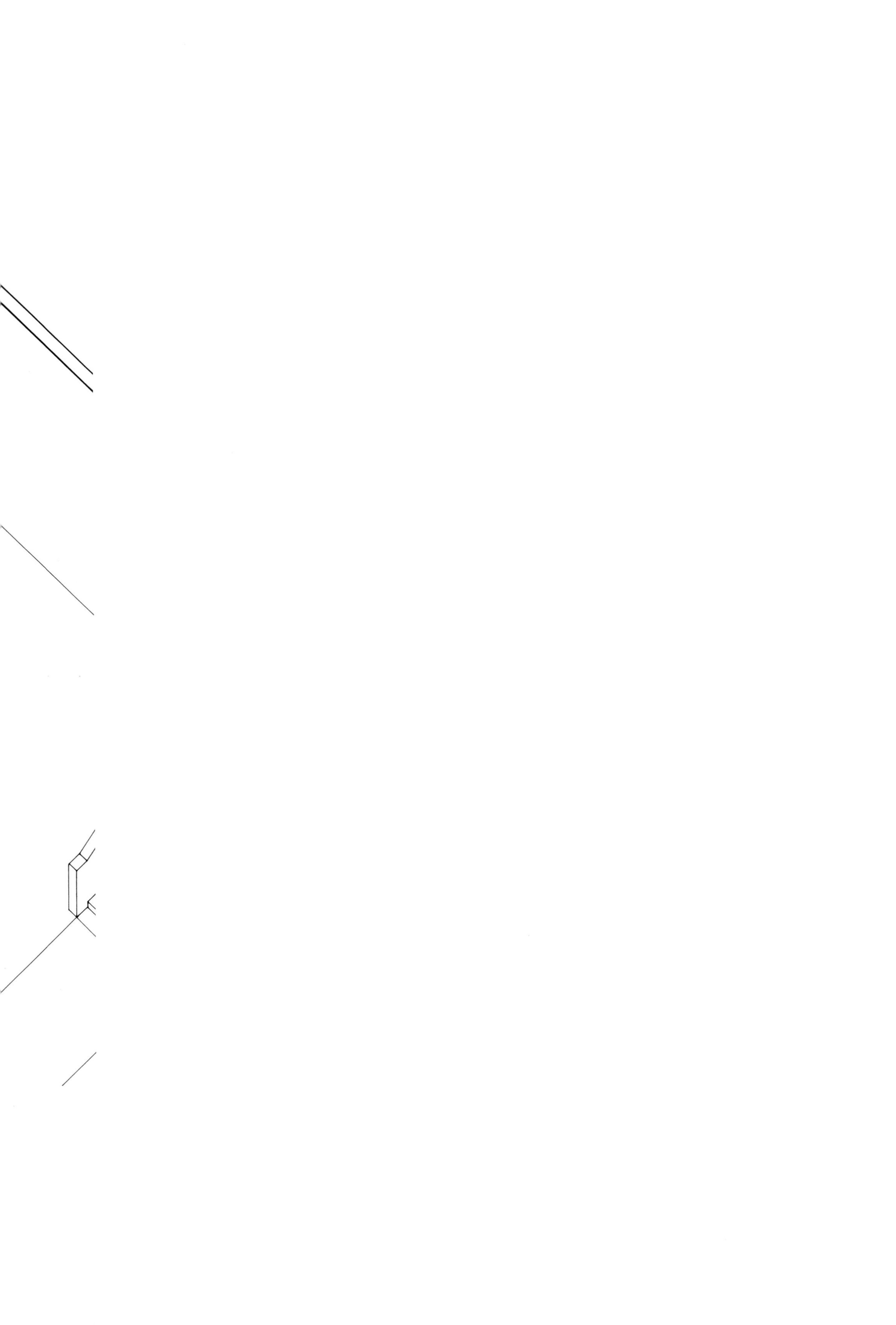

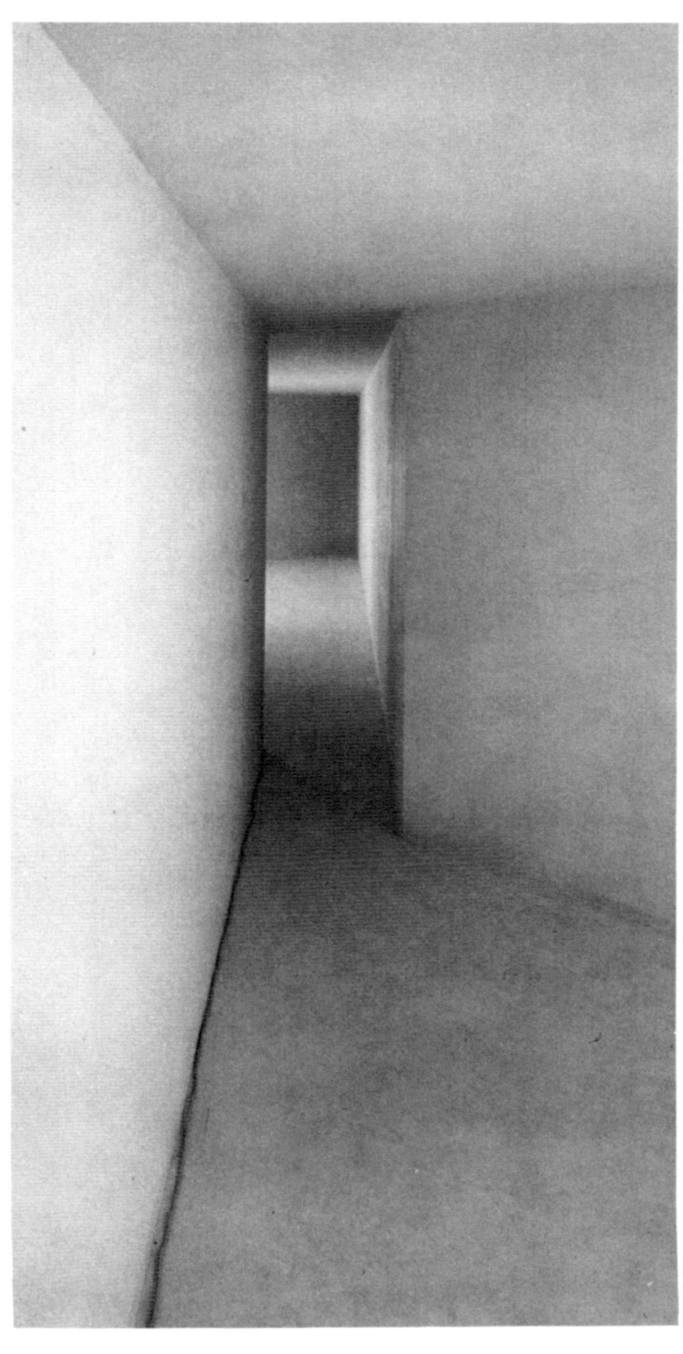

Camera in small triangular area facing passageway into large triangular area. Photo taken with artificial light.

plified in the larger triangular spaces, reaching its highest level at the back wall. With the removal of the main-entry doors, the installation was also directly ventilated from outdoors, and therefore subject to varying climatic conditions.

I originally intended the installation at Pomona College to deal with air movement generated from natural, outdoor sources rather than mechanical means, and to direct that air movement through the gallery. In this regard, the installation was an amplification and variation on my early air works and, specifically, my more recent air works at Newport Harbor Art Museum and the Whitney Museum of American Art, all of which had employed mechanical devices to generate air flow into the exhibition area. The Pomona work was similar to the installation at the Museum of Modern Art in that it collected and structured given exterior elements and integrated them into the work.

While working on the Pomona installation, I realized that it was impossible to focus on one singular element such as the movement of air. All of the various elements, once the space had been literally opened to them, had to become inherent determinants in the production and reception of the work.

The installation shifted formal control from a singular object to a seemingly neutral given architectural structure previously containing that object. The induced and false neutrality of the object had been dependent upon the false neutrality of the container.

The triangular shapes were defined in opposition to the usual architectural context surrounding a work of art. As right triangles, they simultaneously adapted and referred to the conditions of the architectural container.

The arbitrary way in which the exterior elements entered the triangular spaces was as important to the work as the material construction of the installation, if only as a contradiction of the installation's formal control over those elements.

Entering and moving through the installation, the viewer became increasingly removed from the exterior reality, at the same time perceiving gradual abstrac-

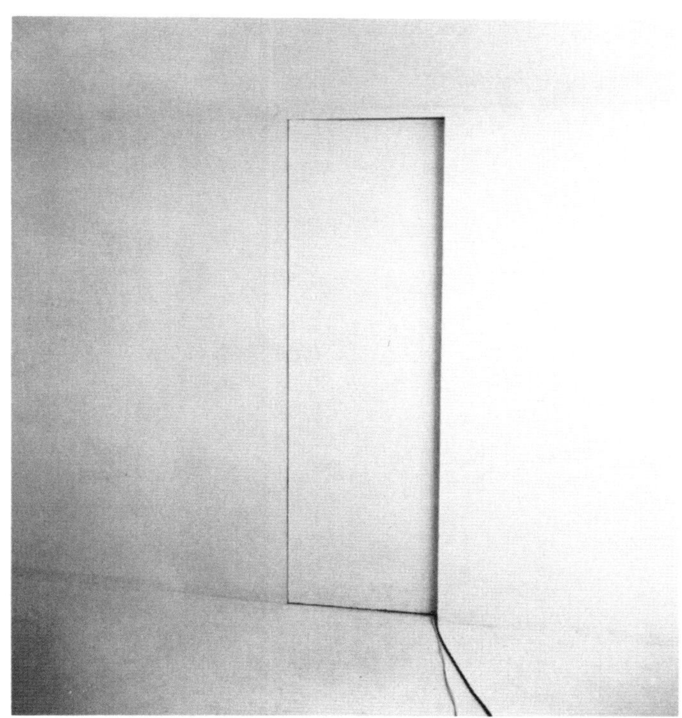

Detail of constructed entry/exit to offices south of installation. Photo taken with artificial light as indicated by electric power cord.

View from front (small) triangular area with constructed office door on the far right, viewing into passageway. All photos by Frank Thomas.

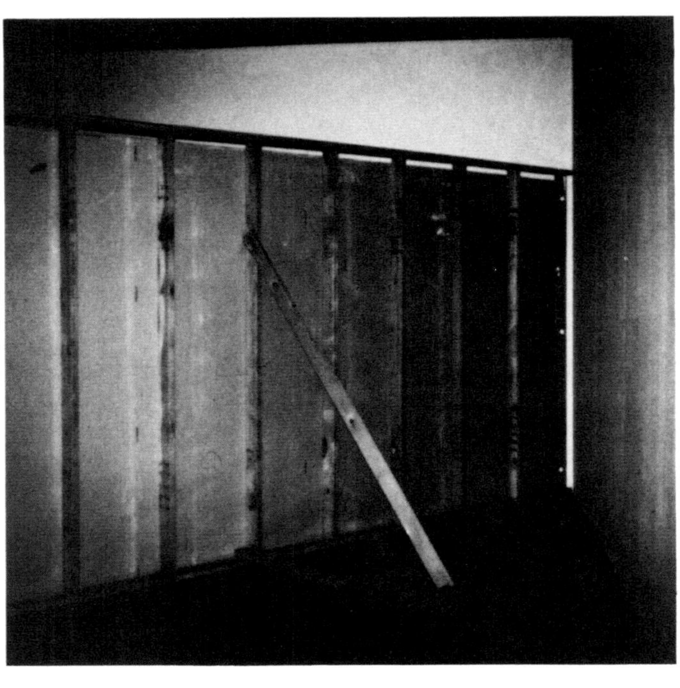

Detail of prop-construction and sandbags from the service area of the gallery after the completion of the installation. Photo by Hal Glicksman.

Small triangular area facing toward passageway. Photo taken with daylight. Photo by Frank Thomas.

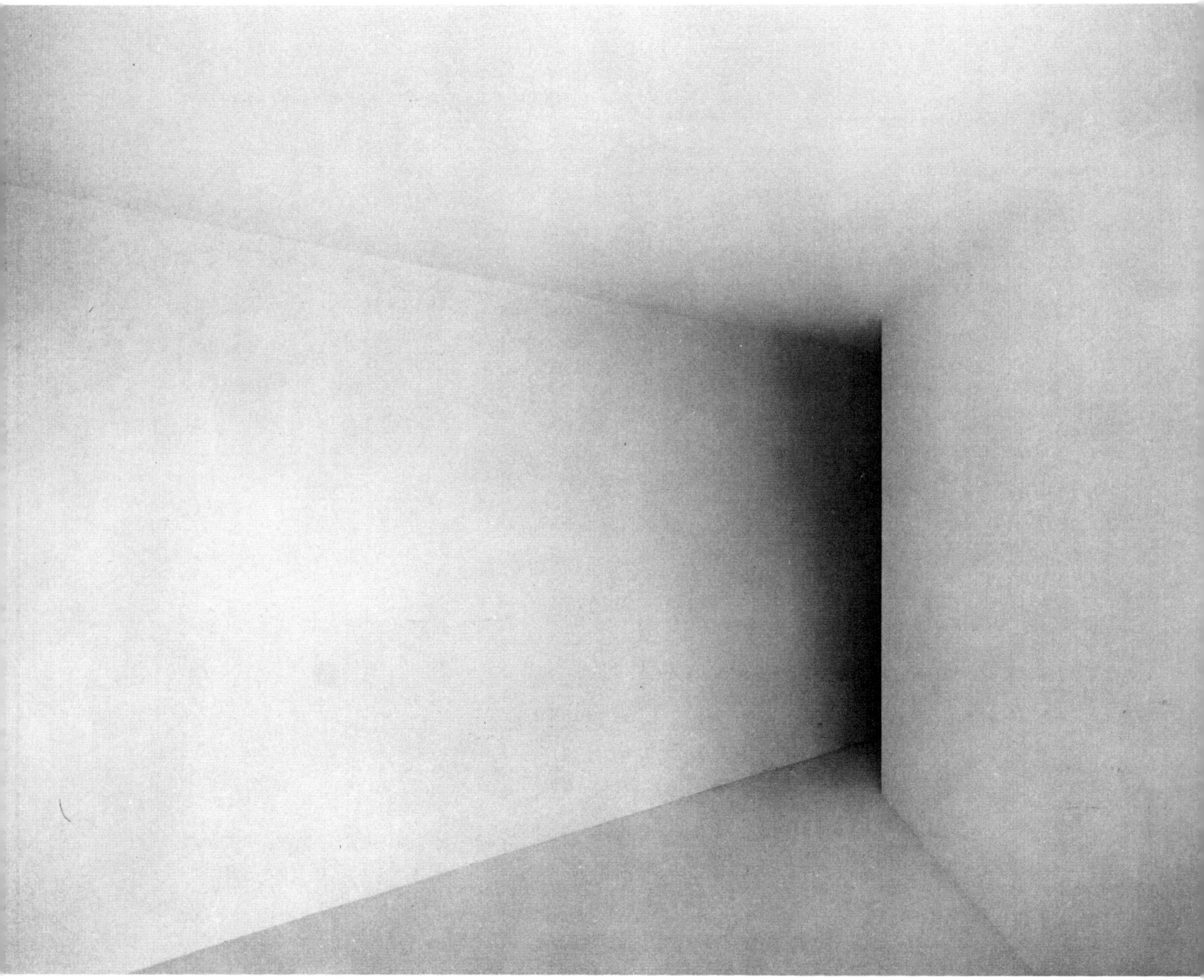

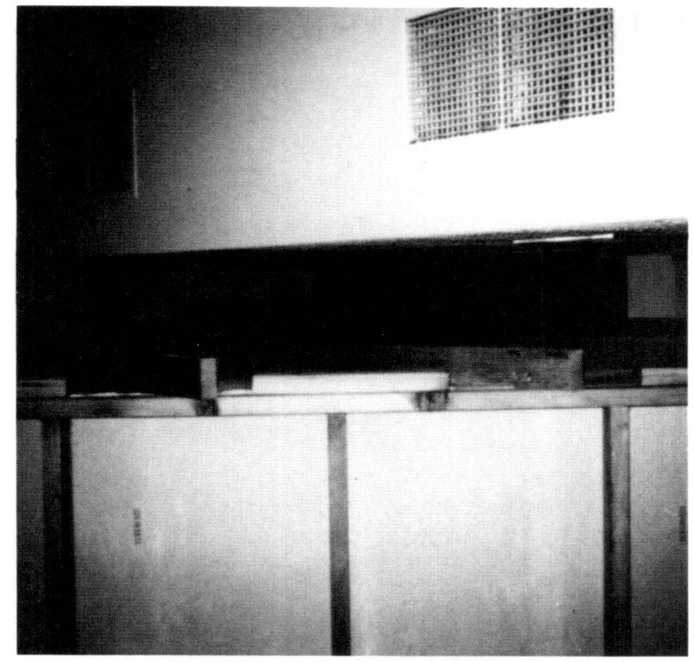

Detail of ceiling and wall junction underneath existing ceiling after the completion of the installation. Photo by Hal Glicksman.

Photo taken from back wall of large triangular area viewing onto front wall of small triangular area. Photo taken with artificial light by Frank Thomas.

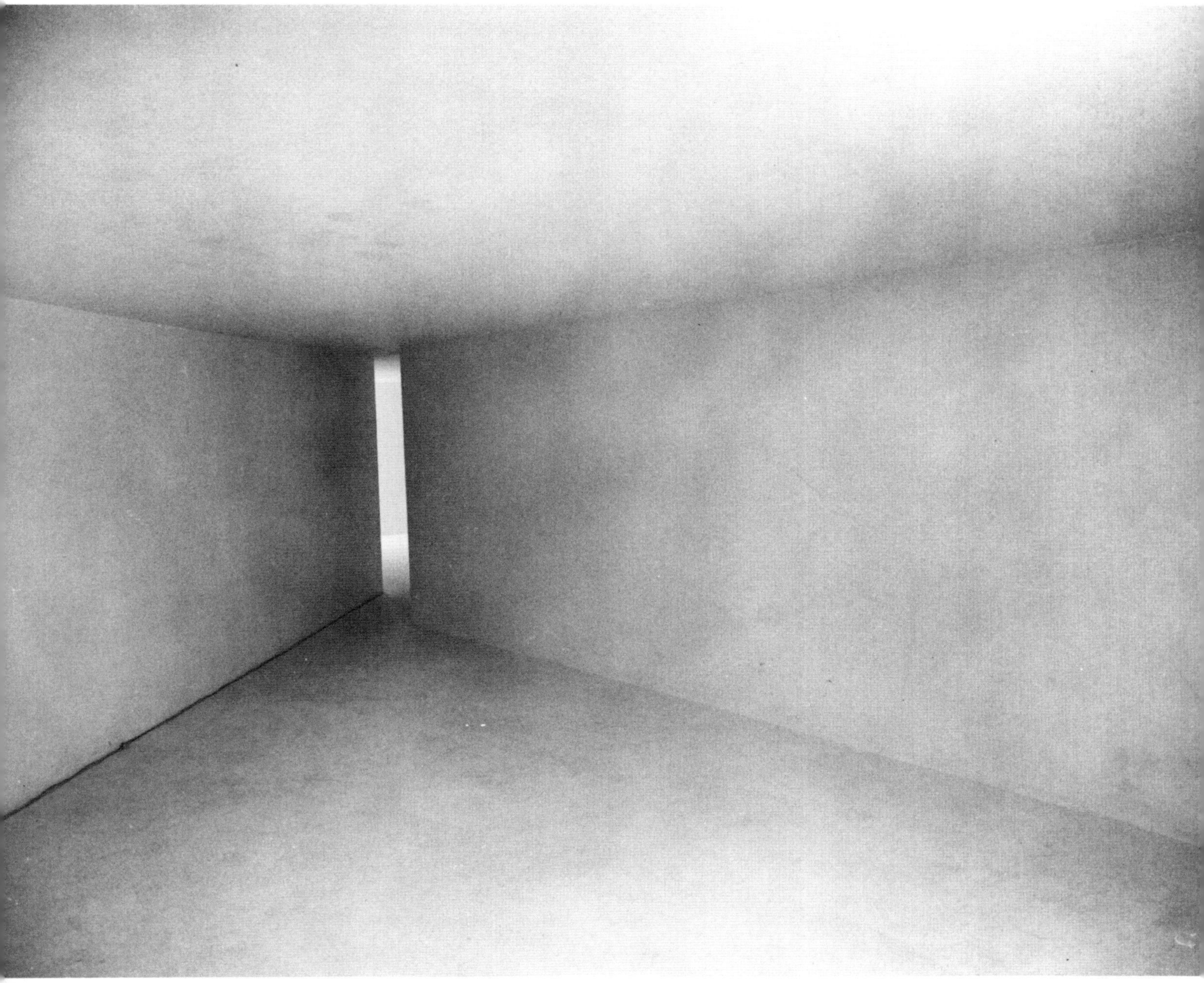

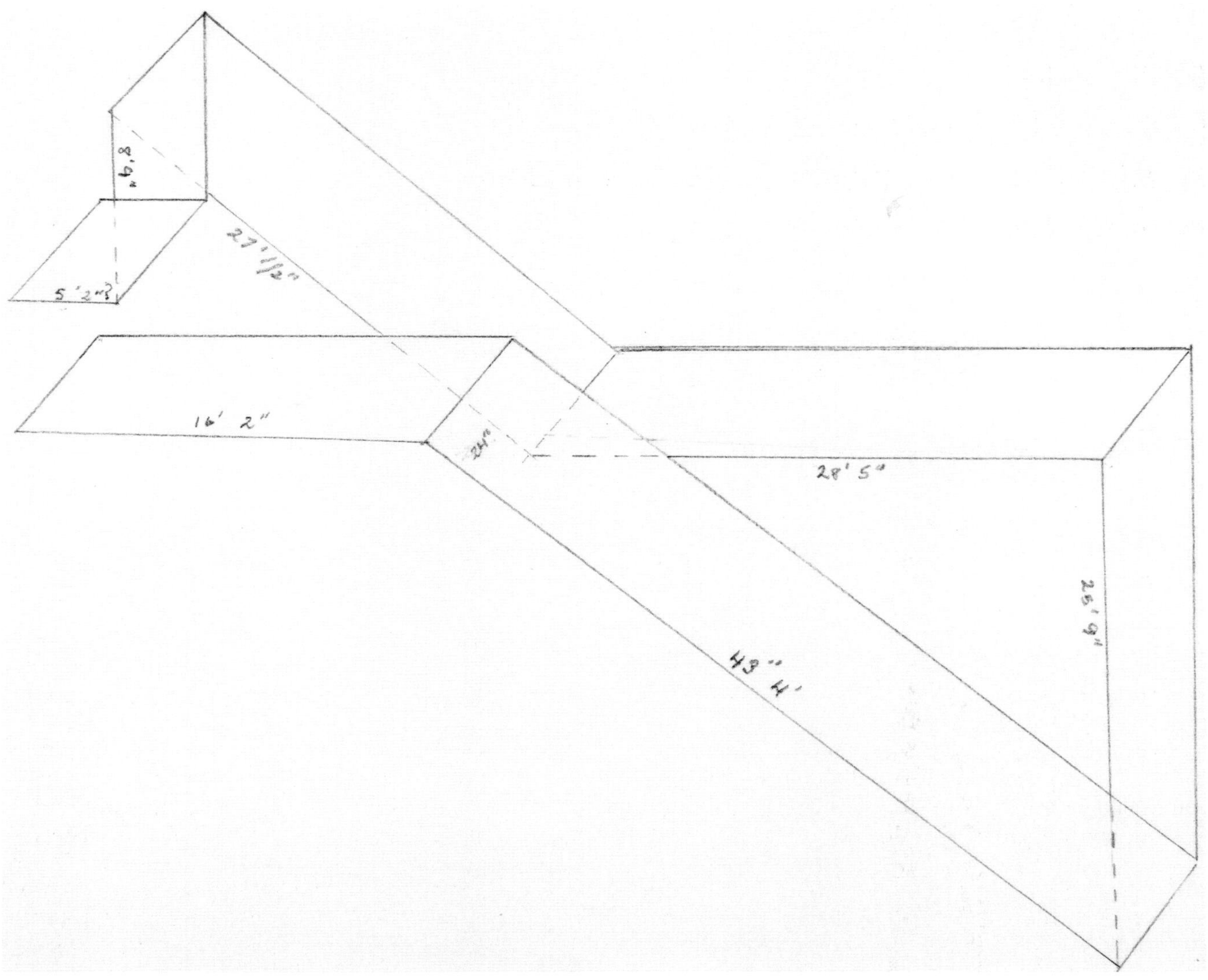

Isometric drawing of walls of installation by Michael Asher.

tions of that reality within a formally determined and controlled space.

Gradually walking back through the two triangular areas, the viewers reconstructed what had previously been abstracted, reaching the point of total reconstruction at the moment they returned to the outdoors. This view of exterior reality was framed by the square entry/exit which was combined and juxtaposed with the final element of the installation's formal abstraction: the 6 foot-4-inch-by-8-foot-9 inch wall panel to the right of the entry/exit square.

The twenty-four-hour time order, a popular structure in the Los Angeles community, was transposed to the operation of the work. This time structure introduced a temporal configuration of reality, opening the work temporally as the entry structure had opened it spatially. Some of my earlier works had also developed a formal temporal structure through the use of sound: sound as a temporal structure determined by its mechanical generation within the work (as in the work at La Jolla), or by the viewer's limited access to the work, which was ultimately determined by the museum's operating hours (as in the work at the Museum of Modern Art).

The sound in this work was the sound of the activity of the community surrounding the work as well as that of viewers who entered it. Because of the twenty-four-hour time structure, viewers activated the work by entering at a time determined by them, rather than according to the museum's usual daytime schedule. The three-week duration of twenty-four-hour accessibility focused on a more generalized understanding of temporal experience.

The visual, spatial, and formal continuity of the installation was dialectically in opposition to the actual continuity of time, sound, light, and climatic conditions. To stage a work that would express these oppositions with ideal clarity, it seemed that certain facets of the reality of the work—its various levels of support, for example—had to be suppressed. The work's specific reality—what it shares with the institution that contains it—remained elusive. This apparent absence derived from conditions created in the work's construction: the demarcation of the existing space and the partial concealment of the activities within that space.

This exhibition, organized by Maurice Tuchman, Senior Curator of Modern Art, and Jane Livingston, Associate Curator of Modern Art, included, in addition to myself, the following artists: John Alberty, James Bradley, Vija Celmins, Ron Cooper, Mary Corse, Robert Cumming, David Deutsch, Guy Dill, Laddie John Dill, Frederick John Eversley, Jack Goldstein, Scott Grieger, Patrick Hogan, Richard Jackson, Peter Lodato, Allan McCollum, Barbara Munger, Peter Plagens, Joe Ray, Allen Ruppersberg, Wolfgang Stoerchle, John White, and William Wegman.

Since the exhibition was scheduled to open simultaneously with the "Art and Technology" exhibition at the Los Angeles County Museum of Art, the artists were given three weeks to conceive and construct their works. My proposal was accepted at the end of the first week, so that—with the assistance of Tahn Hyun—I had two weeks to bring the work to completion.

Two complete rooms and several partitioned, carpeted areas on the fourth floor of the Ahmanson Building were allocated for the exhibition. My work would be in the smaller of the two rooms, which measured 30 feet 6 inches by 29 feet by 15 feet 6 inches.

I had three walls constructed in an area to the right of the passageway leading to the installation area, running on a north-south axis, parallel to the existing west wall of the museum and parallel to one another. These three walls were 5 feet, 10 feet, and 20 feet respectively in length, 15 feet 3 inches high, and 4 inches thick. The 5-foot wall was closest to the preexisting wall, followed by the 10-foot wall, which was followed by the 20-foot wall, each wall separated from the preceding wall by a distance of 4 inches. The walls projected into the passageway at increments of 5 inches (the shortest wall projecting 5 inches, and the longest wall 15 inches).

The 20-foot wall stopped 1 foot 11 inches short of the existing south wall of the installation area, leaving that length of the existing west wall visible, and providing a very narrow access to observe the interior walls. The constructed walls stopped 3 inches short

of the ceiling, to which they were held in place by several angle bars.

The walls were constructed on a piece of plywood flooring which was cut in on one end to conform to the projections of the walls and extended on the other end to the full length of the 20-foot wall. The walls were two-by-four frames covered in plywood. The east and west sides of the walls were covered with drywall. All seams were filled with wood compound and the plywood was treated with a coating to stabilize the grain.

All constructed surfaces, including the plywood flooring, were finished with the same white paint normally used to cover the museum walls, thereby establishing an internal continuity and similarity between the constructed surfaces and the existing walls.

As the viewer approached the passage, the edges of the constructed walls appeared as a serial sculptural relief; abreast of the edges the depth of the walls was revealed against the background of the existing south wall, which they appeared to fragment.

The plane of the 20-foot wall, which faced into the installation area, blocking the view of the interior wall elements as well as most of the existing west wall, appeared to be another full-sized exhibition wall.

The preexisting exhibition wall, recessed 2 feet behind the outer constructed wall, could be seen through the 1 foot 11 inch vertical opening in the southwest corner. The outer wall was therefore often perceived as an integral structural element where works of art were normally installed. Visitors frequently thought it was an unused wall, and they would lean against it to view other works in the exhibition.

As a response to the use of partition walls in museum design, the constructed walls ran parallel to other partition walls in the area where the exhibition was installed; the projecting relief of the constructed walls could only be viewed from the passageway, however.

The solid edges of the constructed walls alternating with the interstices resulted in seven vertical lines, parallel and equidistant. As these edges formed a visual relief, they also constituted the beginning of each

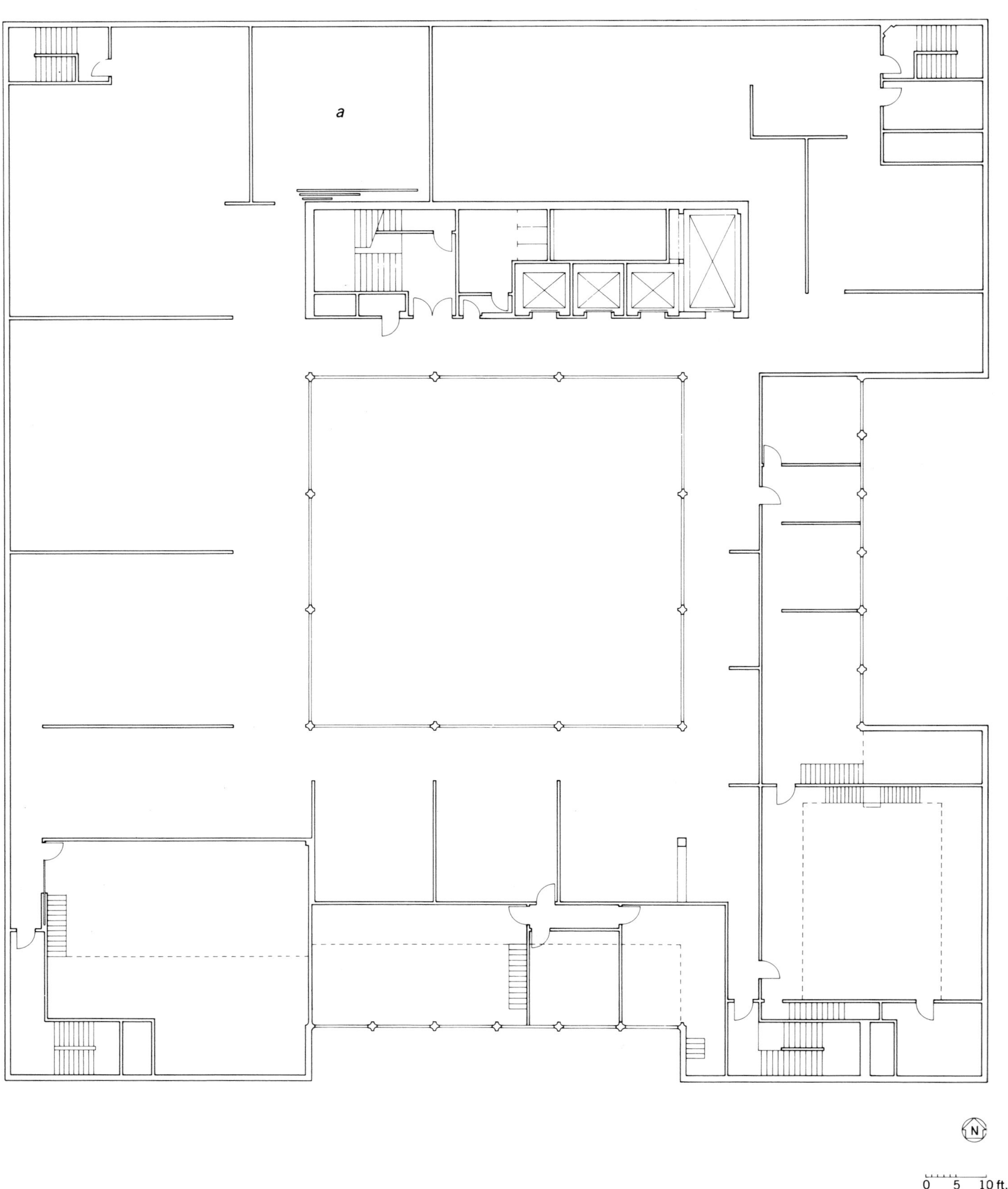

Complete ground plan of fourth floor of Ahmanson Building, Los Angeles County Museum of Art. The exhibition "24 Young Los Angeles Artists" was located in the northwest portion of the building. The north gallery space marked *a* indicates the construction of these parallel walls by Michael Asher. Ground plan by Lawrence Kenny.

Plan of installation area with detail of wall construction. Drawing by Kim Hubbard.

Elevation of wall construction with existing partition wall.
Final drawing by Michael Asher, May 1971.

of the planar wall sections.

The relief structure disappeared when the wall planes were viewed frontally. The outer wall was seen as a white rectangular architectural plane. This outer plane not only covered the internal elements but seemed to compress the internal space against the existing west wall. The internal progression of constructed walls complemented the highly visible progression of what appeared to be a sculptural exterior relief. Through the narrow vertical opening at the southwest corner, the edges of the three walls could be viewed as progressing inward, the 5-foot wall receding furthest into the interior space. The edge of the 5-foot wall within the exterior relief structure was the first to extend 5 inches into the passageway.

Viewed from the exhibition area, the vertical and horizontal edges of the outer wall seemed to cover and frame all other planes and edges of the work.

The outer wall and the internal elements denied the complete 360-degree view traditionally applied to freestanding sculpture, by compressing it against the existing architectural wall and combining it with internal sculptural space and its structural elements.

My previous works—those at La Jolla Museum of Art (see p. 18), the Museum of Modern Art in New York (see p. 24), and Pomona College (see p. 31)— had made use of the complete interior space—walls, floor, and ceiling—to create a fully integrated installation. This work, however, negated the architectural totality of those installations by negating any sense of its own three-dimensionality as a sculptural relief. The completed work was given to the Los Angeles County Museum of Art for their contemporary collection in exchange for a Young Talent Purchase Award, which I had received in 1967. The work was later dismantled by the museum, and since that time has not been reconstructed.

View of museum atrium and passage directed toward installation area and edges of wall construction. Photograph by Michael Asher.

View of wall construction from installation area into passage and general exhibition area. Photograph by Michael Asher.

Detail of progressively recessing edges of wall construction as seen from west side of installation area. Photograph by Michael Asher.

Detail interior view of wall installation as seen from east side of installation area. Photograph by Edward Cornachio. Courtesy of Los Angeles County Museum of Art, Los Angeles, Ca.

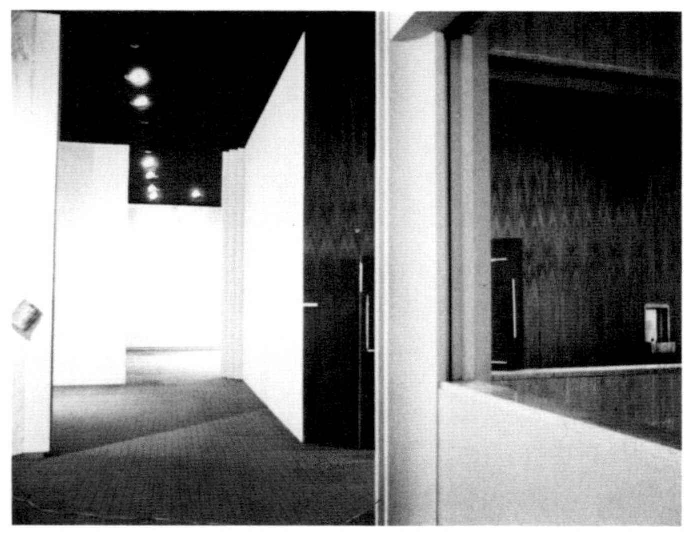

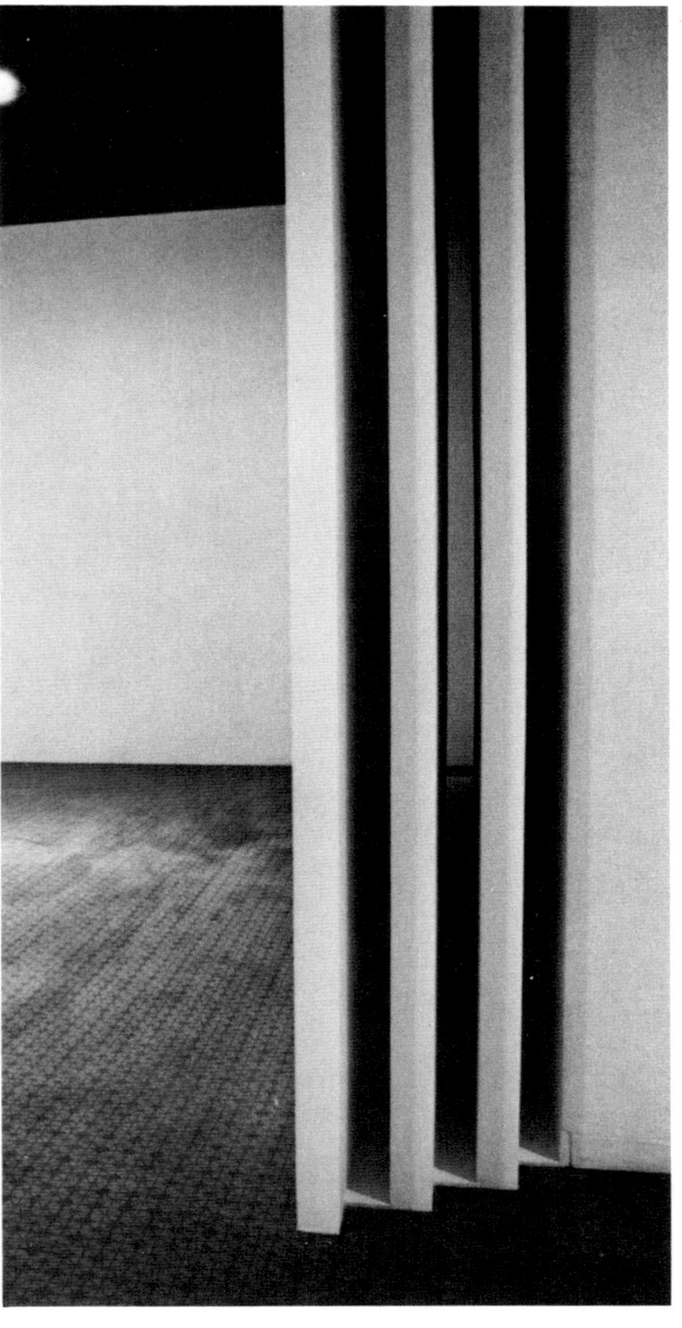
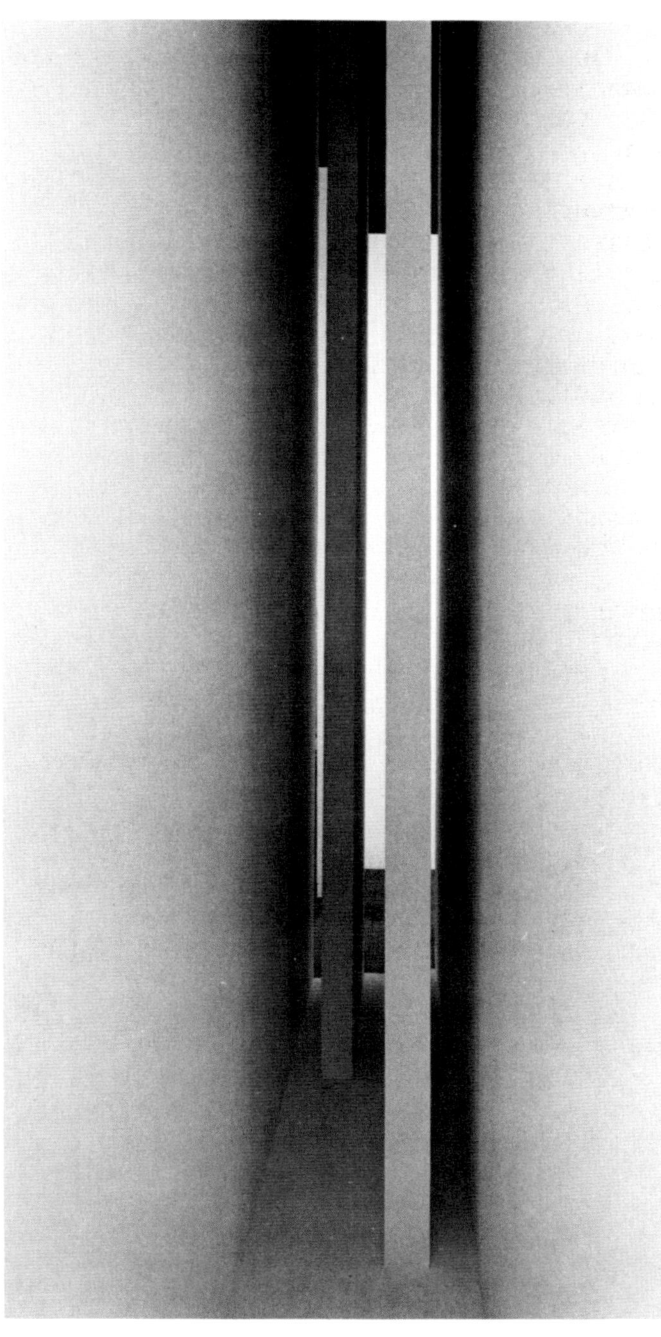

View of outer constructed wall as seen from inside the installation area at 45° angle.

Frontal view of wall installation. Photographs (a-d) by
Edward Cornachio, courtesy Los Angeles County Museum of Art,
Los Angeles, Ca.

View of edges of three constructed walls as seen from hallway.

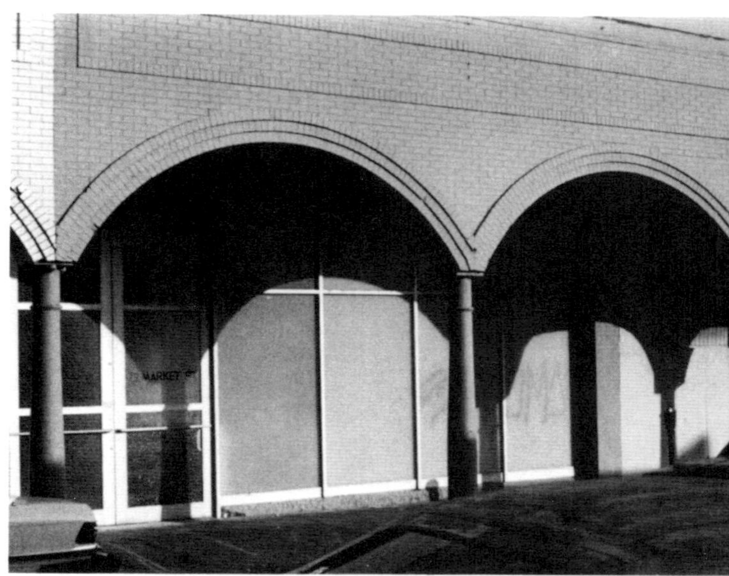

Facade of exhibition space at 72 Market Street, Venice.
Photograph by Michael Asher.

The Market Street Program was a nonprofit, artist-run exhibition program that operated for approximately twelve months in an artist's studio space—later to become a commercial gallery—at 72 Market Street, Venice, California. Market Street Program defined its own aims as follows:

A comprehensive research project classifying and exhibiting the work of professional artists according to their own criteria. The objective of the project was to fulfill the need in any art community for an exhibition program to tie together existing exhibition facilities under a decentralized museum plan while acting as a laboratory for procedures used in the selection and evaluation of art.[1]

The program was set up and participants were selected based on Southern California artists' responses to computer-processed questionnaires. This method of artist self-selection was conceived by Robert Irwin and Joshua Young, who was the adminstrator and organizer of the exhibition program. One question sought the names of artists then working in the area; another asked which artists one would be most interested in showing with.[2] This procedure resulted in my being invited to provide a work for the exhibition.

The existing exhibition area was 49 feet 1 inch by 29 feet 1 inch by 13 feet 4½ inches. Between the north wall of the exhibition container and the south wall, where the main entrance was located, was an office foyer area which measured 29 feet 1 inch by 15 feet 10 inches.

My proposal for the program was approved. It consisted of painting the entire planes of the west wall and the north wall and the entire floor with a matte-black house paint. The entire planes of the east wall and the south wall, as well as the ceiling, were painted with a matte-white house paint. Each painted plane was defined by the floor, wall, and ceiling junctures of the architectural container.

Because the work was determined by the preexisting architectural planes, I found that I could divide the space into a black and a white half without dividing any of the given planes; and the integrity of the original interior plan was therefore maintained. This was unlike the later work at "Documenta V" in 1972 (see p. 57), in which the space was divided by bisecting planes. At the same time this design allowed for disjunctive surfaces.

A wall was constructed from floor to ceiling in a passageway in the north wall to make that wall appear as even and continuous as the other three walls. A standard-sized door was fitted flush within this newly constructed wall, and was butted up as close as possible to the doorframe so as to create the appearance of a seamless surface. The north wall containing the door construction was painted black to further conceal the door and the seam.

There were two skylights measuring 7 feet 8 inches by 5 feet. They were the only sources of natural light in the installation area. Several pieces of white cloth were stretched across the bottom of the skylight wells, flush with the ceiling surface, in order to reduce the intensity of the light and to diffuse the light more evenly throughout the installation area. Two rows of tracklights, which had been installed for the program, were removed for this installation.

The viewer entered through the door in the north wall, which was one of the two black walls. Since the doorway was located near the adjacent white east wall, the viewer tended to feel less visually compressed upon entering.

The view from the two adjacent white walls looking diagonally into the installation, produced an unintended effect: an illusion of a haze spanned the two adjoining black walls, sometimes causing the corner to drop out completely, depending on the intensity of natural light entering through the skylights. The view from the adjoining black corner looking diagonally across to the two adjoining white walls made the installation area appear highly focused and sharply detailed.

Each group—the three black planes and the three white planes—was viewed as self-contained yet interdependent, internally continuous and adjacent. At the

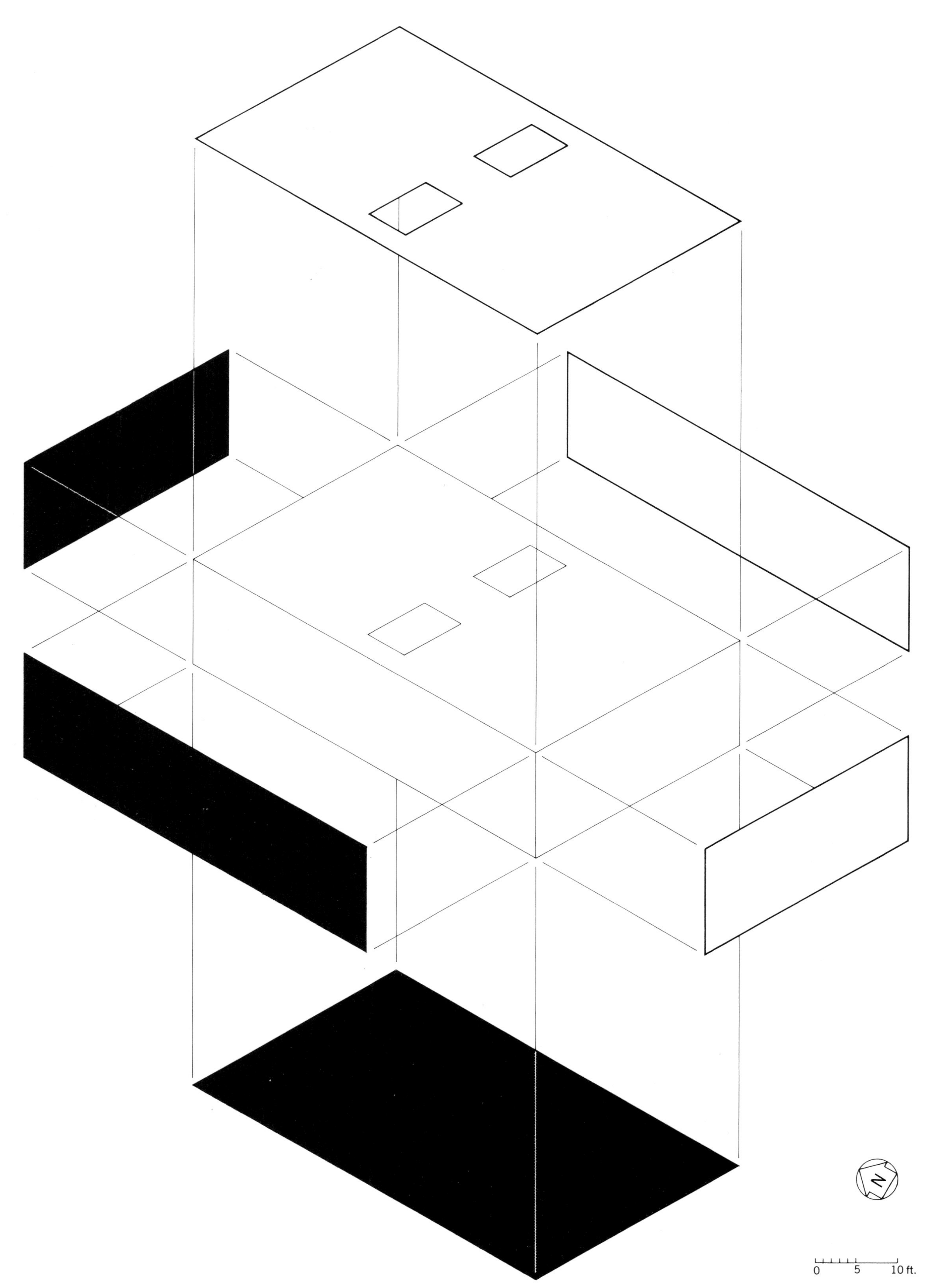

Axonometric drawing of 72 Market Street, the building used for the
Market Street Program exhibition. Drawing by Lawrence Kenny.

same time, the three interlocking complementary planes appeared to form a rectangular architectural container.

Unlike the work at the Los Angeles County Museum (see p. 43), the relief plane and the architectural support plane in this work were compressed to the point of coalescing. The architectural planes, however, remained juxtaposed.

This installation of painted planes was completely determined by the preexisting architectural dimensions. The work thereby clearly contradicted the modernist tradition in painting which claimed that a work's structure was determined by the framing edges of its internal support. Even if this were granted, the scale of the work was totally arbitrary, with one qualification: the painting always had to fit into a specific white architectural container. The edges or frame of the painting attempted to create a discrete mark, and whether or not that mark was positioned on the floor, wall, or ceiling, it manifested its own separate existence while ignoring the architectural container.

To create or materialize a work, conventional practice dictated putting as much material and/or perceptual bulk as possible between the viewer and the display structure in order to identify the autonomous aesthetic object and to distinguish it from its nonaesthetic surroundings. In the Market Street installation, I was questioning the requirement of visual bulk.

By defining the planar elements in terms of the quantity of paint that it would normally take to prepare the architectural container for an exhibition, I directly objectified the space with a material which was familiar to the viewer by common experience. In this way I disengaged the aesthetic object from its supporting surfaces by coalescing its material construction with the support structure itself.

The paint used to cover the surfaces was the standard commercial type used for interior and exterior decoration and protection, and was applied by professional painters using an airless compressor. The paint was unlike industrial materials that have been adapted for art production. (For example, using this paint on a canvas would have transformed it from a stock item into a found material object.) This was also true of other materials that were especially designed, manufactured, and applied to cover wall surfaces in a relief, and that negated their inherent painterly characteristics which had existed previous to the installation of such materials on a wall.

This installation physically made use of a flat or planar surface as in traditional painting. Yet, the wall-sized dimensions of the "painting" were predetermined by the architectural context rather than by a stretcher or armature, which are used to hold paint away from the wall to ensure that its material manifestation is disclosed and framed as a spectacle autonomous and separate from its supporting structure.

---

[1]Michael Leopold, "Computer Mating/Los Angeles," *The Art Gallery*, Summer, 1972 s.p.

[2]Peter Plagens, "Los Angeles, The Market Street Program," *Artforum*, January, 1972, p. 77 ff.

Viewing southwest corner.

Viewing northeast corner.

Viewing southeast corner.

Viewing northwest corner.

Detail of east wall and skylight.

Detail of west wall and skylight.

Photographs by Frank Thomas.

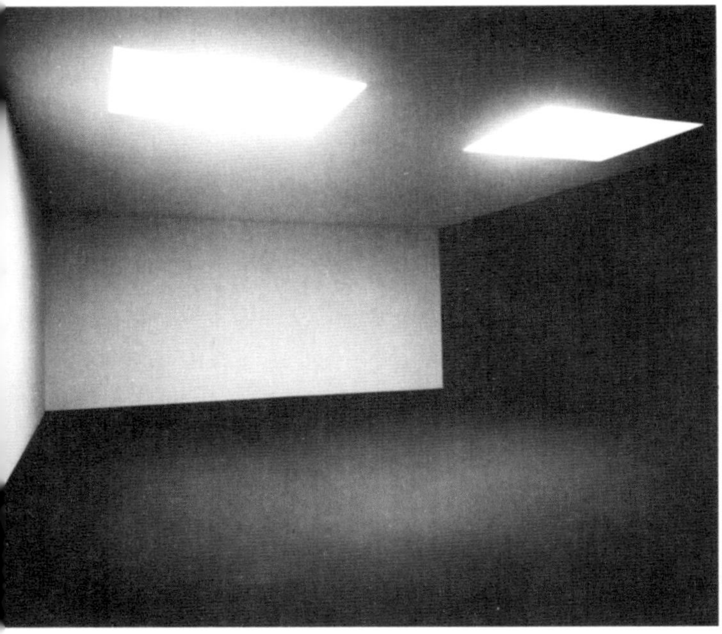

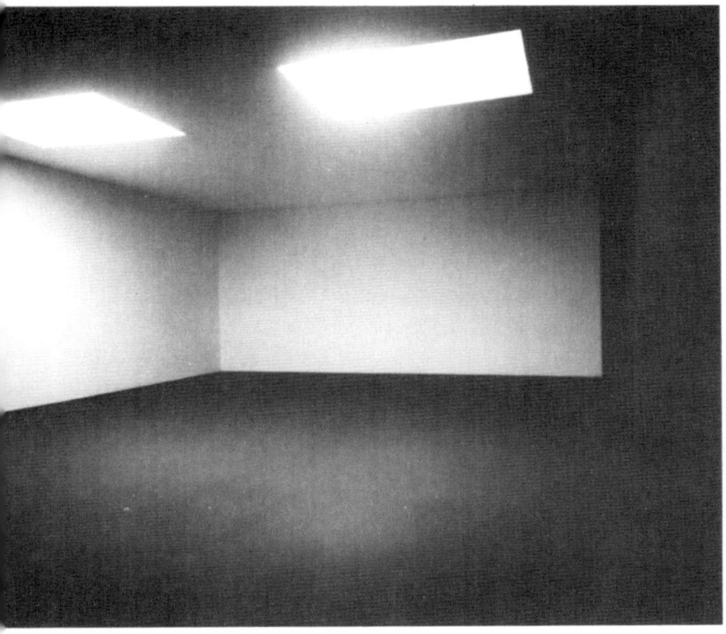

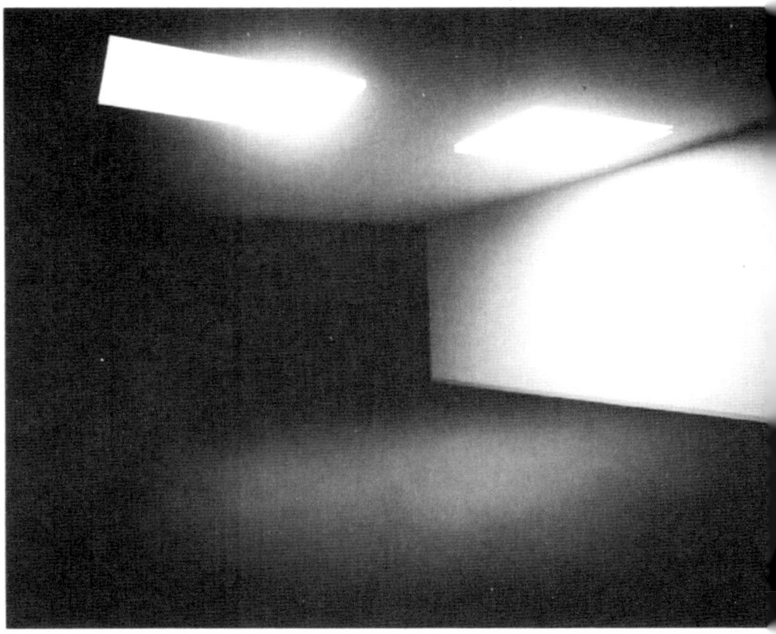

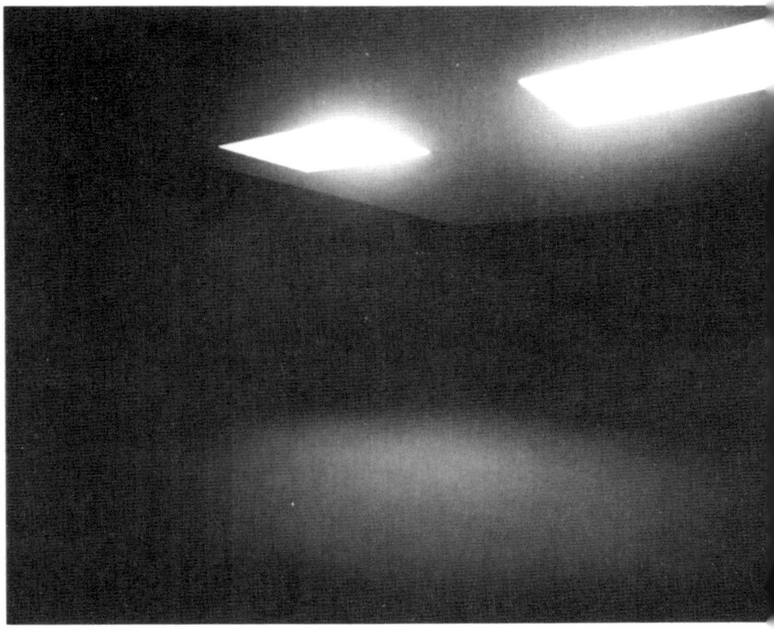

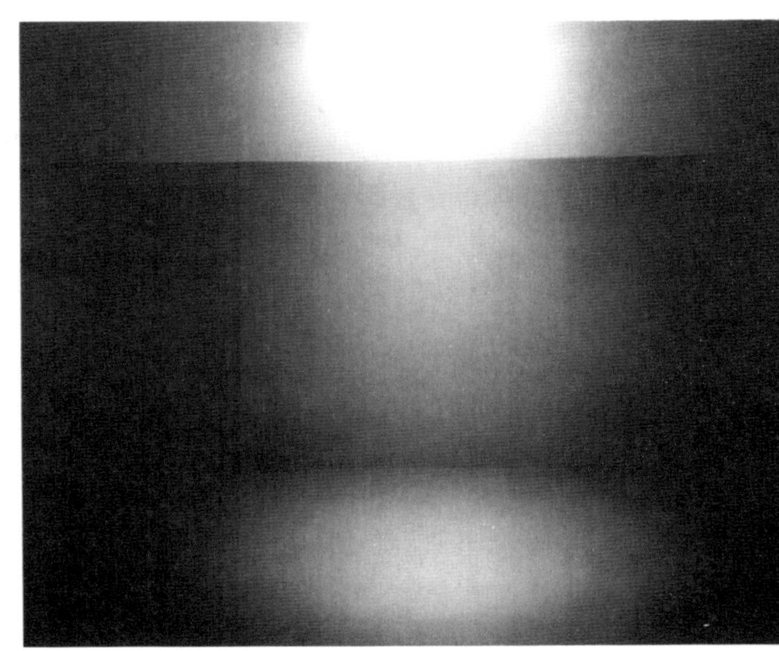

Viewing south.

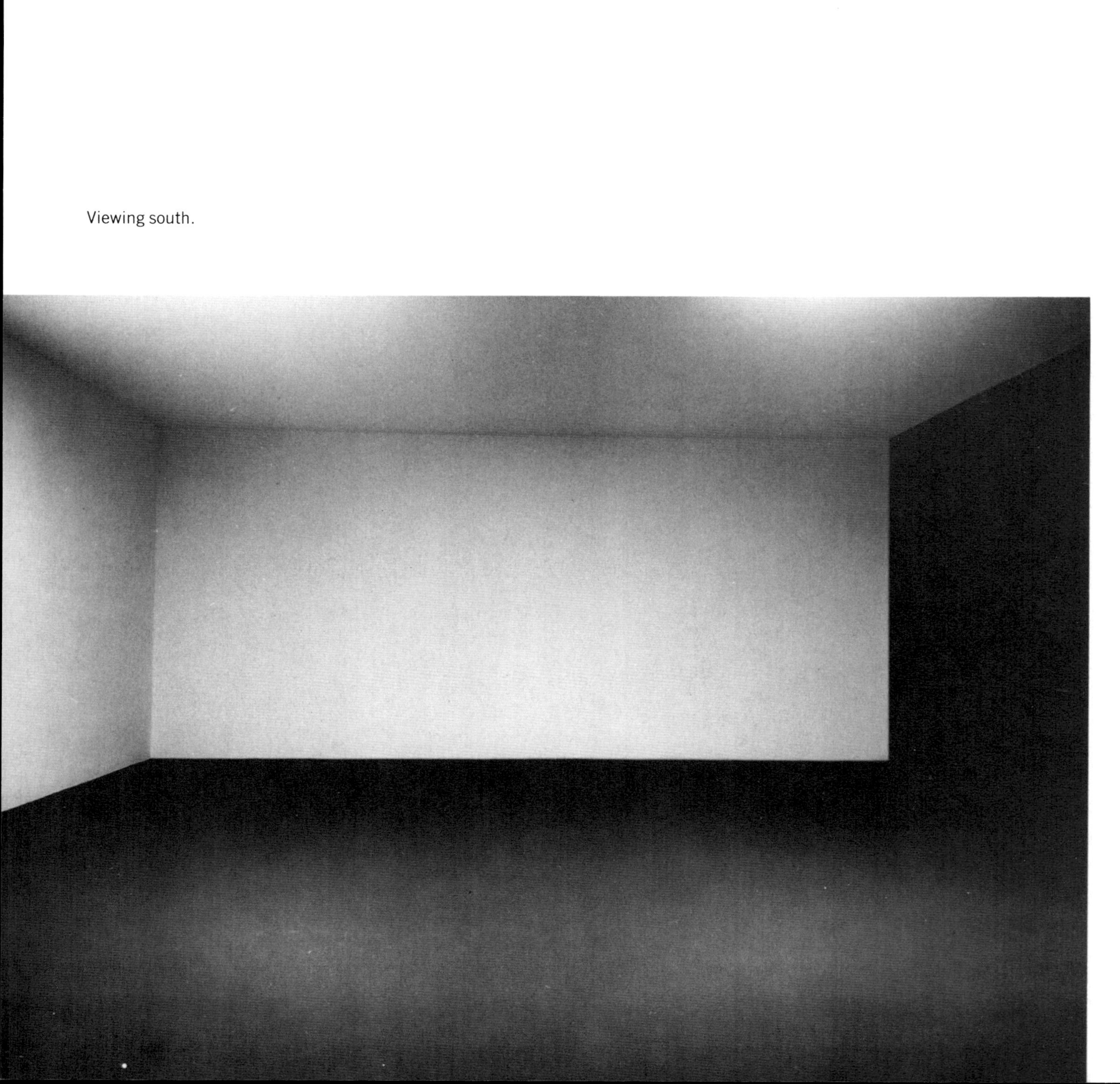

Viewing north. Photographs by Frank Thomas.

Line drawing after completion of installation.
Drawing by Michael Asher.

MARKET STREET PROGRAM 3/72

"Documenta," one of the largest group exhibitions of contemporary art, is staged in Kassel, West Germany, every four to six years. Approximately eighty artists participated in "Documenta V," which was held in 1972, within the confines of the Museum Fridericianum and the Neue Galerie. The director of "Documenta V" was Dr. Harald Szeemann.

In July 1970, Dr. Szeemann wrote to me expressing interest in my work, and in December of the following year invited me to participate in the exhibition. On February 2, 1972, Jean-Christophe Amman, a curator representing "Documenta V," showed me a plan with the assigned space for my installation during his visit to Venice, California. The area that would be available for my work was part of a long hallway, 3.66 meters high, 4.25 meters wide, and 10.97 meters long.

At the time, I was unable to go to Kassel, either to inspect the location, or for the final installation of the work. It occurred to me then to see if another artist could manage to construct my work and modify it if necessary in order to adapt it to its location. It was a challenge to design an installation on paper that would later be constructed in a place I was unfamiliar with. I asked John Knight, an artist and friend, and he agreed to go to Kassel to construct the work. I didn't know then whether I would ever see the finished installation. So, in late March 1972, I made my final plans for a proposal.[1]

My proposal was determined, in part, by the length and width of the available space. The work would be a wood-frame construction of walls, floor, and ceiling measuring 9.65 meters by 3.86 meters by 2.28 meters. The floor would be 10 centimeters from the museum floor and the ceiling 2.28 meters high, so that it would be in the normal perceptual field of persons of average height. Walls, floor, and ceiling were covered with particle board and drywall and were treated with vinyl latex paint.

This proposal focused on issues similar to those addressed at the Market Street Program. Here I wanted to visually divide the interior of the enclosure in half, along the centerline of its longest axis, by painting the north half black, and the south half white. This meant that the ceiling, floor, and two end walls were half black and half white. Whereas the entire north wall was painted black, and the entire south wall white.

Two light wells were constructed in the white half of the container at the east and west corners. These were cut out of the ceiling where the ceiling met the adjacent south wall. Each light well measured 1.83 meters in length and 7.6 centimeters in width. Light from the museum interior passed through the light wells and was diffused, due to a polarizer and a piece of translucent cloth which stretched across the bottom of the light well, flush with the ceiling. I wanted enough light to come through these wells so that, after a short time of eye adjustment, every surface in the enclosure could easily be seen.

The construction was completed by using a 91.5 centimeters wide, light-tight door, mounted flush on the black side of the interior container, for entry and exit.[2]

The standard-grade construction for the walls, floor, and ceiling followed the configuration of the available space, making it long and narrow: an unusual shape, contrary to any enclosure which would normally be used for an exhibition area for the display of artworks. But, by integrating the shape of the hallway into the construction, I was revealing a framework which defined the internal structure of the work. As a leftover architectural element which had been assigned to me for the execution of a work, the 10.97 meter walkway was incorporated in the determination of the work. The hallway due to its formalization, was converted into a function of bodily and visual perception, still mirroring the external architectural structure to which it was bound.

On August 19, 1972, I arrived in Kassel to see the finished work and realized that it was very beautifully constructed. While the white surfaces were immediately visible on entering, the black surfaces in the distance remained below the visual threshold. Eventually, as the eye adapted, the black surfaces could be visually established as contiguous. The black half of the installation absorbed light and was therefore

Detail drawing of light well, plan and elevation by John Knight
for the purposes of his supervision of the installation.

Drawing by exhibition architect Dombois indicating position
and placement of installation in the hallway.

Construction drawing of installation by exhibition architect
Dombois.

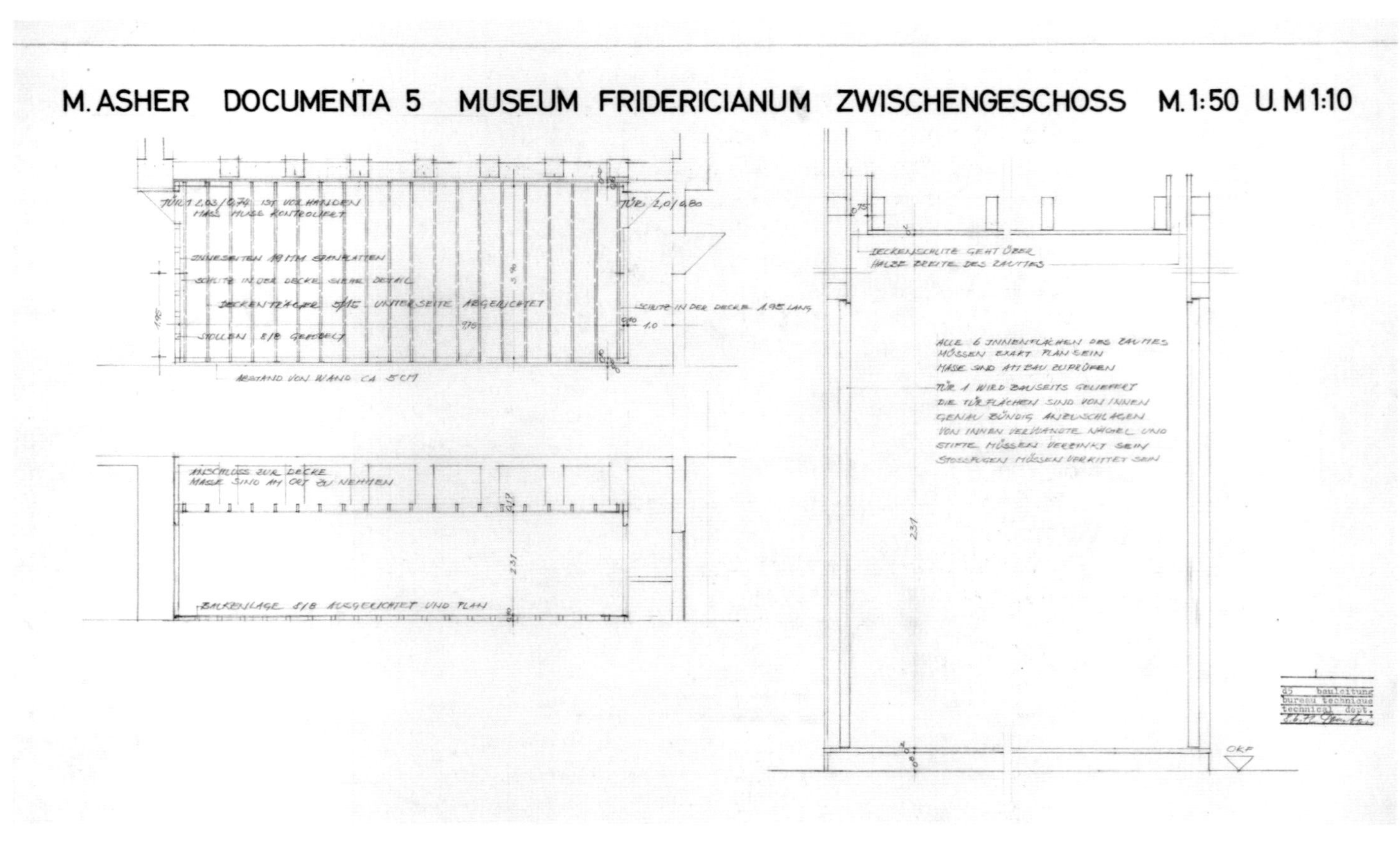

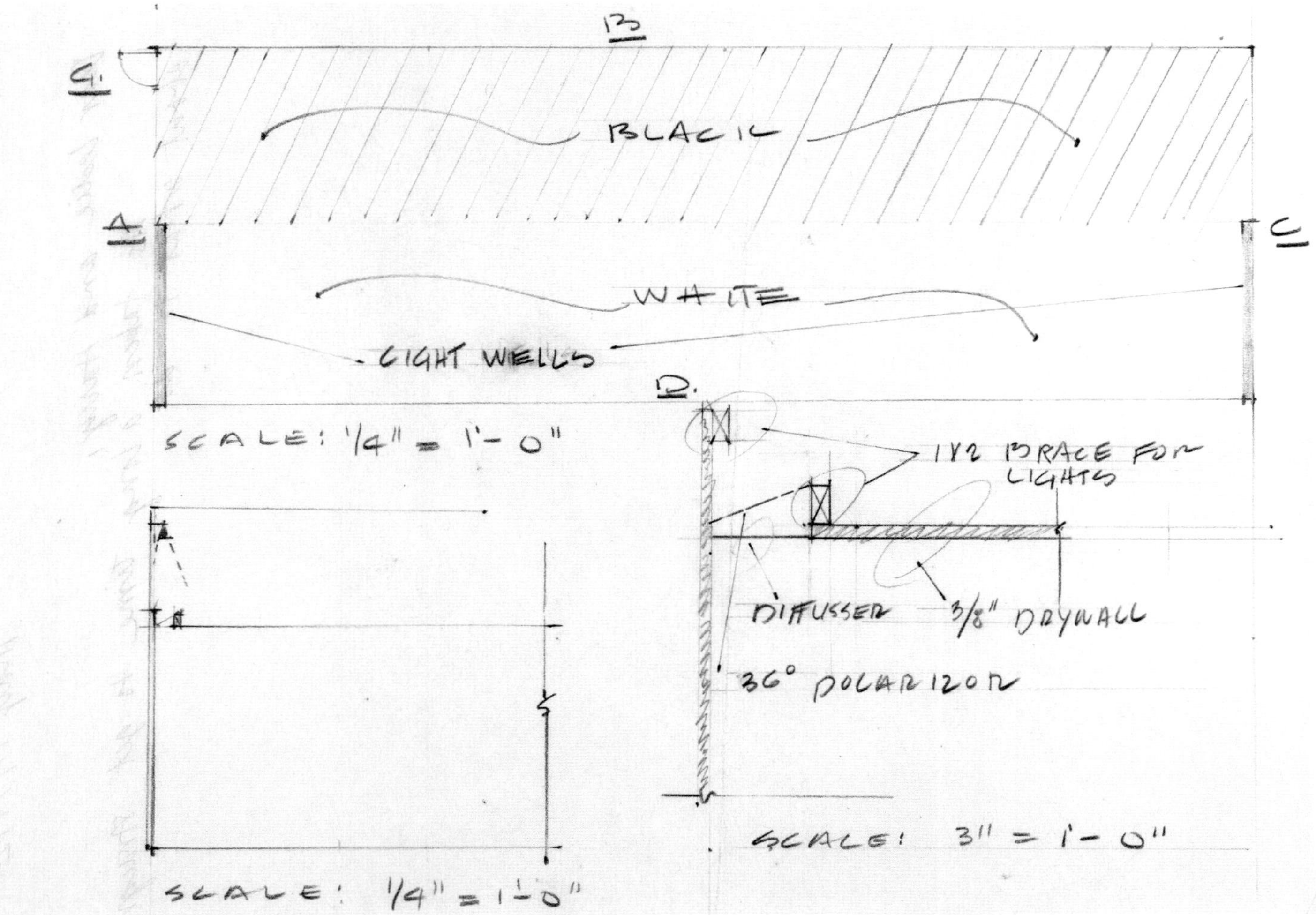

M. ASHER

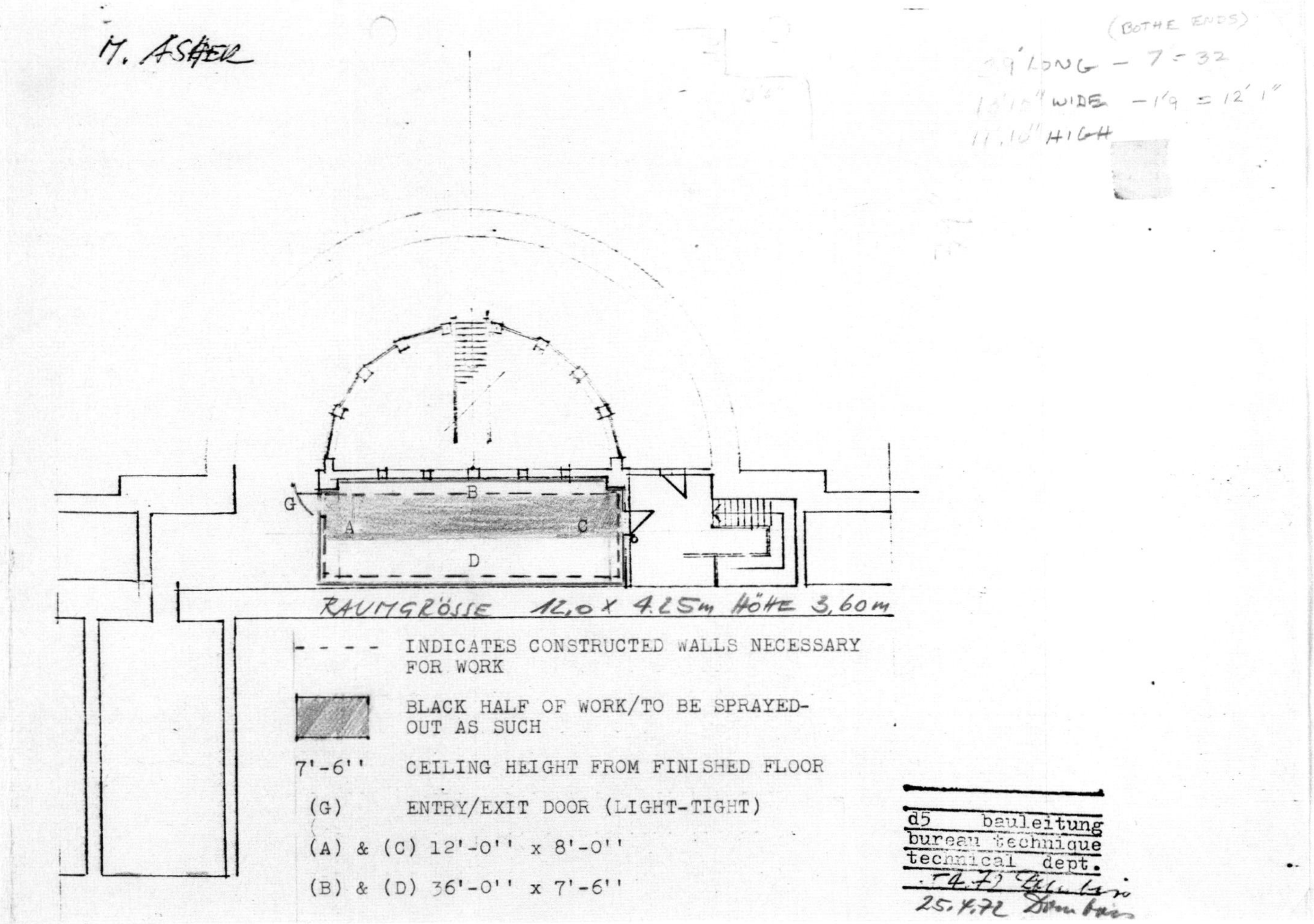

fairly dim; while the white half, illuminated by the light wells at each end, reflected light.

While the viewer was standing in the white half, the work appeared to be all white, although it seemed as if a sheet of smoked glass ran the entire length of the space. The black half seemed to be denser than the white half. While standing in the white half, the viewer formed a strong perceptual image of spatial mass in the opposite black half. Whereas, while standing in the black half, the illusion disappeared.

Although each architectural plane was divided perceptually by paint, there were no physical obstacles to prevent the viewers from walking across the floor plane in any direction they chose.

Bisected and encompassing the viewer, this enclosure could not be seen in its entirety from any one point of view. Each view from zone to zone, as well as each diagonal view found its complementary spatial and chromatic perception in the projection of the visual axis behind the viewer.

All of the planes in this installation were assembled *and* distinguished as adjacent pictorial planes. Therefore they also became planes or elements constituting a sculpture. The installation was not, however, viewed in the round as conventional sculpture; rather, the sum of the six planes constituted a volumetric, rectangular body, forming an enclosure around the viewer. The entire sculptural volume was viewed from within, was walked through, over, and upon. By being an enclosure or housing, the assembled planes were simultaneously experienced as an *architectural* container.

The door defined a transition from the actual exhibition space into the actual sculptural and pictorial space. Upon returning to the general exhibition space, the viewer was cut off from the formalized perceptual mode which equated bodily and visual perception. Once outside, the viewer's perception was once again fragmented into its various functions.

The wood-frame construction was a stage or mediation for the paint. The paint was not applied to the given architecture, as in the Market Street work. Rather,

it was applied to the work's separately constructed surfaces, thereby contradicting the work's original intention as a method of directly articulating the given architectural support.

By formalizing its own purpose within the exhibition, this installation—as a stage—reflected the cultural stage which "Documenta"—as an exhibition—occupied. As a spatial enclosure, it occupied an autonomous position; yet the enclosure did not define the more general conditions of the viewer's experience at the exhibition. The implied autonomy of the work could only be seen within the context of most of the other works, each of which operated within their own separate framework. The work seemed to seclude itself from the rest of the exhibition, while it was actually subject to and receptive of its conditions.

---

[1] This work is extensively reviewed in Carter Ratcliff, "Adversary Spaces," Artforum October, 1972. pp. 40–44.

[2] The door was shipped from the Market Street Program.

Detail of light well on the east side of the installation. All photographs by Karl-Heinz Krings.

View of installation from west wall.

View of installation from northwest corner.

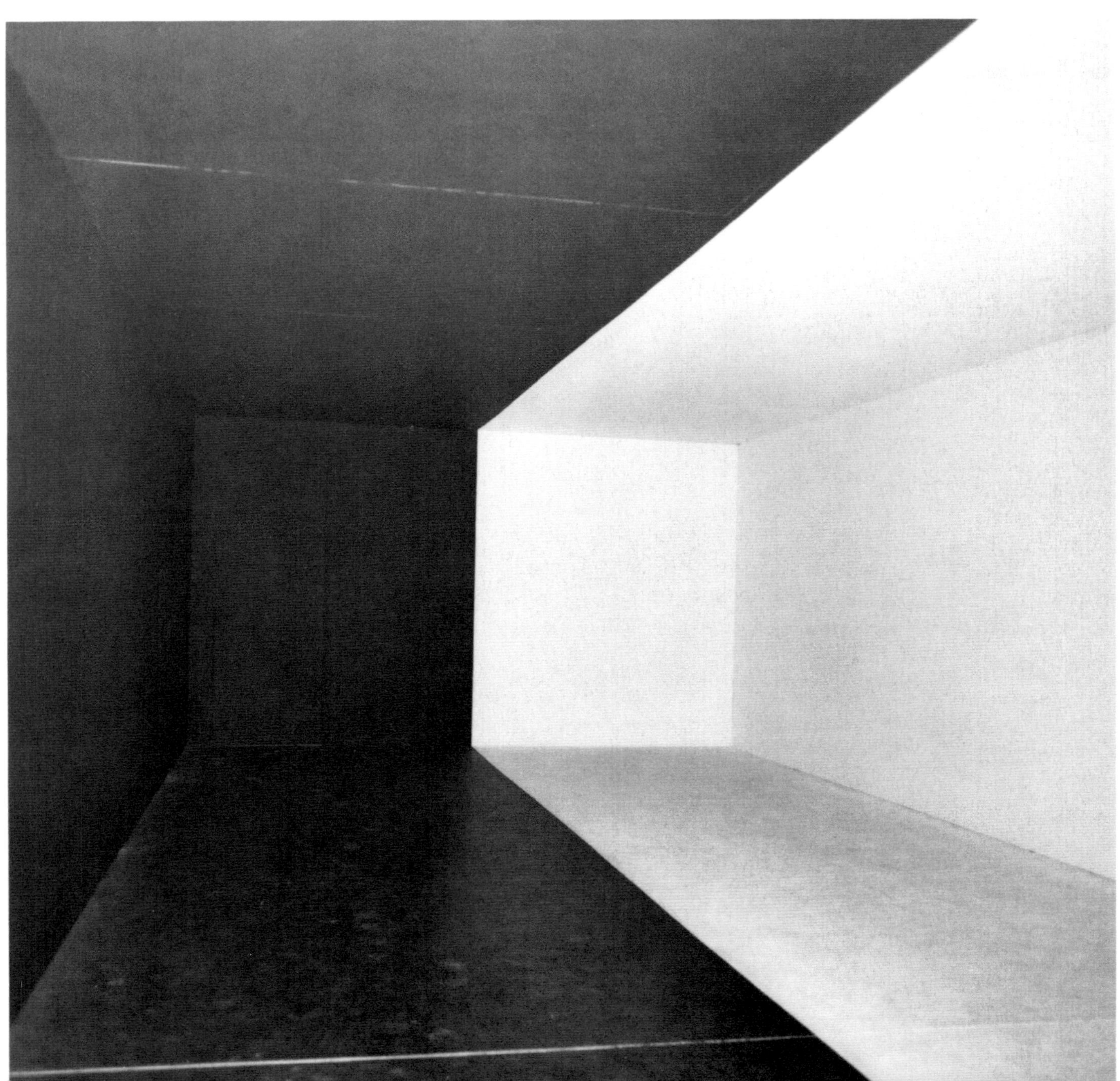

View of installation from southwest corner.

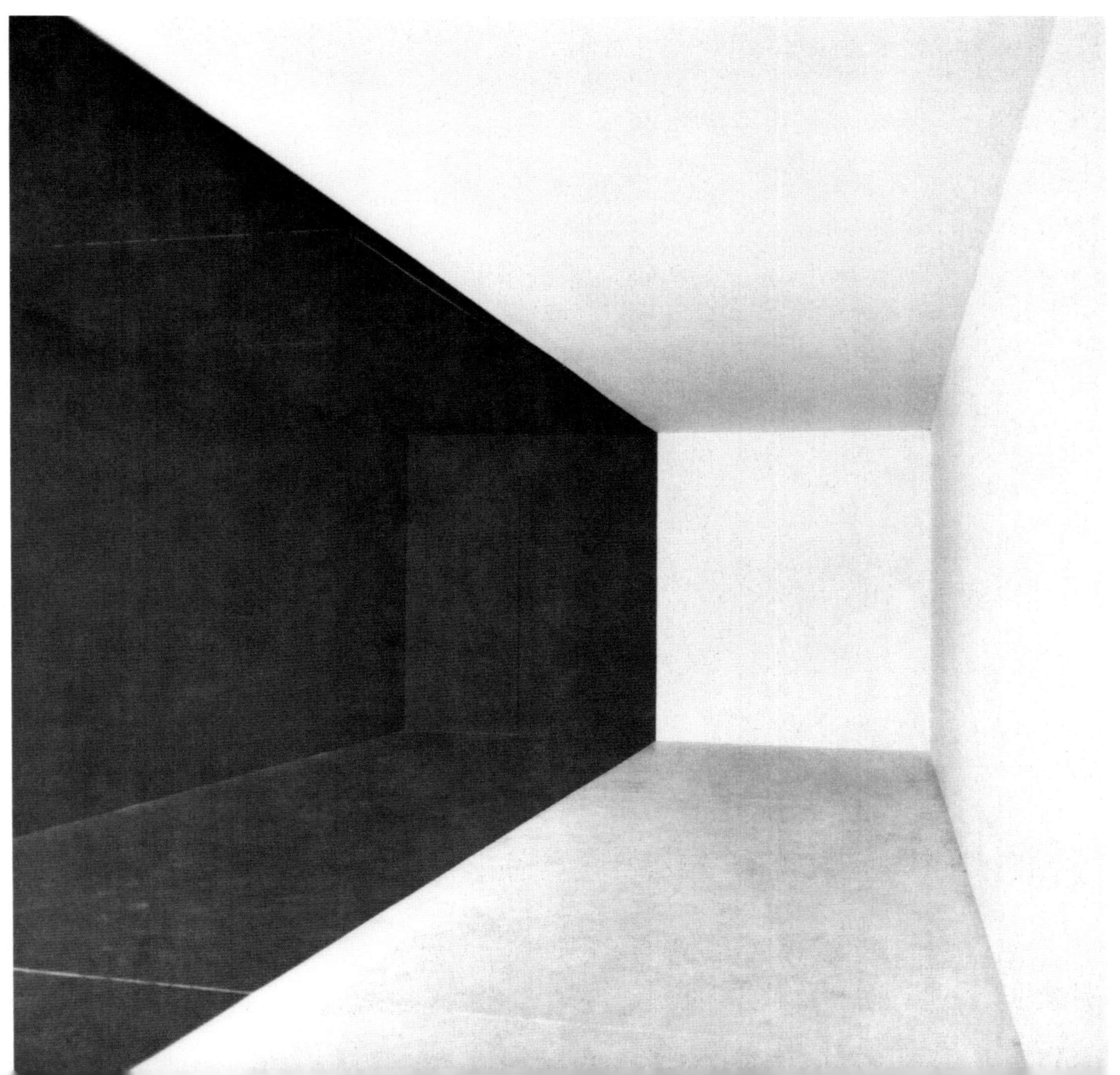

Gallery A 402 was a student-run gallery where exhibitions were organized by Suzanne Kuffler, who was at that time a graduate student at the California Institute of the Arts. The gallery functioned as an exhibition space for both artists and students to make their work accessible to the Institute community. In late 1972 I was invited to exhibit a work there.

The gallery measured 27 feet 7 inches by 16 feet 8 inches, with a ceiling height of 9 feet. Two rows of fluorescent light fixtures—the gallery's only source of light—extended the entire length of the room. The floor was covered with brown wall-to-wall carpeting. A series of rectangular wall facets—floor-to-ceiling wall projections which formed short strips of wall surface or wall planes on a north-south and east-west axis—interrupted the exhibition wall planes, breaking up any continuity that the installation space might have had as a rectangular volume. There were two rectangular wall projections on the east side and one large 6-by-9-foot wall projection on the west side. Looking straight ahead into the southeast corner of the room, there was another short rectangular wall projection. All of these projected wall surfaces were permanent and accommodated utilities and air-ducting. Only the southwest corner was not interrupted by any projections.

Given this architectural configuration, I developed a proposal for all of the white wall surfaces. My idea was to paint the six parallel, opposing surfaces on the north and south side with the white *Dunn-Edwards* paint that was normally used for wall surfaces throughout the Institute. The seven east-west surfaces I wanted to leave as they were, yellowed, spotted with fingerprints, and broken through in various places.

It didn't occur to me to tell the gallery director what I planned to do, other than saying that I would paint the gallery. The morning I arrived to do the installation, I found all the walls freshly painted. I was really shocked because it was like having painted the work away. After thinking about it for a couple of hours I decided to adapt the idea slightly. I kept all the east-west opposing wall surfaces painted with *Dunn-Edwards Beau-T-Wall-White* since the gallery or-

ganizer had used that paint. On all of the north-south opposing wall surfaces, I then applied *Sherwin Williams Nu-White*. Both paints were matte-white, and close in tone and value, but the *Nu-White* was intended to diffuse the light from the fluorescent fixtures while the *Dunn-Edwards* carried the light. The interior surfaces were identified therefore in terms of their distinct response to light rather than their chromatic difference.

The one set of double doors at the entrance to the gallery and the removable doorhead were dismantled, making the passage to the gallery an open span from floor to ceiling. This made the gallery accessible at all times during the exhibition. The doors —two rectangular planes—were normally part of the gallery's interior. With the doors removed, the viewer became aware of the function utilities (fire hose, water fountain, utility-room door, and elevator) in the outside hallway framed by the open doorframe of the exhibition space. Viewers also became aware of their own static positioning within the formalized space as they watched people passing in the external space of the hallway. Visitors entering through the doorframe thus established a connection between exterior dynamics and interior stasis.

The two different whites of the painted surfaces were reduced to a consideration of axis of location and amount of light absorbed. There resulted from this an increased awareness of the interior functional elements (power outlets, air vents, light fixtures, sprinkler system, and wooden floor molding), which were continued and reflected in the exterior functional elements visible through the doorframe.

My work was a formalization of the gallery's architectural surfaces as well as the preexisting architectural order that determined the configuration of the interior gallery space and the exterior hallway. The art-display function of the gallery container appeared within the larger multiple-function architectural container. Just as the appearance of a box within a box was obviated by the removal of the doors, the separateness of the wall planes, emphasized by their

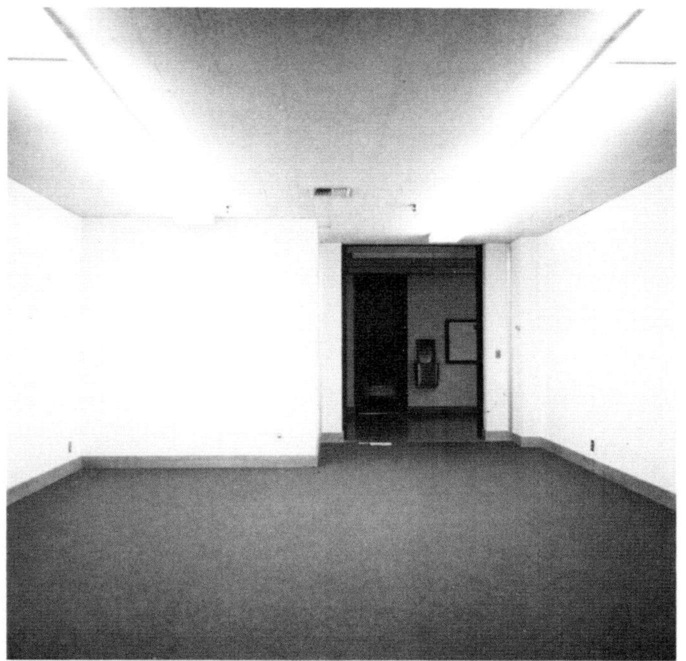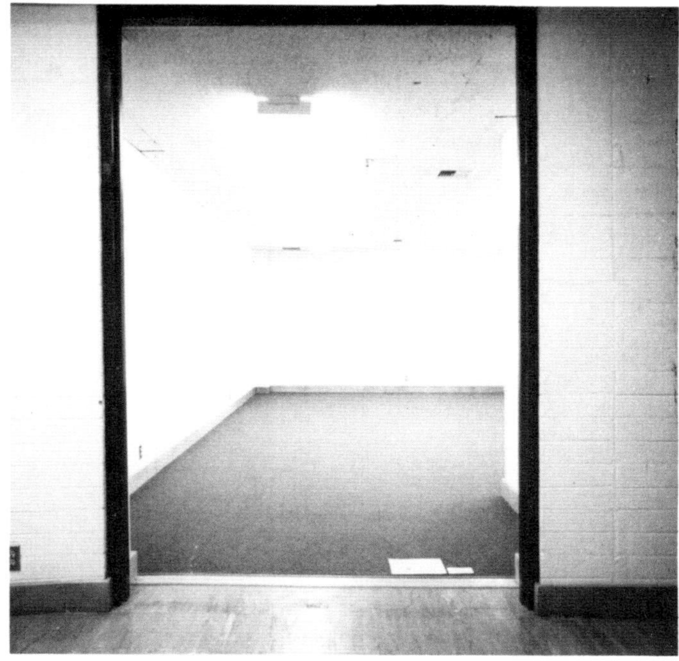

painted surfaces, decomposed the white gallery container.

As a consequence of integrating the outer hallway and gallery interior the passer-by, following the normal traffic pattern through the building, could have entered the perceptual range of the viewers facing the doorframe. Thus the viewer's more or less static perception of the spatial configuration was interrupted. The people passing through the hallway were unaware of the viewer's static position while assessing the work, but the viewer's perception was activated by becoming aware of the movement in the hallway. The simultaneity of these two viewing modes brought about a shift in the way in which the viewer perceived the seemingly autonomous structure of the installation.

Modernist tradition has created cultural boundaries within which aesthetic production is viewed as being autonomous and particularized: usually those of institutions such as museums and galleries. There the works of art, as objects, are solely interactive with the viewer, disallowing any other routines or reality to take place within the field of the viewer's perception. On the other hand, the Institute installation did not negate the reality of different movements and routines (e.g., entering and leaving the gallery space) that may have been ancillary to the process of perception.

Camera inside of installation viewing north into hallway.

Camera in hallway viewing south into Gallery A 402 and installation. Photographs by Alvin Comiter.

Study plan of Gallery A 402 with notes on exhibition project
by Michael Asher.

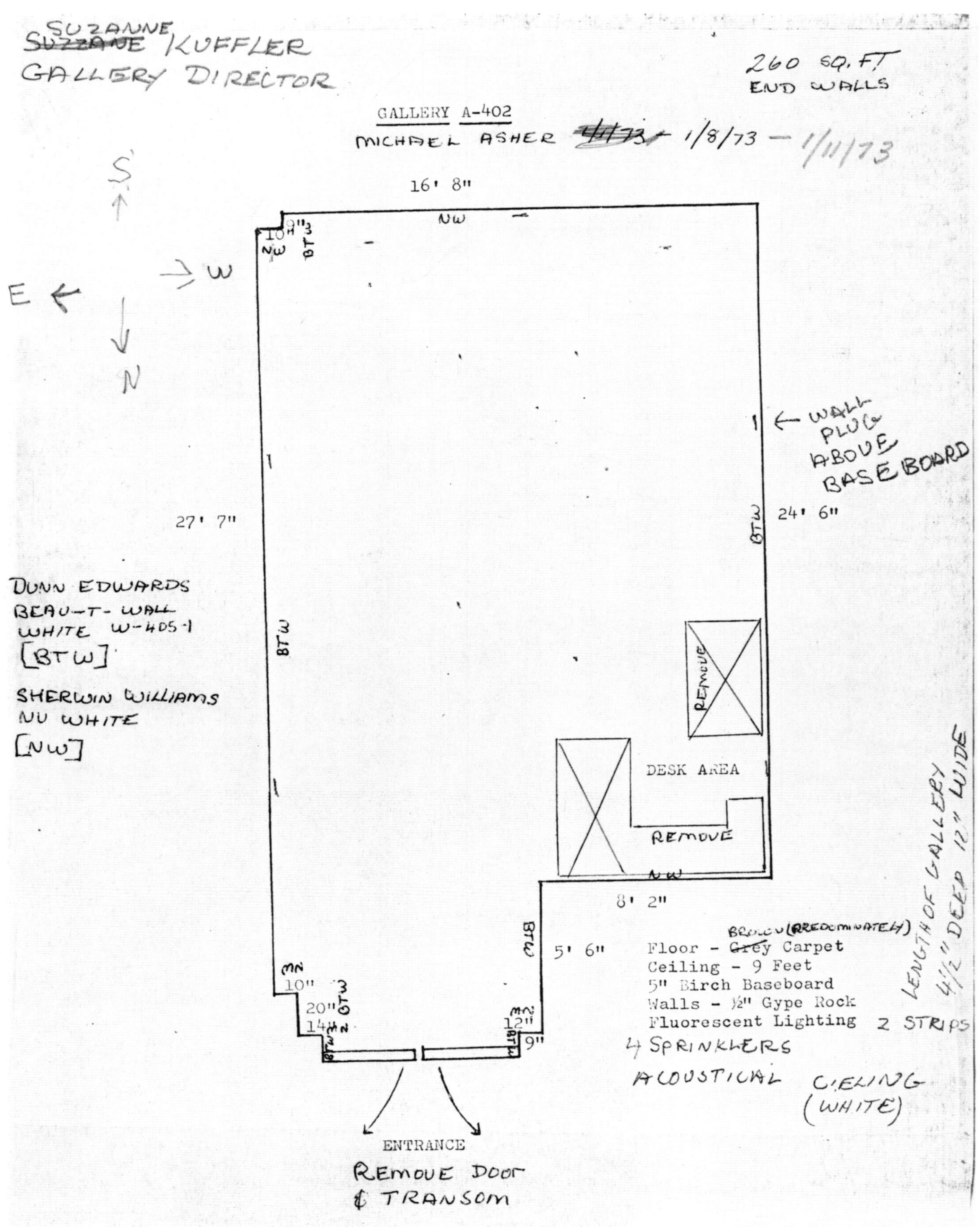

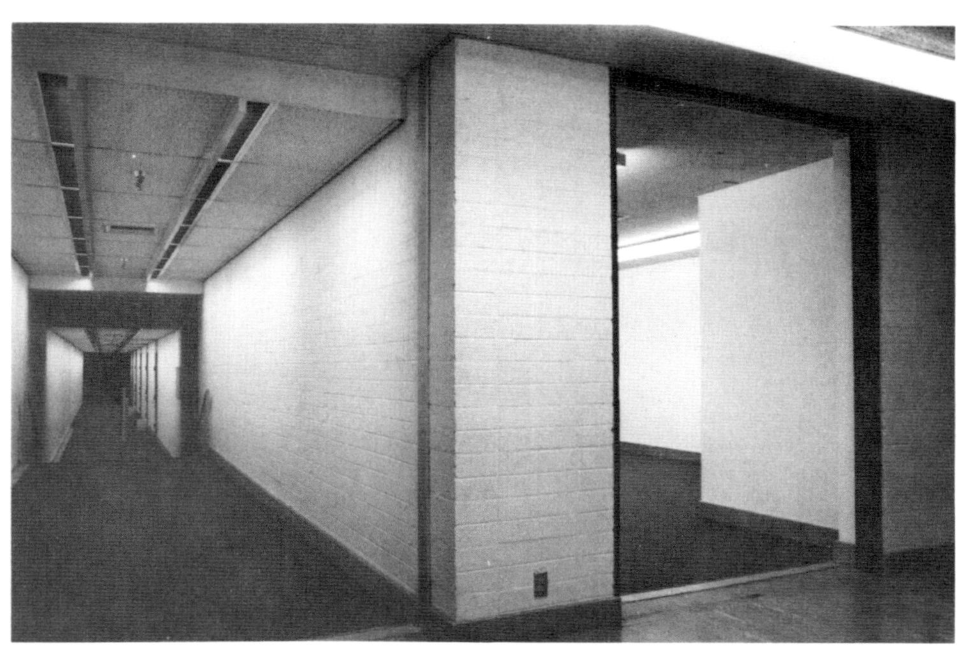

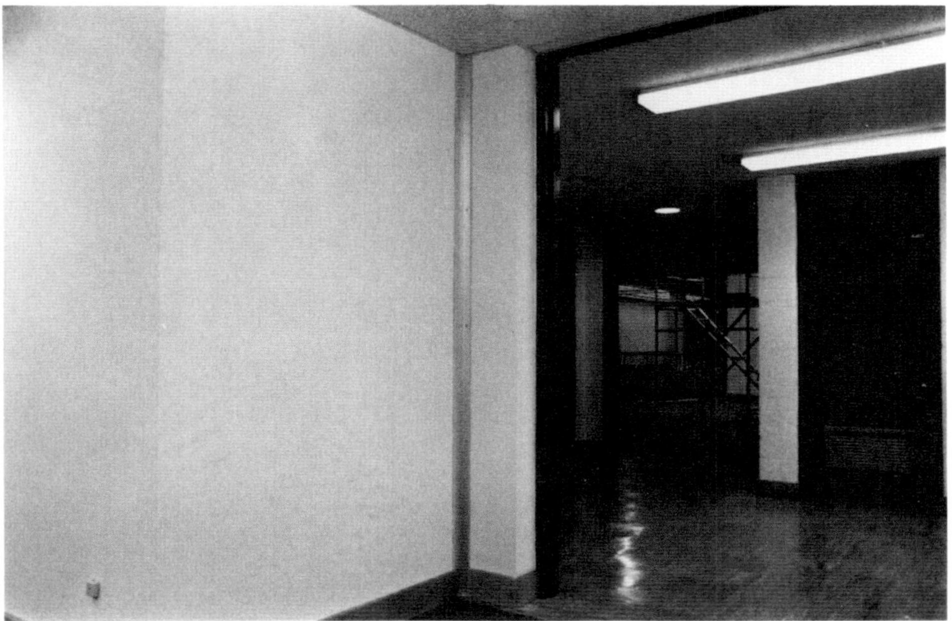

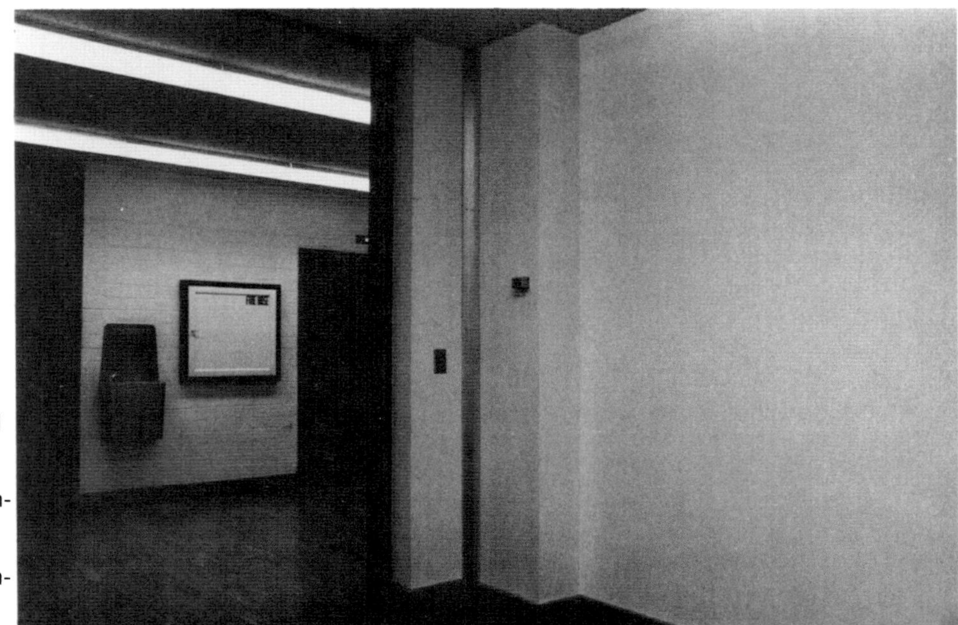

Camera viewing southwest into hallway and installation space simultaneously.

Camera viewing from installation area northwest into hallway and mezzanine.

Camera viewing from installation area northeast into hallway and mezzanine.
All photographs by Michael Asher.

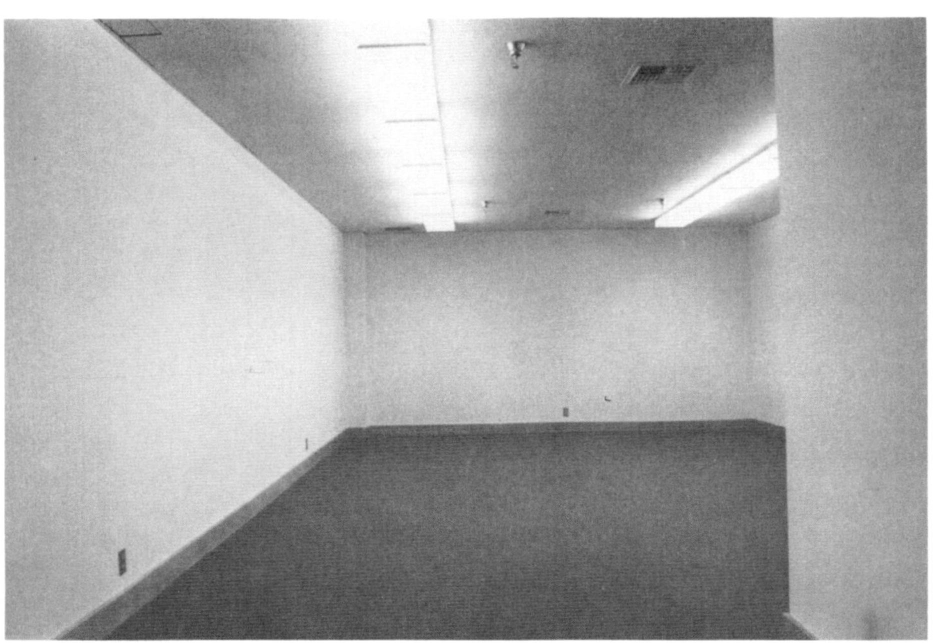

Camera inside installation area looking at south wall.

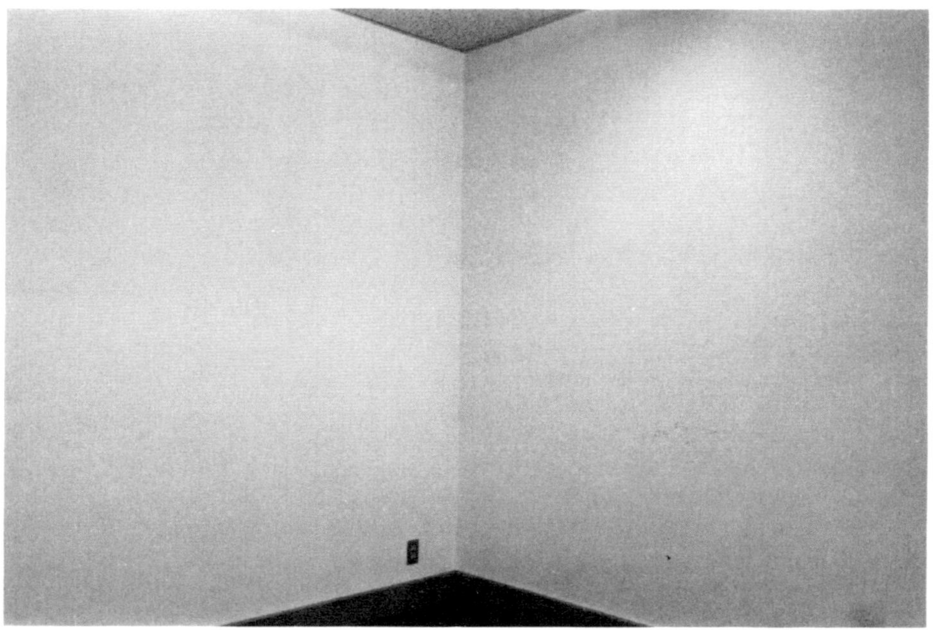

Camera viewing northwestern area of installation toward north wall adjacent to utility shaft. North wall painted with Sherwin Williams Nu-White. West wall painted with Dunn-Edwards Beau-T-Wall White.

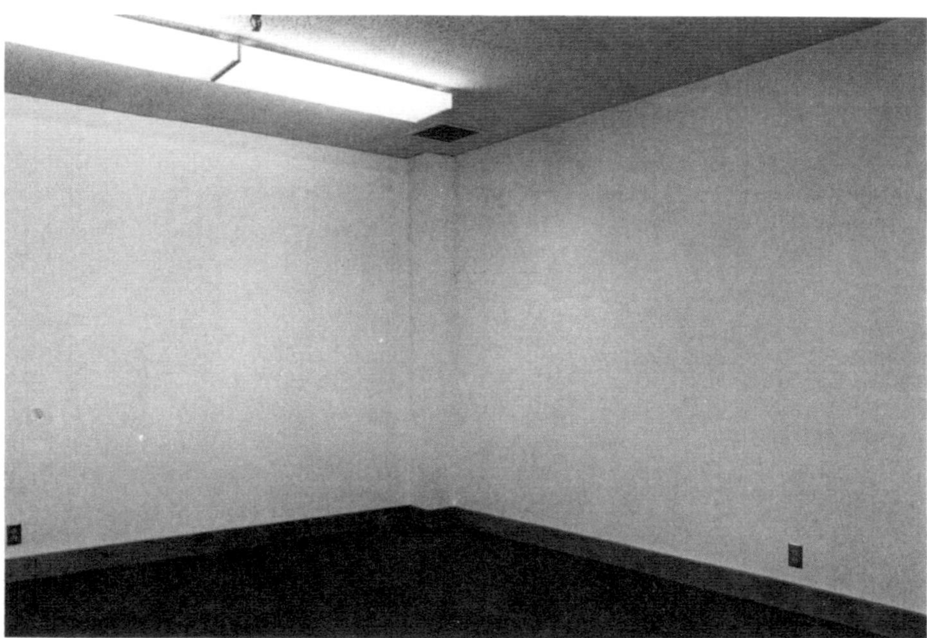

Camera viewing into southeast corner of installation space. East wall painted with Dunn-Edwards Beau-T-Wall White. South wall painted with Sherwin Williams Nu-White. All photographs by Michael Asher.

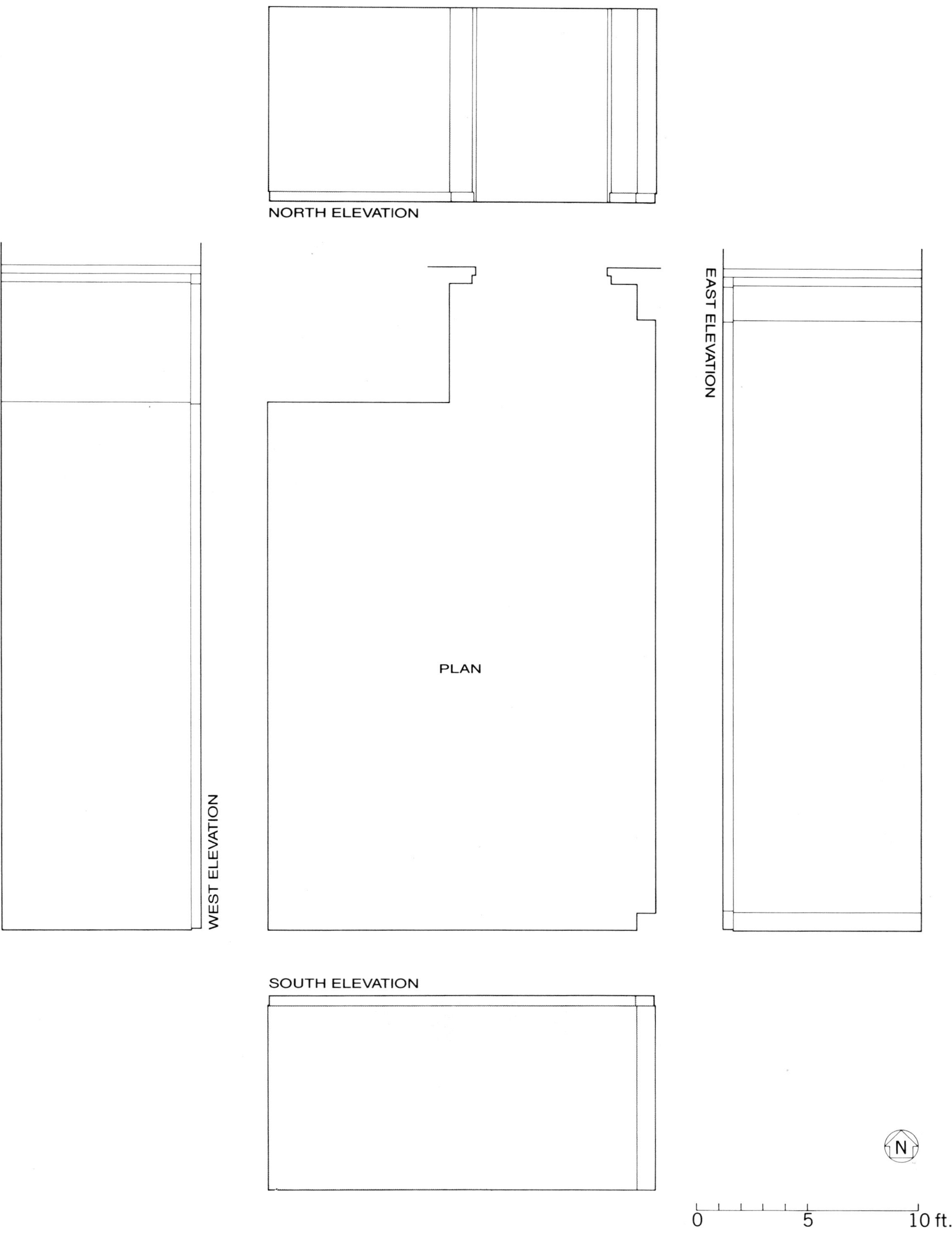

Ground plan and elevations of Gallery A 402.
Drawing by Lawrence Kenny.

May 14–May 18, 1973
The University of California at Irvine, Gallery 167
Irvine, California

MARNETTE ANDERSON
MICHEAL ASHER
STEVE CARSON
LESLIE DAVIS
ERIC DIESSLIN
LUCY DUBIN
MARY BETH ELLIOTT
BARBARA FILET
BETSY GERACE
ALEXANDRA GREVATT
JANET GROVE
ANDREW HARRIS
DEBBY HEDUCK
KIM HUBBARD
JIM JAHN
JOHN KNIGHT
JANE REYNOLDS
ROBERT SENOUR
STEPHANIE THOMASSON
PHILIP TIPPETT
ERIC WALT
TERRANCE WILLIAMS
WAH HO YOUNG
ELINOR YERKES

RECENT WORKS:
GALLERY 167 MAY 14– MAY 18
UNIVERSITY OF CALIFORNIA, IRVINE

I had the opportunity to teach as a replacement instructor in the Studio-Problems Class, at the School of Fine Arts, University of California at Irvine, during the second quarter of the school year. At the end of the term the students organized an exhibition, requesting that both faculty and students who had participated in the class be represented in the exhibition. As a participating faculty member I agreed to contribute to the exhibition.

The exhibition was installed in a small room on campus and contained primarily drawings and photos framed behind glass, as well as a few paintings, some sculpture, a work with audiotape, and a work dealing with temperature. I proposed for my contribution that each piece of glass that was used in the exhibition for protection and display be measured, and that their total lengths and widths be computed and averaged. The result was a 14 inch-by-14 inch glass square, which was attached to the wall at eye level with four finishing nails. This piece of glass was thus installed as the other works.

My work framed a 14 inch-by-14 inch section of the wall. The surface of the glass reflected light and was thus distinguishable from the matte-white wall surface. The four finishing nails holding the glass square against the wall were also clearly visible.

The structure of the work addressed the particular presentation elements used in a university art exhibition, which the students considered part of their education. I therefore assembled the work with the materials necessary for such a presentation. The work was unmediated by paper or other support materials, which, by themselves, block the wall or immediate structural support. My use of isolated presentation elements disclosed the existence of mediation devices as functioning elements in their own right.

By isolating the 14 inch-by-14 inch section of the wall without the intervention of paper or other materials between the framing glass and the support-wall, the texture of the rolled paint over the drywall and the color of the wall became objectified. I employed display and presentation materials that were generally part of the context of the exhibition: glass, nails, and wall surfaces of rolled paint. Therefore, what functioned as a backdrop for the other works in the exhibition became the content of my own. Particularized in my work, the paint on the gallery walls could then be perceived in its usual function as well as a backdrop behind all of the other works on the wall.

The glass in my own work was meant to function as the object of perception, not the focal point of the work. The work did not claim attention for itself as an object, but, rather, as a device whereby modes of presentation and their constituent elements could be analyzed, ranging from the architectural container, to the glass which normally protects and frames the work, to the nails used to support the glass, to the wall, the white backdrop for the works of art.

Detail of glass square and its support. Photograph taken after
actual installation by Michael Asher.

Installation of glass square on wall. Photograph taken after
actual installation by Michael Asher.

Announcement card for Project, Inc.

An invitation to do a work came from Paul McMahon, at Project, Inc., a nonprofit, community arts project that shared a building in Boston with other similar programs. I decided that this work would involve the use of film and film projection. I had experimented with videotape, using mostly a static camera, since early 1973. Video and film could be used with media technology in a way that would be analogous to my previous use of various materials in existing architectural contexts. For example, I had produced 30 minutes of tape and had run it through a tapedeck to pick up the deck's signal, without the use of a camera. This work had been rejected.

In the Project, Inc. work I used film and film production in a way similar to my earlier use of videotape. I wanted to make a medium-gray frameless film without a camera, using only the processing equipment and chemicals usually employed for development.

This film was meant for only one screening at Project, Inc., because, after being shown once the medium gray would inevitably be fractured with scratches which would then be perceived as moving lines within the projected picture plane.

With the assistance of Mark Whitney, a professional filmmaker, I made some trial runs with a camera so that the technicians processing the film would know exactly the sort of gray I was looking for. I did this with a Super-8 cartridge, the least expensive way possible. Shortly afterward the camera was put aside and test runs were begun as 16mm film stock was put through the chemicals and processing machinery. For each run the amount of light and the voltage used in the processing equipment was changed. Each test was recorded so that it could be referred back to. The results ranged from dark to light gray.

After going through various screenings, a very fine grain film stock (Eastman Kodak 7302) was chosen. This was split from 35mm to adapt it for 16mm use. The final film, 15 minutes in length, was sent through the processing chemicals at light 5 and at 68 volts. The final print was not screened before its first presentation in Boston.

Enlarged detail of actual film strip.

The location of Project, Inc., at the Arts and Crafts Center in Boston, turned out to be inappropriate for a screening. Therefore I used one of the vacant dormitory rooms at Cambridge School in Weston, Massachusetts, where Paul McMahon lived and worked during the summer. The projector was set up on a wooden bedside table, among other institutional furniture. The projected film frame was approximately 3 feet wide and the quality of the film turned out to be uniformly excellent. It had a completely consistent medium-gray tone with a very fine, even texture. The projected film had only two technical events, consisting of the appearance of the splice of clear leader and film stock at the beginning and end of the film. Ideally, I would have liked to project the film in a temporally unlimited, continuous loop, without any variation whatsoever.

Due to the absence of visual events, viewers withdrew their attention from the projected frame, while the light, which was cast back onto them, increased their awareness of themselves as viewers. Without a camera-directed point of view located within the film, viewers recorded their own points of view, external to the picture plane. The light from the cinematic frame was reflected back, as well, to its source of generation —the projector—and onto other material objects and the room itself.

Viewers were not only made aware of themselves, but also of the projection process, the functioning projector, and the objects and architecture surrounding them. All of these elements, therefore, became the "content" and "representation" of this cinematic event. The "action" existed external to the cinematic frame, opposing its static image. The narrative structure of the film's temporal sequence was evidenced by its two technical events, defining its opening and its closure.

Each step of mediation was disclosed, starting with the film itself and its projection, then the projector, the wall, the architectural container, and the audience. What the viewers saw was therefore differentiated from the representation of the projected image.

Both material processes—that of cinematic production and cinematic projection—were, in separate and parallel ways, decomposed into their constituent elements. And while they were only referring back to themselves, they represented themselves upon reconstruction as film and film projection. Both processes were synthesized and became congruent in real time as a pictorial projection on the plane of a given architectural container.

Image of film during projection.

Close-up of film image during projection.

Photographs by Paul McMahon.

August 24 – September 16, 1973
Lisson Gallery
London, England

Announcement card of exhibition.

After visiting "Documenta V" in Kassel, Germany, on my first trip to Europe in 1972, I went to the Lisson Gallery in London at the invitation of Nicholas Logsdail, the owner of the gallery, who had asked me to do an exhibition there. Since the gallery was then undergoing renovation, I didn't see the completed exhibition area until I returned to actually do the work in August of the following year. I did take notes, however, which I consulted on my return to Los Angeles. Inspecting a gallery space and taking notes was an essential part of my method, since my work never consisted simply of adding preconceived or completed objects to a space for exhibition purposes.

On my return to London in August 1973, I discussed several proposals for the exhibition with Nicholas Logsdail, all of which turned out to be impractical for the available space. A proposal was finally deemed feasible for a basement exhibition area which the gallery owner had originally described as being "unsuitable for any kind of installation."

The dimensions of this gallery space were 16 feet 8½ inches by 13 feet 9 inches. The height to the bottom of the untreated wooden beams of the open-beam ceiling was 7 feet 4 inches and to the actual ceiling plane, 8 feet 3 inches. On the east and west walls of the gallery there were two vertical structural reliefs extending from floor to ceiling and projecting 6½ inches and 7 inches respectively into the room, both having a 9-inch width. In the southwest corner there was a floor to ceiling recess 1 foot 4 inches wide and 7 inches deep. The walls were composed of brick, cement, and plaster and finished with a white acrylic emulsion. The floor was reinforced concrete, finished with gray polyurethane.

There was a door 30 inches by 62 inches and a window 34½ inches by 50 inches in the south wall opening to a garden patio which was 24½ inches above the basement floor level. Furthermore, there was a passage 75 inches by 40 inches in the east wall which connected the basement with the upstairs galleries. The basement area was illuminated with natural light from the patio door and window, and with artificial

Detail of southwest corner, showing reveal and ceiling beams.
Photograph by Nicholas Logsdail.

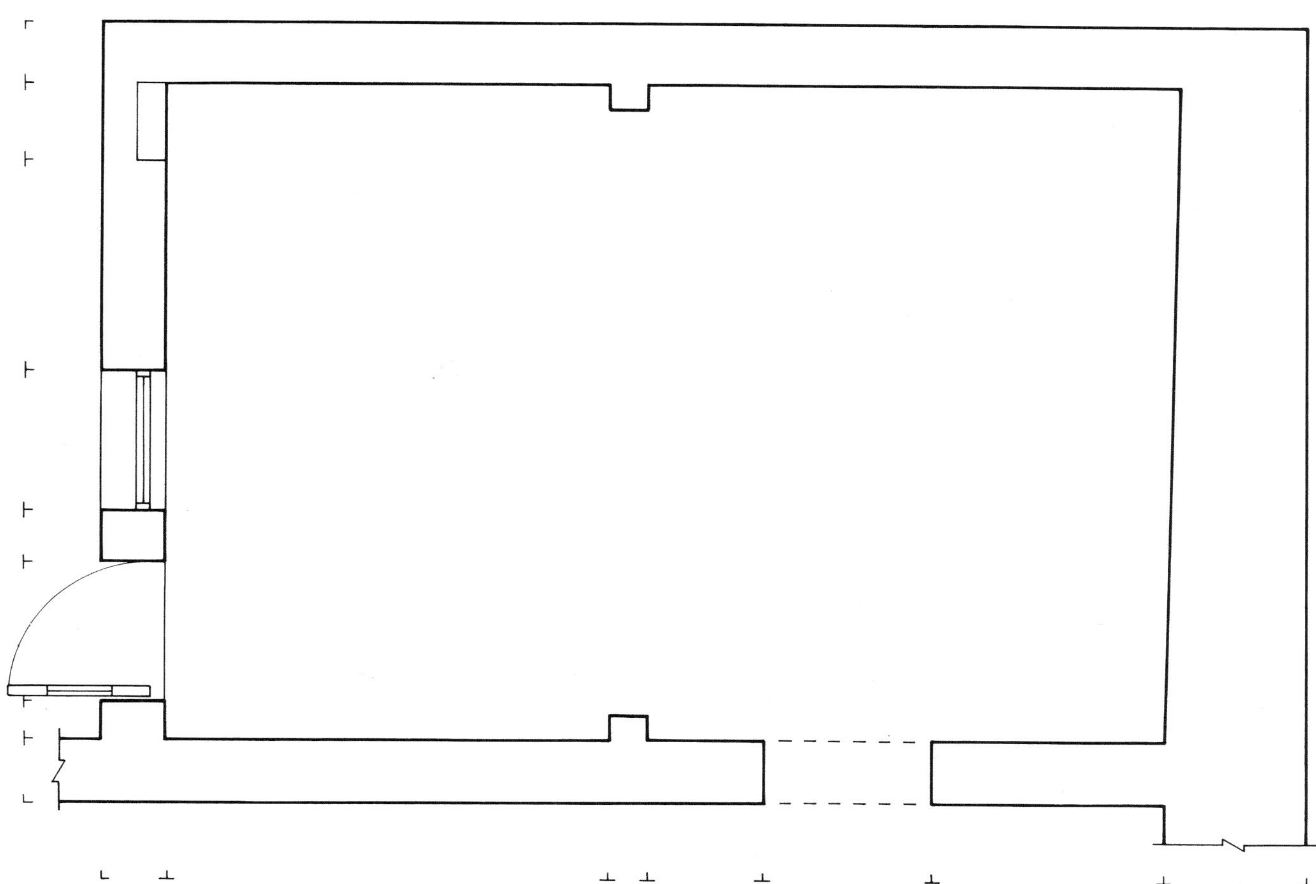

Ground plan of exhibition space.

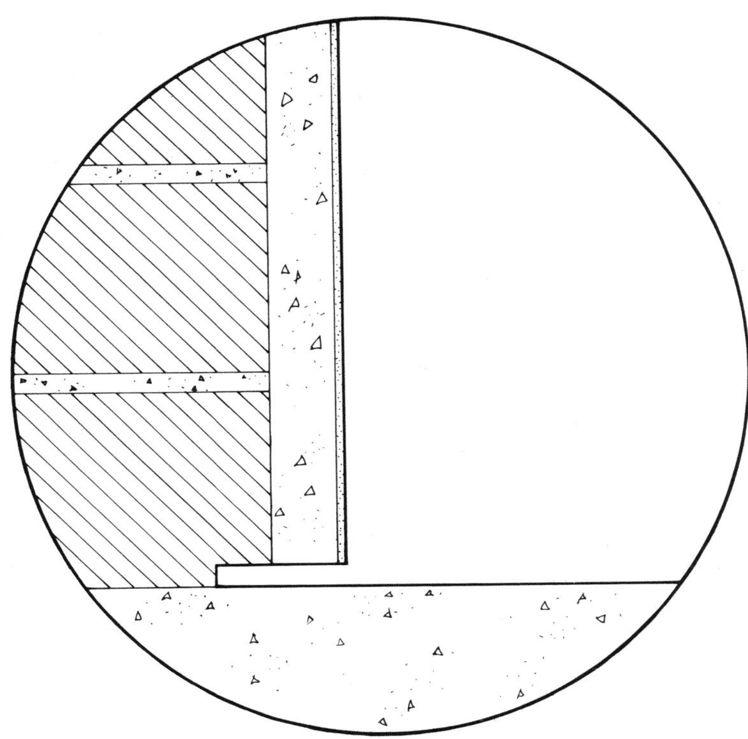

Detail of wall and architectural reveal.

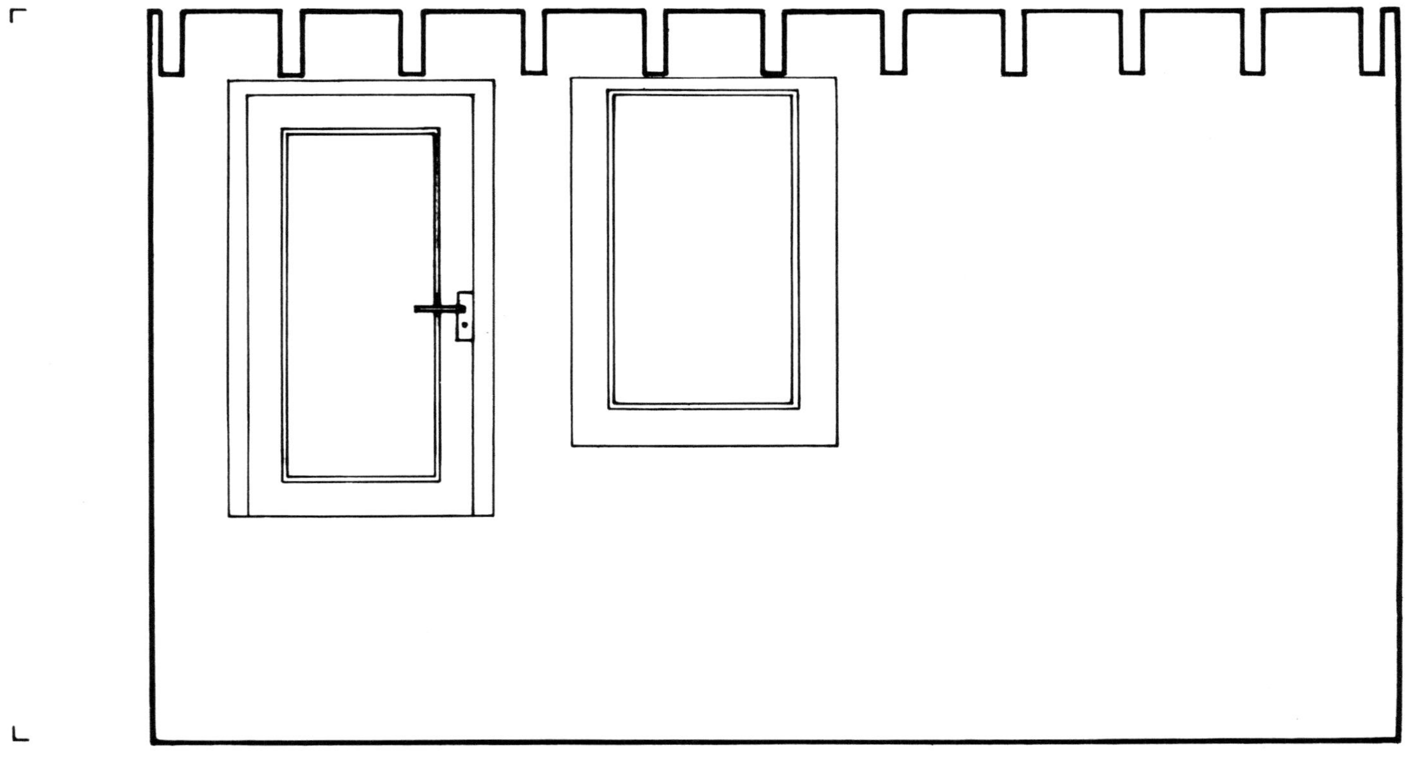

South elevation. Indicated are ceiling structure, window and
door to garden of the gallery.

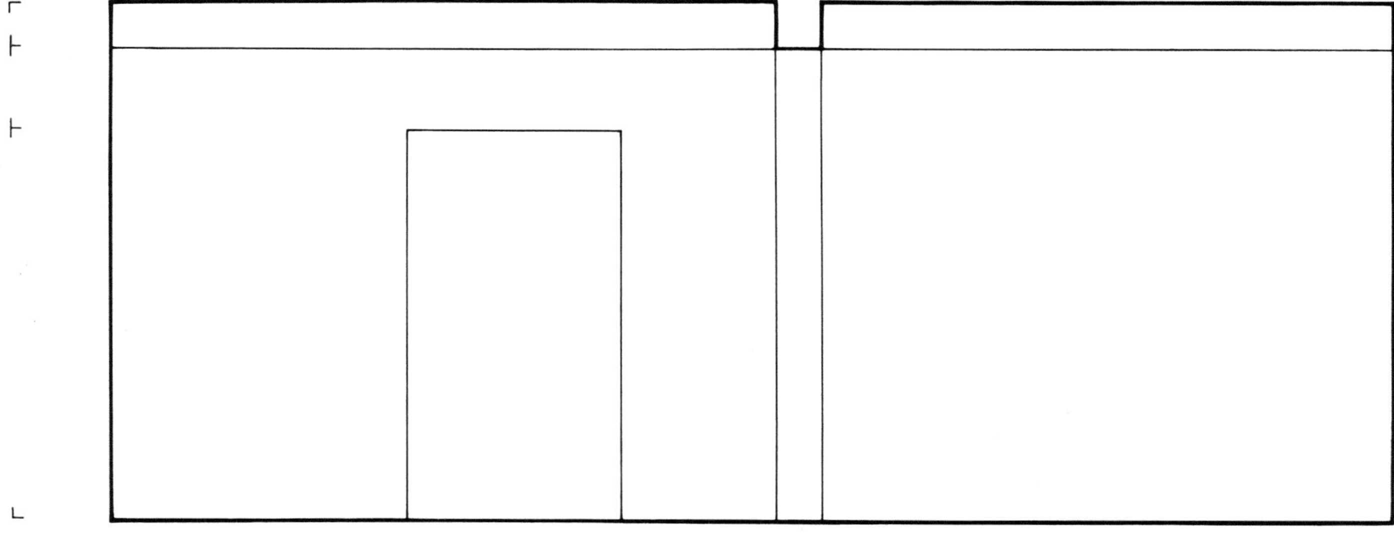

78 East elevation. Indicated is passageway to adjacent gallery
space. Drawings by Nan Legate.

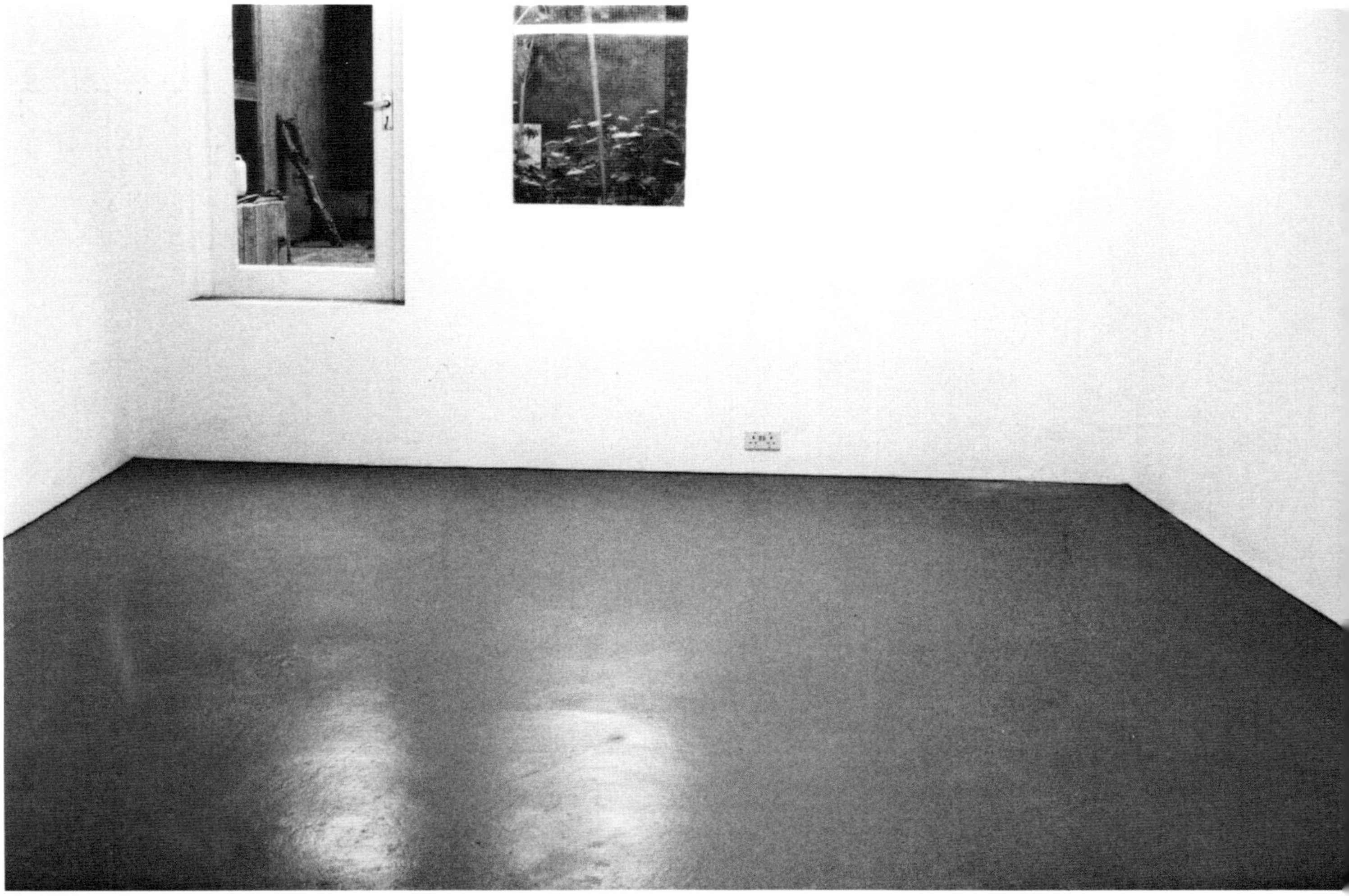

Installation view, south wall.

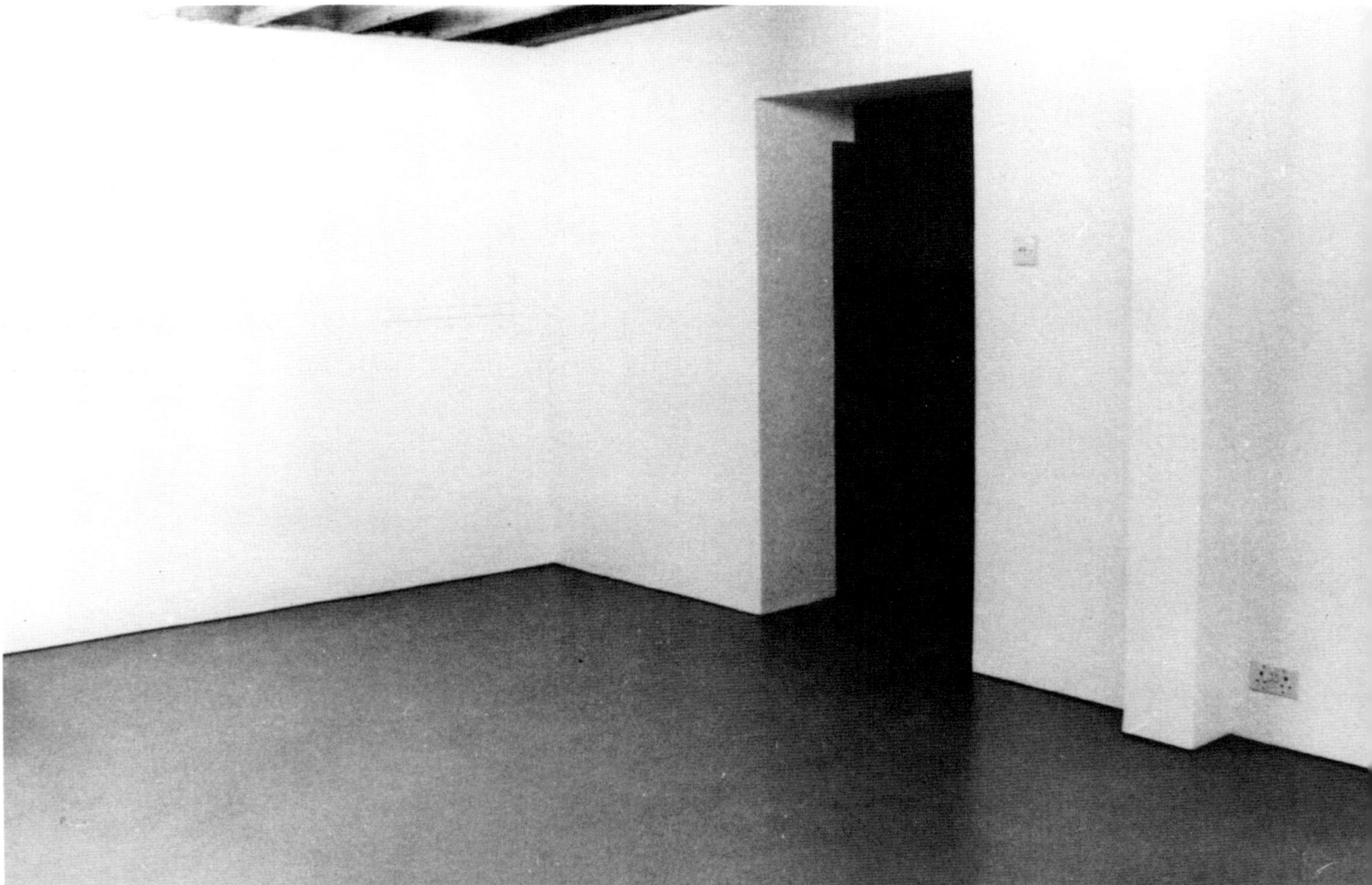

Installation view, northeast, with entry/exit passage. Photographs by Nicholas Logsdail.

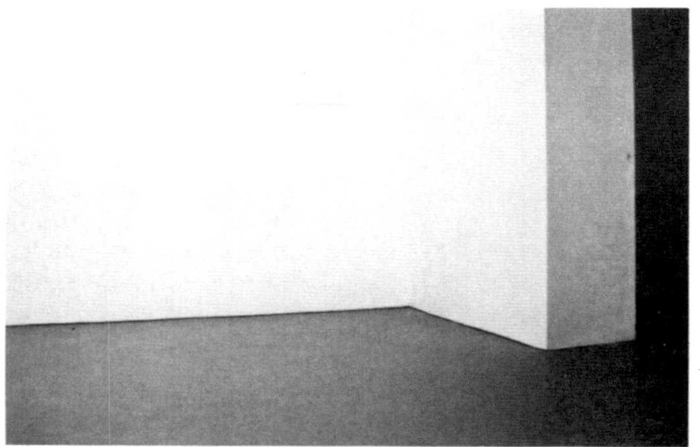

Detail of entry/exit passage, the point where the reveal is completed.

Detail of architectural reveal around perimeter.

Detail of reveal in corner. Photographs by Nicholas Logsdail.

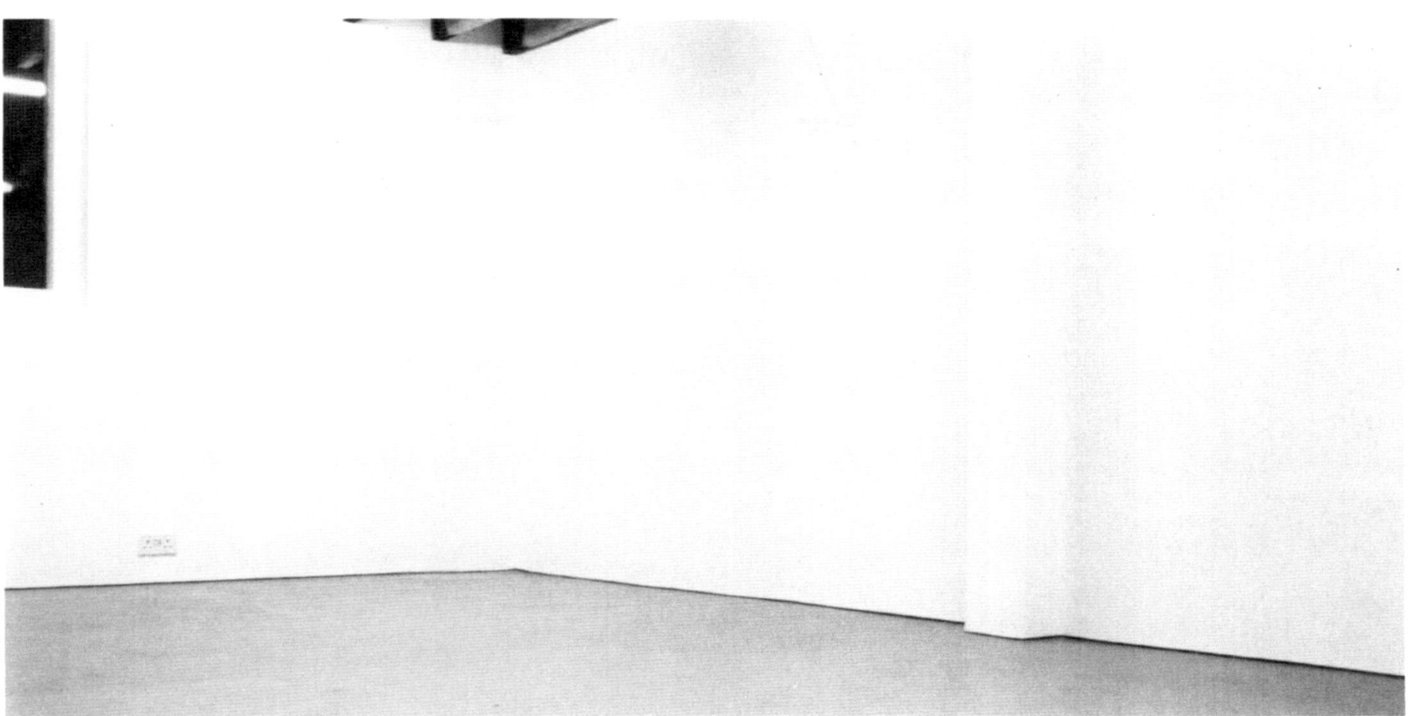

Installation view, southwest. Photograph by Nicholas Logsdail.

light from two overhead fluorescent light tubes.

My proposal for this space was to cut an architectural reveal, ¼ inch wide and 1½ inches deep, into the wall at floor level, around the perimeter of the room. The architectural reveal began and ended at the entry/exit passageway, without turning into the passageway, since that functioned as a transition zone between two exhibition spaces. Because the reveal followed the perimeter continuously, it was necessary to cut around and into the vertical projections and the recess. A masonry grinder was used to cut into the wall, making a recess averaging 1½ inches deep, so that the floor line became indistinguishable.

The creation of a pictorial or sculptural sign traditionally involves the addition of materials to an initial support until some sort of resolution is brought about. The work at the Lisson Gallery reversed this process by creating a mark or sign through a process of material subtraction, in which existing materials were withdrawn from the architectural support. This procedure of material withdrawal was similar to that used by Lawrence Weiner in several works he did in 1968 in which he removed materials from gallery floors and walls. (For example. "A removal to the lathing or support wall of plaster or wallboard from a wall," in: Lawrence Weiner, *Statements*, New York, 1968, n.p.)

The walls of the white container stopped where the open-beam ceiling began. The open-beam construction seemed, therefore, to be excluded from the presentation area, yet was at the same time essential to it, functioning to delineate and frame the display walls, as did the vertical structural reliefs and the vertical recess in the corner. The constructed reveal at the juncture of the wall and the floor—receding from the wall surface and the gallery space—and the open beams at ceiling height, framed the walls and visually located them as pictorial planes for hanging artworks.

The vertical wall surfaces remained part of the architectural container, while being visually isolated between floor and ceiling. The isolated floor plane could therefore be seen as analogous to the wall's pictorial planes. At the same time, the recess at the base of the walls defined the walls as volumetric masses.

At that point in the historical development of art, any process that involved the adding, structuring, or assembling of materials on a support was acceptable within aesthetic practice. The procedure of withdrawing material interrupted and questioned the continuation of that practice. The additive process was partially the result of the traditional avant-garde concern for innovation, whereby materials were synthesized and contextualized in a manner that was alien to their own materiality and method of production.

In this work, the subtraction of materials from the site of both, production and reception, disclosed and defined the structure of the production, as well as its contextual determination.

September 4–September 28, 1973
Heiner Friedrich Gallery
Cologne, West Germany

The installation at the Lisson Gallery was my first individual exhibition in a commercial gallery; my next two one-person exhibitions would also be in European galleries. When I visited the Heiner Friedrich gallery on my return from "Documenta V" in 1972, I was invited to do an exhibition there. The gallery seemed to be well finished, particularly in the detailing of its hardware (radiator ledges, window blinds, doorknobs, etc.). Structurally, however, the wall and floor junctures were quite rough in places, and the surface of the walls was wavy. In fact, on closer observation, one could see that the floor and wall did not always meet. The space was broken up into what, at the time, seemed to be a disorder too incomprehensible to work with.

At the gallery entrance, a foyer adjoined an opening to a rectangular exhibition area on the right. This exhibition area measured 8.50 meters by 3.87 meters. The ceiling height was 3.50 meters and was consistent all through the gallery area. Three windows provided natural light and a system of fluorescent light fixtures provided artificial light. Leading directly ahead from the entry and foyer was a hallway, 7.95 meters in length and 1.35 meters in width, which provided access to the second exhibition space and the offices. To the left of the foyer was a door to the bathroom and next to it, a door to the kitchen. Perpendicular to the kitchen door, a double door gave access to the secretarial offices. This office area was a rectangular space measuring 7.45 meters by 3.70 meters and had two windows. At the end of the hallway another door led to a second, more private office, measuring 5.80 meters by 3.60 meters, with one large window. The hallway merged at the end into the second exhibition space, a semirectangular area measuring 11 meters by 6.05 meters, set askew, so that, on the ground plan of the whole gallery, it appeared as an appendage of the otherwise perpendicular layout of the gallery. This area was evenly lit by two windows.

The floor throughout the gallery was brown-tinted black asphalt; whereas the opposing horizontal surface, the ceiling, was painted white, as were the existing

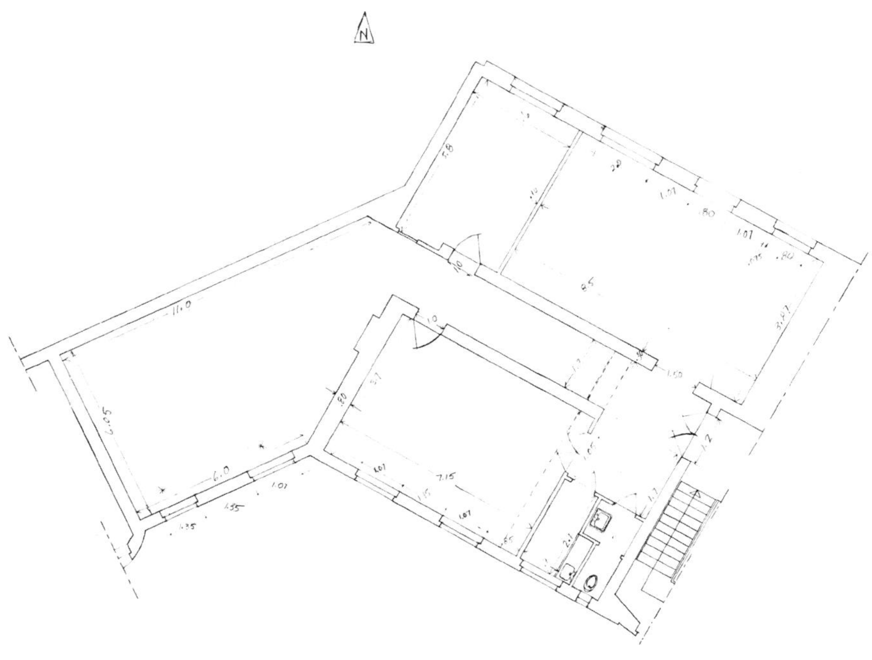

Ground plan of the Heiner Friedrich Gallery
by Kim Hubbard.

vertical surfaces, the walls.

My proposal for the gallery focused on the ceiling and the floor, the only two interior architectural surfaces that were identical in size and shape, but not in color value. I proposed that the tint of the floor be duplicated in a latex-paint mixture and applied to the entire ceiling surface, within the perimeter of the gallery. The paint was mixed and applied by professional building painters. Meanwhile, I filled in all spaces where floor and wall did not meet. This entire procedure was completed during my stay for the installation of the work, and it was the only material addition and visual change brought about by the work within the gallery.

The paint color that was mixed was a slightly darker tone than the color of the floor, in order to compensate for the high light reflection on the ceiling during the day. The two surfaces, therefore, appeared to be similar, yet the actual difference in tone and texture remained evident.

The chromatic similarity effected a visual continuity without achieving an illusionary congruence, which would have controlled the viewers' experience, as opposed to allowing the viewers to visually assemble the discrete parts of the installation. Because of this visual similarity, all horizontal surfaces throughout the gallery area apeared to be the same dark brown color; whereas all vertical surfaces retained their original white finish. This meant that all opposing horizontal surfaces were a similar brown and all vertical surfaces, opposing or adjacent, a similar white.

Each and every part of the gallery was linked by the newly painted ceiling, establishing an actual visual continuity and therefore integrating the exhibition areas with those areas normally not on view. By visually unifying the various areas, their functional interdependence was revealed to the viewer who, in order to perceive the work in its totality, had to have access to all of the gallery areas. The normal procedures and functions of the gallery became integrated into the exhibit as the work focused upon them as the content of the exhibition.

The color of the ceiling and its conjunction with the limits of the perimeter walls, demarcated the activities and properties of the gallery. At the same time, the corresponding color of the floor and ceiling created a relationship of accessibility/inaccessibility. The ceiling was inaccessible to foot traffic, but, by painting it a "floor" color, its properties as a ceiling became visible as structurally fixed and integral to the gallery. The floor and ceiling sandwiched mobile features such as office equipment, furniture, works of art, appliances, and hardware. In contrast to the static nature of the relationship between floor and ceiling, the arbitrary nature of the placement of these mobile elements became emphasized, as for example in moving them from room to room, or replacing and updating them. No matter how arbitrarily these objects were placed within the space, their function would remain the same.

The works at both the Lisson Gallery and the Heiner Friedrich Gallery were conceived for and determined by the site and context of each institution. Like earlier works that had been produced for museums and public exhibition spaces, these works for commercial galleries were defined equally for and by the situation into which they were inserted. Therefore these works remained outside of the conventions of relocation or adaptation.

The intention of the installation at the Heiner Friedrich gallery was to formally define and materially differentiate the function of aesthetic production from the architectural structure and from the activities within the gallery. These activities usually served to abstract the aesthetic production for its commercial adaptation. The gallery was therefore called upon to authorize itself to define the purposes of the work of art, which supposedly was congruent with the actual purpose of the producer. Even though the gallery dealer did not participate in the production of the work, it was ultimately the dealer who fixed the commercial value of the work and its potential for surplus production, regardless of its function as aesthetic production.

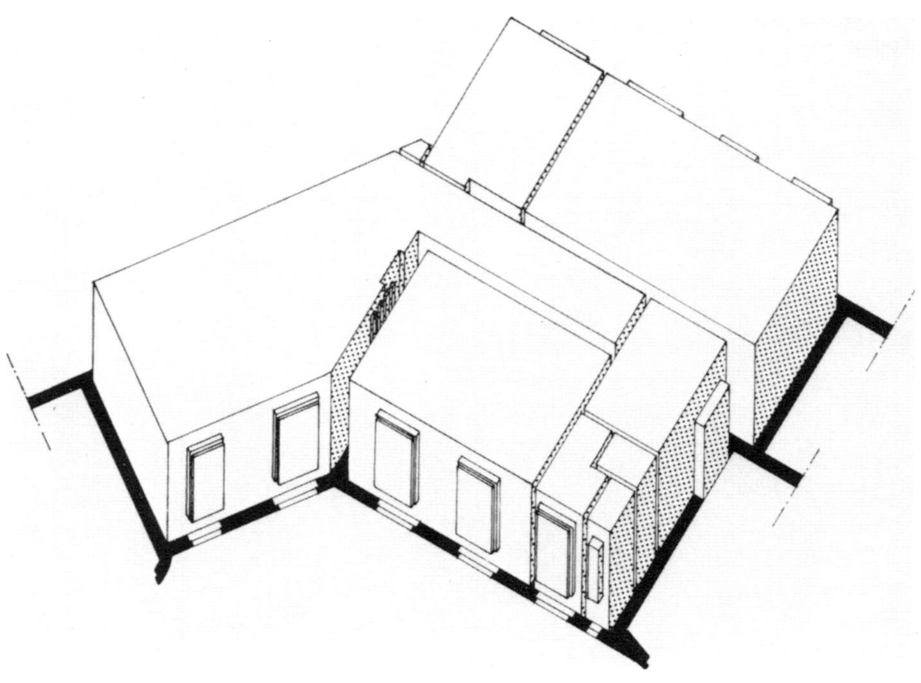

In this way, the gallery was more like a brokerage firm where commerce was carried out, representing neither the actual production, nor the interests of the community, nor the interests of the individual producer, nor any concern for the work's historical context. The gallery could have served the same function if it had been an office with some filing cabinets.

In this work, the viewer could see the relationship between the gallery's office space activities and the gallery's exhibition space activities, which visibly appeared as opposed functions in that the fixed nature of the work (the whole gallery) came into opposition with the commercial functions of the gallery. In a sense, the exhibition suspended the commercial function of the gallery.

The work was proposed and accepted for an average exhibition period of one month, a temporal determination inherently given with the work. The proposal requested that the work should be painted over after completion of the exhibition. Even though the ceiling was not repainted as requested, the work ceased to exist as defined by the proposal. Instructions are an integral part of my work since they define the time frame and the context in which the work exists. Since the work was not painted out, it existed beyond my definition and control, and the continued perception of the work necessarily falsified my original intentions. The material placement and temporal duration which I had defined both became misappropriated and misconstrued by the entrepreneur's motivation. A work of art that is inserted into and determined by the architecture of a commercial enterprise lends itself to being manipulated as though it were the property of that commercial establishment. The work then constitutes an irresolvable conflict between the author's intentions and the entrepreneur's interests. As a visual fact, the work could be perceived as anything ranging from a remnant of an aesthetic production to interior decoration. It could be perceived as a vestige of aesthetic production—for example, a dissassembled installation —but only if the artist were to define it as such.

East view of general office space with sculpture by Dan Flavin. Photograph by Timm Rautert.

Axonometric drawing of the Heiner Friedrich Gallery by Maurizio
Mochetti

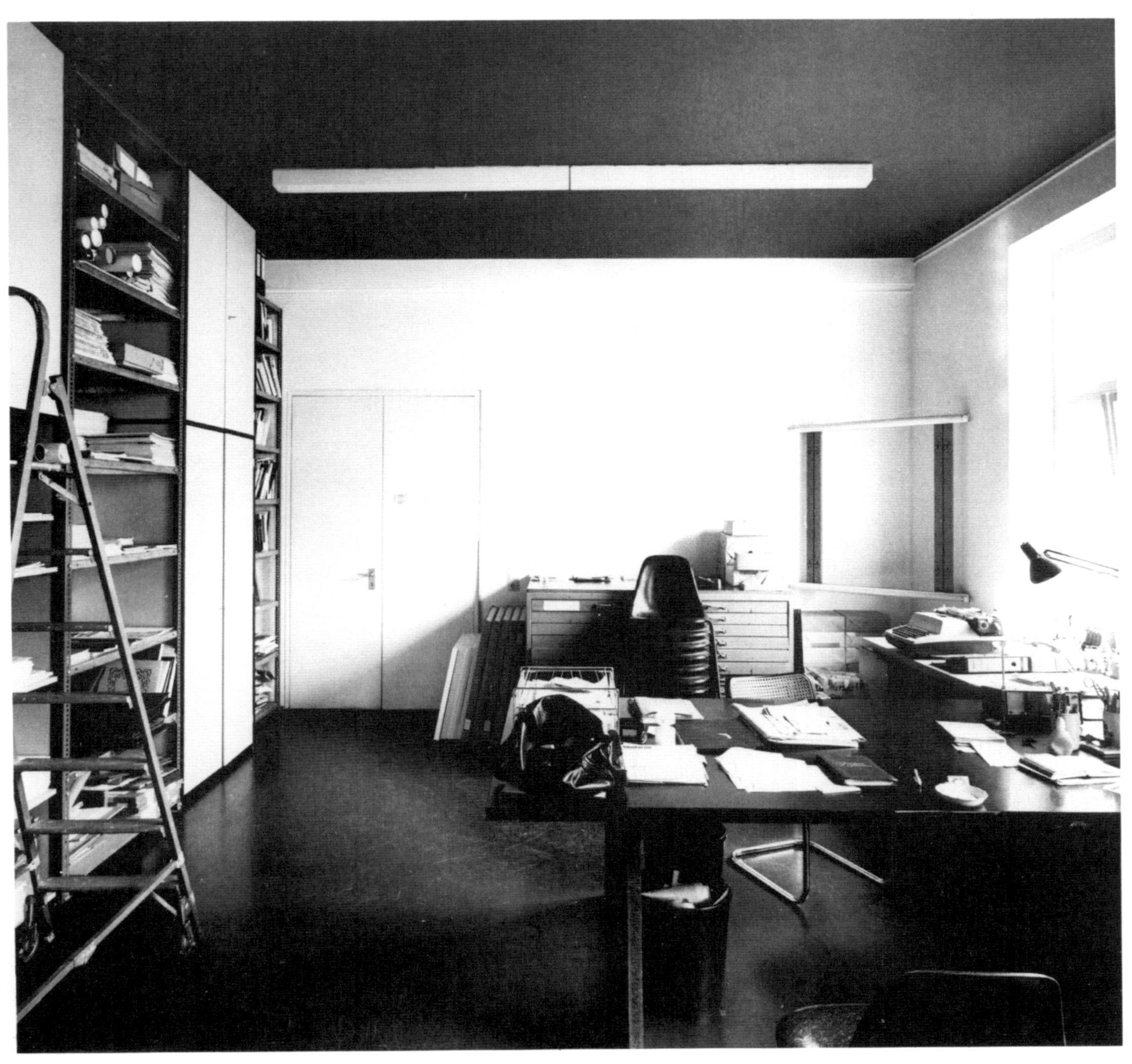

West view of general office space.

View of director's office space with sculpture by Dan Flavin.

Hallway viewing into back gallery.

Hallway viewing toward front entrance.

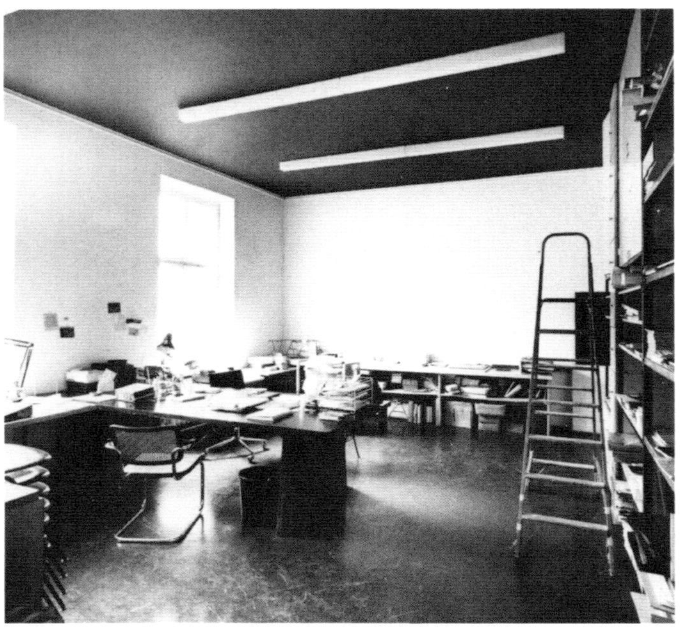

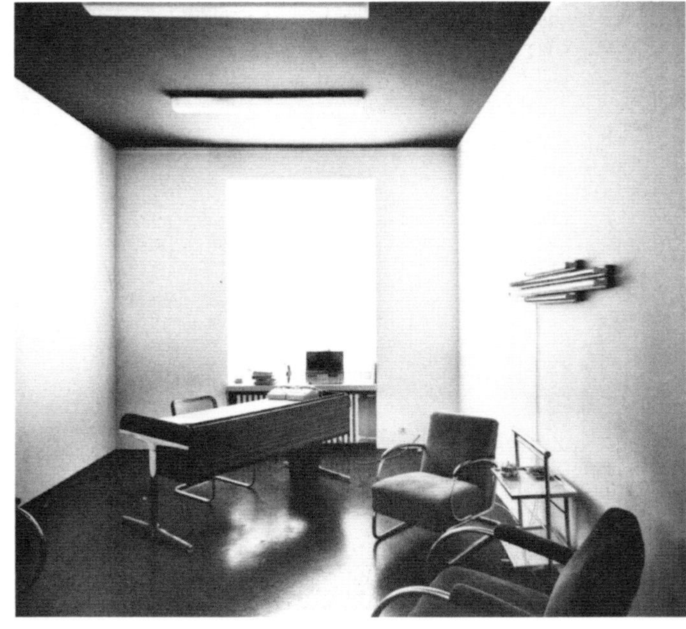

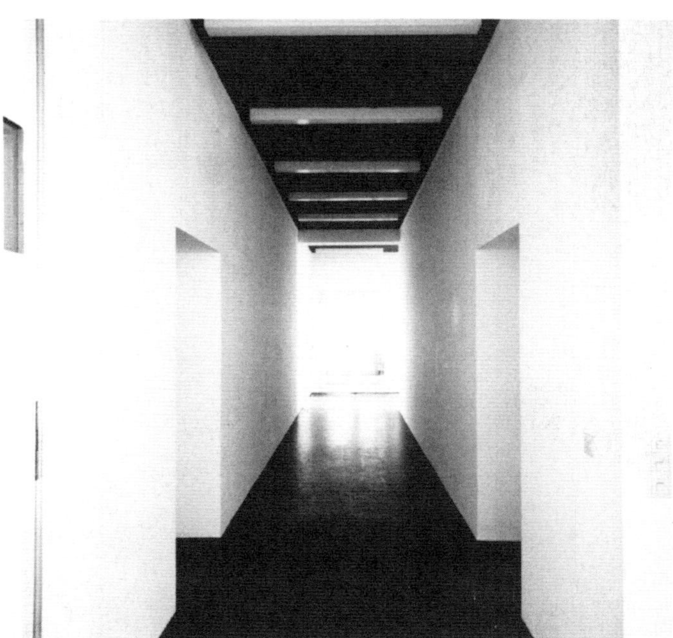

View of gallery lobby during exhibition.

Front gallery viewing northwest wall.

Back gallery viewing southwest wall.

Back gallery viewing northeast toward hallway.
Photographs by Timm Rautert.

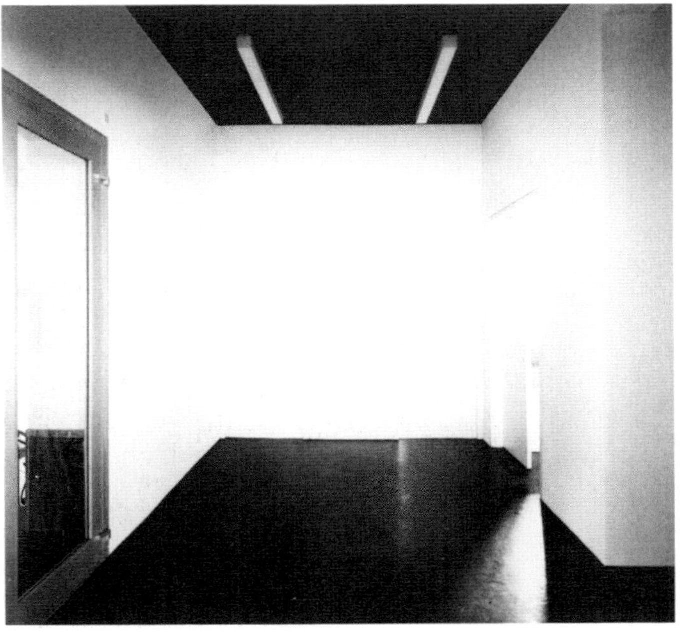

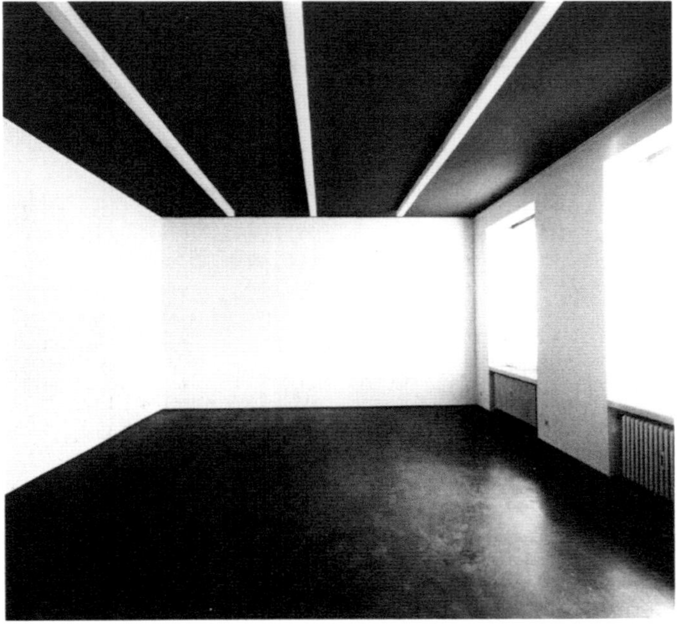

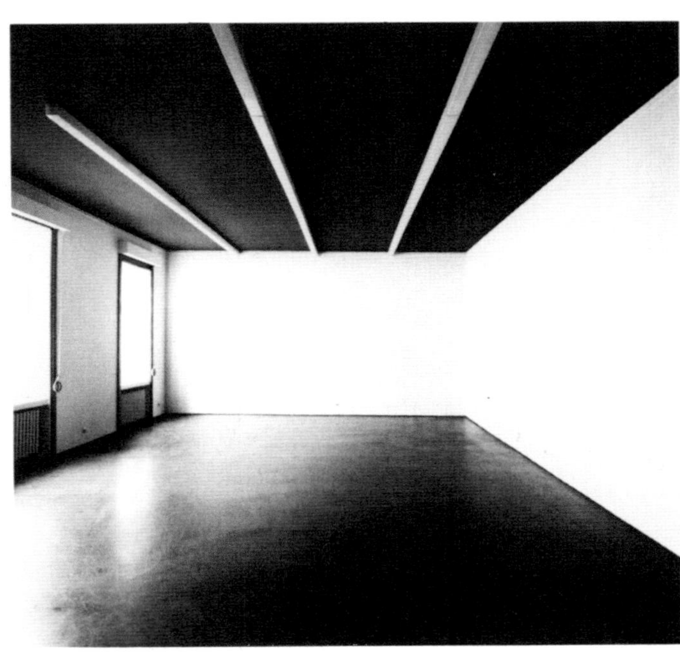

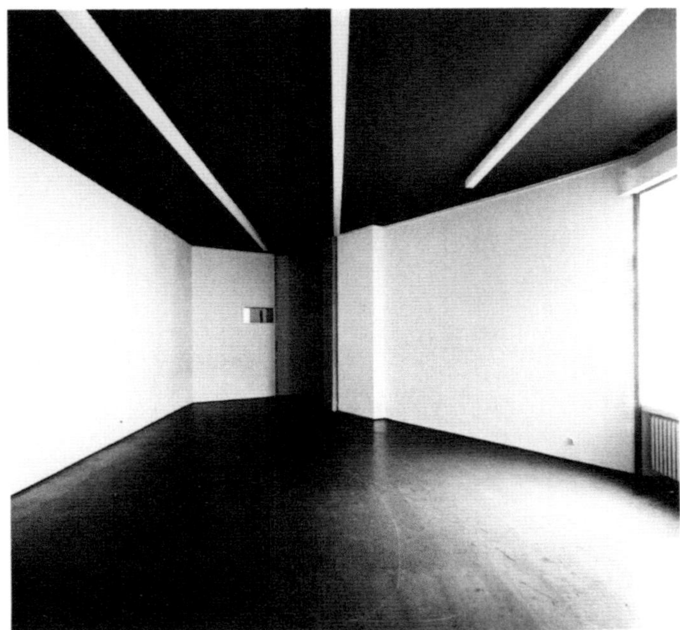

MICHAEL ASHER

13 SETTEMBRE - 8 OTTOBRE 1973 GALLERIA TOSELLI VIA MELZO 34 MILANO

My last stop during my trip to Europe in 1973 was the Franco Toselli gallery, a commercial gallery in Milan. Franco Toselli had previously invited me to do an exhibition; we had exchanged letters, I had seen plans of the gallery, and I had some idea of what I might want to do. But since I had no specific project for the Toselli Gallery—unlike the Lisson and Heiner Friedrich galleries, where I had been able to visit the exhibition space in advance—I went there with the hope of doing something, but with the agreement that a work did not necessarily have to result from my visit.

Visitors to the Franco Toselli Gallery, which is located in a lively residential neighborhood, enter through a cobblestone courtyard. From the west side of the courtyard five steps lead down to the gallery, which is situated below ground level. The gallery space is expansive, resembling an industrial warehouse or machine shop. The east-west axis of the gallery is an unencumbered space, 17.10 meters long. The ceiling height is 4.90 meters. The maximum width on the north-south axis is 11.90 meters. The width of the space is interrupted by a series of 50-centimeter-square columns with bevelled edges which support a beam of the same square dimensions, extending the entire length of the gallery, 3.50 meters from and parallel to the south wall. In the far half (the southeast area) of the gallery, the spaces between the columns have been filled in to form a 9.13-meter-long wall which, together with a short perpendicular wall, encloses a space used for an office. The rest of the columns are open, 4.40 meters from floor to ceiling beam, partially framing an enclosed stairwell which provides residents of the dwelling above with access to the courtyard. Three windows in the west wall admit natural light from the courtyard and two rows of fluorescent light fixtures on the ceiling provide artificial light. At the time of the exhibit, the floor was gray concrete with a nonskid surface. The walls and ceiling were finished with numerous layers of white paint from previous exhibitions.

My proposal for this exhibition was to have the walls and ceiling sandblasted, so that every trace of the many layers of white paint which had been applied over the years would be removed and the underlying plaster exposed. Once the proposal was approved, work began immediately. It required the labor of four people for four days to complete the paint-removal operation and the following clean-up.

Sandblasting revealed a brown plaster surface on the walls and ceiling. The columns and ceiling beam were a lighter brown than the plastered-wall sections between the columns. Just as there were regular chromatic variations in the brown plaster of the sections between the columns, the opposite wall also had regular tonal variations, indicating where windows had been filled in some time after construction of the building. On the same wall, a darker horizontal plane along the floor was possibly a sign of moisture below street level. (See photograph p.91)

Hardware in the gallery was also sandblasted: two pipes entering through the ceiling and passing through the wall at a 45-degree angle, and an electrical conduit near the door. Once the gallery was sandblasted,

Installation view of an exhibition by Robert Mangold at the Franco Toselli Gallery. Photograph by Giorgio Colombo.

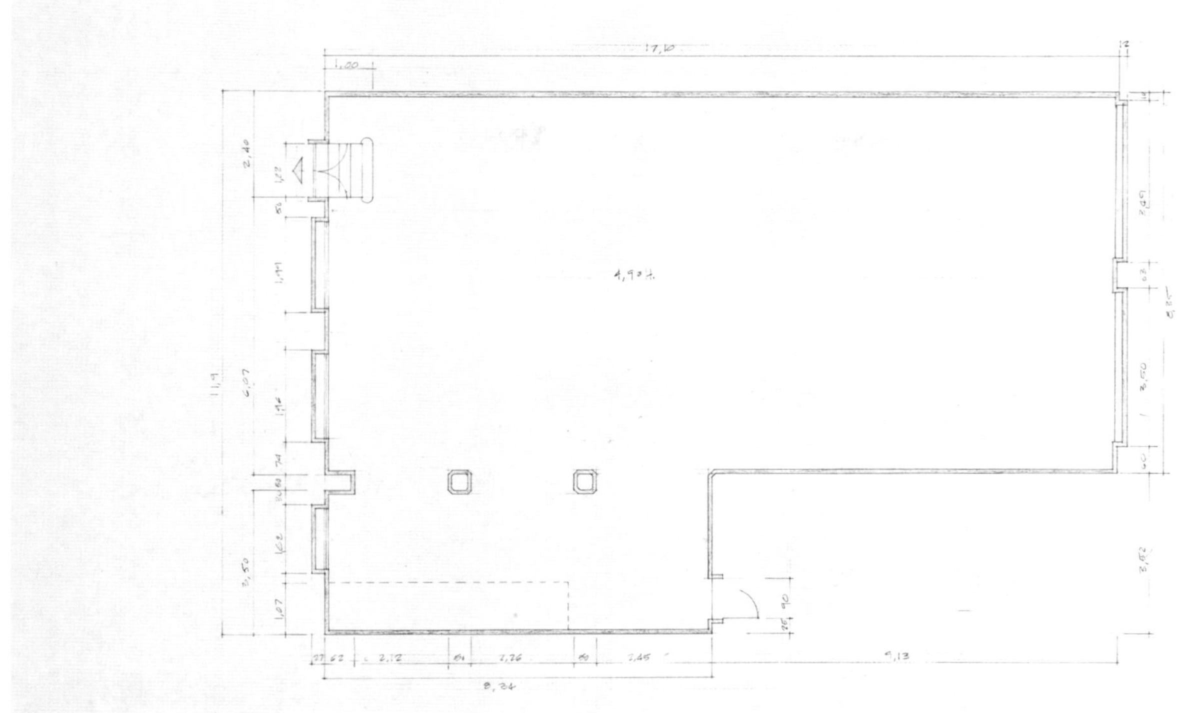

Ground plan of the Franco Toselli Gallery. Drawing by John Knight.

only natural light was used to light the interior.[1]

What was explicit in the floor—the uncoated concrete—had been implicit in the wall and ceiling surfaces before sandblasting. Once the plaster had been exposed, the walls and ceiling had the same property as the floor—no coating. The walls, ceiling, and floor were thereby identified in terms of a common condition, and this established a surface continuity.

The work cast the gallery in its most rudimentary state, appearing to be either under construction with its surfaces yet unfinished, or at a stage of dismantlement that would uncover the record of the gallery's past. The bare plaster was reminiscent of a construction site before any finishing coats of paint have been applied to interior surfaces. In addition, the wall between the columns, which was filled in with one kind of plaster, and the filled-in windows, where another kind of plaster was used, served as a possible historical document.

The variations in brown earthen chroma were visually rich compared to the consistent white of the gallery container. These brown hues—paradoxically, once used in the visual arts—were particularly surprising here since the usual surface color for gallery display is white paint. In this work, a large exhibition space had been totally stripped of all the conventional coatings that had built up over the years on its display surface. The brown plaster surfaces resembled the common, indigenous outdoor plaster walls of the community. The previously concealed plaster essentially brought inside an outdoor material, disclosing a relationship between the gallery and its surroundings.

The complete material withdrawal—a process of subtraction—was also a process of addition, since the exposed plaster could also be viewed as an added material. The withdrawal of the white paint, in this case, became the objectification of the work.

For the realization of this proposal the gallery had to temporarily dispense with its conventional display surfaces for a material alteration or withdrawal. This was a strategy I had not used in any of my previous work. It meant that the gallery had to forego a certain amount of its property in exchange for a work of art which appropriated and dismantled the gallery's display surfaces. In addition, should the new display surfaces turn out to be nonfunctional for the purpose of display in future exhibitions, the exchange also committed the gallery owner to reconvert and restore the surfaces to conditions which would allow for conventional usage.

Prior installations of my work had consisted of material application or construction. This work, however, deployed a procedure of material withdrawal. More than any other prior work, it integrated its materials with the actual materials of the gallery display surfaces, and it was simultaneously joined and synthesized in its totality with its own architectural location and support structure.

Compared to the works at "Documenta V" or the Market Street Program, which could still be perceived in terms of a figure-ground relationship, the work at the Franco Toselli Gallery substituted a material withdrawal, which encompassed the totality of the exhibition space, for a figure-ground relationship (addition of material marks). The ceiling and walls revealed the marks of this commercial gallery's architecture rather than an author's predetermination to organize and place marks as part of a painted surface, or even to arrange elements in order to penetrate or add to the surface. Even though the work at the Lisson Gallery employed to a certain extent a procedure of material withdrawal similar to the work at the Franco Toselli Gallery, it was still operating as a material extension of a conventional manner of mark-making, in this instance a linear volume used to frame the wall surfaces of the gallery space.

Marking by disclosure, rather than by constructing figure-ground relationships, revealed the building's construction history. At the same time, it established the integral totality of both exhibition space and work, without isolating either one, or any single element within them. It escaped a traditional formulation by synthesizing both the gallery and work as an objectification of the exhibition and the exhibition space. At

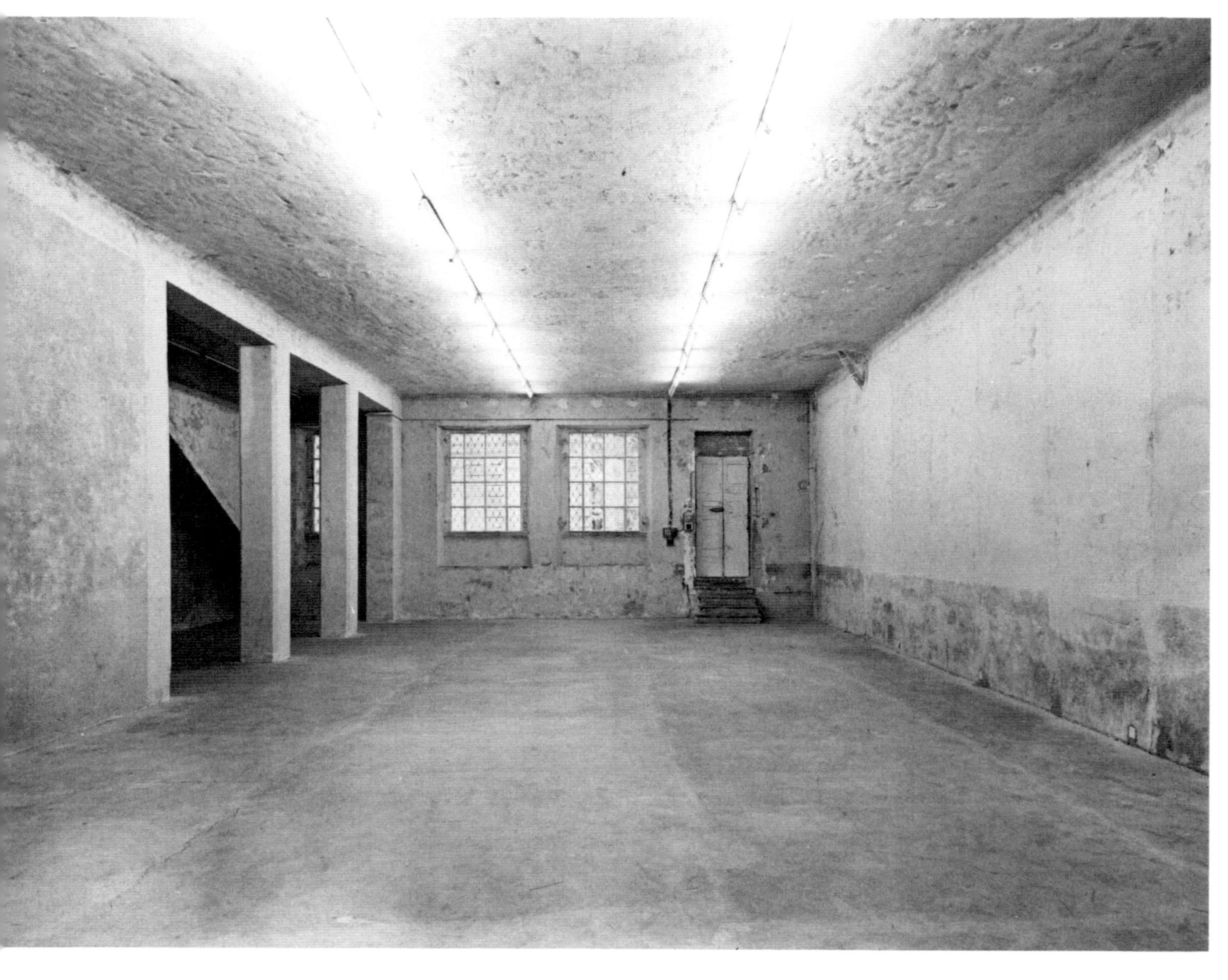

Viewing west during exhibition at the Franco Toselli Gallery.
Fluorescent lights have been illuminated for the purposes
of photography only.

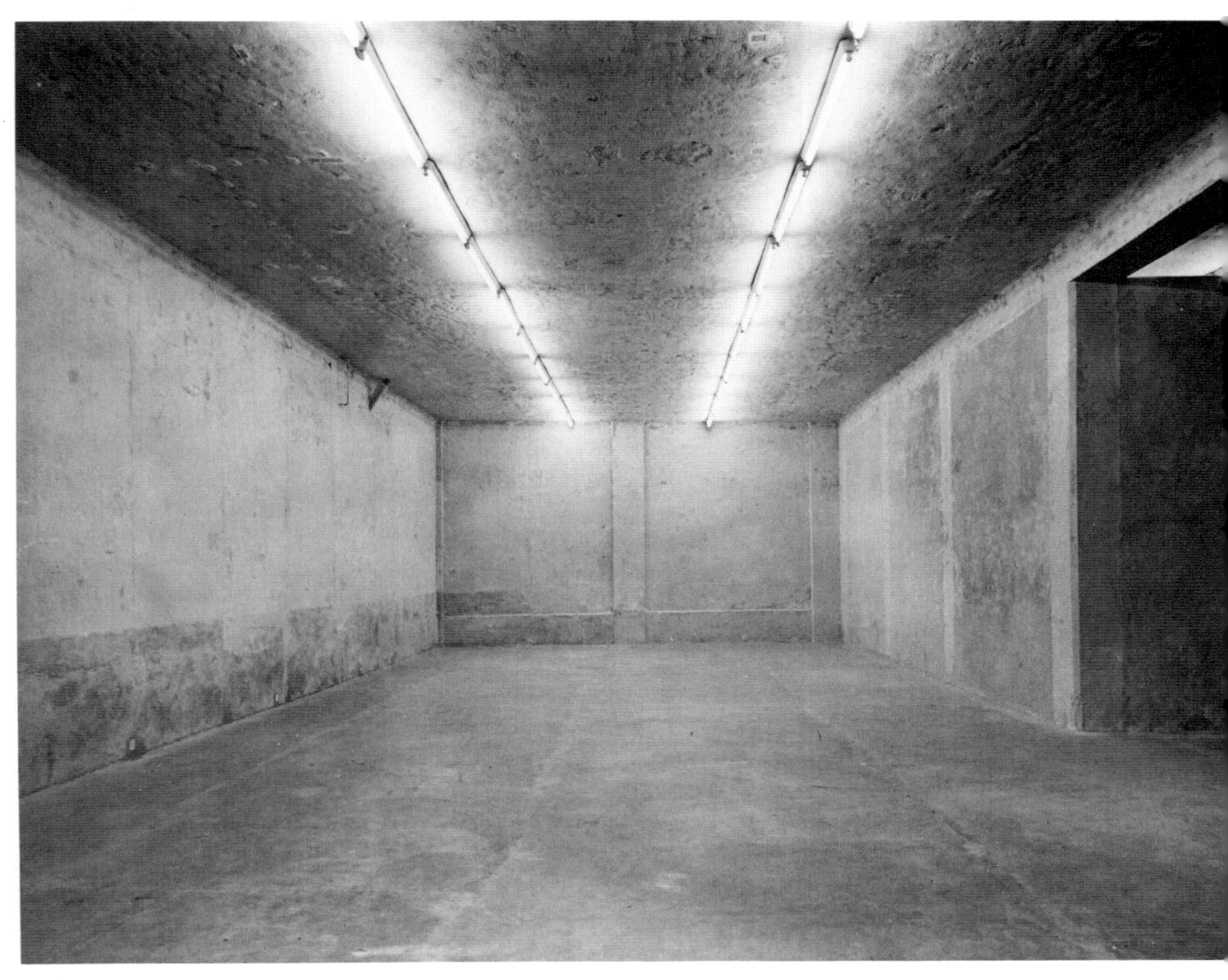

Viewing east in installation. Photographs by Giorgio Colombo.

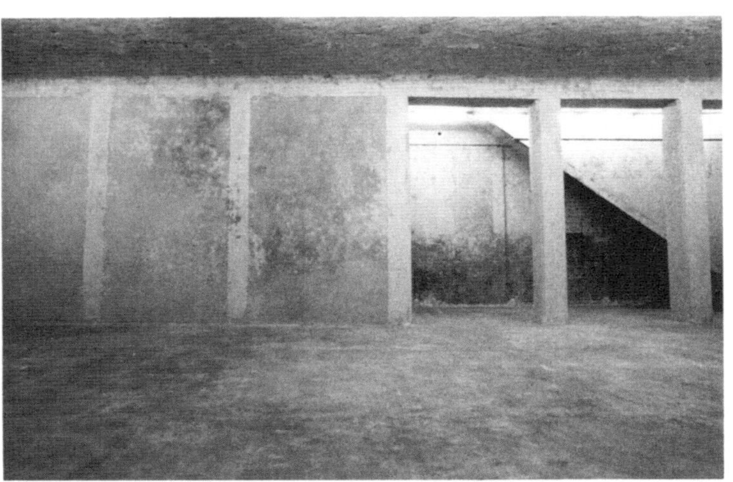

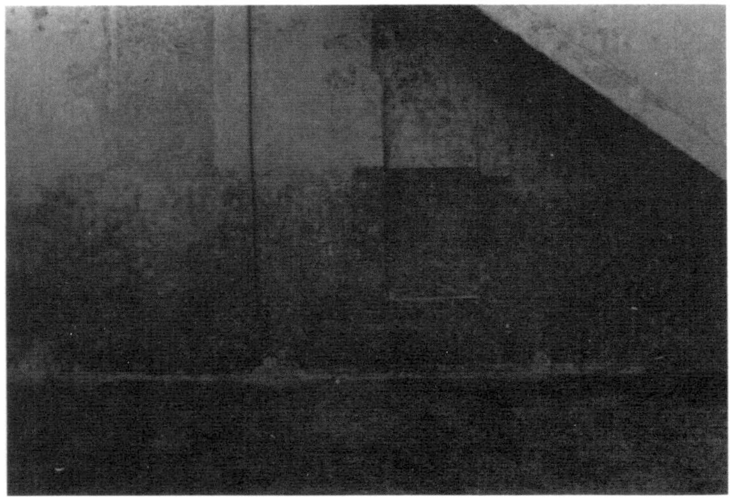

Viewing south wall and part of stairwell with artificial light.

Detail of stairwell in south wall.

that time I considered this work to be the most specific materialization of the history of a gallery's construction and functional properties.

Traditionally, the white interior of a commercial gallery presented an artist's production within an architectural setting of false autonomy. If, through its absence, the viewer was reminded of the white paint, an interesting question, was then raised: How does the white "partition" of paint affect the context of art usually seen on that support surface. At the Toselli Gallery, I used a procedural approach, attempting to materially withdraw an author's sign and responsibility. Usually an artist's sign, as an addition to a given architectural space and a discrete, visually identifiable element, guides and restricts viewer awareness and shifts it from the problems inherent in the gallery space and the work to an arbitrarily formalized insert.

The method of defining this work was still dependent on the Minimalist idea of specificity. The term "specificity," as it occurred in Minimalist discourse, described materials as being unmediated. Therefore the perception of a work incorporating such materials was understood to be equally unmediated. The installation of my work at the Toselli Gallery was structurally comparable to this concept, except that it differed from sculptural objects by its expanded dimensions, coalescing the display-structure with the work.

Furthermore, by integrating the work with its actual exhibition space and the actual materials of the display surface, it went beyond the specificity of materials, as defined in Minimalist discourse, by not introducing any materials whatsoever. It therefore became materially more specific to its own operation, not withstanding the totality of its site and context.

In clear contrast to Minimalism, the work did not assume that the viewers' perception could go unmediated, but instead revealed every single aspect of the way in which the viewers' perception of the work was materially mediated within the conditions in which the work was inscribed.

The white display surfaces—one of the fundamental elements normally taken for granted and suppressed as part of the presentation of works in a gallery—had been withdrawn. A feeling of relief, resulting from the recognition of traditionally suppressed visual elements, activated a perceptual and cognitive process. The ideological deconstruction of the architectural surfaces of the commercial gallery occurred simultaneous to their material deconstruction.

If viewers assumed that the space had been liberated from the white paint support, they had only to view the plaster to appreciate an inherent paradox: the plaster, as another support surface (another coating), was as much an integral part of the gallery as the white paint.

---

[1] The lights were switched on when some of the photographs of the exhibition were taken.

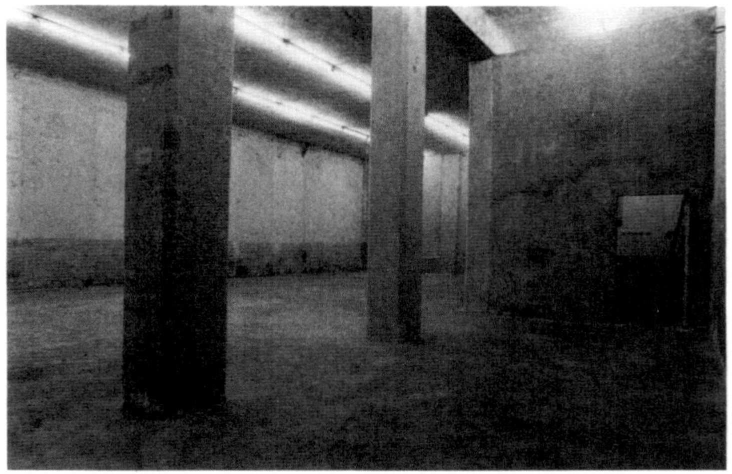

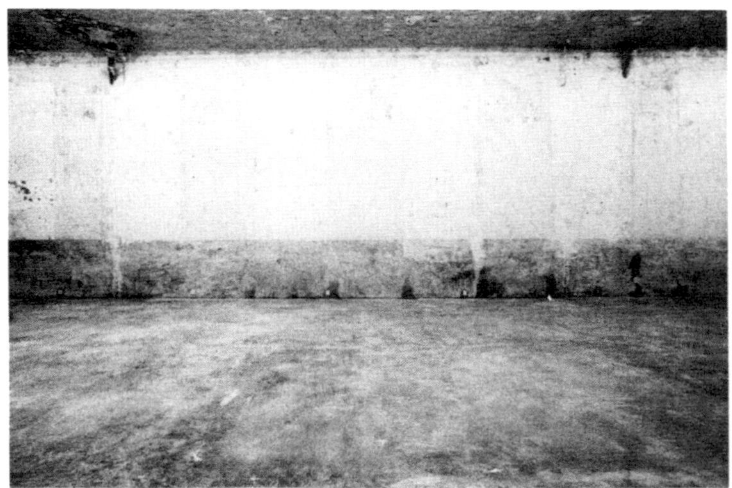

Viewing east into office area and exhibition area.
Photographs by Franco Toselli.

Viewing north wall during exhibition.

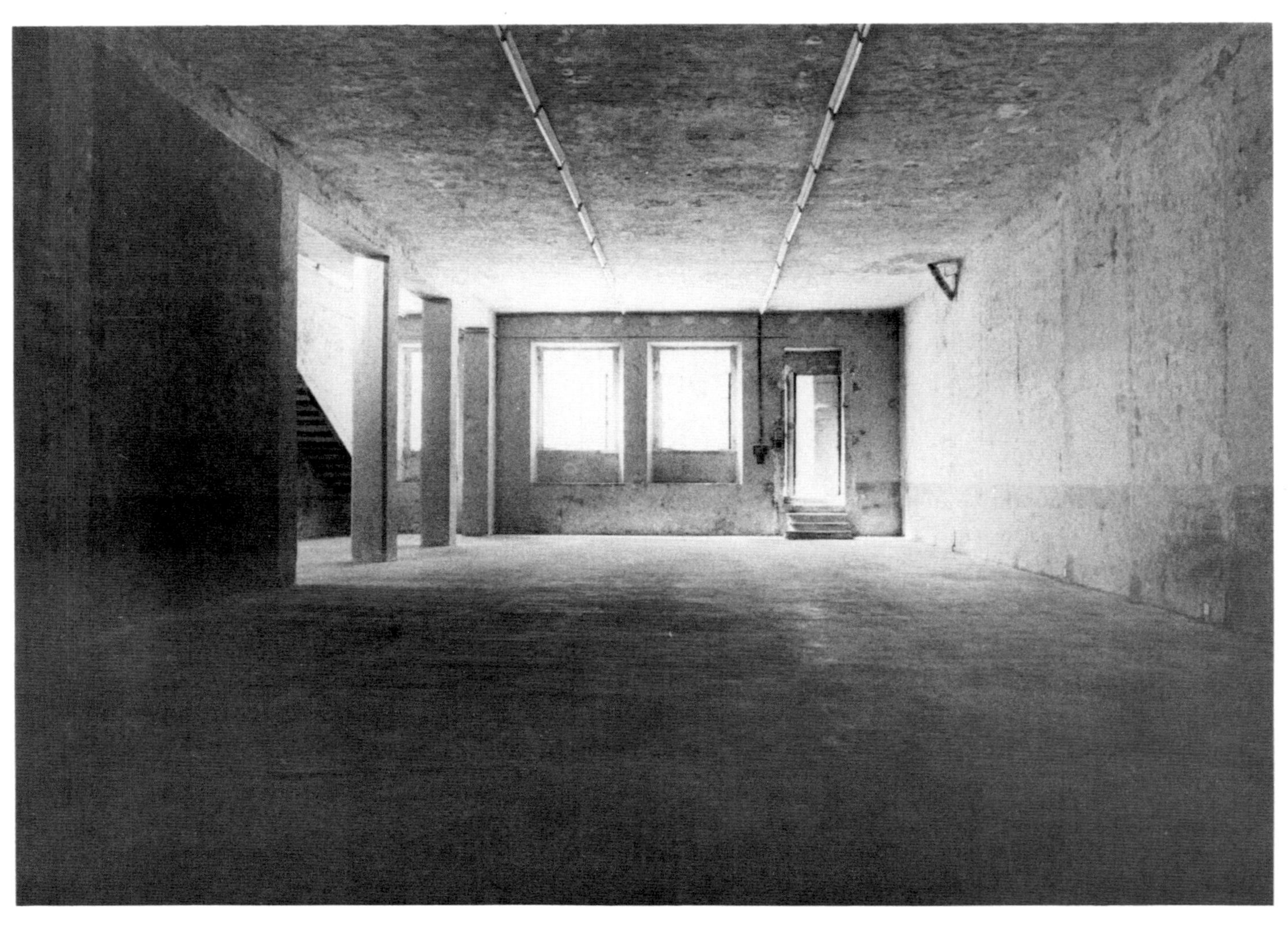

Viewing west under natural light conditions.
Photograph by Franco Toselli.

A year after the exhibition of my work at the Franco Toselli Gallery in Milan, I did an installation for the Claire Copley Gallery in Los Angeles. It was my first individual exhibition in a commercial gallery in North America.

The gallery was located on La Cienega Boulevard, one of the city's major north-south thoroughfares, where most of the other commercial art galleries in Los Angeles were located at that time, and where there was a constant flow of pedestrian traffic. The gallery space, which originally had been a multipurpose storefront, was entered directly at street level. A storefront window facing the street measured 6 feet 8 inches by 5 feet 4 inches. The gallery from front wall to back wall measured 53 feet 7¼ inches; its width was 14 feet 4½ inches and height 11 feet 2¾ inches.

A partition wall separating an office area from the front exhibition space extended floor-to-ceiling 10 feet 8⅜ inches across the width of the gallery at a point 16 feet 5¼ inches from the back wall. The partition ended 4 feet 2⅛ inches short of the opposite wall, forming a passage connecting both areas. The office area contained office furniture and equipment, artworks in storage, and a separate utility area. The white wall surfaces of the larger front area were maintained as a backdrop for exhibition purposes.

The work I proposed was the dismantling of the partition wall for the duration of the exhibition. The idea was to integrate the two areas, so that the office area and its activities could be viewed from the exhibition area, and the exhibition area opened to the gallery directors' view.

Once the proposal had been accepted, the entire partition was removed. Its drywall surfaces were stripped from its frame, which was then disassembled and stored until reinstallation after the exhibition. Remnants of the partition's original construction, such as seam compound, were removed, and a small piece of rug cut out to make way for the partition, had to be replaced.

Since the work also meant to restore the display surfaces of the gallery to presentation standards, it

CLAIRE S. COPLEY GALLERY, 918 N. LA CIENEGA, LOS ANGELES

SATURDAY, SEPTEMBER 21 THROUGH SATURDAY, OCTOBER 12, 1974

was necessary to fill in cracks and cover over any features that might have become objects of perception, so that the entire interior would appear to be an integrated and continuous flawless container. In the north wall large cracks marked by waterstains had to be caulked from the outside and filled with cement on the inside. In the south wall cracks caused by the joining of plywood against plaster also had to be filled in. All cracks were finished with drywall compound before the walls were painted. Wall and ceiling surfaces were then treated to the usual gallery white with an airless sprayer, and they were finished by being "fogged" out. The office and storage area was painted in the same way as the exhibition space, but was otherwise left untouched. Once the wall surfaces were finished and everything was in place, the exhibition area walls seemed to vignette the office area and its activities and turn them into the content of the exhibition.

A sign over the storefront window identified the gallery by name and served to frame the gallery's operation for passersby. Once inside, the viewer could hear as well as assimilate more readily the various private and business activities with museum staff, collectors, artists, and friends usually screened from view. Also, artworks could be clearly seen in storage in the exhibition/gallery, as opposed to being placed on the gallery walls for exhibition.

I left instructions with the gallery dealer to inform viewers who requested information about the work that I had produced it, and that by removing the partition wall the day-to-day activities of the gallery were disclosed to the viewer in the unified office/exhibition space. In the same way that gallery personnel seemed to become increasingly aware of their activities, viewers also became more aware of themselves as viewers.

The viewers were confronted with the way in which they had been traditionally lulled into viewing works of art and, simultaneously, the unfolding of the gallery structure and its operational procedures. Works had been perceived from a safe cultural distance which generally prevented the viewer from questioning the issues involved. Without that questioning, a work of art could remain enclosed in its abstracted aesthetic context, creating a situation where the viewer could mystify its actual and historical meaning. As a commentary, this work laid bare the contradictions inherent within the gallery structure and its constituent elements.

The gallery dealer is—in the viewer's understanding—the knowledgeable, responsible mediator of the work in the many steps of its abstraction from its context. The dealer's prime function is to commodify the work of art, to transform the work's aesthetic use-value into exchange-value.

To accomplish this aim the works are generally isolated on the white walls of the gallery, clearly separated from the area of business activity. Once they are returned to the storage area, that is, the area of business operation, they have been reduced to their essential commodity-function.

Because the gallery dealer must give the work an economic value, the dealer is often unable to reveal its actual function. Paradoxically, the reality of the work can be viewed only through this conduit in which it undergoes the initial abstraction in the accrual of exchange-value.

The function of the work at the Claire Copley Gallery was didactic: to represent materially the visible aspects of this process of abstraction. For this reason, the work's structure was circular in order to reveal its affiliation with the production, the mediation, and the reception of culture. In one sense this could be viewed as a concomitant of economic interest, while other cultural aspects could come under scrutiny as well, from the handling of money to the selection of exhibitions. Works in storage—those preserved in cabinets and those leaning against the wall—were now also visibly accessible. The material reality of the gallery operations surfaced as questionable and problematic even though the author and viewer might find the gallery to be the most efficient way for the public reception of works of art. If the viewer saw the Toselli Gallery display surfaces perhaps as a definition of the architectural structure and, further, what that structure implies, then the work at the Claire Copley Gallery could be defined as an analytical model of the actual operations of a gallery behind those display surfaces.

The removal of the paint at the Toselli Gallery was in part a reference to the traditional concern in painting of the processes of adding and subtracting materials to a two-dimensional plane. The two-dimensional plane was generally determined by its contour and its support structure, which in turn implied further architectural support structures as well as covertly operational support systems. From a similar point of view but in a different way, the volume of the partition determined the actual space and its functional operations; its removal from that space disclosed the office volume and juxtaposed it to the exhibition volume which was necessary for the exhibition to take place. The Claire Copley work was rejecting the conventional functions of the space it occupied to make the space function as an exhibition/presentation.

A critical analysis of the gallery structure was developed by a small number of artists in the late sixties and early seventies, at a time when they viewed their role as artists as that of individual producers with the

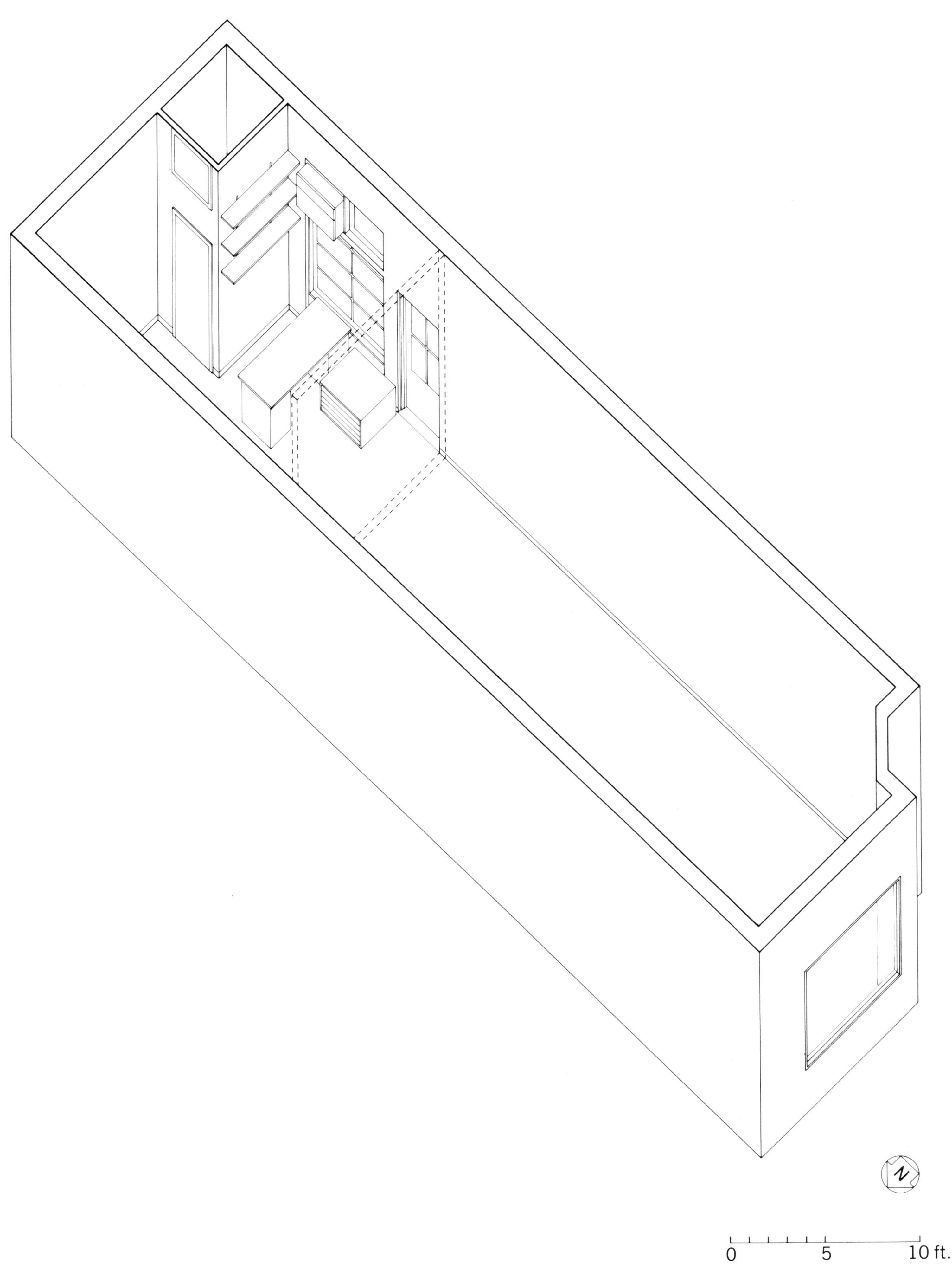

Axonometric drawing of Claire Copley Gallery. Ghostline showing removed wall. Drawing by Lawrence Kenny.

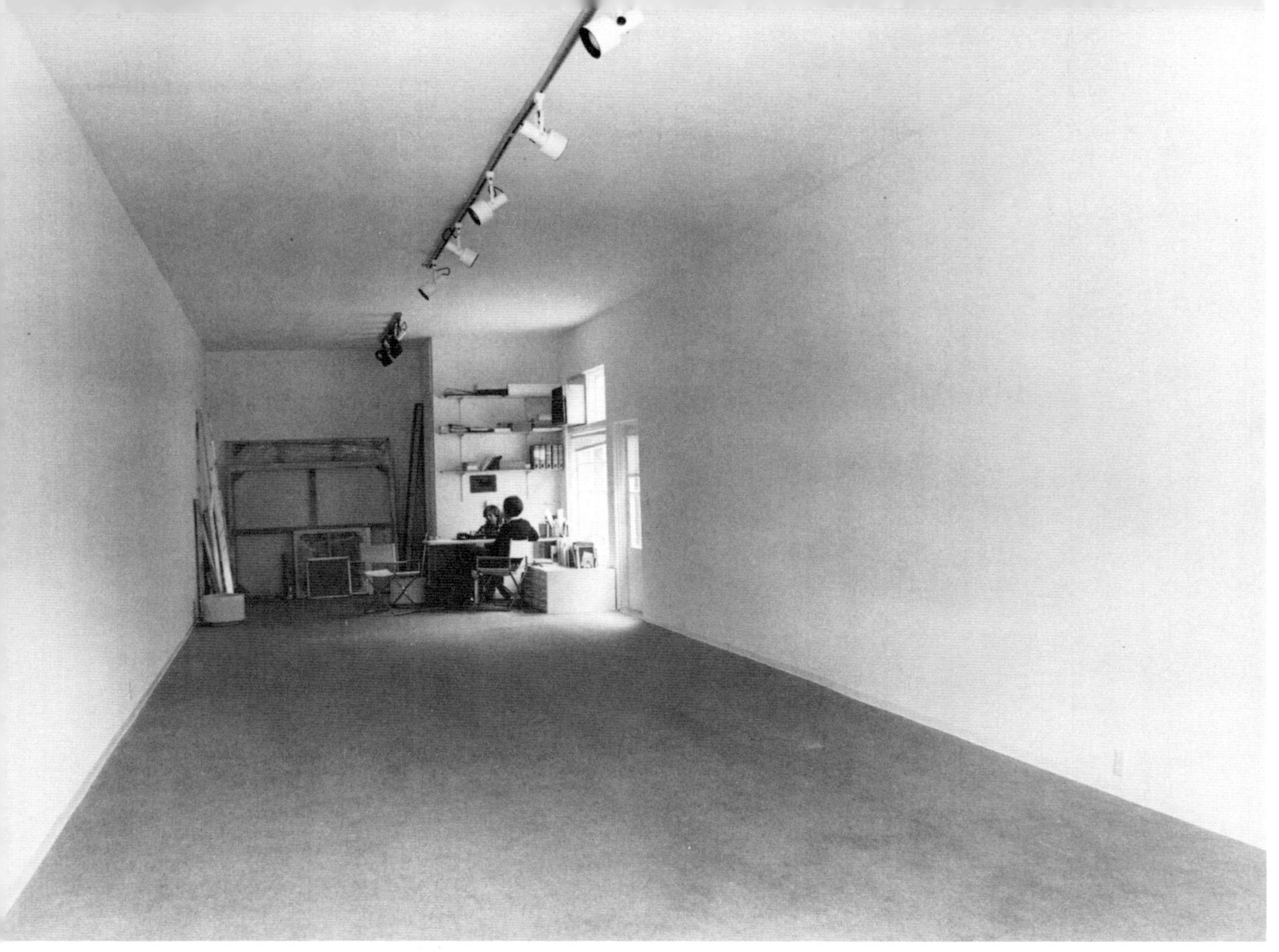

Installation at Claire Copley Gallery. Viewing through gallery toward office and storage areas.

Viewing through gallery toward entry/exit and street. Photographs by Gary Krueger.

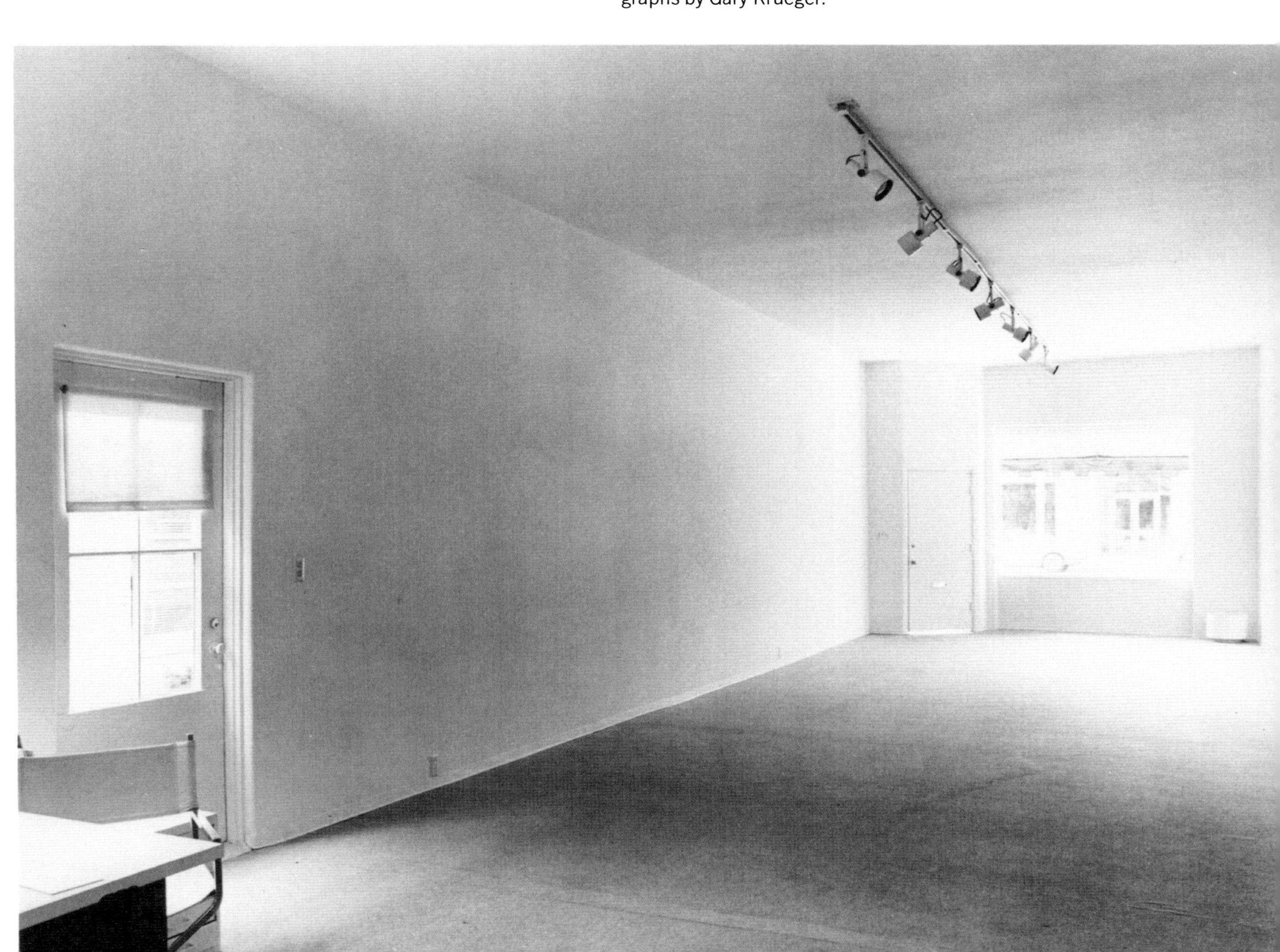

right to control totally not only the production but also the distribution of their work. They believed that artists of previous generations had accepted uncritically and without qualification a distribution system (the gallery/market) which had often dictated the content and context of their work. These artists found themselves in a paradoxical situation; they either had to suppress the intentions of their work when it intersected with the gallery/market or they had to forgo the conventional distribution system altogether and give up their role as individual producers; or they could exhibit outside the traditional exhibition context, with the hope that a new production and distribution system could be developed. When their work conflicted with the commodity status required by the gallery system, these artists had no choice but to develop a new cultural context for their work before they could expect to function within the gallery nexus.

Interestingly enough these works were often seen as "nonmaterial" since they seemed to function outside of the traditional context of the marketplace. Instead of deriving their cultural meaning from the conventional exhibition support, they functioned in a variety of locations. Ultimately, in the late seventies, it was shown that these works had at least an economic materiality of their own and did not in fact operate outside of the cultural context. Some younger generation artists considered this discrepancy of theory and practice sufficient proof that once again the interdependence between production and distribution in the work of art could be totally ignored. The work as object reinstated the dealer and the distribution system to its original status. Some artists of this younger generation, possibly seeking a way out of object-production and gallery/museum distribution similar to that of artists of the late sixties and early seventies formed production collectives, which attempted to keep their non-object—oriented production outside of the confines of the cultural industry.

Another phenomenon of the early seventies, deriving from artists' anticommercialism and concern with the problem of commodification was the development of the alternative space system for exhibition although not necessarily for distribution. The alternative space relied for its funding on outside sources rather than the market for which the work was primarily produced. Alternative spaces made more works more frequently accessible than the commercial galleries, yet they falsified the work's commodity status, assuming that visibility alone would complete the reception process and that exchange value was not one of the work's features. The alternative space system provided visibility for the work regardless of specific interest, but it did not necessarily stand behind the work, with the full support necessary for reception within the culture. Paradoxically, the only way for a work to be fully received is through its initial abstraction for exchange value. To resolve these contradictions between the artist's interests and the functions and capacities of the alternative space, these institutions finally had to assume the role of being either a commercial gallery or a museum.

I felt at the time and still feel that the gallery is one essential context for the cultural reception of my work. What came under scrutiny in the Claire Copley work was the question of whether a work of art whose discourse disclosed the system of economic reproduction could possibly, at the same time, engender that economic reproduction for itself. Just as the work served as a model of how the gallery operated, it also served as a model for its own economic reproduction.

MICHAEL ASHER

OCTOBER 7 — OCTOBER 10, 1974

ANNA LEONOWENS GALLERY
NOVA SCOTIA COLLEGE OF ART AND DESIGN
6152 COBURG ROAD
HALIFAX NOVA SCOTIA
CANADA

While teaching as a visiting instructor at the Nova Scotia College of Art and Design in the fall of 1974, I was invited to do a work at the College's Anna Leonowens Gallery, which was then directed and curated by Alan McKay.

The College was then located in a residential area where the campuses of several other universities are also located. The gallery building was set back approximately 40 feet from the street on its front or north elevation. The gallery had a floor to ceiling window-wall 15 feet 4 inches high. Each window section is 8 feet 9 inches wide and was framed by vertical steel columns. The building containing the gallery also housed the classrooms, workshops, and library of the College. The entrance through the gallery area was used as the main access to these facilities. This entrance consisted of a double door which was set under a metal canopy, placed 9 feet 6 inches from the northeast corner and projecting 8 feet into the interior gallery space. The actual dimensions of the gallery were 40 feet on its north-south axis and 57 feet 10 inches on its east-west axis.

Five feet four inches from the north window-wall and parallel to the east wall at a distance of 5 feet ran a partition wall 17 feet 4 inches long, which formed a storage area. The secretary's desk was placed in front of the partition wall. These two elements were constructed or placed within what was otherwise an uninterrupted rectangular volume. Plaster coated steel columns were spaced 8 feet 6 inches along the south wall. These columns extended from floor to ceiling, at a height of 15 feet 4 inches, where they stopped at the exposed corner of the ceiling. At the east corner of the south wall there was a double door entry/exit, which was the main access to the building's elevators and the library. At the west corner, a doorway lead to a stairway to the mezzanine level, 9 feet above the main gallery. The mezzanine gallery was 23 feet 1½ inches by 22 feet, with a ceiling height of 8 feet.

For the purposes of this installation, I did not alter the gallery or any of its materials or architectural details in any way, leaving everything, including the lighting fixtures, in exactly the same position and condition inherited from the previous exhibition. During the exhibition I did not turn on any of the lights in the gallery. I wanted the space to be perceived solely as an architectural volume uninflected by details or fixtures. For the same reason I also took the tinted sunscreens off the top of the window-wall, since they were not a part of the original design and would have modified the normal quality of interior light. I did not want the walls to be painted, so all of the interior surfaces were left in the condition they were in after the previous exhibition. I had the floor swept clean, but not polished. I also asked that the secretary not be present every day since the gallery space was regularly open and accessible to the general public and the school. A bulletin board, outside of the gallery, announced the exhibition.

Unlike my earlier works, this work was concerned with the minimal amount of modification to the gallery space itself. In part, it showed that any place defined as a gallery would be perceived as such by the viewer, whether or not objects were being exhibited there. The absence of objects, in this case, first objectified the architectural space and design details and then shifted the viewers' attention to their own preconceptions of what an exhibition should look like. Ultimately, the viewers were left to decide to what degree they might have been the subject of this exhi-

Anna Leonowens Gallery, Nova Scotia College of Art and
Design, Halifax. Viewing west with office equipment before
removal and opening of the installation.

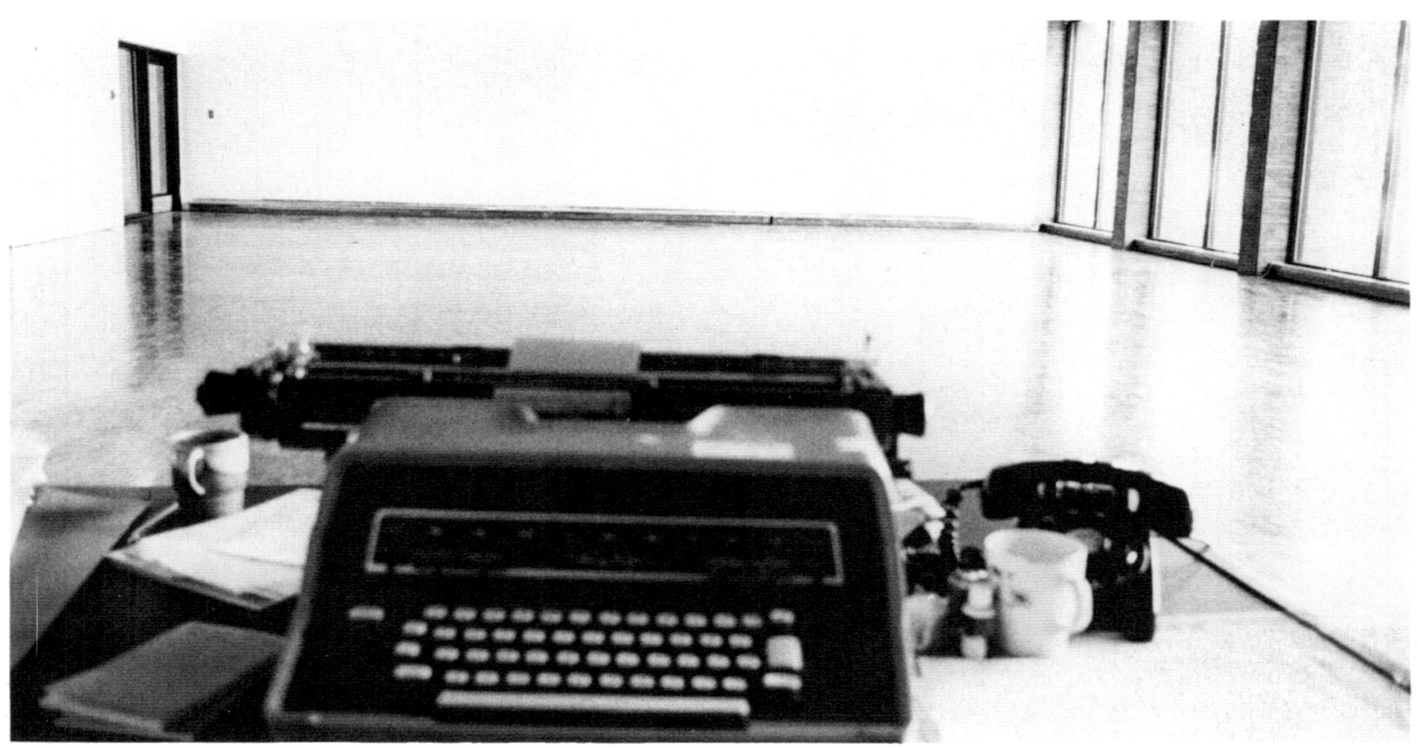

bition or whether they were supposed to project some imaginary exhibition into the space.

Viewers may have perceived the installation as an exhibition by Michael Asher, particularly if they were aware of the announcement posted on the bulletin board; as an architectural container waiting for a function; or as an empty gallery space between exhibitions. Audience perception could also have been directed back upon itself, since the installation was set up with no object or person as its focus. Finally, the *method* of the work, in the tradition of designation or declaration, could have been seen as its dominant feature. Unlike a designatory work, however, this installation was located within an existing exhibition space continuing to function as a gallery. While all of these possibilities were inherent in the work, the sequence of perception was determined by the viewer.

Should an exhibition institution generate exhibitions, or does the given institutional space, time, producer, and receiver suffice to define the experience of the exhibition? For an exhibition to concretize and demarcate itself within a culture, it will generally require a public's presence and awareness within a specific time and place, as determined by the producer. A work such as this generates its own historical mode of production. At a minimum, it affects its own discourse. At a maximum, within artistic practice, it demands the receiver to take a critical position within the material world. After the conclusion of the exhibition, the work continued to exist as an abstraction of the original context and experience.

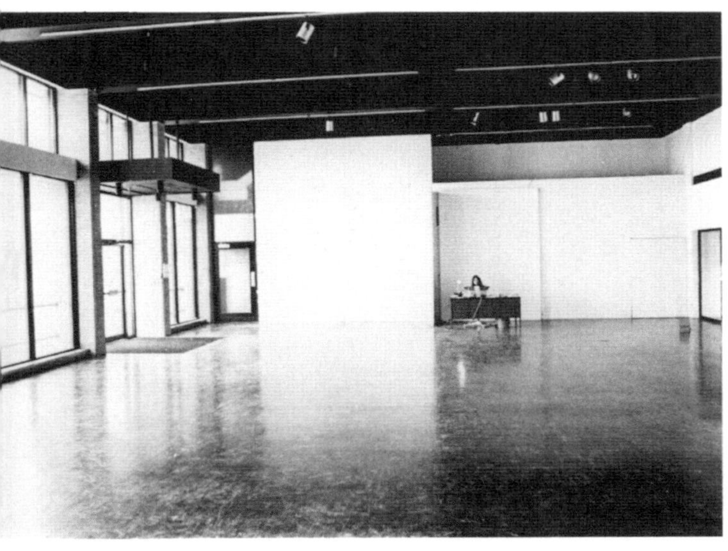

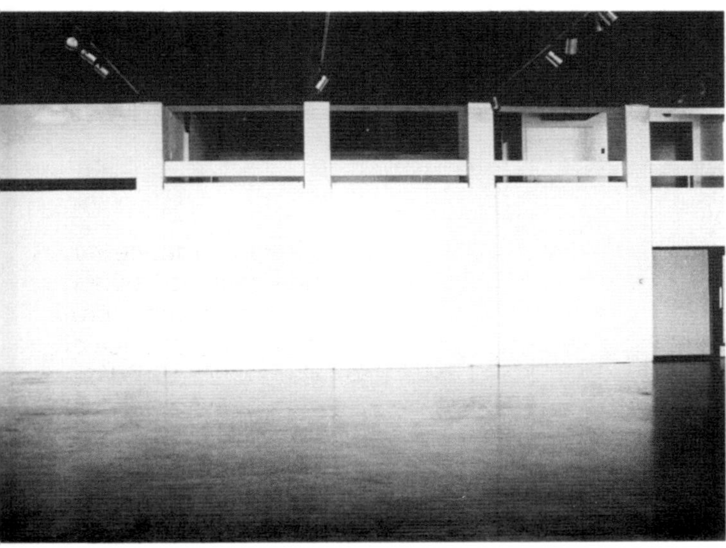

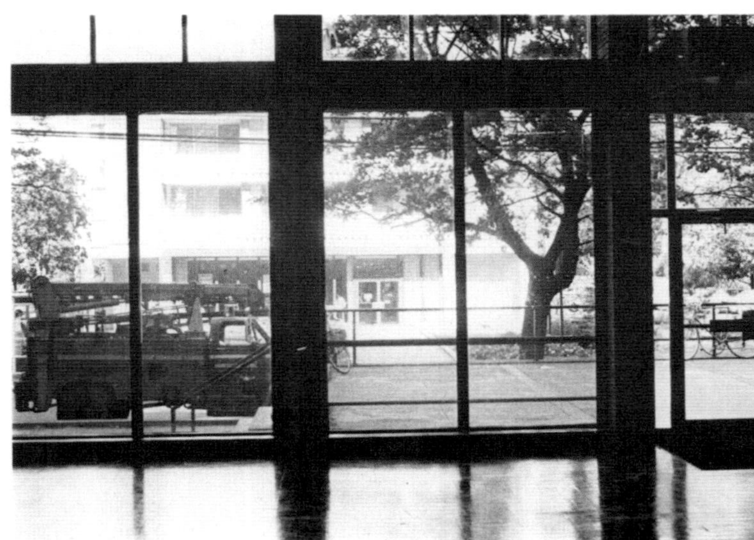

Viewing east in gallery toward office area before the opening of the installation.

Viewing south wall and mezzanine gallery.

Viewing west wall of gallery during exhibition.

Viewing north. Detail of glass curtain wall and entrance canopy of gallery. Photographs by Michael Asher.

February 24–March 9, 1975
The Gallery of Otis Art Institute
Los Angeles, California

OTIS ART INSTITUTE and OTIS ART ASSOCIATES
invite you to an exhibition by

MICHAEL ASHER
February 24 - March 9, 1975

OTIS ART INSTITUTE GALLERY FOYER
2401 Wilshire Boulevard, Los Angeles, CA 90057

GALLERY HOURS
Monday—Thursday, and Saturday: 10:30 am to 5:00 pm
Sunday: 10:30 am to 5:00 pm, closed Friday

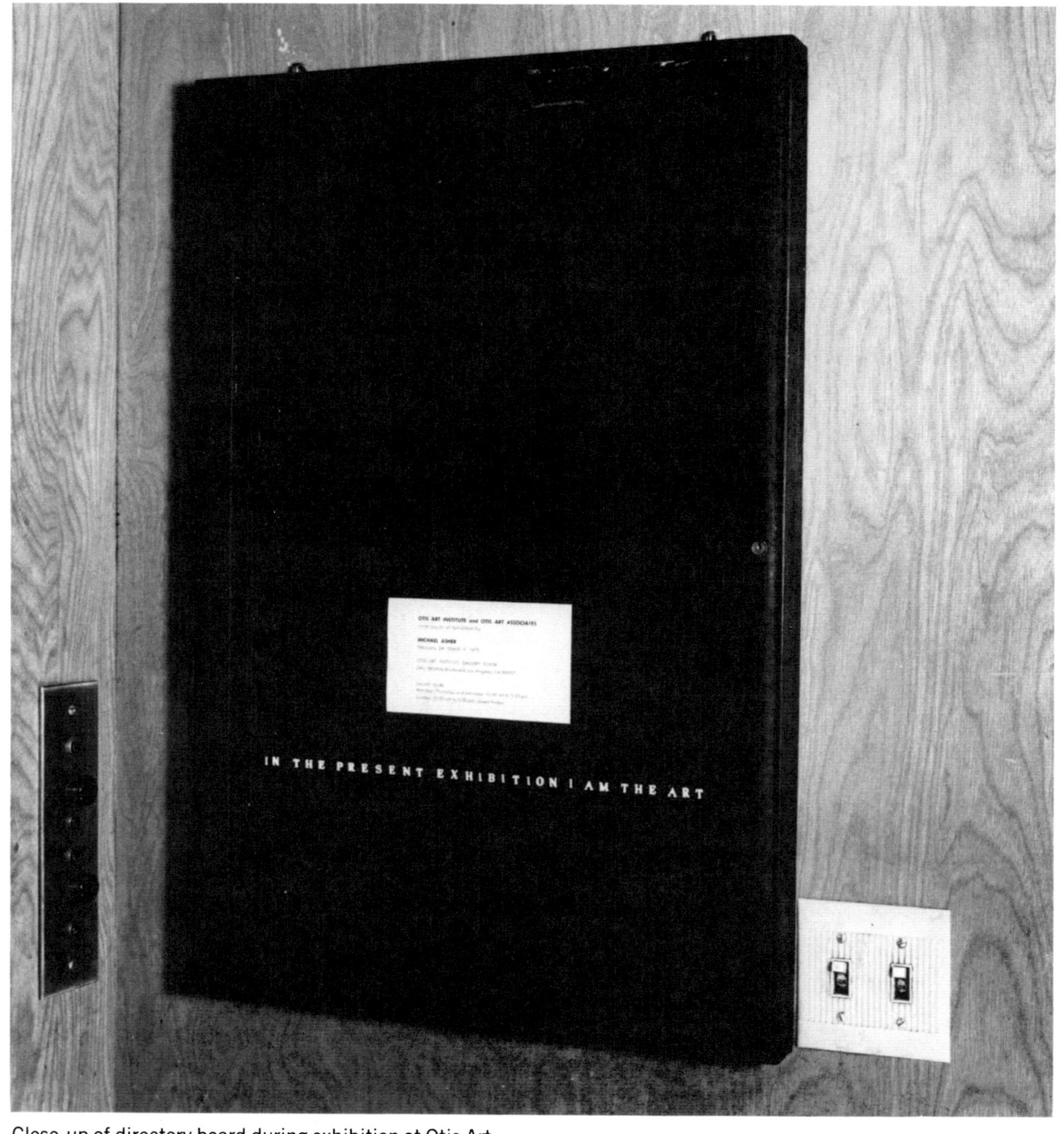

104 Close-up of directory board during exhibition at Otis Art
Institute. Photograph by Frank Thomas.

Gurdon Woods, director of the Otis Art Institute, extended an invitation to do an exhibition at the gallery of Otis Art Institute, which is located directly on MacArthur Park, one of the largest and most visited parks in downtown Los Angeles. The park consists of two areas on each side of Wilshire Boulevard, a major east-west axis; it is a recreational facility used by families, older residents, and different ethnic groups. Situated on the park, the gallery is visited by passersby who frequent its exhibitions. From a double-door entry/exit, a foyer leads into the main gallery's exhibition area.

The gallery measured 99 feet by 33 feet 3 inches by 16 feet 6 inches. The walls were finished with wood panels painted white, which were evenly grooved from floor to ceiling for hanging paintings. A wooden grid structure, painted black, formed a false ceiling which contained the lighting fixtures. I decided not to use this space, however, because its interior decoration seemed inconsistent with the sort of installation I had in mind. The doors to the exhibition area, therefore, remained locked for the length of my exhibition, and I used the foyer with its double doors to the street for the installation. The foyer measured 11 feet on the north-south axis and 11 feet 6 inches on the east-west axis, with a ceiling height of 8 feet 6 inches. The walls of the foyer were wood paneled from floor to ceiling and varnished. Along the south wall was a built-in illuminated display case with a floor-standing ashtray beneath it; on the north side there were elevator doors and a drinking fountain. The locked doors to the exhibition area were on the west side. Permanently mounted on the east wall and next to the doors to the street was a glass-covered, black-felt directory board, 2 feet 6 inches high and 1 foot 8 inches wide, which was designed for the mounting of molded plastic letters. Approximately three-fourths of the way down from the top of the directory board, I placed letters which spelled out the following phrase:

IN THE PRESENT EXHIBITION I AM THE ART

And just above that I attached the mailer sent out by the Otis Art Institute which read:

OTIS ART INSTITUTE AND OTIS ART
ASSOCIATES
invite you to an exhibition by
MICHAEL ASHER
February 24–March 9, 1975
OTIS ART INSTITUTE GALLERY FOYER
2401 Wilshire Boulevard, Los Angeles, CA. 99057
Gallery hours
Monday–Thursday, and Saturday: 10:30 A.M. to 5:00 P.M.
Sunday: 10:30 A.M. to 5:00 P.M., closed Friday

The work at the Claire Copley Gallery had directed viewers' attention to the way the gallery functioned, and therefore focused primarily on the gallery director; the work at the Nova Scotia College of Art and Design had directed the viewers' attention primarily to themselves. The work at the Otis Art Institute, however, directed the viewers' attention primarily to the artist; in this way these works circumscribed the production, distribution, and reception of the artwork.

The statement on the directory board was read as an objectification of the producer as subject. It reflected the producer's principles regarding production at the time of the exhibition. The statement implied that the author was not separate from his own manifestation and that his work had developed from and was integral to his experience. It further implied that if there were no separations between the aesthetic manifestation of the work and the author, the aesthetic production would have its own dialectical relationship with history. Perhaps alienation begins when the artists view their production as materially separate from themselves, or as a product existing independently from their own consciousness; while the viewers consider it necessary to isolate the aesthetic production from the author in order to generate their own vision of the artist's production, which is partly fictionalized through projection. This separation is concurrent with the transformation of the work of art into a commodity which negates the role of the producer. When art is placed in its historical context, the separa-

Otis Art Institute Gallery. West view of installation area.

Northeast corner of lobby during exhibition.

Exterior and entry/exit to lobby. Photographs by Hal Glicksman.

Otis Art Institute Gallery ground plan with details of lobby, elevation of display case and rear entrance. The directory board inside the lobby that was used for the exhibition is not indicated on the plan. Courtesy Otis Art Institute Gallery.

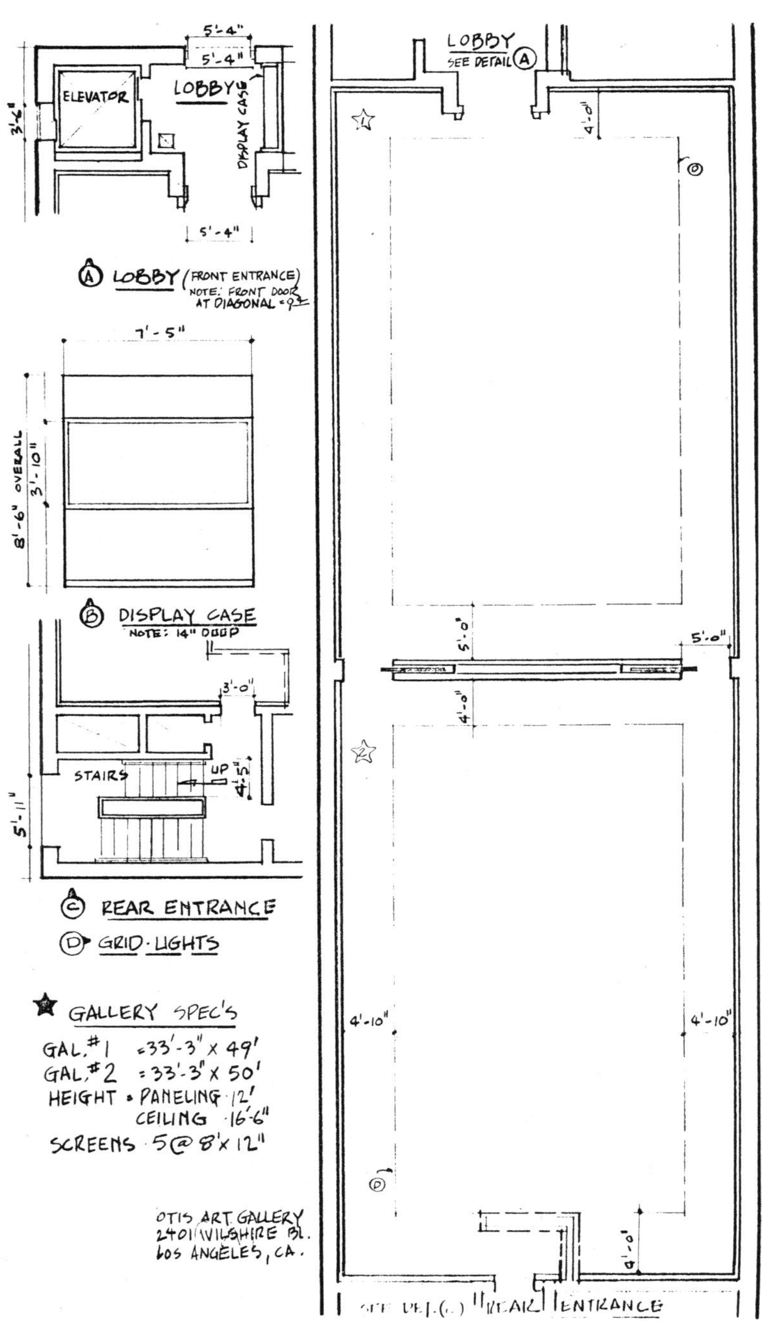

tion once again occurs within the culture, which divides author from production and negates the work's dialectical relationship with history.

By using a written statement to integrate the author's experience with his production, the paradox of the work's own aesthetic reality is stated. Experience, in this case, might have finally been understood as a question of "life," as the personal pronoun "I" seemed to suggest, but subjective experience alone did not contain the impulse of aesthetic production, since that would have precluded all of the other factors necessarily determining the work.

I was trying to discover if it was historically possible to integrate author and production in a specific work. The work perhaps defined the meaning of the separation between author and product by juxtaposing its material presence (lobby, directory board, statement in plastic letters) with the abstraction of the written statement. Those viewers who identified themselves with the "I" of the author chose their own subjectivity over a confrontation with the artist's statement.

But can the materialization of the work's own aesthetic principle be located and identified? As a material entity, it seems to contain a great number of contradictions. Is it the actual installation, the statement itself, or the "I" in the statement (the author of the statement) where the materiality of the principle is located? Which of these constituents or which of their interrelationships incorporates the proclaimed aesthetic principle and how does that principle operate?

Language can point to a material or visual problem, or it can proclaim a principle in aesthetic production which can be verified within and through language. I used language in this work to define a principle that contradicted itself in its material presentation. This work is the only one to date that I have defined in the medium of language.

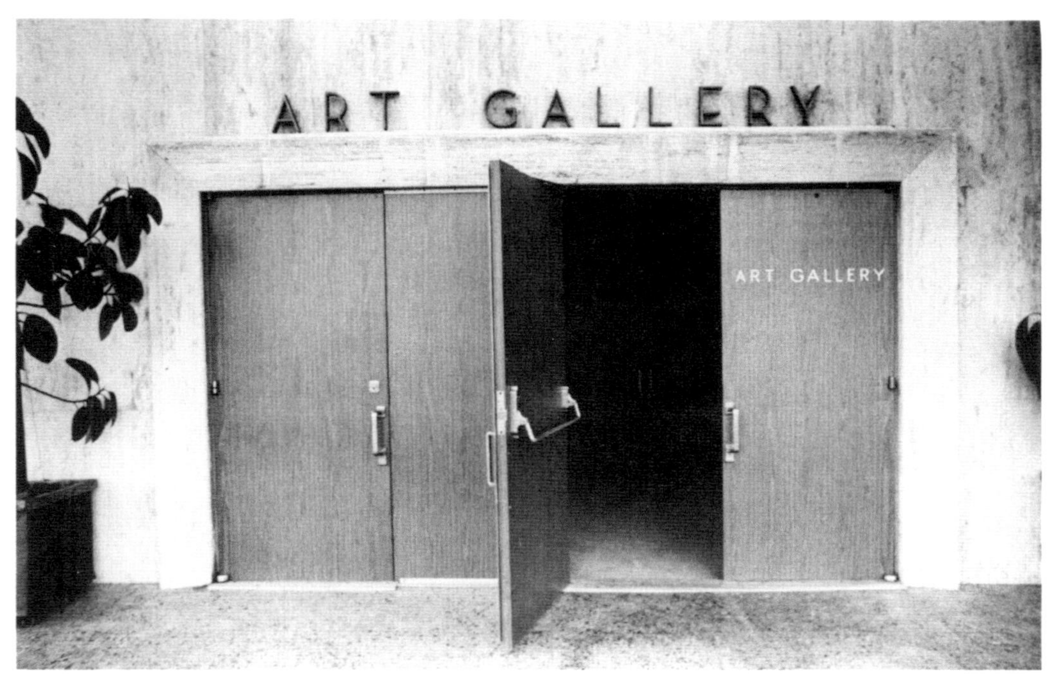

ART GALLERY
ART GALLERY

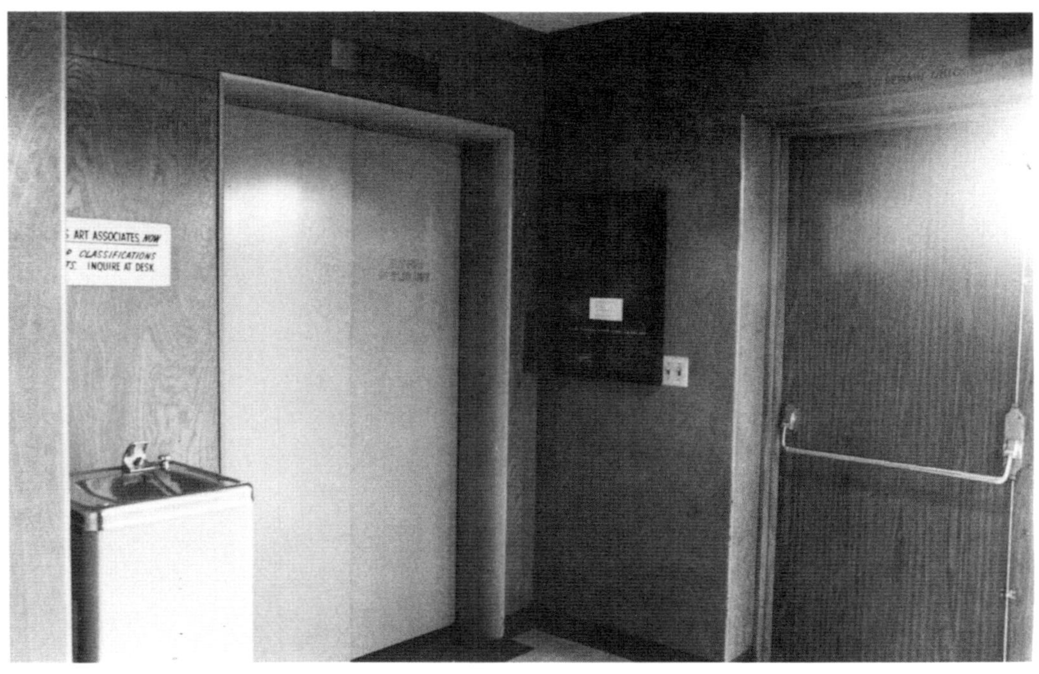

ART ASSOCIATES NOW
CLASSIFICATIONS
INQUIRE AT DESK

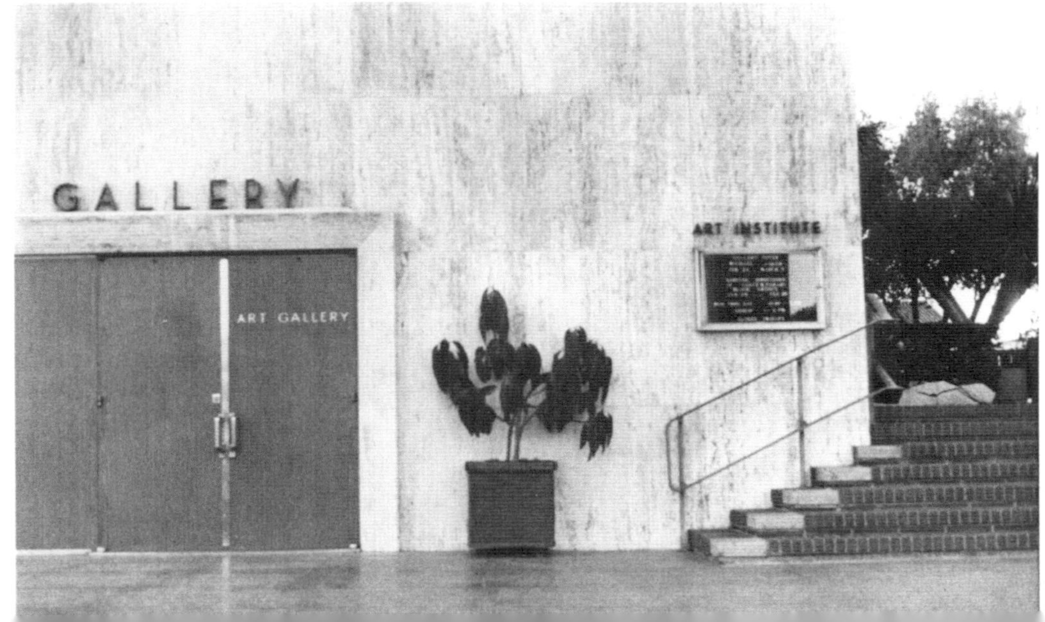

GALLERY
ART GALLERY
ART INSTITUTE

September 1975
Vision, *Number 1*
edited by Tom Marioni, published by
Kathan Brown Crown Point Press,
Oakland, California

In August 1975, I was asked by Kathan Brown and Tom Marioni, who planned to publish the first issue of *Vision* magazine, to contribute to this issue which focused on artistic production in California. The concept of the magazine was presented to me in a letter by Kathan Brown, defining the main features and function of the magazine as follows:

> *Vision* will be a publication by and for artists.... Each artist will present his own work in whatever way he chooses.... The page size is standard legal paper, 8½"x14", but since the work of an individual will always be shown on two facing pages the effective working size is 16"x14".

Tom Marioni, the editor, defined the purposes of the magazine in the first issue as follows:

> It is the purpose of *Vision* to make available information about idea-oriented art. It is an artist-oriented publication, presenting works and material only from artists, each issue devoted to a particular region of the world. In this first issue we have included California artists who have had an influence on the region or the world, and have created work that has the character of the region as well as an individual style. This section of the publication functions like an exhibition space where the artists were invited to show whatever they wanted to represent themselves. (*Vision*, no. 1, p. 11.)

During this postconceptual period, I thought the magazine would probably carry primarily texts, photos, and documentation presented as original works of art. It seemed necessary, therefore, to find a way to produce a work which, in the context of the magazine, would embody and represent the material conditions of its presentation.

My reply to the letter inviting me to contribute to the September issue of *Vision* magazine, dated August 16, 1975, outlined my proposal as follows:

Kathan Brown:

Thank you for your letter concerning the proposed publication of *Vision*. As I have mentioned to Tom Marioni, I would like to participate in your publication. My contribution will be to permanently adhere the two facing pages of my presentation together in order to form one leaf. It is important that the proper adhesive be used so there is no wrinkle or distortion over the page surface and edges are permanently bonded. Possibly a dry-mount technique will solve this problem. I am interested in having all three edges line up edge to edge and have them conform to the registration of the other pages in the book. I'm also interested in having the page numbers read consecutively so those on my two pages might possibly be lost. I leave it to your discretion to not print the page numbers for my presentation. If you have an index or table of contents, I wish to be included. If there is any hitch or you have any questions, please feel free to contact me directly. Best wishes for *Vision*.

Sincerely,
Michael Asher

Even though only a very short time elapsed between the proposal and the production of the work, it was finished in a very satisfying manner. All aspects of the outline of the work given in the letter were realized.

Glue was used to bond together the two 8½ inch-by-14 inch pages allocated for my contribution. The edges of the pages were flush and the front and back surfaces of the two bonded pages were smooth and even. The two bonded pages formed one leaf which differed in weight and thickness from all of the other leaves in the magazine. Stabilized in this way, the two bonded pages did not easily fall to either side when the magazine was opened, but stood out from the seam. When leafing through the magazine, the increased tangibility of the two bonded pages was distinctly noticeable.

The work denied readers'/viewers' expectation of textual or visual information. Since any representation of this order was withheld, the work's increased tangibility was set in opposition to the work's decreased readability and perceptual presence.

The work followed page 41 and preceded page 44. Only the page numbers 42 and 43 and my name were printed and they were printed in the same way and in the same place as they were on all of the other pages. Due to the adhesion of the two pages, however, the printing on the inside was almost unreadable. My name was listed in the table of contents and the contribution was identified as beginning on page 42.

The material presence of my work was contextualized with the visual and textual representations of the two contributions by Douglas Wheeler and Bruce Nauman (diagrams and a poem) preceding and following the bonded pages. By merging three distinctly different works, both visually and materially, the viewer was led to question the necessity of their usual presentation in isolation, since such a form of bracketing tends to induce a comparative reading and cross-referencing of the works. The bracketing of individualized works serves to deny their stylistic individualization and isolation; this in hope of consciously opening up an inquiry into their historical relations and contradictions.

The textual and visual representations of the two contributions that preceded and followed my work were cross-referenced with my work and with each other. In this manner it became apparent that, as representations, they were abstracted from their original context and intention in order to fit into the magazine format. A material construction (in terms of the magazine format), founded upon the material elements of the framework of the presentation, the work seemed to deny its own status as representation, and in doing so also questioned the representation of the other works (in terms of the magazine format).

At the same time, the work did not escape from being appropriated by the conditions of the framework into which it was inscribed, similar to the way in which it appropriated the work adjacent to it through contextualization: it became subject to the cultural reception of an aesthetic discourse which was exter-

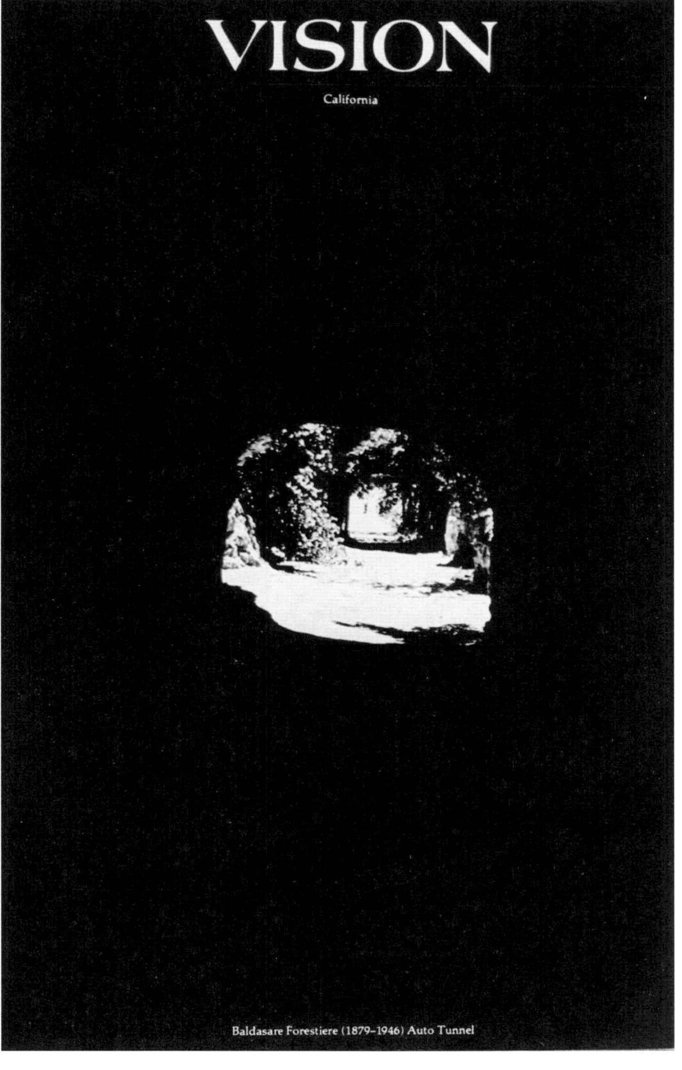

Cover of *Vision* magazine, Number 1, 1975.

nal to the magazine. It was all the more subject to inevitable aesthetic appropriation, since the work's claim to be a pure material presence and an essential formal practice was crucial to its function of dismantling isolated formal material practice. Operating within this traditional aesthetic practice, with an immediately apparent formal or material presence of its own, the work reduced itself to a historical device of disjunction.

Through the denial of its own presence, the work distanced itself from this practice while it simultaneously constituted itself within the discourse of artistic production. The work therefore derived its meaning from inscribing itself into the framework of formal modernist practice. The interpretation of this practice imposed meaning upon the work which caused it to be perceived as a historical reality; but at the same time, as a discursive device, it became a fiction in its attempt at distancing itself from aesthetic production.

The work as an object of perception within the display system of the magazine interrupted the display system materially. At the same time this rupture revealed itself to be dependent upon modernist conventions, such as: withdrawal of perceptual information, declaration as a designatory tool, transparency of material construction, self-referentiality and contextualization. These strategies imbued the work with the specific features of modernist art practice, self-reflectiveness, empirical verifiability, denial of aesthethic illusion, critical negativity and a claim for autonomous existence.

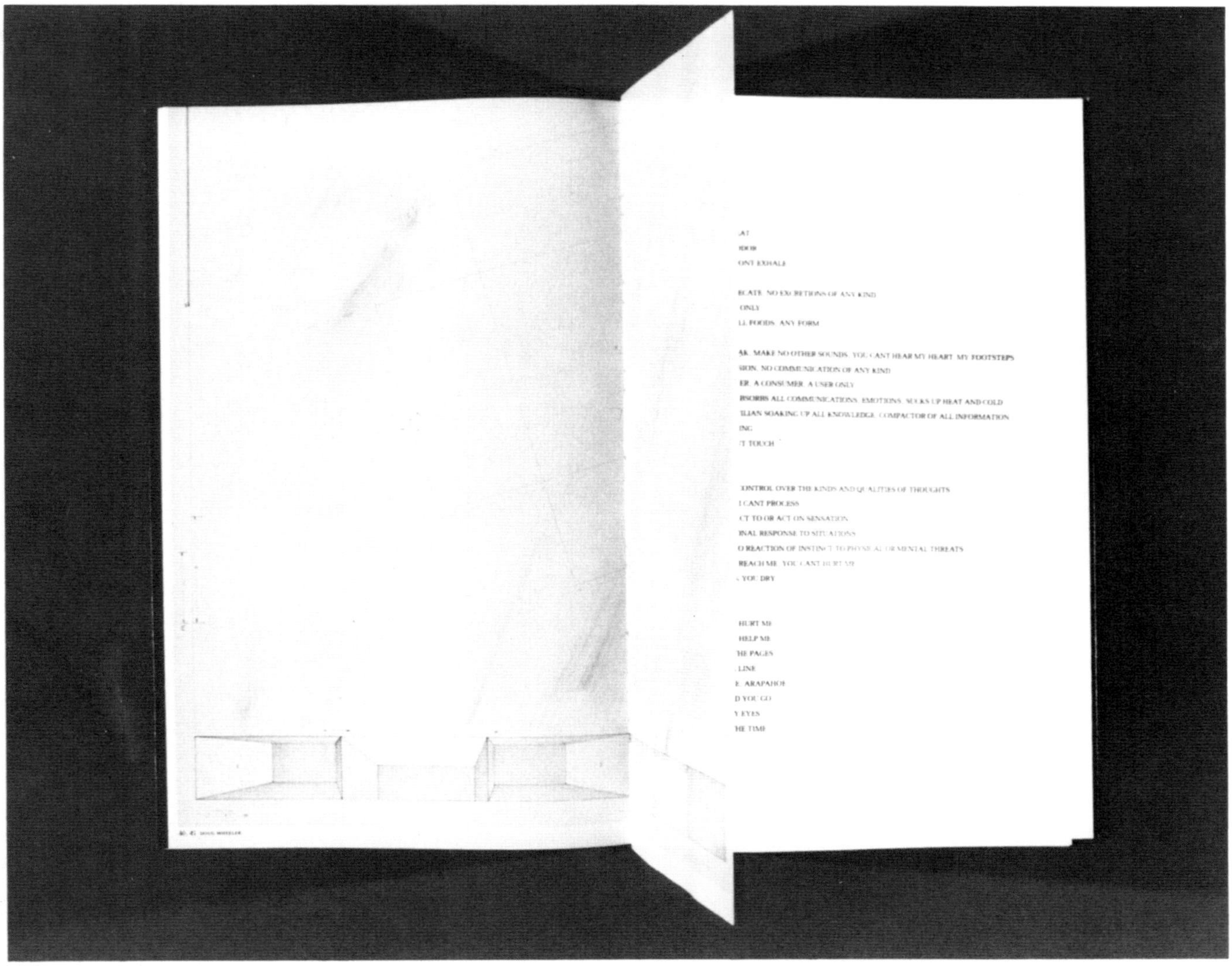

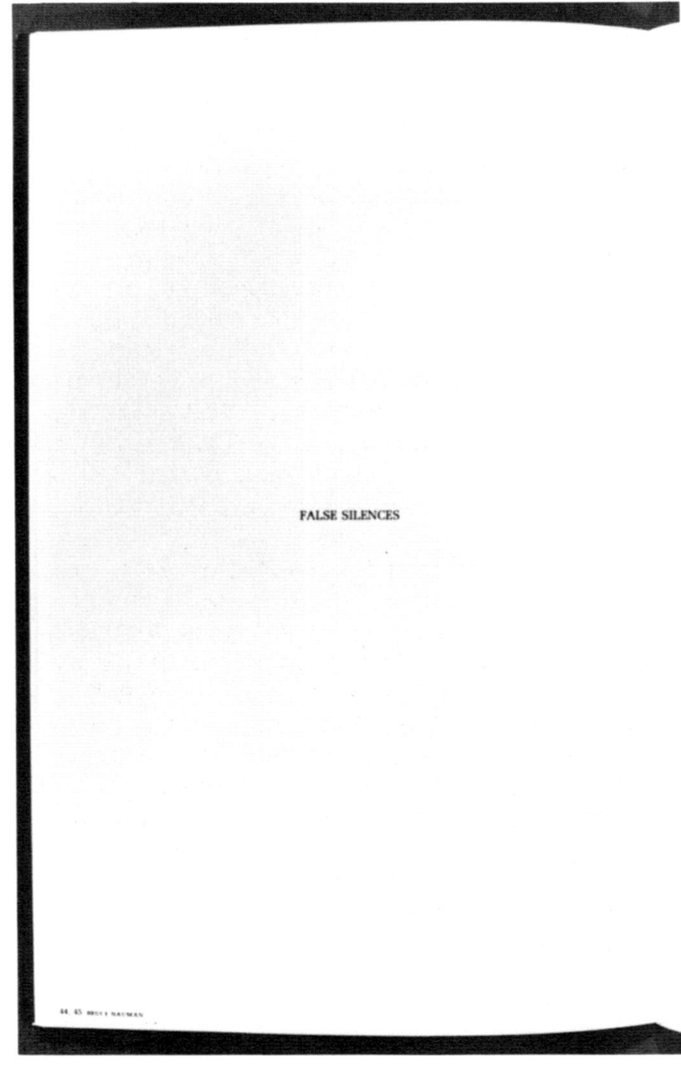

The contribution by Michael Asher to *Vision* magazine as to be seen between pages 41 and 44. Photographs by Louise Lawler.

January 8–February 8, 1976
Via Los Angeles
Portland Center for the Visual Arts
Portland, Oregon

SUNDAY JANUARY 18TH

KATU-2-ABC 233-2422
KOIN-6-CBS 228-3333
KGW-8-NBC 224-8620
KOAP-10 229-4892
KPTV-12 222-9921

* DENOTES COLOR PROGRAM

6:00 6 FAITH FOR TODAY*
6:05 8 DOXOLOGY/NEWS DIGEST*
6:15 8 SOUND OF TRUMPETS*
6:30 2 REV. CLEOPHUS ROBINSON*
     6 THIS IS THE LIFE*
     8 SIGNS OF LIFE*
6:45 8 DAVEY AND GOLIATH*
     12 NEWS HILITES*
7:00 2 MUSIC & THE SPOKEN WORD*
     6 IMPACT*
     8 HOT DOG*
     12 JERRY FALLWELL*
7:30 2 AGRICULTURE, U.S.A.*
     6 LAMP UNTO MY FEET*
     8 VISION ON*
8:00 2 CHRISTOPHER CLOSEUP*
     6 LOOK UP & LIVE*
     8 VEGETABLE SOUP*
     12 KATHRYN KUHLMAN*

8:30 2 OPTIONS*
     6 INTERNATIONAL ZONE*
     8 8 LIVELY ARTS*
     12 REX HUMBARD*
9:00 2 GENERATION III*
     6 OUTDOORS WITH BUD BEACHWOOD*
     8 GETTING IT TOGETHER*
9:30 2 REFLECTIONS*
     6 PREGAME SUPER BOWL X*
     8 GARDENING WITH ED HUME*
     12 ORAL ROBERTS*
10:00 2 URBAN FOCUS*
     8 MEDIX*
     12 DAY OF DISCOVERY*
10:30 2 DEVLIN*
     8 VIEWPOINT*
     12 IT IS WRITTEN*
11:00 2 BUMPITY*
     6 SUPER BOWL X*
     8 MEET THE PRESS*
     12 A NEW WAY TO LIVE*
11:10 3 JOT*
11:15 3 DAVY & GOLIATH
11:30 2 MAKE A WISH*
     3 INSIGHT*
     12 THE GOOD NEWS*

AFTERNOON

12:00 2 ISSUES AND ANSWERS*

     3 MUSIC & THE SPOKEN WORD*
     8 N.B.C. RELIGIOUS SPECIAL*
     12 BRUNCH THEATER
"The Buster Keaton Story" . . . starring Donald O'Connor and Ann Blyth.
12:30 2 DIRECTIONS*
     3 REX HUMBARD*
1:00 2 THE ROCK*
     8 8 LIVELY ARTS*
1:30 2 JACK IN THE BEANSTALK*
     3 GRACE CATHEDRAL*
1:45 12 KIPLINGER LETTER*
2:00 8 THE LANGE CUP*
The world's best pros compete for ski-racing's top prize down Sun Valley's famous Baldy Mountain.
     10 LEONARD BERNSTEIN AT HARVARD*
     12 SUNDAY MATINEE
"Who Killed the Mysterious Mr. Foster?" starring Ernest Borgnine, Will Geer, J.D. Cannon.
2:30 2 MONSTER MOVIE
     3 LIFELINE TO TRUTH*
     8 HOGAN'S HEROES*
3:00 2 PHOENIX OPEN GOLF*

TV SPORTS OF THE WEEK

SUNDAY, JANUARY 18
Super Bowl X: Ch. 6, 11 a.m.
The Lange Cup: Ch. 8, 2 p.m.
Phoenix Open Golf: Ch. 2, 3 p.m.

THURSDAY, JANUARY 22
Wrestling from Grand Theater: Ch. 3, 10:30 p.m.

SATURDAY, JANUARY 24
NCAA Basketball: Ch. 8, 1 p.m.
Boxing from Olympic: Ch. 2, 2 p.m.
Bing Crosby National Pro-Am: Ch. 2, 3 p.m.
NCAA Basketball: Ch. 8, 3 p.m.
Pro Bowlers Tour: Ch. 2, 4 p.m.
Sports Spectacular: Ch. 12, 4:30 p.m.
Wide World of Sports: Ch. 2, 5:30 p.m.
U. of O. Basketball: Ch. 12, 8 p.m.
Portland Wrestling: Ch. 12, 10:30 p.m.

—2—

Page from *TV PREVUE*, Portland, Oregon for the week of Sunday, January 18th—January 24th, 1976, indicating the 1 p.m. time slot of Michael Asher's television installation.

Mel Katz of the Portland Center for the Visual Arts invited me in the fall of 1975 to participate in an exhibition of the work of six Los Angeles artists. The exhibition, curated by May Beebe and Mel Katz, included the artists Chris Burden, Bryan Hunt, Channa Horwitz, Allen Ruppersberg, and Alexis Smith. My contribution to this exhibition was a 30-minute television broadcast on January 19, 1976, at 1:00 P.M.

My proposal for the 30-minute television broadcast segment was as follows:

The television program I propose is intended to utilize a half-hour of broadcast television time, alternating live television with commercial breaks, including titles and credits in the structure. I wish to focus a camera with an audio pickup upon the master control area of a television station. The camera and audio pickup will record the usual studio activities of the technicians and equipment. It is important that the people in the studio pursue their tasks as they do normally. In this respect, there is no conscious attempt to direct the viewer's response.

Juxtaposed against this are commercial breaks which have been carefully composed to direct the audience's attention upon a specific notion or object for a fifteen- or thirty-second time span. The commercial breaks also function to impose the usual progression of program format.

The program should be scheduled to integrate with other regular programming at times of the day when it is not critical to consider the viewers' location or what they might be doing. An announcement in the newspaper is desirable so the program will not appear as a mysterious event and may easily be referred to by the viewer.

A slightly different version of this proposal was displayed at the center for the duration of the exhibition and functioned as a description of the work. This display also indicated date, time and channel of broadcast. The work was announced in spot-announcements on television and in the local television guide *TV-Review*, as well as in the local newspaper, so that

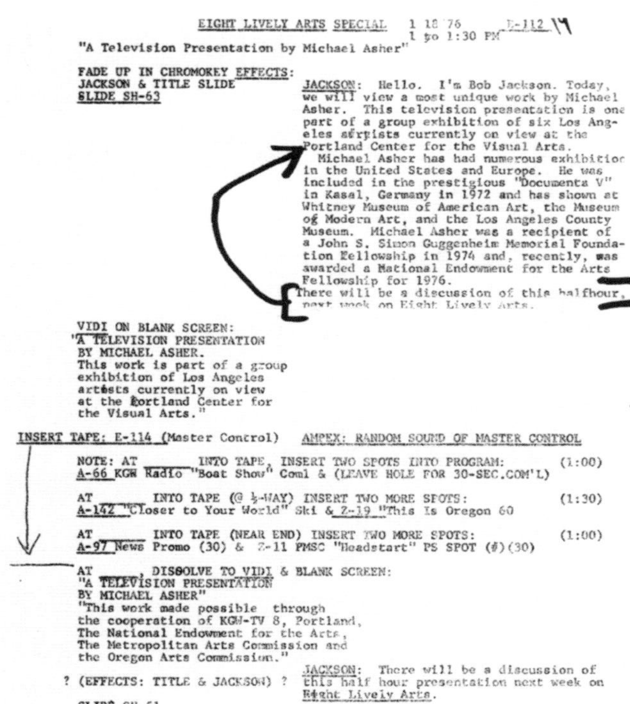

Time-line sheet for *Eight Lively Arts* television program on January 18, 1976, 1 p.m.

the public would be informed and the audience would not be alienated.

The commercial television station KGW, the NBC affiliate in Portland, agreed in principle to produce and broadcast the work proposal in the context of its weekly cultural program "Eight Lively Arts." This half-hour time slot determined the time frame for my work.

Mel Katz contacted an individual at KGW who was able to interest the station in producing and broadcasting the work. The program director was finally persuaded to approve the proposal, and, in December, the station called me to discuss certain questions that they considered problematic. After the proposal was approved the station still attempted to postpone the work because of what they believed to be the implication of its use of "dead air time."

The master-control area in this television broadcasting station kept track on a bank of monitors, of all incoming and outgoing programming, network, live, tape or film. It was also responsible for maintaining the programming schedule and implementing transmissions. The essential equipment of the master-control area consisted of tape decks, film islands, monitors, and switching panels for outgoing and incoming programming as well as a large storage area for videotapes of advertising and spots.

The dimensions of the master-control area were 65 feet by 30 feet. The walls enclosed windowless space, with the exception of one partial glass wall facing the main corridor of the building. The corridor behind the glass wall provided access to two studios, the master-control room, and the main stairwell leading to the offices on the second floor. A static television camera was locked in place for the recording of the activities in the master-control area and was able to view about one third of the space. In the center of this area an audio pickup was installed to record the sound from the broadcast activities. A cluster of switches and monitors was in the foreground of the image picked up by the camera. The glass wall to the left of the camera was in the background of the image and through it one could see the corridor. The camera recorded the ordinary activities that took place at the station during a broadcast; personnel passing in and out and interacting with those people on the job in the master-control area.

The camera recorded the activity of one of the seven production technicians who ran the master controls and lined up promos for public-service announcements. This technician was watching the monitors while talking (audible to the viewer) to the technical director and his assistant who were located in a booth upstairs from the master-control area. Equally audible but not visible was a technician who set up tapes of prerecorded commercials.

These technicians are the heros behind the television scene. But since there are no cuts or fades, no close-ups or dramatic angles, the visual codes used to produce televison fiction are not present and ultimately the viewer, used to reading those codes, loses interest. While the technicians continue to implement reception for home viewing, they are not part of the narrative fiction and therefore do not attain visual credibility for television delivery. The images of the technicians do not make good TV: there is nothing to take seriously, no manipulation to obey or lifestyle to be bought. Viewing these images, the audience realizes the degree of mediation necessary to the production and reception of TV images. The audience also understands that the TV image is an electronically generated depiction of real space on a flattened plane at a reduce scale with light and sound representations recorded by camera and sound equipment.

In the broadcast image the monitor to the left showed color bars for color registration. The middle monitor recorded the camera's own image. The monitor on the right showed a constant flow of network television, some of which was taped for viewing on KGW later in the evening.

I asked the station management to insert six thirty-second breaks, the standard number or commercial and public service announcements for a 30-minute program. Of the six breaks, two were spots for the television station, one was commercial for a savings

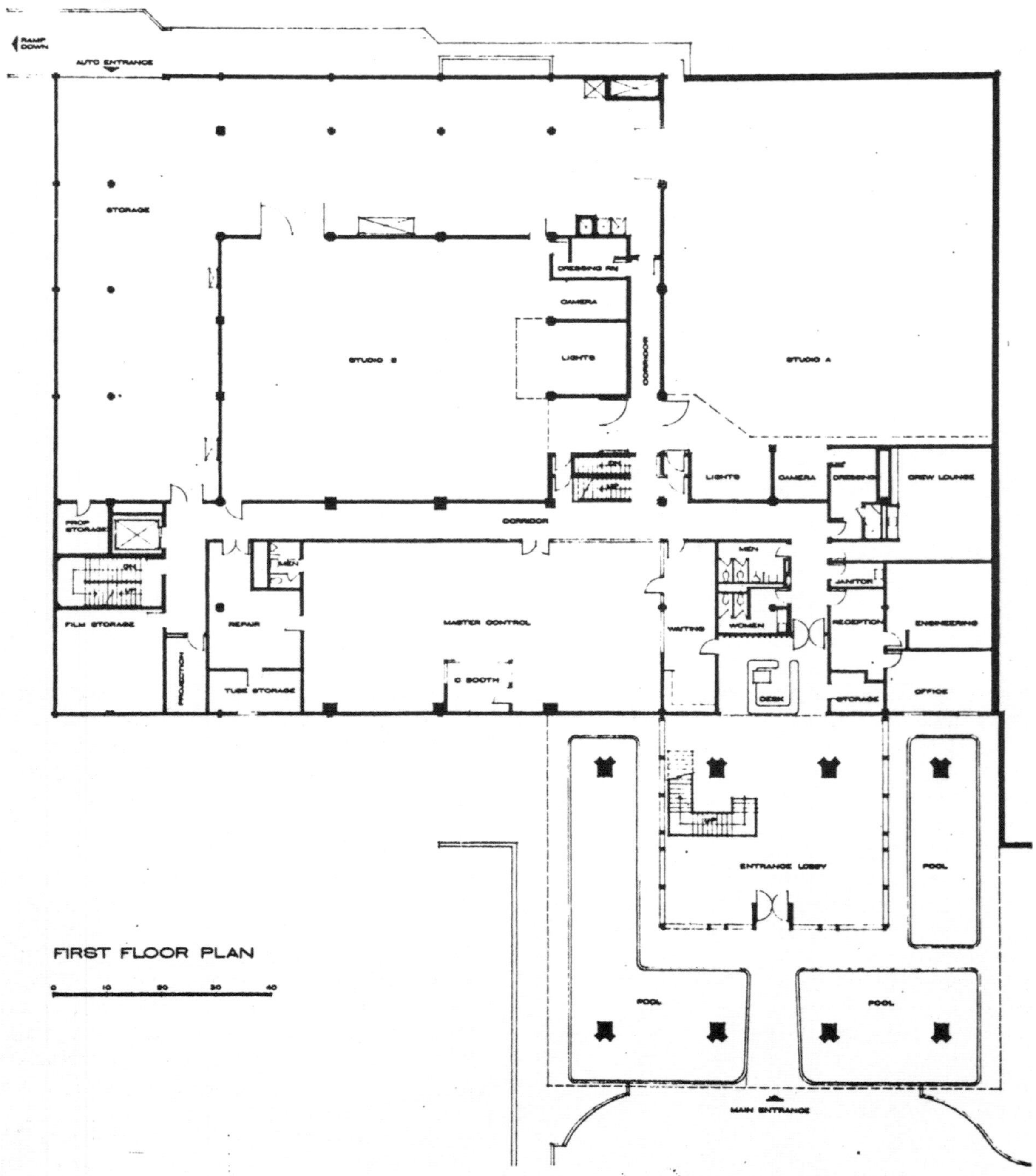

FIRST FLOOR PLAN

0 10 20 30 40

KGW RADIO & TELEVISION BUILDING

FRED BASSETTI & CO, ARCHITECTS

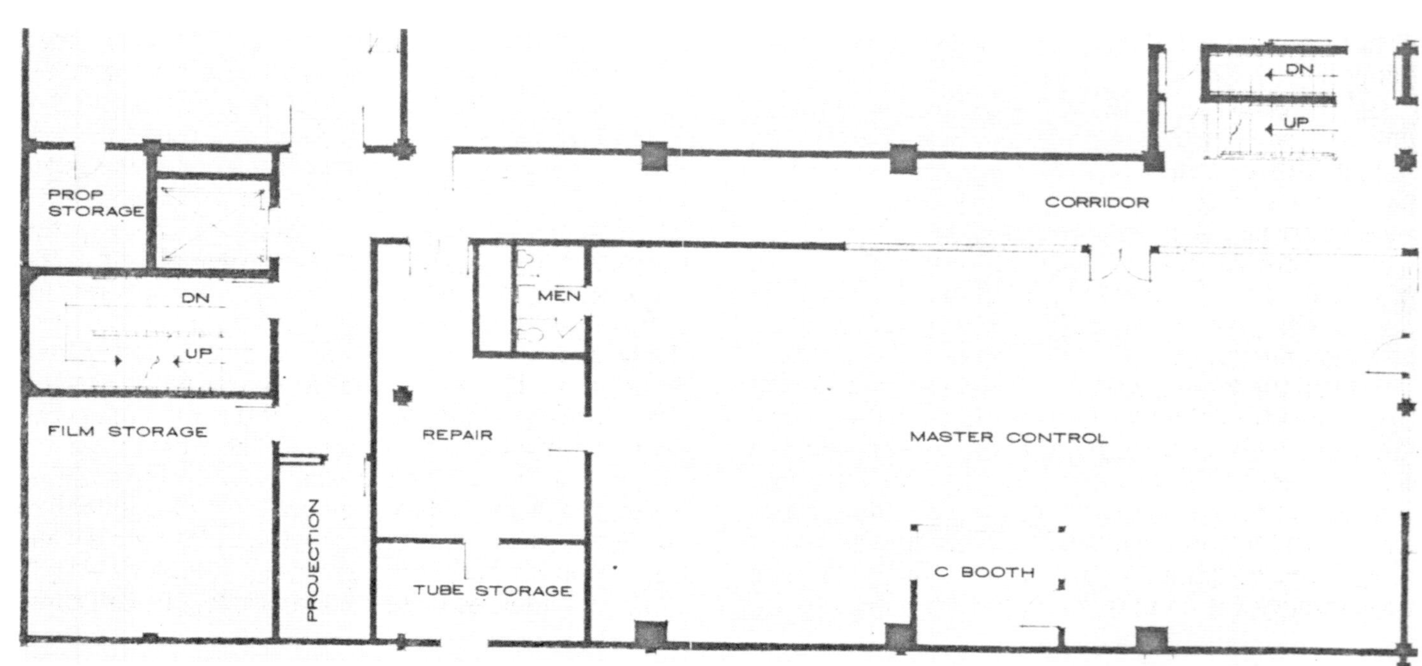

bank, and three were public service announcements, one showing a travelogue of Oregon, the second announcing a local boat show, and the third promoting the Head Start Program in Portland.

My original intention had been to produce the work in real time. Two different camera angles were tried in advance, offering an alternate view and giving me some idea of what to expect during the live recording and broadcast. I would have liked to continue to examine different camera angles, but the administration declined further experimentation.

Just before the real time broadcast, the program director refused to air the program live and instead confronted me with the option of either using the pre-recorded material or cancelling the broadcast of the work altogether.

The explanation for this decision revolved around questions of cost, technicians availability, and the stations's obligation to the public. This response seemed unusual in light of the fact that I was enlisting the services of only those people who were available at the time of the broadcast, and within the parameters set up by the station. Neither was it clear what the program director meant by "obligation to the public."

The recording itself turned out extremely well, however, perhaps because the technicians working in the master-control area avoided appearing self-conscious and did not attempt in any way to direct viewer response. Before the recording session, the technicians were told that the tape would not be used for broadcast. Shortly before the actual broadcast, however, the program director had to obtain their consent, as I assumed he would.

Even though the work appeared to be a fiction, it had a paradoxically natural look about it due to the absence of self-consciousness. In my original plan, the self-consciousness of the participants might have concealed their natural behavior, even though it was broadcast in real time. Both recorded and real-time broadcast images are mediated technically in almost identical ways through the camera, tape, transmission, and re-

ception (monitor or TV set), and are physiologically perceived in identical ways. Therefore, it became clear to me that the traditional distinction between actual space and real time on the one hand, and representation and recorded time on the other was no longer functional in regard to the production of television imagery. Furthermore, the broadcast image could not be broken down in terms of self-referentiality since the relationship between the real temporal and spatial locus and its representation could, ultimately, not be verified. yet the television image is considered the most reliable testifying device of any mode of visual representation. At the same time, however, the work was situated and specified both temporarily and spatially in two different contexts: in an institutional context (an exhibition grouping together artists whose works originated in a location different from that of the exhibition), and in the context of a television transmission attracting the largest American television audience of the year: the live broadcast of the "Superbowl."

Since the master-control sequences could not be viewed as good television, they could be dismissed by the viewer as inconsequential fantasies. In the framework of television, an inactive image generates "dead air" and is thought to produce an unreal viewing experience. On the other hand, whatever sells a product or a lifestyle appears to be active and is therefore considered a part of reality. The commercials and spots fulfilled the viewers' expectations of television reality, and therefore became dominant compared to the master-control sequences, ultimately becoming the prime content of the program. By polarizing the commercials and spots with the master-control sequences, the program emphasized content over style, rather than merging the two as is done in regular programming. The usually latent dominance of the commercials became manifest and transparent in this broadcast.

At the time of the broadcast, I was at the station answering phone calls along with Mel Katz and the two KGW receptionists. Approximately 140 phone calls were received during the program, indicating a wide range of viewer responses. For example, one call came

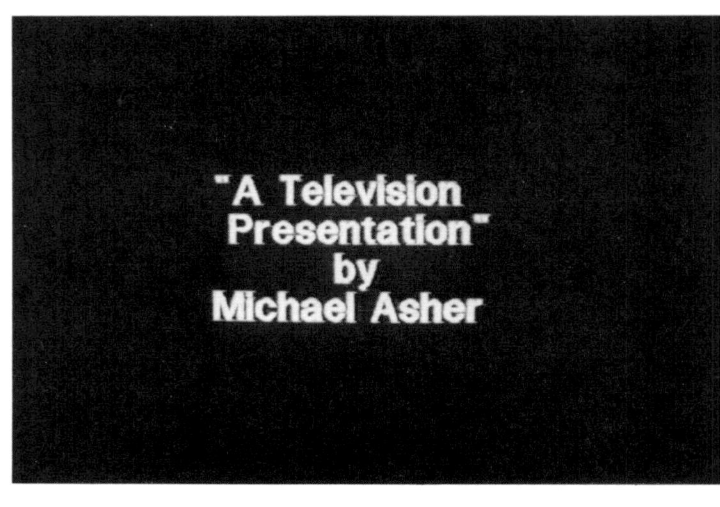

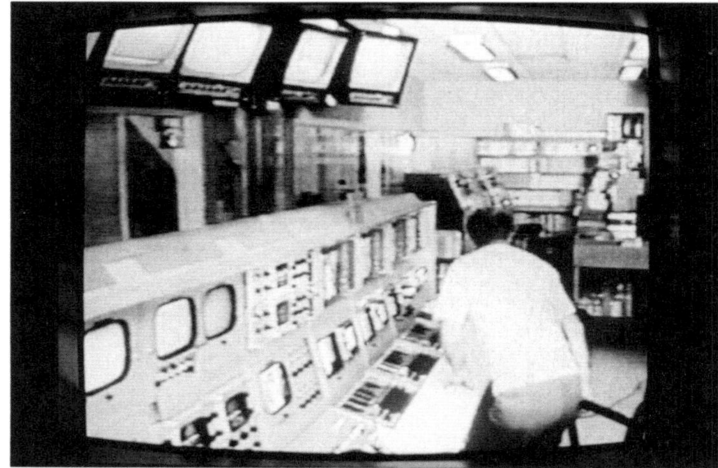

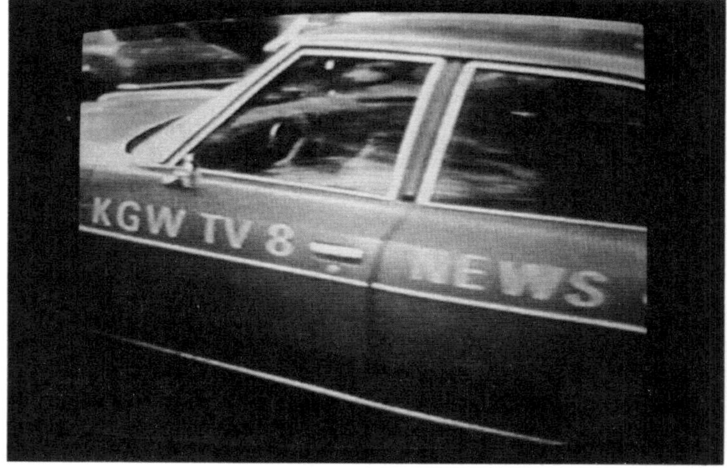

from a television technician 246 miles south of Portland who, thinking there was a faulty transmission, called the station to let us know that there was a camera in the master-control area. A number of other callers from the Portland area also communicated the same observation, some of them noticably upset. Another group of callers thought they understood the program and congratulated the station for this type of programming. Most callers were satisfied to hear that the program was a work of art and did not carry the conversation on from there. Some callers, however, asked for more detailed information about my activity as an artist and about the potential of a collaboration between broadcast television and the visual arts in the use of videotape. Bob Jackson, the announcer of the broadcast, "Eight Lively Arts," introduced and closed the program by informing the audience of a follow-up discussion of my work, which actually occurred a week after the broadcast and was paneled by three people and the announcer. During the discussion it became evident that the panelists saw the work as a possible solicitation for participatory television. Although this option was not excluded, as an alternative it seemed difficult with the current centralized television delivery system. It would also have reduced the work to a simple proposal for a change of programming of television and it would have reduced the problems inherent in the television delivery system to a merely technical level.

This work was in part a response to a work by Dan Graham, "Yesterday/Today," which I had seen installed at the Otis Art Institute during September—October 1975. My work attempted to reintegrate video technology into the mode of production from which it originated: television technology. It did so by reintegrating representation within its social-institutional origins and material elements of production.

12 stills from the 30-min. television program/installation taken at various intervals and representing the different types of actions/imagery that were broadcast during this period. Photographs by Michael Asher.

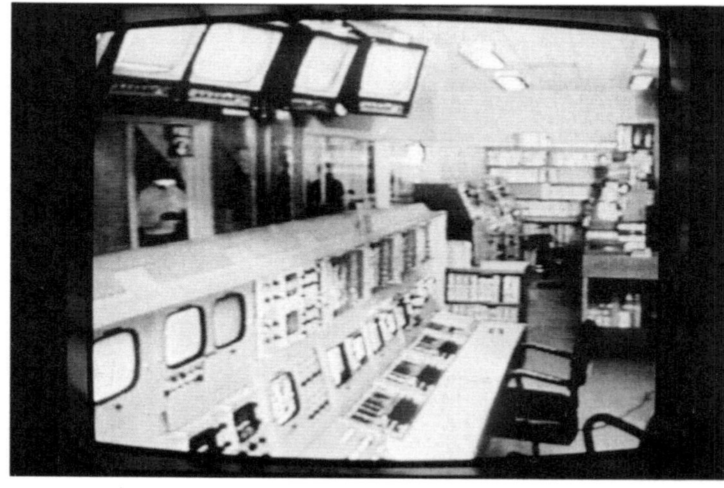

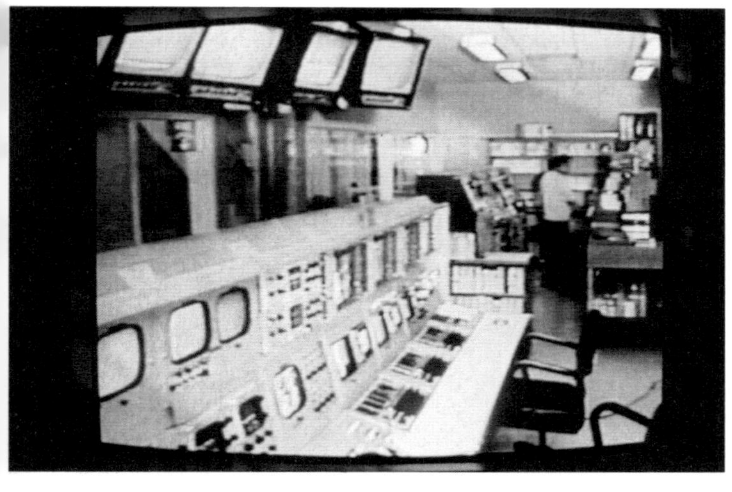
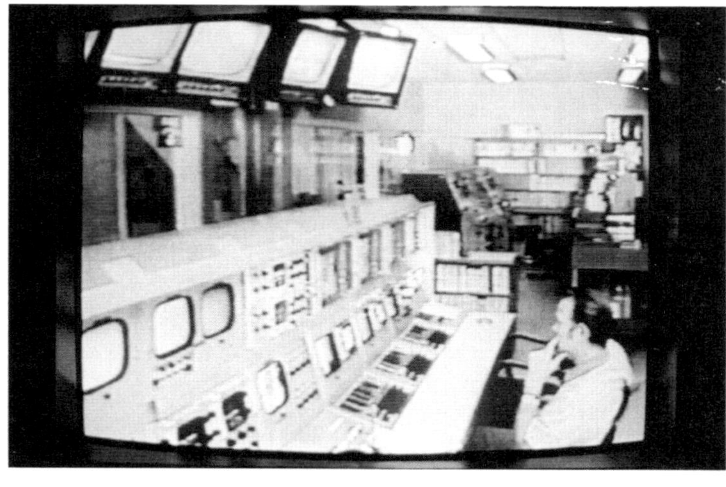
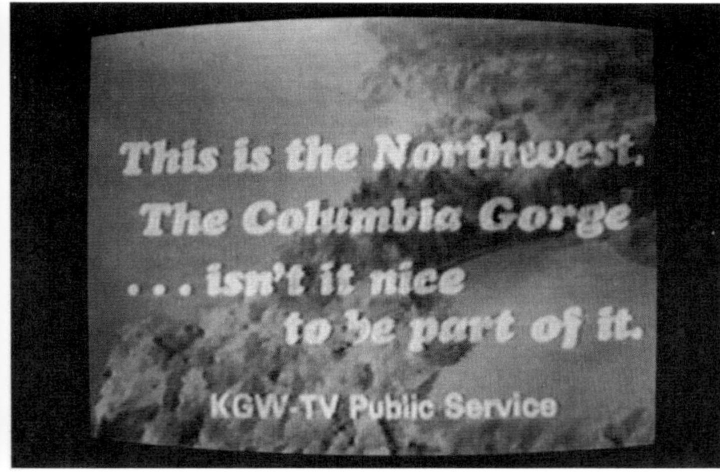
This is the Northwest.
The Columbia Gorge
... isn't it nice
to be part of it.
KGW-TV Public Service
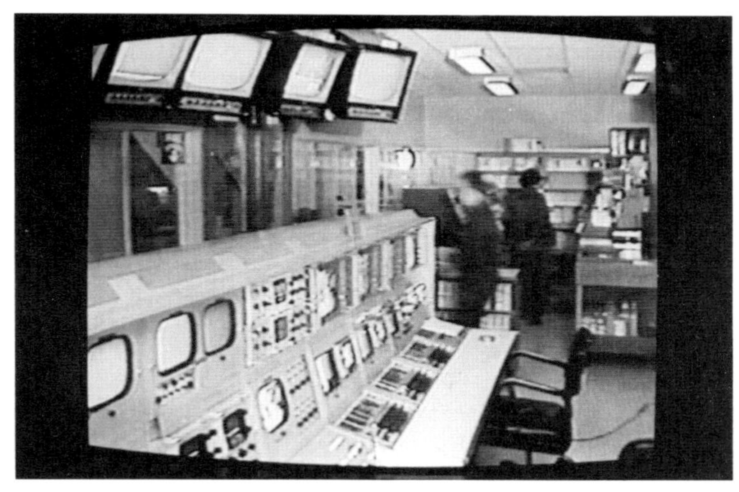
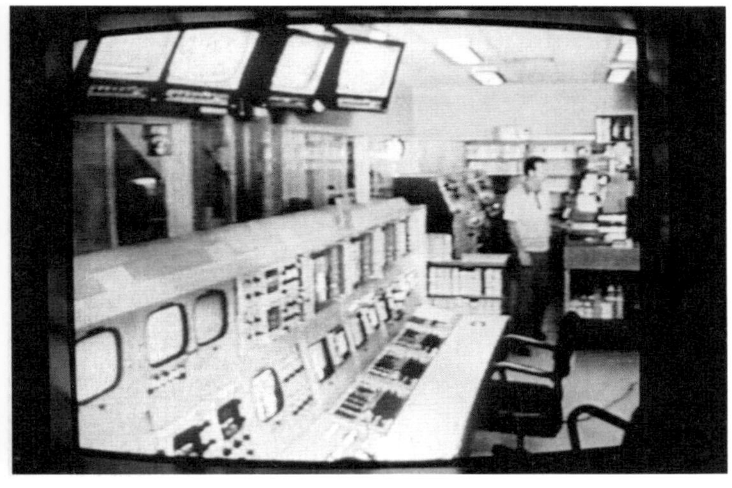
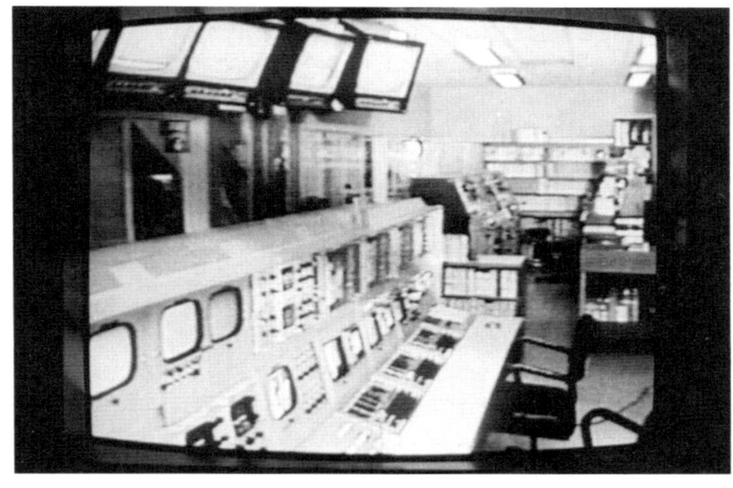
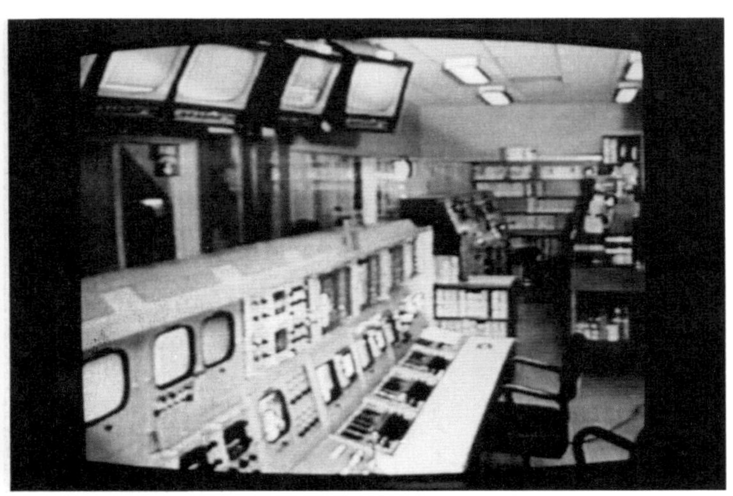

This work made
possible through the
cooperation of
KGW-TV 8, Portland,
The National Endowment
for the Arts, The
Metropolitan Arts
Commission and the
Oregon Arts Commission

MICHAEL ASHER
3661 SACRAMENTO STREET
MAY 1 - 22, 1976
24 HOURS A DAY

SPONSORED BY:
THE FLOATING MUSEUM

Lynn Hershman, curator of the Floating Museum, invited me to propose a work for the temporary museum which was planned to be in operation from October 1975 through June 1976. The concept behind this "alternative" to the existing alternative spaces was to set up a program without an architectural context of its own, where administrative structure would be reduced to a minimum, that would directly present projects by artists with support of public (tax) and private (tax deductible) dollars. The idea was to have an exhibition area independent of an architectural setting and institutional framework that would create a broader cultural base for a larger audience. As the director stated at the time: "One hundred seven members joined by paying a tax-deductible fee. Their participation was the nucleus of a community collective that not only exhibited art work but actually caused the works to be made. By tapping into the resources of the area it was possible to make use of public spaces in the community, from free television and radio time to billboards to sandblasting equipment to paint."[1]

Late in 1975, I agreed to participate in the Floating Museum program, and I subsequently traveled to San Francisco to inspect sites for a possible installation. The most accessible sites were those belonging to members of the museum, such as the Garden Mall Shops on Sacramento Street, the Landor Corporation, a public relations and advertising company, or the KPIX radio station. Eventually, I proposed a work for the Garden Mall. Lynn Hershman approached the tenants of each of the fourteen shops in the mall and they agreed to have the work installed. Architects Scott Wood and David Robinson supplied me with six photographs of plans for the mall renovation, which acquainted me further with the mall's·construction.

There had originally been three separate buildings on the site, which were renovated to form an intimate mall. Two of the buildings were adjacent to Sacramento Street and were three stories high. The three buildings formed a courtyard which was landscaped with trees and bushes. In order to make these buildings function as a shopping center, they were

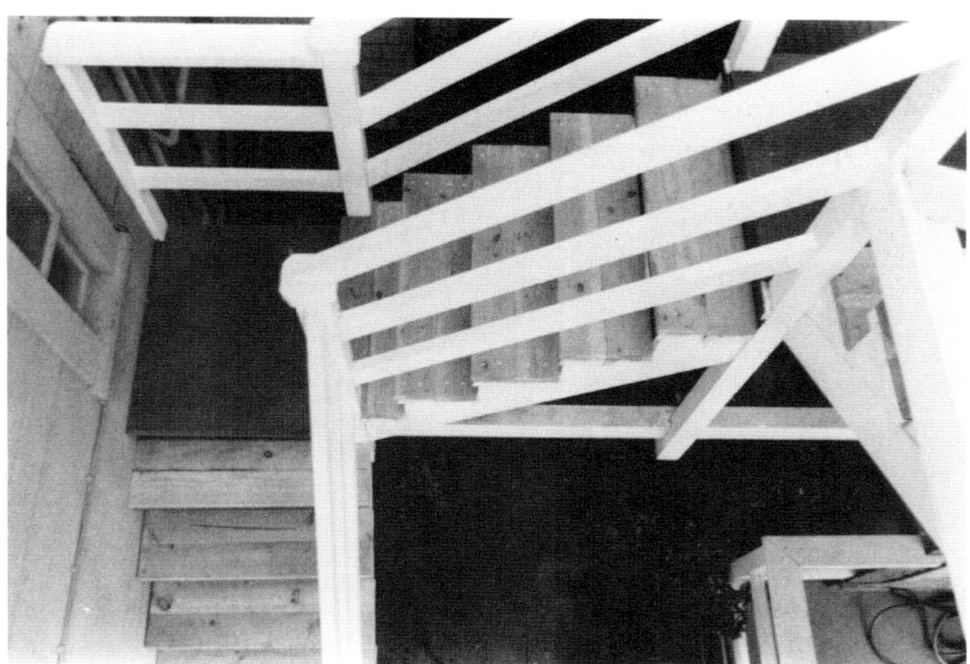

Detail of landing and steps.
Photograph by Michael Asher.

connected by wooden pathways and staircases built along the courtyard walls. The staircases, leading from the ground-floor level to the third storey, were interrupted arbitrarily by landings and changed directions circuitously at every landing and level. The courtyard and constructed pathways gave access to the various shops in the mall. At the same time, the staircases and pathways fulfilled a distinctly decorative function. The staircase and its railings were of wood construction with the treads painted gray or red, and the railings white. The two pieces of wood that formed the tread of the steps were made of construction grade 2 foot-by-6 foot boards.

For this work I nailed to each tread (approximately 100 steps) two pieces of 2 foot-by-6 foot Douglas fir. These two pieces of wood were of exactly the same size and material as the boards used to construct the treads of the new staircases during renovation. Unlike the existing treads, which had been painted different colors, these treads were left unpainted, and as such, created a visually unified effect. The difference between the renovation and my installation could be detected if the staircase was viewed from the front or from the side, since the unfinished edge of my installation treads was clearly superimposed on and flush with the painted edge of the existing steps. All the staircase landings and the pathways were left unaltered, and were thus also juxtaposed to the unpainted wood surfaces of my installation.

The juxtaposition of individual treads was quantitatively enlarged in the juxtaposition of groups of unpainted treads with the painted surfaces of the landings. This juxtaposition was further enlarged and repeated in the combination of whole sequences of unpainted treads with the extended surfaces of the painted pathways. The work matched the given number of existing painted treads with an equal number of unpainted treads. However, the unpainted wood was only added to those surfaces used for ascending or descending, while the platforms and pathways which were used for horizontal movement were left unaltered.

While standing in the courtyard, the viewer could look around and see the quantity, distribution, and location of the work's units as horizontally placed, discrete sculptural elements or as varying levels of vertical and spatial distance. The actual details could only be perceived from a fluctuating point of view by the viewer/visitor using the stairs, since the work was intricately connected with the architectural function of its location.

At first it seemed that the immaculate surface of the newly applied, unfinished material deterred the viewer's/visitor's use of the stairs. But once footprints had accumulated on the raw wood, use returned to normal.

In spite of the addition to the tread, the height of the steps in the staircases appeared to be consistent. Perception of uniform height was disrupted, however, between sequences of steps. The last step leading up to every landing and pathway appeared to be reduced in height (by approximately 2 inches); while the first step beyond every landing appeared to be increased in height (by approximately 2 inches).

Unlike previous sculptural work, which had defined itself as *place,* but which had essentially become arbitrary in its placement, this work was determined entirely through its situational context. Unlike previous distributional sculpture, which had attempted to define itself according to a notion of perceptual field rather than as a specific volume in space, but which had in fact remained within the confines of traditional volumetric perception, the visual elements of this work were located in a totally decentralized 360-degree arrangement within a given architectural context. Because the work's structural entirety was always external to the viewer's perceptual field, the work was defined at any given moment, in any fragmented part, by the viewer's random choice of direction within the architectural structure.

The constituent parts of the work were placed neither by chance nor random distribution. Nor were the material elements amorphous or unprocessed, but highly determined in their distribution and material definition by the function of the structure as a whole

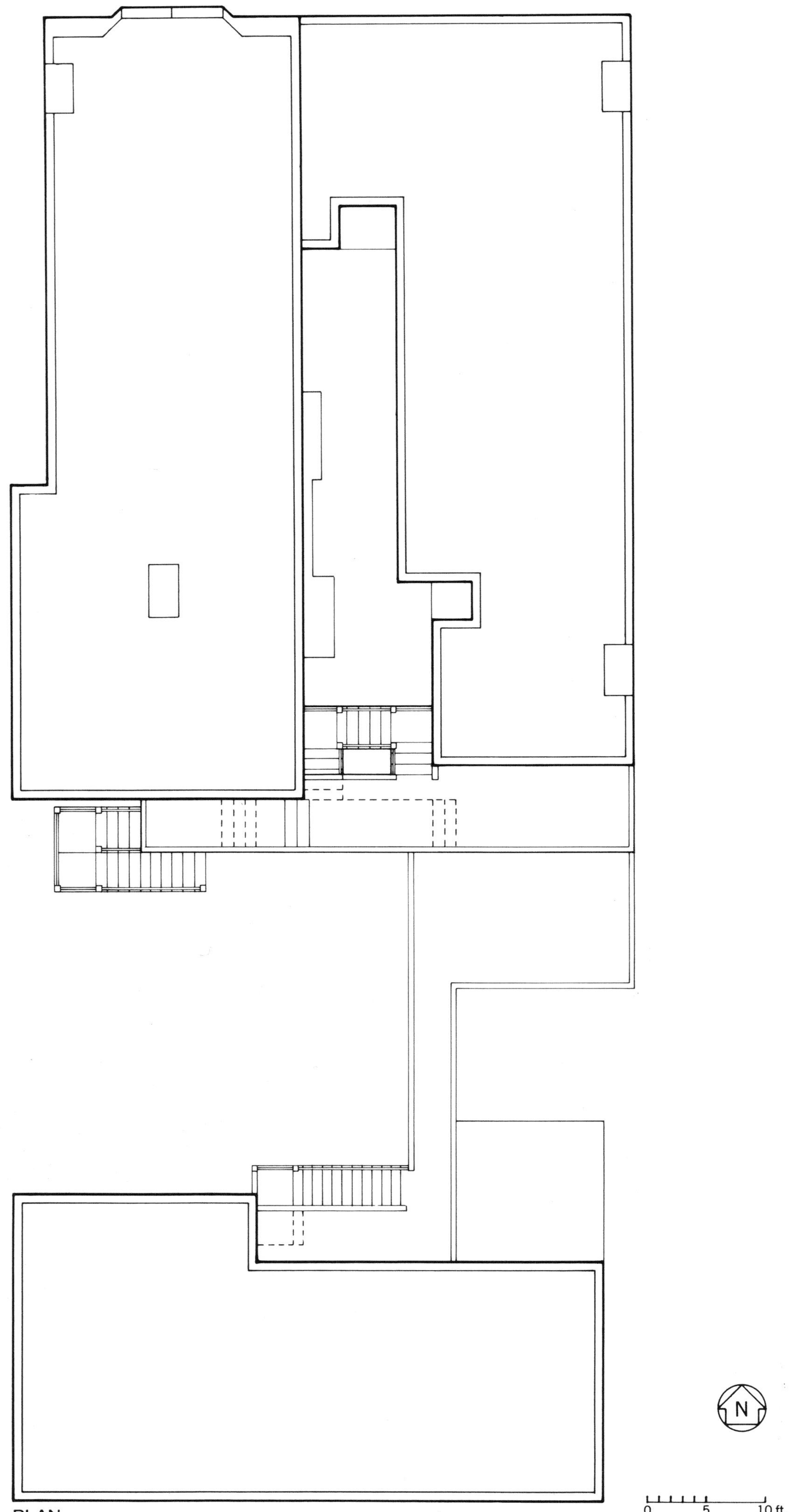

PLAN
0 5 10 ft.
N

and the specific units of the structure into which they were inserted (staircase and step).

The transitional and forward movement from one step to the next situated the viewers' stance on two elevations simultaneously, at any given moment. This was different from a traditional position in front of or on top of a sculptural work. This alternation of positions in relation to the work generated a unified visual and bodily perception and located this perception in the visitors'/viewers' movement through the work, which was integrated with the architectural structure.

This work foregrounded the problems involved in the type of renovation that tries to recreate historical codes within a contemporary architectural idiom, and, in so doing, becomes a visual display system for individualized consumption. This installation not only paralleled the method of hybrid architectural renovation (addition and superimposition), as it combined and overlapped architectural elements to create a period fiction, but it also imitated and revealed the actual (material) elements and ultimate simplicity of this transformation.

On May 22, 1976, the exhibition ended. At that time, my installation at the Garden Mall was dismantled and the stairs were restored to their original condition.

---

[1]Lynn Hershman, *The Floating Museum, Inc.*, original texts and translations, ed. Ciacia Nicostro.

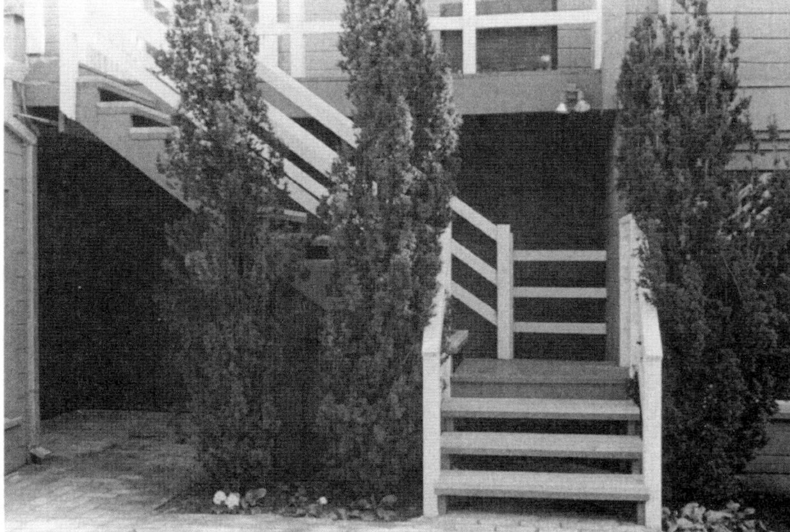

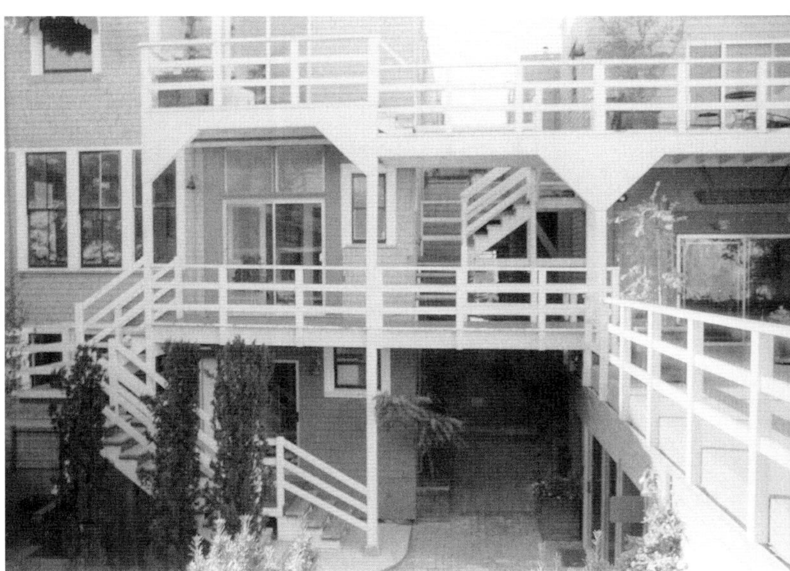

Detail of staircase and landing in courtyard. Photograph by Edmund Shea.

Inner courtyard opposing street side. Photograph by Michael Asher.

Working drawing of architectural renovation:
Elevation of courtyard.

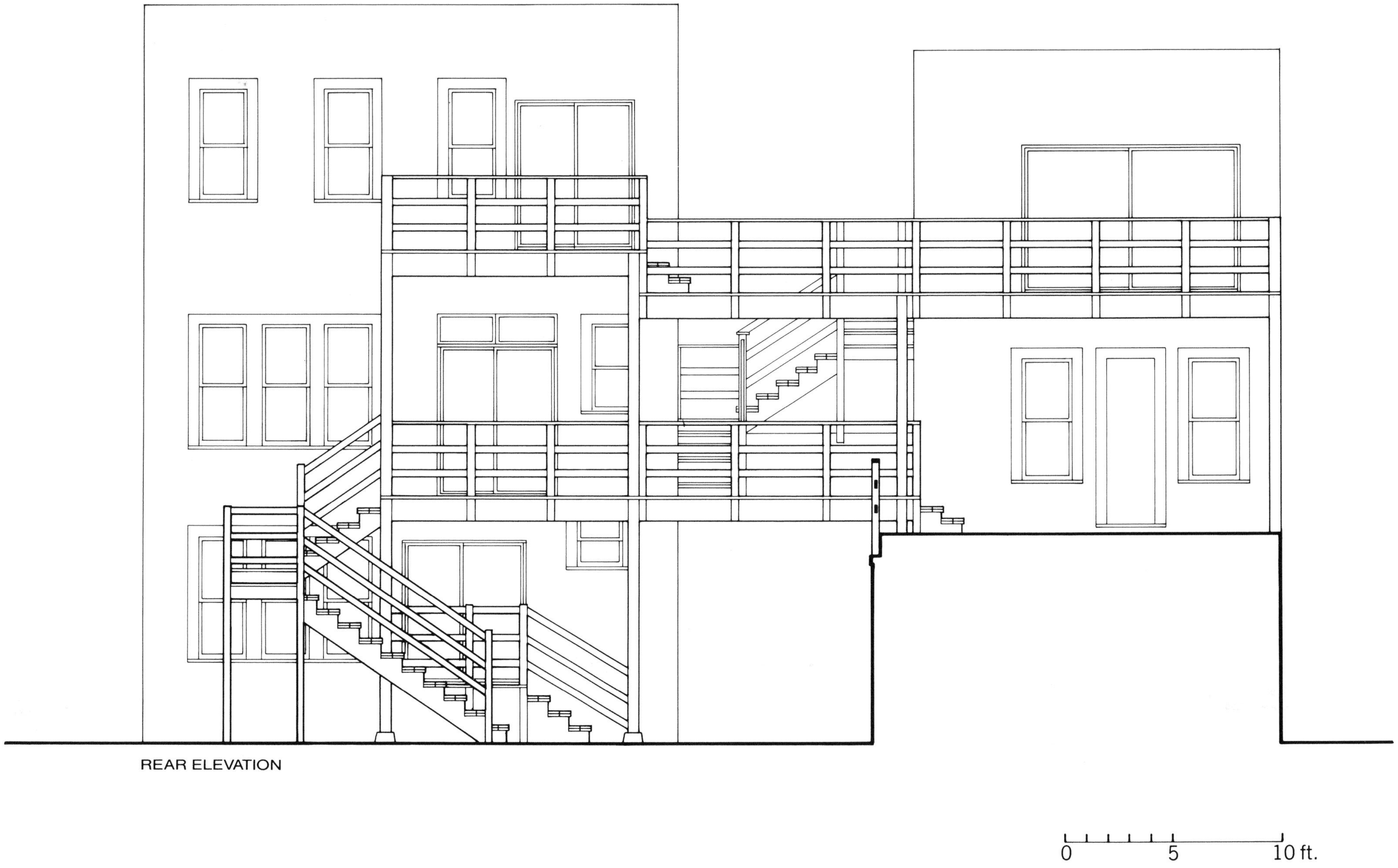

REAR ELEVATION

0   5   10 ft.

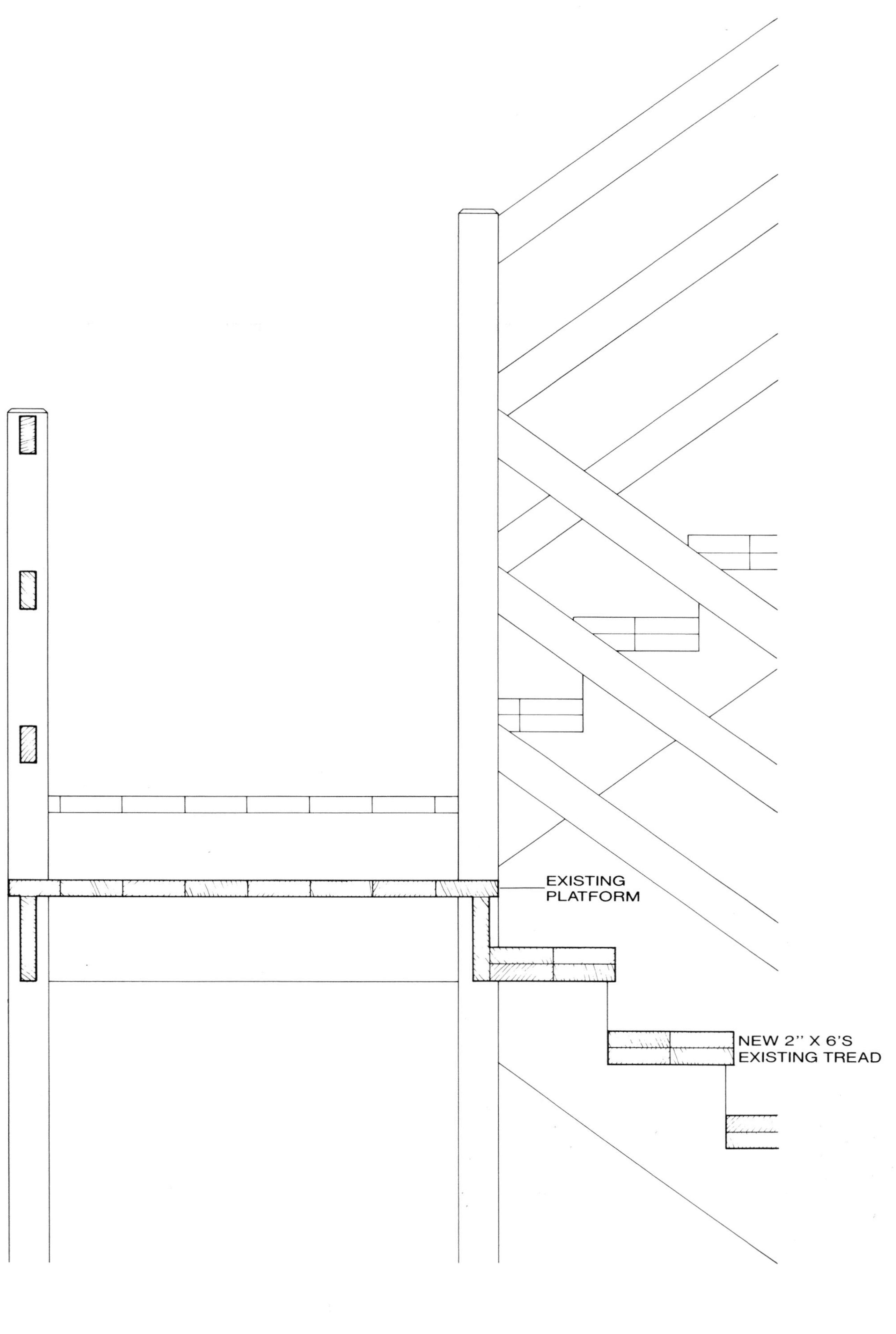

Detail of installation with additional step construction on existing staircase. Drawings by Lawrence Kenny.

Inner courtyard near street. Photograph by Michael Asher.

Detail of landing and steps. Photograph by Edmund Shea.

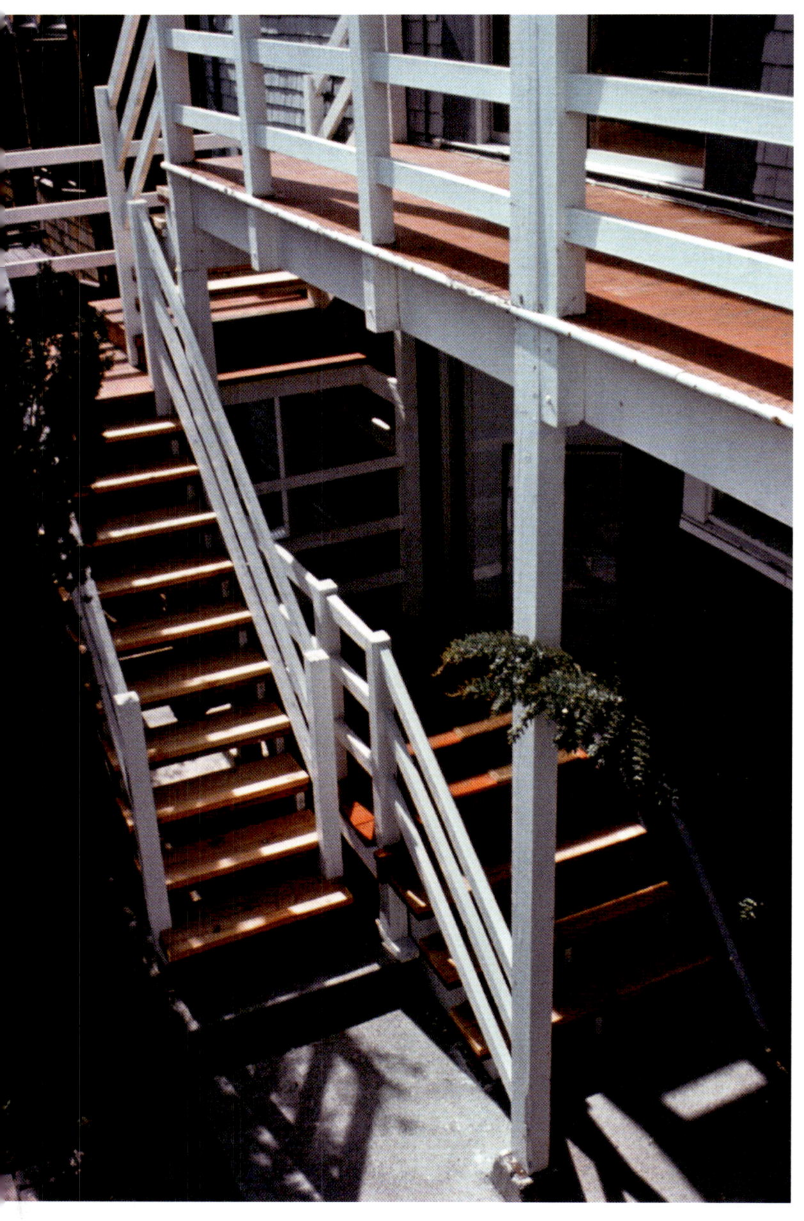

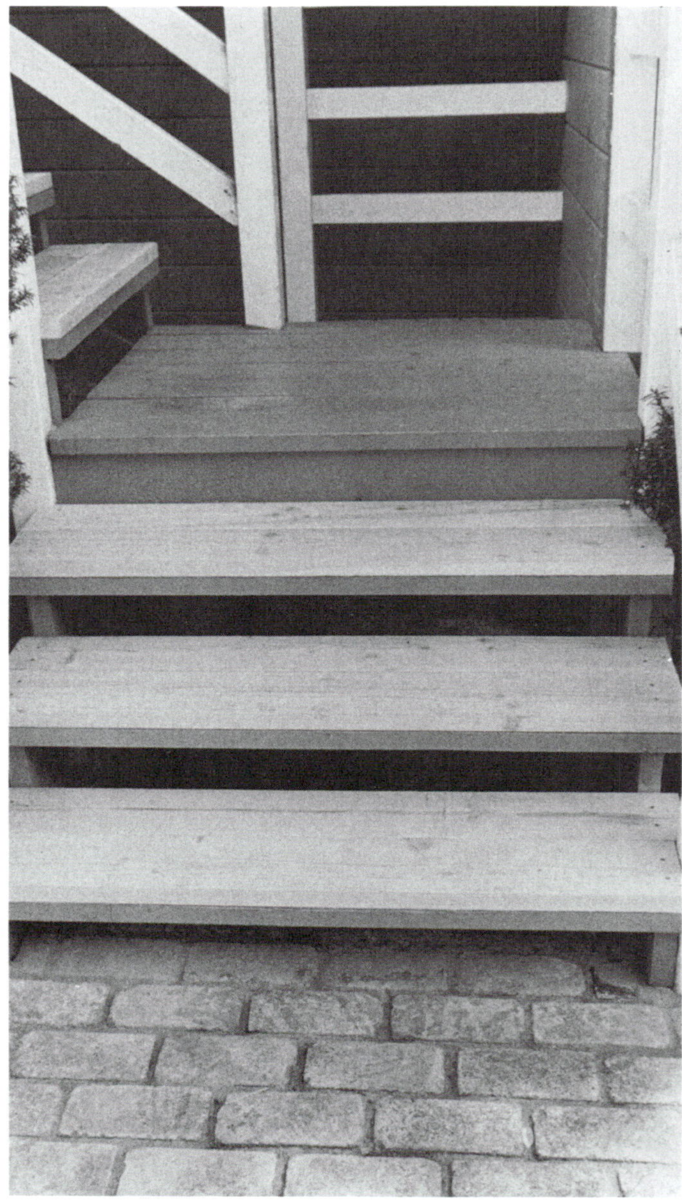

The director of the Clocktower, Alanna Heiss, at the suggestion of Kasper Koenig, invited me to do a one-person exhibition which was to open on March 20 and last until April 10. The Clocktower, an alternative space operated under the auspices of the *Institute for Art and Urban Resources*, a nonprofit organization, is located at 108 Leonard Street, at the corner of Broadway and occupies the thirteenth, fourteenth, and fifteenth floors of the building. Constructed in 1870, the building's three top floors and a clocktower were added in the 1930s. The actual clocktower contains a clock 12 feet in diameter which can be read from all four sides of the building.

Late in December 1975 and early in January 1976, I was in New York and had the opportunity to see the space that would be available and to consider a proposal that might function for this particular setting.

Because they were a later addition to the building and were used for different purposes, the three floors allocated for the exhibition were of greatly varying size and were detailed and finished in significantly different ways. Unlike most other museum and gallery spaces, the interior of this space was not very well finished and maintained and its wall surfaces were frequently interrupted by windows, doors, heaters, pillars, and moldings.

The interior dimensions of the thirteenth floor were 58 feet by 56 feet by 13 feet. There were eight windows varying in size and proportion from 5 feet by 2 feet high to 2 feet 6 inches by 18 inches. All window frames began 8 feet 4 inches above the floor and were set back in the wall with a bevel as part of the window sill. Other visual characteristics of this floor included five pillars supporting the ceiling, plaster walls, and a parquet floor.

A hallway entry/exit on the thirteenth floor led to the exhibition space and, unlike the fourteenth and fifteenth floors, here there were no doors opening to the exterior porches and balcony of those floors. A stairwell led from the thirteenth to the fourteenth floor.

The interior dimensions of the fourteenth floor

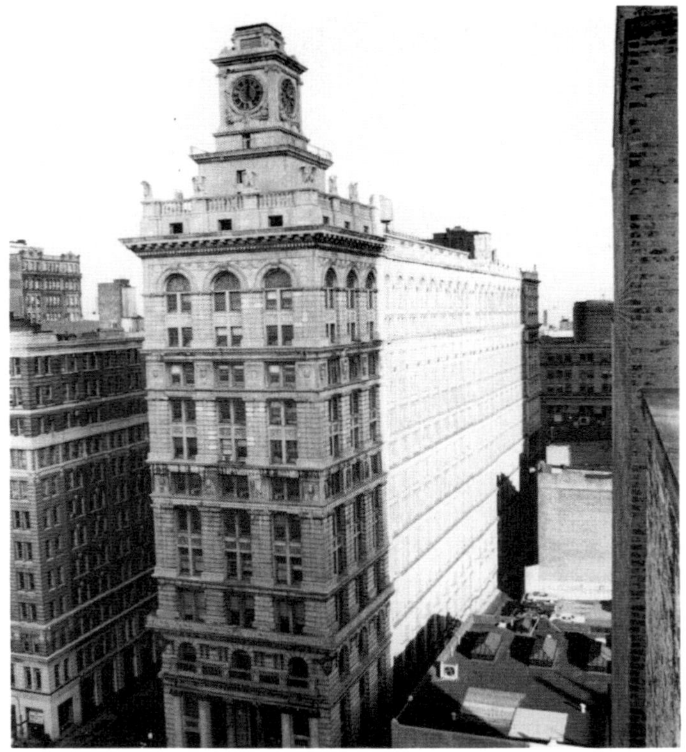

General view of Clocktower building. Photograph by Michael Asher.

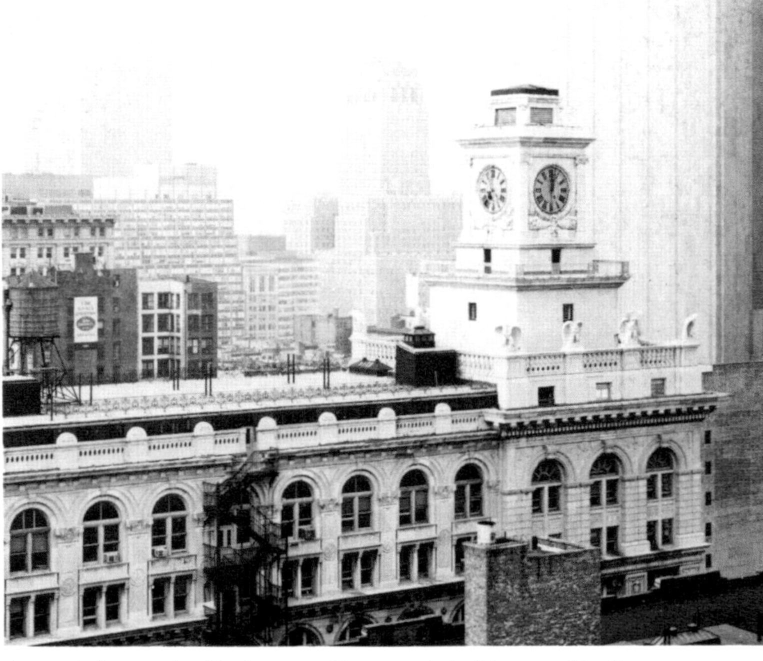

General view of the Clocktower. Photograph by Thomas Struth.

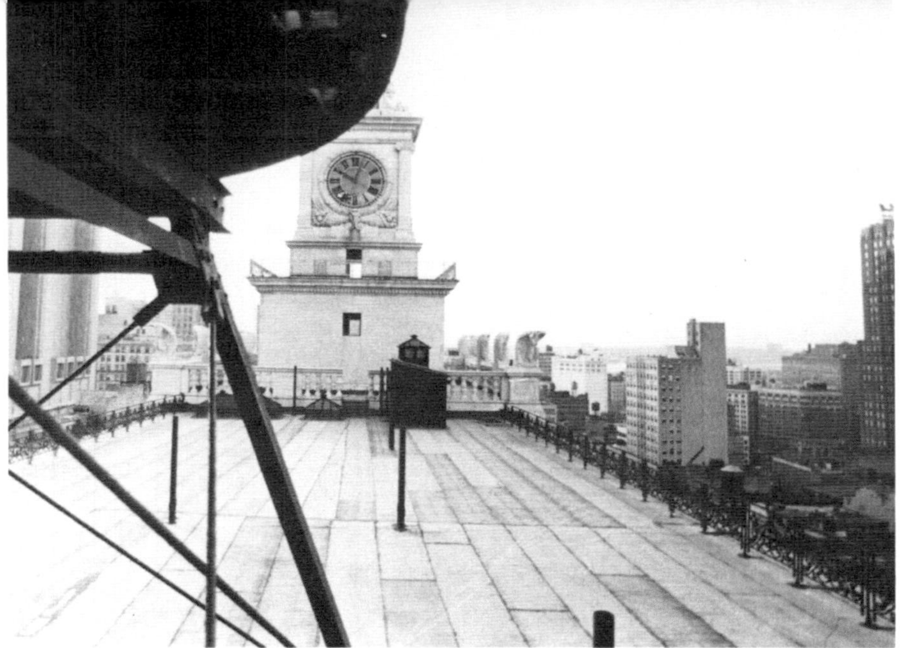
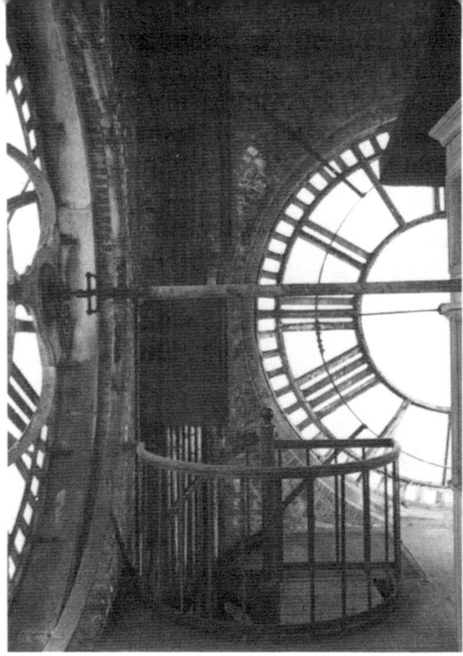

Viewing west toward the Clocktower from roof of adjoining building. Photograph by Daniel Buren.

Interior detail of clockworks. Photograph by Michael Asher.

were 31 feet by 31 feet, with a 22 foot 6 inch ceiling height. On either side of the room was a window set one foot into the wall, measuring 4 feet by 3 feet. Each window was located 11 feet 3 inches above the floor and was horizontally centered. A 3 foot by 7 foot-4 inch door on the northwest side led to a 9 foot-wide exterior porch which continued around the perimeter of the fourteenth floor. The exterior walls, from the fourteenth floor on, were of quarried stone, as was the railing around the fourteenth-floor porch. Representations of the American eagle, approximately 8 feet high, were sculpted out of the same stone and placed at a 45-degree angle on top of each corner of the railing. Also, on the east side of the porch, several steps led to the rooftop of the rest of the building. The interior of the fourteenth-floor exhibition area was defined by brick walls, a cement floor, and steel-girder supports which ran across the corners of the ceiling. There was also a cast iron spiral staircase which led to the fifteenth floor and the actual clocktower above that floor.

The interior dimensions of the fifteenth floor were 20 feet by 18 feet by 13 feet. There was one door in the center of each wall which led to a balcony 7 feet wide, with a wrought iron railing which surrounded the floor on its exterior side. A 4-by-4 foot box contained the pendulum and weights for the clock in the tower above. The floor was covered in red tile.

The interior dimensions of the clocktower itself were 18 feet by 18 feet, with a 16 foot 6 inch ceiling. The clocktower housed an elaborate gear mechanism for the clock which was not running at the time of the exhibition. The clock faces, which were made of frosted glass and featured metal roman numerals, were set into each of the four tower walls. Since the staircase was designed to reach the clocktower through the fifteenth floor, I left it unencumbered and therefore had to consider the clocktower as part of the exhibition area.

After considering several ideas, I made a proposal for a work that comprised the three top floors of the building. The proposal took into consideration architectural details, such as doors and windows leading to the exterior, which were part of the design on all three floors. The viewer would enter the exhibition space at a level where there were only windows, pass through an area with doors and windows, and then finally climb to a space which had only doors. My proposal stipulated that all exterior doors and windows on all three floors be removed and kept in storage for the length of the exhibition.

The intention was to enable viewers, once having entered the interior of the installation, to find the exterior to be as important to the work as the interior. So that they would pay as much attention to the exterior of the exhibiton space as they normally would to the interior. I wanted to merge interior and exterior conditions, that is, exterior noise, air, light, and pollutants with the conditions existing in the interior. I also wanted viewers to be able to identify familiar views, north, south, east, and west, each view framed by the windows in the interior and seen in its complete context from the balcony and porch.

The windows had, for the most part, been covered over with frosted glass and the doors had been closed to the public, since, before this installation, the space had been used as an exhibiton area insulated from the world around it.

The exhibition was defined by the existing space and was meant to take place without distorting or changing the architectural integrity of the area in any way.

Because of the horizontal and vertical discontinuity of the three floors I wanted to use the whole space as an exhibition area. I wanted the verticality of the spiral staircase and the horizontality of the walkways to delineate pathways from which the viewer could perceive the work: the material subtraction of standard architectural details which had originally been fabricated and fastened in place in order to enclose the space.

The viewer approached the work with the formal criteria attached to the notion of modernist art. This included perceiving the total space as an installation, modifications within that space, movement of light across interior planes, climatic conditions (spring) on

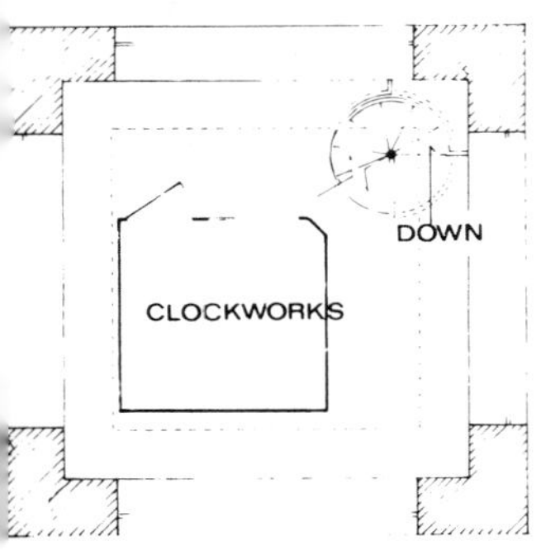

th floor

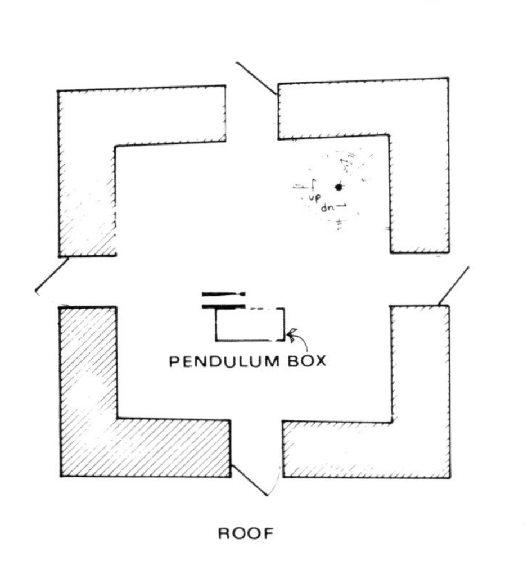

5th floor

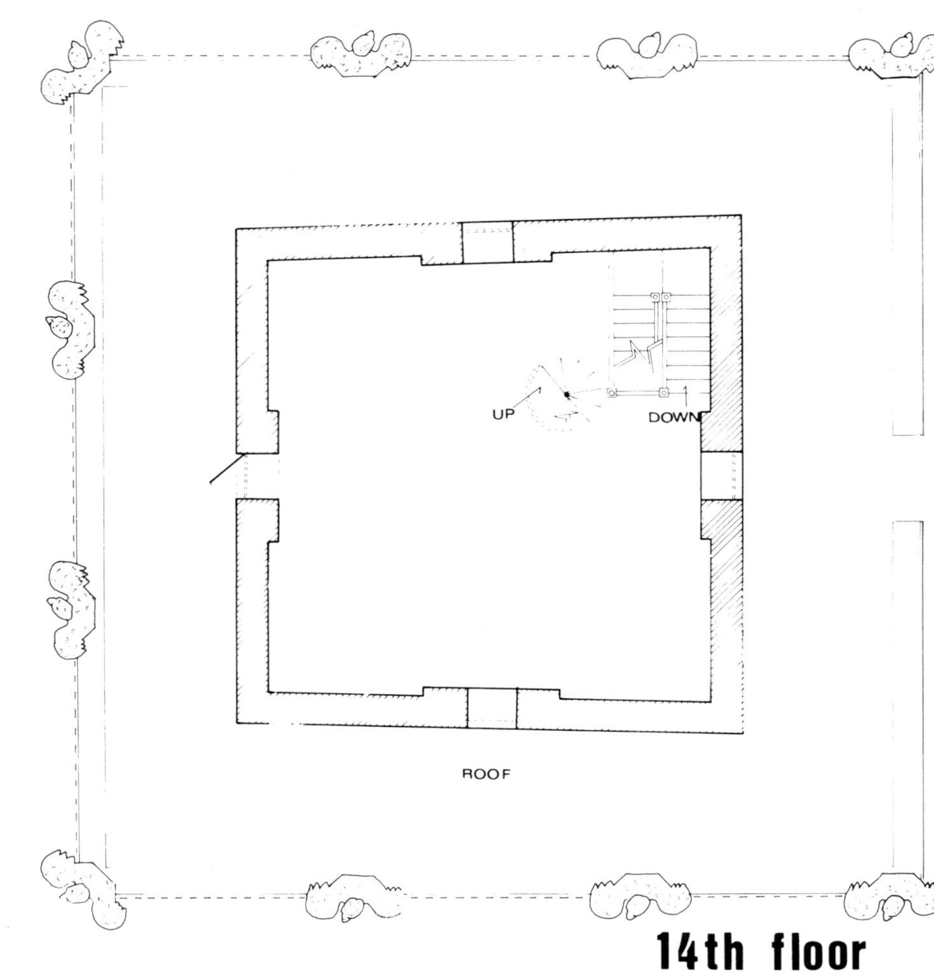

14th floor

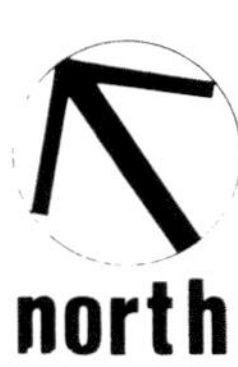

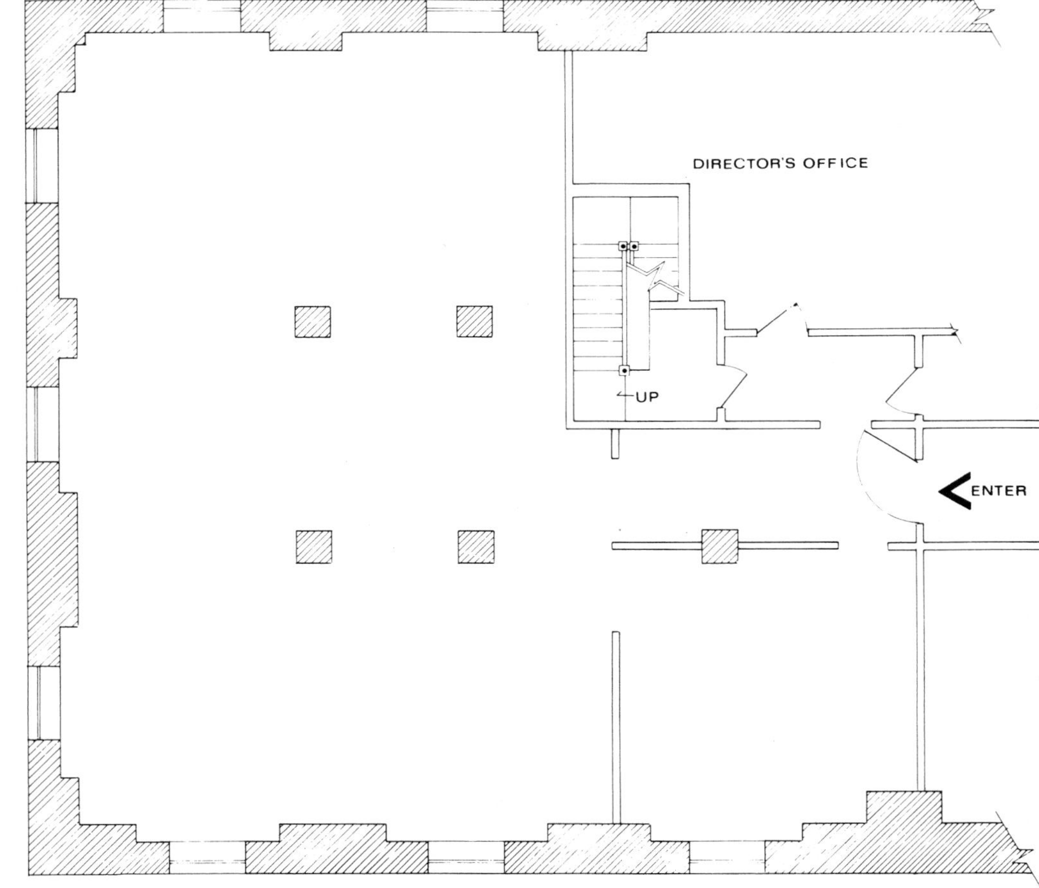

13th floor

THE CLOCKTOWER

Ground plan of the 13th, 14th, 15th floors and the clockworks of the Clocktower,
New York. Courtesy: The Institute for Art and Urban Resources, N.Y.C.

Section of the 13th, 14th, and 15th floors of the Clocktower, the areas where the installation was located. Drawing by Lawrence Kenny.

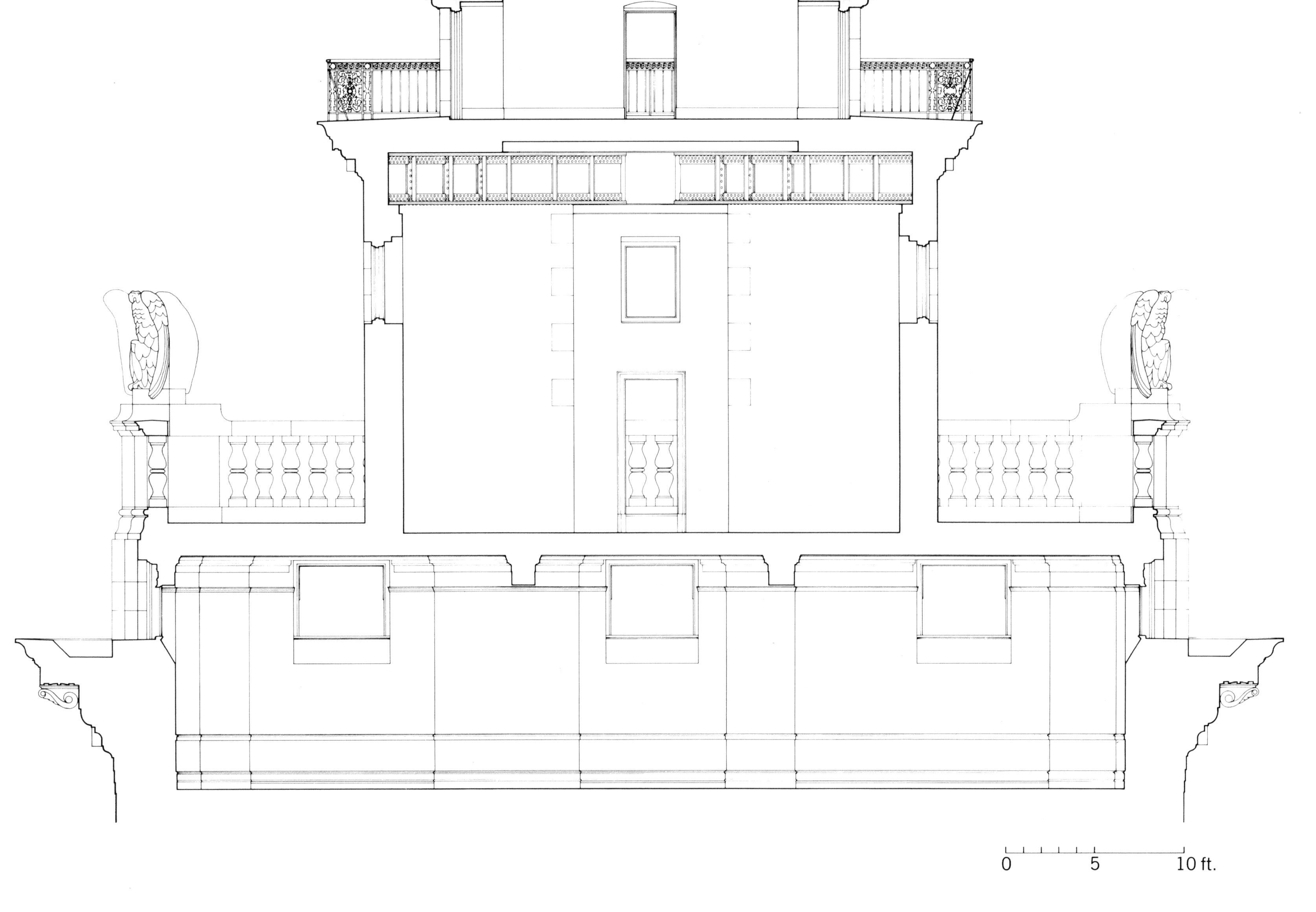

0   5   10 ft.

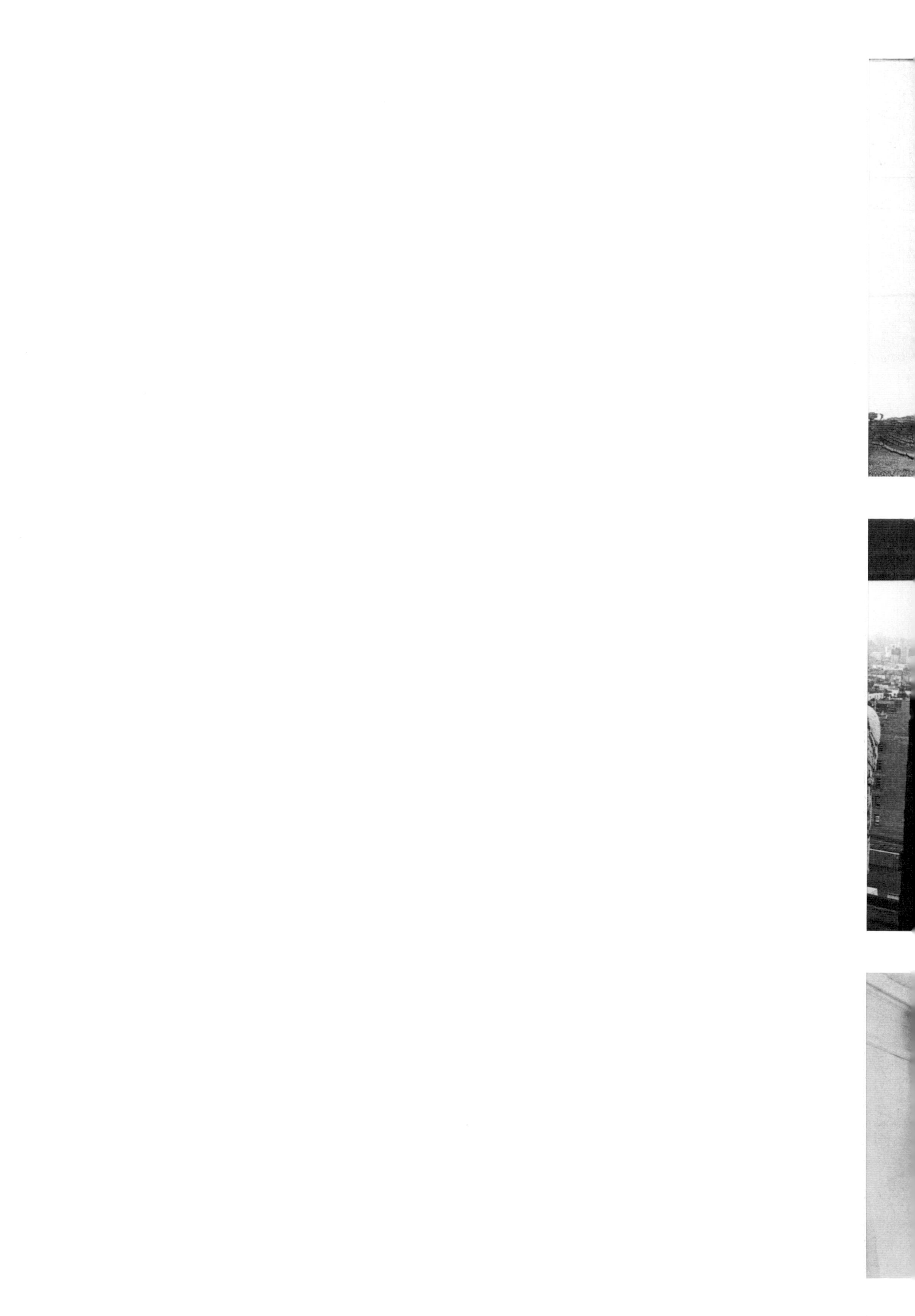

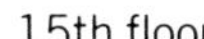

15th floor

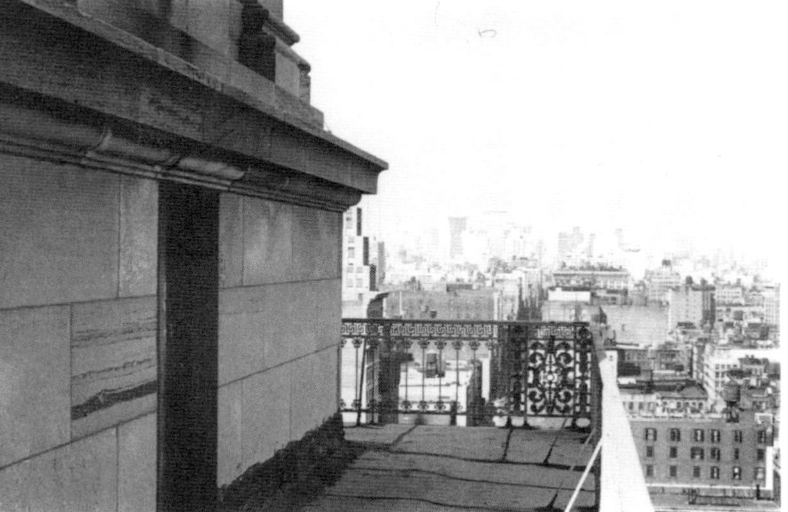

South view of fifteenth-floor porch during installation. Photograph by Balthasar Burkhard.

Viewing north on fifteenth floor during installation. Photograph by Daniel Buren.

Viewing south on fifteenth floor during installation. Photograph by Daniel Buren.

Viewing east on fifteenth floor. Photograph by Daniel Buren.

Viewing west on fifteenth floor. Photograph by Michael Asher.

North view of fifteenth-floor porch during installation. Photograph by Balthasar Burkhard.

14th floor

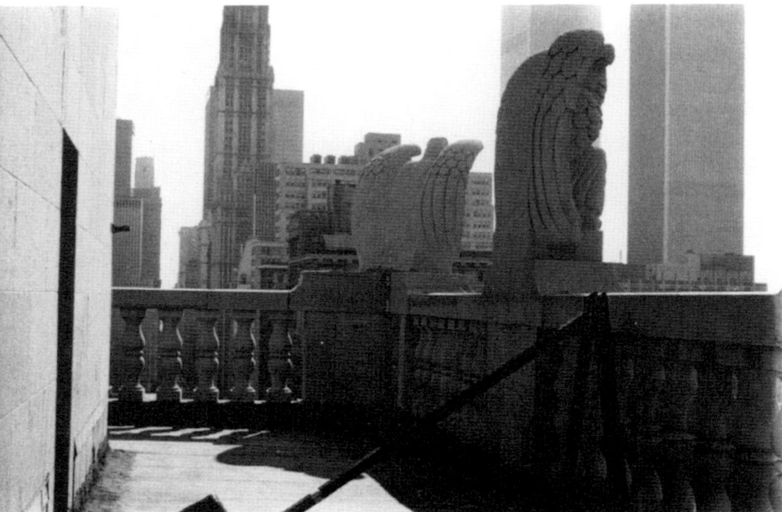

South view of fourteenth-floor porch during installation. Photograph by Balthasar Burkhard.

Viewing west on fourteenth floor. Photograph by Michael Asher.

Viewing east on fourteenth floor. Photograph by Helen Winkler.

Viewing west toward staircase on fourteenth floor. Photograph by Michael Asher.

Detail of architectural ornament of the fourteenth-floor porch. Photograph by Daniel Buren.

South view of fourteenth-floor porch during installation. Photograph by Balthasar Burkhard.

13th floor

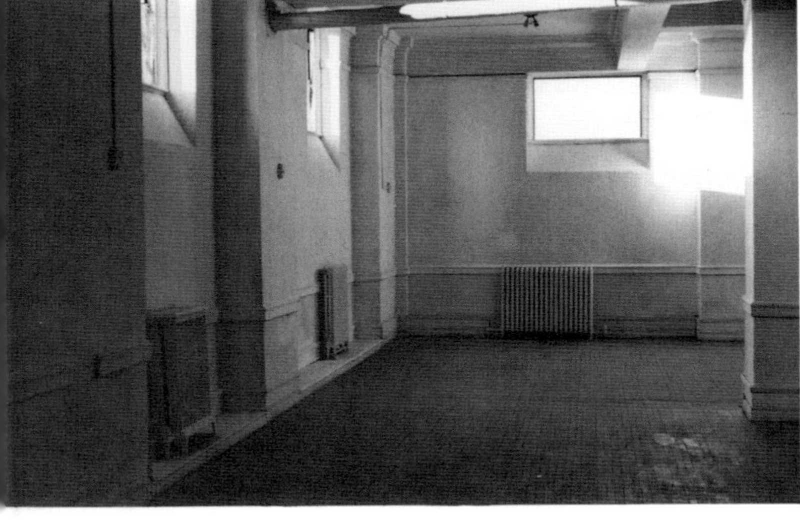

Thirteenth floor, viewing east toward office of exhibition space during installation. Photograph by Michael Asher.

North view of installation in thirteenth-floor exhibition area. Photograph by Balthasar Burkhard.

Window detail of thirteenth floor, viewing southwest during installation. Photograph by Balthasar Burkhard.

Installation view of thirteenth-floor exhibition area. Viewing north. Photograph by Helen Winkler.

133

Fourteenth-floor window detail, viewing south on Broadway.
Photograph by Daniel Buren.

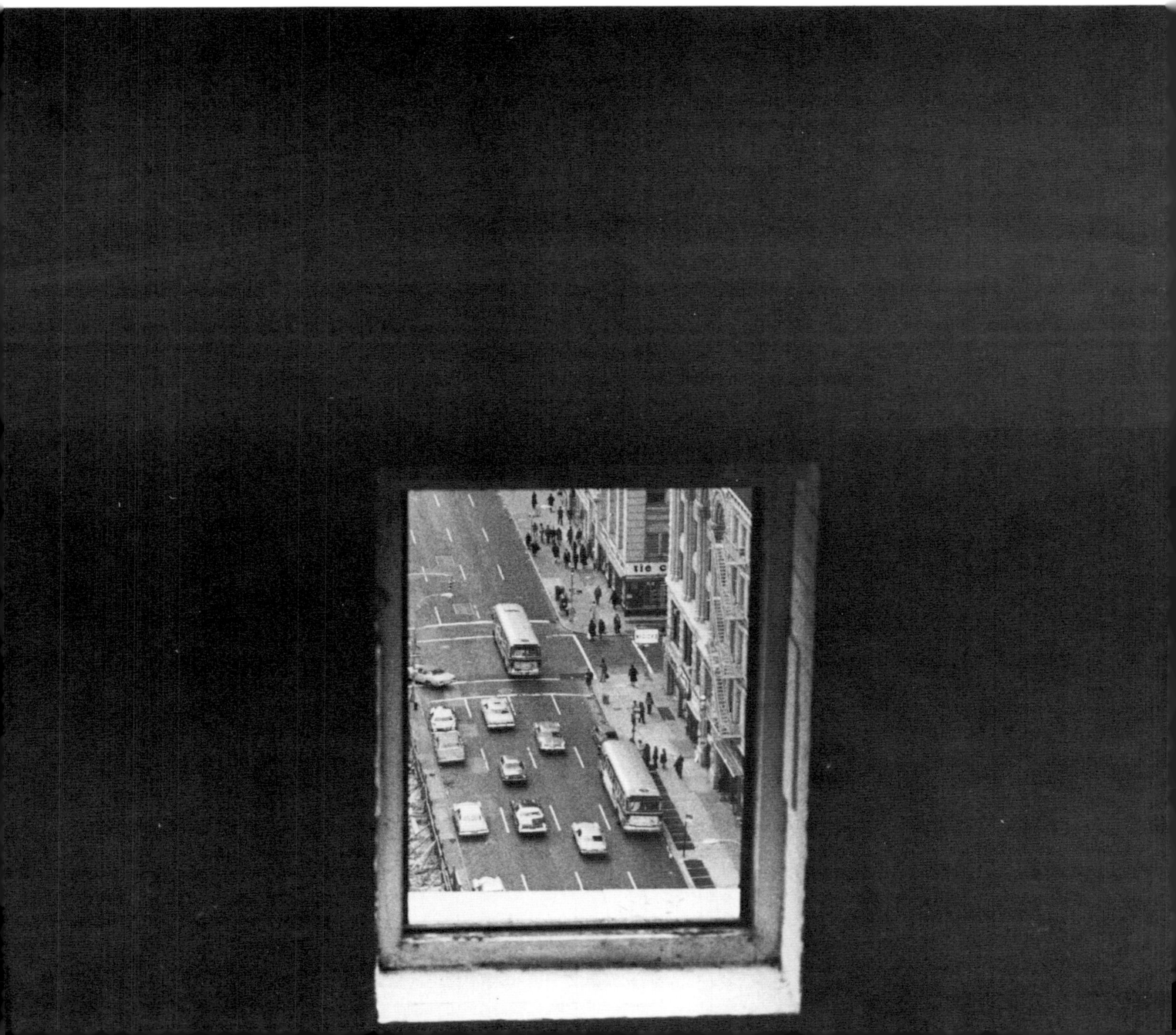

the thirteenth, fourteenth, and fifteenth floors, sounds displaced from the street into the exhibition area, and the resulting disjunction in the exhibition context. Since there were no specific objects, from the inside the installation first appeared to be a tour path, guiding viewers to inspect each direction and level. From the outside the exhibition container was a two story architectural addition functioning as a base for the clock tower, which, prior to this installation, had simply been an interior exhibition space.

If the work was a metaphor for the unfolding of visual experience, it was because that exhibition area was materially and concretely defined as having been actually opened to the outer world. Yet from the inside, as well as the outside, the Clocktower installation only revealed the way in which it was situated within the reality of the cityscape in contrast to its former isolation as an exhibition space.

The traditional way of viewing sculpture was possibly altered in this installation since the outside was objectified and integrated through the opening of the once hermetically sealed doors and windows. Viewers were therefore unable to abstract the exhibition space and its contextual surroundings. And this loss or reduction of the ability to abstract the installation from its surroundings caused a change in viewer self-awareness within the installation and possibly an altered mode of perception of the surrounding architecture. The viewer was thereby freed from the perceptual convention that had become reified in the format of recent museum and gallery installations.

It now seems that any means I used to effect a decomposition (such as in this installation), became all the more the focus of objectification. That is, the installation objectified what had been used as a de-objectifying device. The problem with this type of decomposition was that the extent to which the viewers' mode of perception could be affected relied on, was embedded in, objectification itself. For example, in this case, an objectively determined sequence of external visual events had been juxtaposed with the interior architectural frame. This was manifested in the

way viewers would ascend the staircase, freezing and framing images of the city outside from within the empty exhibition container.

Material subtraction and addition have become interchangeable methods of working within the discourse of art. Historically, the producer affects the aesthetic discourse by adding material constructs that are designed and designated for that discourse (any piece of manually worked bronze is automatically registered as sculpture) or by subtracting such constructs in a material negation designed to enter a material discourse.

The designatory method includes elements in the aesthetic definition of a work which would not normally be applied to its aesthetic discourse. For the purpose of this installation, designatory elements were claimed and enlisted as determinants not only for the structure of the work, but also for the context of the discourse into which it was inserted (the alternative space, the building's architecture, the New York skyline, etc.). Even those elements—in this instance the windows and doors—which had been removed through subtraction became designatory in their absence. Subtraction became a mode of declaration in the work by declaring what the subtractive method had revealed. The designatory method implies the objectification of the elements it appropriates. But those elements are inserted into a historical moment of discourse where both the objectification and the discourse are contingent upon one another for deconstruction.

Detail view of north wall during installation. Photograph by
Helen Winkler.

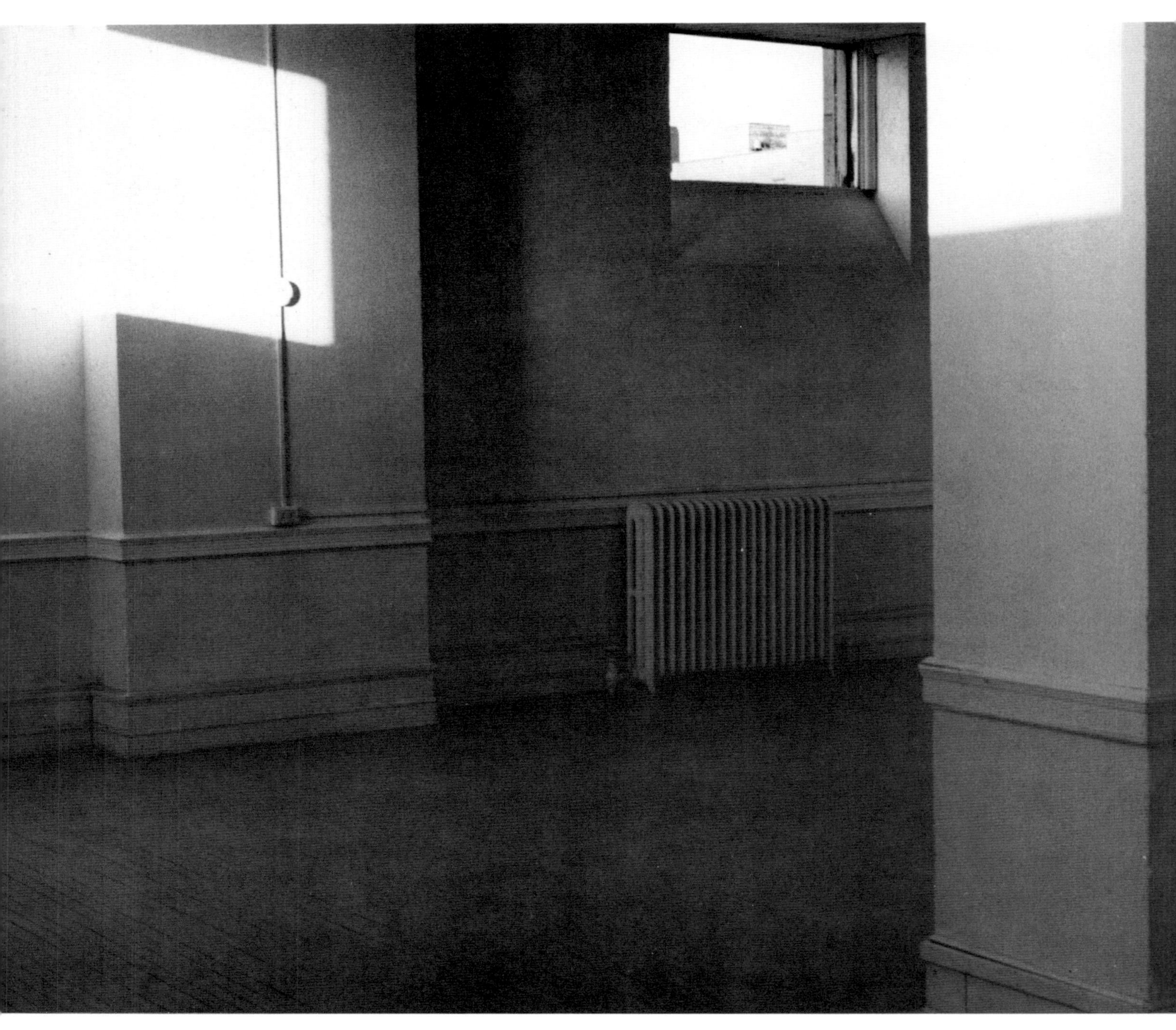

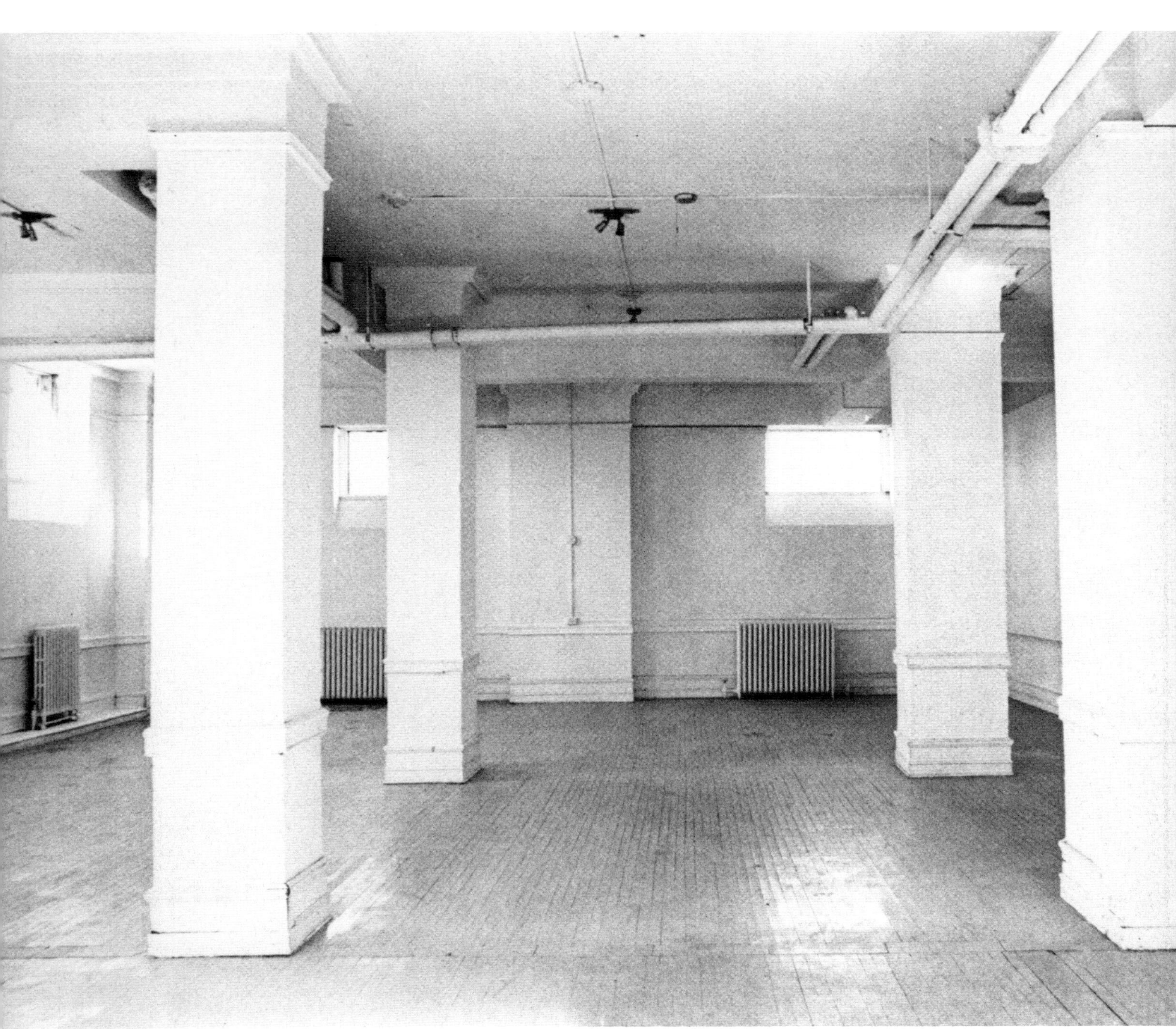

North view of thirteenth-floor exhibition area during installation.
Photograph by Michael Asher.

In late December 1975, I received an invitation to participate in a special exhibition which was organized and curated by Germano Celant in the context of the Venice Biennale, to be held from July 18 to October 16, 1976.[1] The Ambiente Arte Exhibition was divided into two sections, one historical and the other contemporary. The historical part suggested an ongoing continuity of environmental installations in twentieth-century art, while the contemporary section would include installations/works by artists as divergent as Vito Acconci, Joseph Beuys, Daniel Buren, Dan Graham, Robert Irwin, Jannis Kounellis, Sol LeWitt, Mario Merz, Bruce Nauman, Maria Nordman, Palermo, Doug Wheeler, and myself. By the end of the following March I knew that the contemporary section of the exhibition was to focus on installation works which, in one way or another, were supposed to relate to the given architectural structure of the exhibition building, the Italian Pavilion.

On April 1, 1976, I sent a proposal for a work to Germano Celant and by mid-April I had received floor plans of the pavilion for more detailed and specific planning. At the time, my proposal read as follows:

As for my contribution to the Biennale, I have a specific idea for a work in mind. This is to put together a lounge area in front of, or near an entry/exit of the exhibition area. If, by any chance, lounge areas have been designated for the pavilion, I would like to develop them. My thinking of a lounge is a comfortable place where visitors may communicate with one another on a social level. It should be conducive to meeting and sharing in a quiet and relaxed atmosphere. The idea will be comprised by putting the lounge in a specially constructed area away from an entry/exit or immediate access areas to the pavilion. Being functional, and very natural, is important for the idea and the inquiry into it.

At this point I am considering using sofas, chairs, and low tables. The designs should have some continuity. Do you have any access to modern design or institutional furniture which would be considered indoor lounge furniture? I would like to keep the design as simple as possible for each element. If it is necessary, I would also like to have access to floor coverings such as carpet or coco mat. I would like the chairs and sofas to be at the same height and the tables a little lower. If possible, I would like to have access to natural daylight with a simple incandescent lighting to supplement daylight and be used during the evenings. The amount of furniture and the way in which it is arranged will be dependent on the given area. This might be a good time to send floor plans and any other visual information, such as photos, which you think I might need to further prepare.

In the contemporary section, each of the artists had a separate space for his/her contribution so that each work was isolated from the works around it. Individual installations were connected by passageways.

I received and studied the floor plan and saw that an area had been set aside for a coffee bar. Germano Celant's proposal that I use a nearby space, adjacent on the southside to an outdoor patio east of the coffee bar, seemed acceptable for my installation, which would assume the functions of a lounge. In a letter dated April 11, 1976, I replied to Germano Celant with the following statements:

Next, I wish to inquire about the area on the floor plan you have suggested for my use. Can the corridor wall be removed or perhaps the first half be removed? Is the open space in front of the building and coffee bar covered with a roof? Is this a patio area? Would it be possible to integrate the coffee bar (if it is working) and the open space in front, if it is enclosed? Perhaps this would keep my contribution to the Biennale more true to a lounge, with institutional or designers' furniture in a lounge area, rather than a room . . . . I am still thinking that it is, perhaps, best to keep the furniture as casual and simple as possible. An architect and a couple of institutions have been used for resource materials. I am now looking for benches without backs and

1. Balla, Depero, Pannaggi, Tatlin-Yakulov, Rodchenko, Puni, Lissitskv De Pisis

2. Kandinsky, Davis, Delaunay, Vordemberge-Gildewart, Burchartz, Huszar, Mondrian, van Doesburg, Tauber-Arp, Schlemmer, Gorin, Strzeminsky

3. van Doesburg, Dada-Messe, Duchamp, Schwitters

4. Arp, Radice, Sartoris, Gorin, Duchamp, Ray, Surrealist Exhibitions 1938/1942/1947, Pollock, Fontana, Gallizio, Klein, Kaprow

5. Nevelson, Klein, Manzoni, Arman, Segal, Kaprow, Oldenburg, Ben, Watts

6. Christo, Oldenburg, Paolini, Colombo, Schneeman. Accardi, Warhol, Pistoletto

7. Information 1966/1976

8. Palermo
9. Buren
10. Graham
11. Beuys
12. LeWitt
13. Merz
14. Nauman
15. Kounellis
16. Acconci
17. Irwin
18. Nordman
19. Wheeler
20. Asher

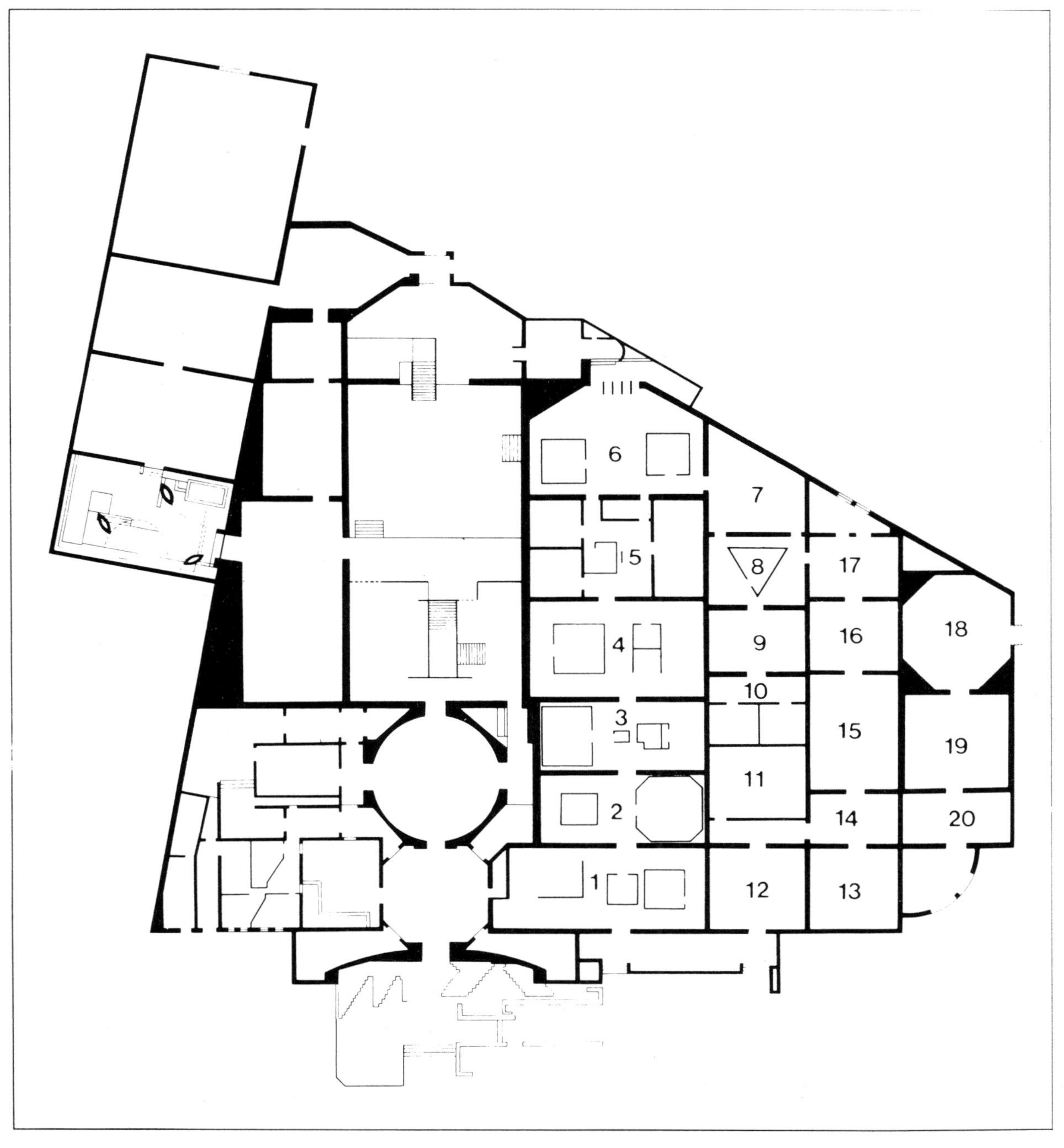

Diagram of the various installations at the Ambiente Arte Exhibition, Padiglione Centrale Giardini di Castello, July 18—October 16, 1976. Courtesy: La Biennale di Venezia.

some type of folding chair, but I still must see the Biennale site before a selection can be made. I feel the furniture should definitely be of the country's origin that is sponsoring the exhibition in order to signify certain symbols and feelings of that country.

Since the patio functioned as a main entry/exit, I thought that it might be used as an outdoor area where chairs from the proposed installation could be conveniently moved by the visitors. The installation could then function as an indoor lounge with access to a garden patio surrounded by landscaped areas where visitors could rest, much like those found in museums and office and apartment buildings. The patio area formed on the south-east side an off-set radius of 7.2 meters on the east-west axis and 5.00 meters on the north-south axis. At a height of 6.00 meters an overhang completely covered the patio and followed its perimeter.

On the north side of the area allocated for my installation, space had been designated for the installation of a work by Douglas Wheeler and on the west side an area had been designated for the work of Bruce Nauman. The actual interior installation area set aside for my use measured 10.49 meters by 5.00 meters by 8.38 meters. On the north side of the area was a passageway of 2.72 meters high and 1.80 meters wide, while a second passage 2.97 meters high and 1.67 meters wide led from this area into the patio. A skylight in the center of the room—9.03 meters by 3.00 meters, more than half the size of the ceiling—provided natural light. I had the walls covered with stucco and then painted white. The parquet floor was sanded and treated to highlight the grain.

An original interior passageway that I had planned to use after seeing the photographs of the designated area, had been closed off shortly before I arrived. This passageway was as necessary to my work as the passageway to the exterior since it guaranteed that viewers had access to and from my work and the adjacent exhibition area. The passageway also reinforced the function of my work as a lounge area for exhibition visitors.

The curator and architect of th exhibition refused, however, to have this passageway reopened, which delayed the installation of my work and resulted in a seemingly unresolvable conflict. From June 21 to July 21, 1976, I continued to work on this project in Venice (interrupted by several trips to distributors and manufacturers in Minal and Bologna in search of chairs for the installation), whle trying to resolve the impasse.

On July 18, the day of the opening, seven artists —Dan Graham, Vito Acconci, Daniel Buren, Jannis Kounellis, Maria Nordman, Mario Merz, and Palermo —signed a petition which had been draughted by two of them. It read as follows:

"Ambiente" represents a very unique situation, where, from concept to execution, artists' proposals and their realization have been developed in a spirit of open rapport between organizer and artists, and also between artists. The exhibition functions as a totality, altering or losing any one work detracts from every other work and sense of the original intent for the exhibition. For this reason the signers of this statement believe that if the work of Michael Asher cannot be executed exactly as he intends, not only is this work lost, but the purpose of the exhibition destroyed.

The petition was presented to the curator and he took notice of it. I believe it was on the strength of this petition that two days before I left Venice, a passageway was finally cut into the northwest corner of the area allocated for my work. The passageway measured 4.27 meters high and 60 centimeters wide. It was cut through the west wall, between my installation area and that of Bruce Nauman's work. Its height was determined by the height of the ceiling in Nauman's installation area (where an additional ceiling construction had been installed at a lower level specific to the purpose of his work). Finally, the passageway was stuccoed and finished like the rest of my installation area.

I decided to use twenty-two folding stools to cre-

Product information on stool used in the installation (front).

Product information on stool used in installation (back).

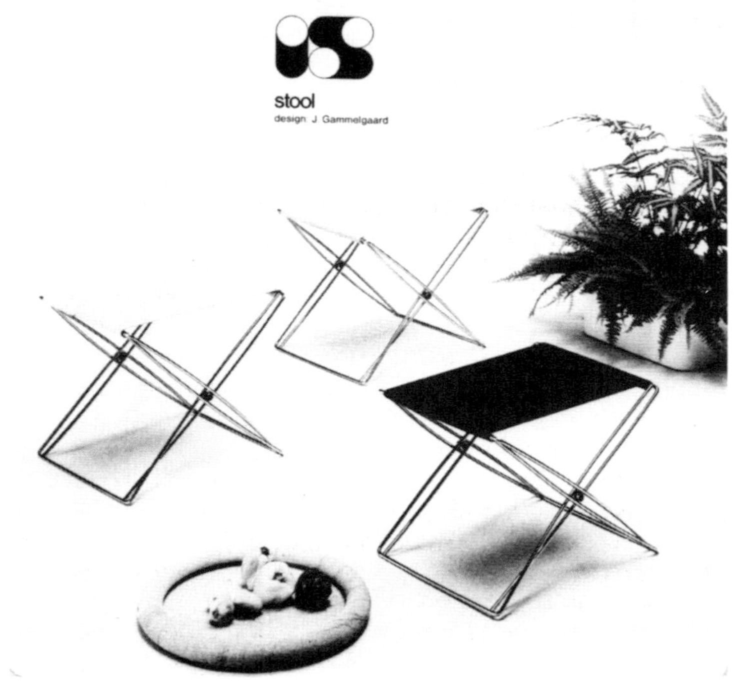

ate a seating area. The actual stool model, which I had seen in a number of Italian design journals before I left Venice, California, was designed by J. Gammelgaard and was produced in Italy by Strutture d'Interni of Bologna, under license from Design Forum. Unfolded, the stool was 57 centimeters long, 46 centimeters wide and 40 centimeters high. Chromium-plated steel with a natural canvas seat, the stools could be easily moved and visitors could cluster them in different patterns as they chose. I wanted the stools to be of designer quality, the kind that might ordinarily be found in a living room or lounge along with other fixtures, such as designer tables, chairs, and sofas, rather than simple wooden ones with no particular design or function. I decided to use a light stool not only for practical reasons, but also as an alternative to the usual, ponderous institutional seating arrangements which, in many instances, allow for no variation in physical points of view.

I decided on the number twenty-two after measuring the available seating area, in order to avoid overcrowding and to allow at the same time for the comfortable arrangement of various sized groupings.

The stools arrived from the manufacturer before the interior passageway was constructed. Soon after my departure, they were placed in the installation area when the passageway was completely finished.

This work was specifically designed for the Ambiente Arte Exhibition at the Venice Biennale, a unique event with high visitor attendance. The work ceased to exist after October 16, 1976, when the installation was dismantled and the chairs were dispersed.

The intention of the Venice Biennale work was to establish a relationship between a seating area and its architectural setting. This was in opposition to the exhibition theme which was not directly concerned with the functional elements of the architectural context. Instead of focusing on an abstract notion and tradition of architecturally related art, the work shifted its intention to an actual architectural function within exhibition practice, such as the functionally neces-

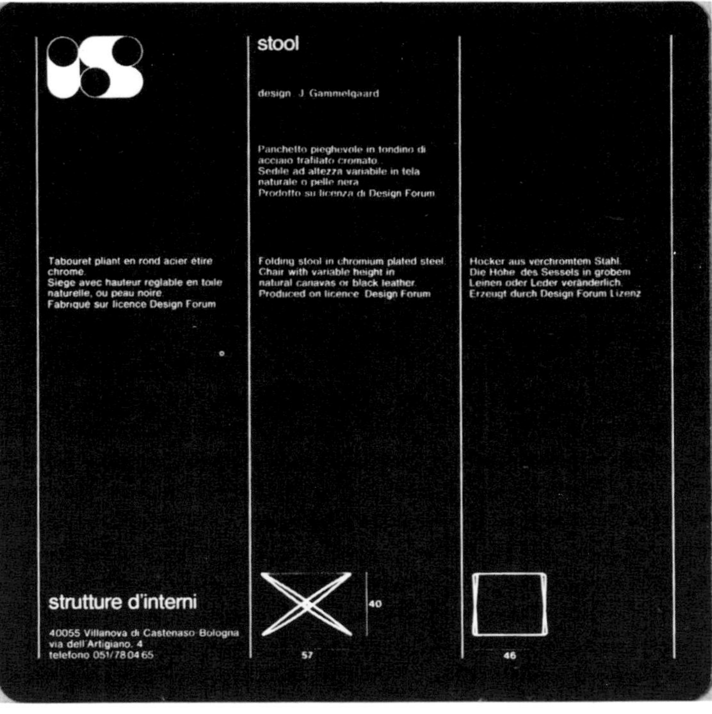

sary lounge or seating area for visitors. The work thereby avoided being read as just another work within the historical discourse of architecturally situated works.

The work attempted to indicate to what extent traditional modes of aesthethic production (e.g., painting and sculpture) took on architectural claims in certain environmental works. At the same time, the work tried to clarify the extent to which these architectural claims aestheticized and reified the functional appearance of architecture by depriving it of its use-value. This work therefore attempted to dislodge the problem inherent in works which, having their source in color-field painting, extracted a new aesthetic practice from an architectural tradition that had suffered from the fallacy of assuming that social progress would automatically coincide with architectural function and aesthetic practice. It is only through the work's essential limitation as a functional lounge or seating area in this particular exhibition context that it can redeem itself, as aesthetic practice, from these false claims.

By being limited to this specific exhibition and its thematic and temporal frame, the work allowed for an explicit subject-object relationship, whose utilitarian features were valid only within that framework. As a contextually bound, unique instance of actual use-value, this work denied, at the same time, the claim for use-value as a universal condition or possibility within artistic practice.

It was different, in this respect, from installations which were disguised as architecture, but were actually made of props. These may have created the impression of a redistribution of architectural space, through the use of false walls and lighting, to specify and determine the way in which the viewer should perceive the work. For the same reason, these installations may have displaced or destroyed elements that were originally integral to the architectural space. By ignoring both the architectural givens and functions of the space, and the viewers' interaction with those givens, these installations extracted functions from architecture, and objectified the viewers' experience by overshadowing their perception of the preexisting architectural context.

Furthermore, this type of work did not respond to the specific purposes of the architecture, as *exhibition architecture*, but instead transformed it into a spectacle in order to confirm the ideological presuppositions of the exhibition topic. My work, on the other hand, confirmed the exhibition topic, by negating the topic's validity in direct response both to the architectural situation where the exhibition was installed, and to the viewers' needs within that situation.

Another type of work in the exhibition tried to animate a given space with alien elements or materials that were abstract in relation to their spatial context. But, paradoxically enough, these were perceived as particularly concrete elements. The intense presence of these objects in their abstracted spaces was the result of a theatrical disjunct between the exhibition's and the viewer's reality. While the *architectural* installations pretended that the viewer's experience was exclusively determined by abstracting perceptual elements from architectural conditions (e.g., light, surfaces, volume, and color), the *theatrical* installations asserted that only objects, independent of their surrounding architectural frame (as well as their historical and social frames) could determine the experience of the viewer.

In my work, the presence of the theatrical prop, and the illusion of the architectural prop, were excluded by foregrounding the object's potential use-value. In spite of the fact that exhibition-value was unavoidably imposed on the objects within my work, they maintained their use-value as their primary quality. The objects in the theatrical installations transformed their potential use-value into exclusive exhibition-value by suspending their potential function, thus becoming a unique and momentary illusion in reality.

The methodology of the ready-made framed objects and abstracted them from their use-value to imbue them with exhibition-value alone. The methodology of this work negated that, however, since the objects of my installation retained their common use inside the exhibition. My work responded both to the historical conditions and to the present state of installation work. First of all, the context of the exhibition, in all its ideological and concrete dimensions, determined the choice of objects and materials. These elements were defined by their use-value within this situation. Simultaneously, by opposing both the suspension of use-value in the ready-made, and a strict functionalist reduction of the object in an over-determined use-value situation, the design objects in the work functioned as a quotation from the contemporary vernacular. Furthermore, in contradistinction to the other installations in the exhibition, which reaffirmed the distance between author and audience, this work emphasized the viewer's presence and needs.

The stools I had chosen were specifically identifiable as designer objects. Yet the fact that they were mass-produced and looked mass-produced allowed them to be seen as mere raw material. I felt that they could be seen as nothing more than raw material, in the same way that the stucco walls or wooden floor could be seen as raw material. To all appearance, the stools were authored and produced under conditions which were external to my work. The artist's determination of the material and formal elements of the work was denied by the appropriation of a given object from contemporary design vernacular. At the same time, individual authorship was negated as a result of the viewer's potential use of the work. The negation of authorship also questioned the claim to uniqueness that tended to define the architecturally related works in the exhibition. This claim was implicit in their method of installation. Authorship in my case consisted of assuming responsibility for the actual operation of my work and for its insertion within the given discourse; although it did not involve defining material production. That would have individuated the author.

This work introduced a mass-produced cultural artifact into a unique high-art context in the same way that unique objects of high culture can enter the design vernacular and acquire the status of mass-produced functional objects.

While the appropriation of a supposed high-art object and its transformation into a commodity are taken for granted culturally, the functional integration of a designer object/commodity into a supposed high-art context seems to be very problematic, if not culturally unacceptable. The concept of utilitarian practice is unacceptable within the traditional definition of high art. Since high-art practice continues to maintain the idea of an autonomous, purposeless practice, its conflict with utilitarian practice cannot be resolved by attempting to integrate utilitarian practice within high art.

The functional and vernacular quotations within the work were not sufficiently particularized to be immediately located and identified within the discourse of high culture. At the same time, they were not sufficiently generalized and anonymous to be automatically identified as a feature of popular culture. The hybrid of contemporary design seems to represent the historical possibility of an integration of aesthetic practice with utilitarian practice. Certain contemporary artists seem to be increasingly attracted to the supposed integration of utilitarian design and aesthetic production, since this integration would resolve the split between social-political practice and aesthetic practice. In fact, rather than resolving this split, this integration actually falsifies any political perspective since it shifts the artist's attention from the actual social conditions to an exclusive concern with matters of design. This kind of utilitarian practice generates and stylizes the reification of social-political goals. In this way, my work in Ambiente Arte attempted to deal with the modernist tradition of high-art practice which is totally isolated from the social-political goals of a utilitarian practice within the historical context of an exhibition.

Design language embodies the myth of individuality in the form of supposedly functional, industrially produced commodities. The deliberate use of designer stools, rather than simple functional objects, mirrors the myth of individual artistic production in the aesthetic reality of the work. Since the designer stools

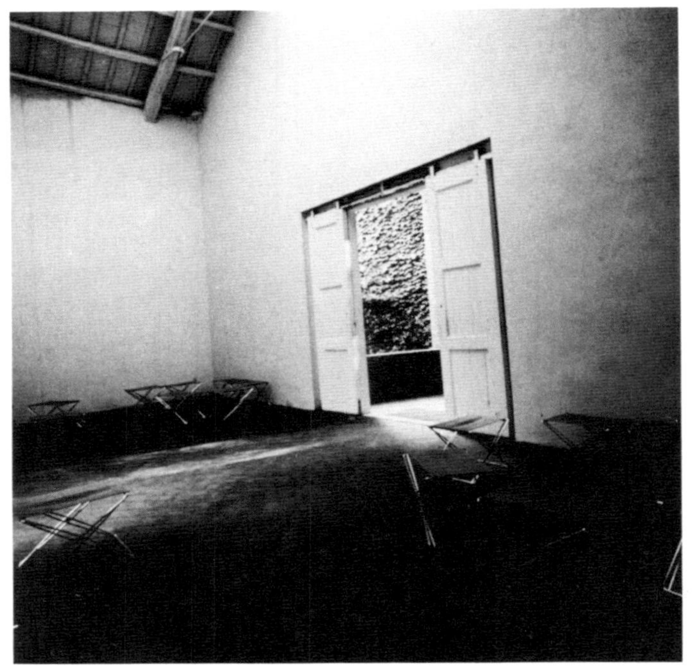 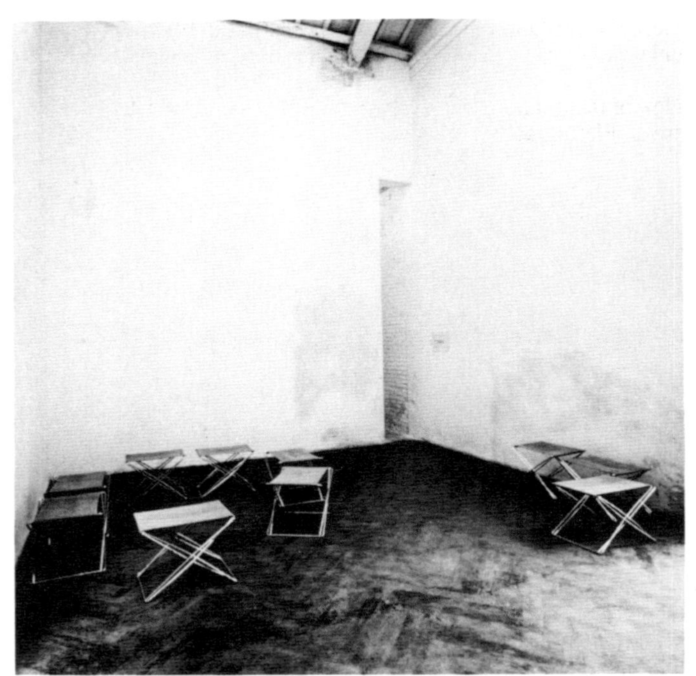

operated in the work as both a quotation from design language and a functional object of use-value—one seemingly negating the other—they became a model which revealed the degree of contradiction within individual aesthetic production.

[1] Contrary to the information given on page 20 in the catalogue *Michael Asher Exhibitions in Europe 1972–1977*, Stedelijk van Abbe Museum, Eindhoven, 1980, the Venice Biennale Ambiente Arte Exhibition did not open until July 18 and ended on October 16, 1976.

Facsimile of letter of support with artists' signatures.

View of installation with entry/exit toward patio. Photographer unknown.

View of installation with passage toward other exhibition areas. Photographer unknown.

Exterior of patio with entry/exit to installation area at the Padiglione Centrale. Photograph by Michael Asher.

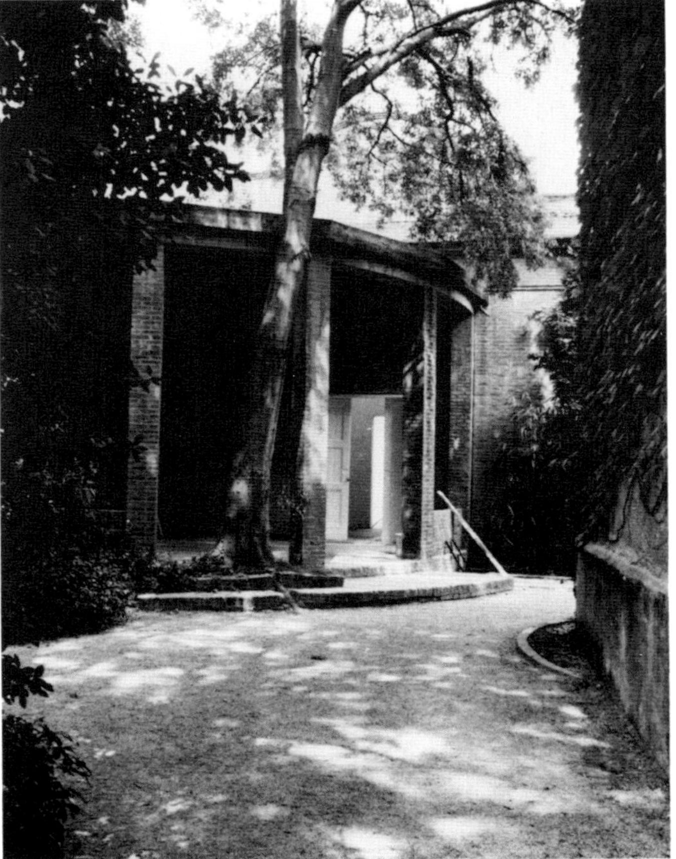

January 15–February 10, 1977
Los Angeles Institute of Contemporary Art
Los Angeles, California

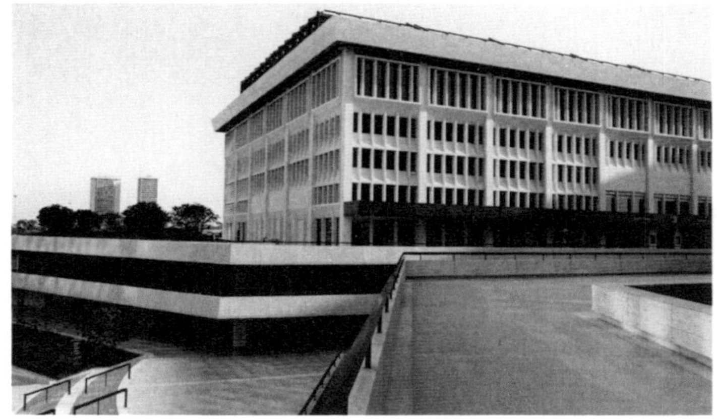

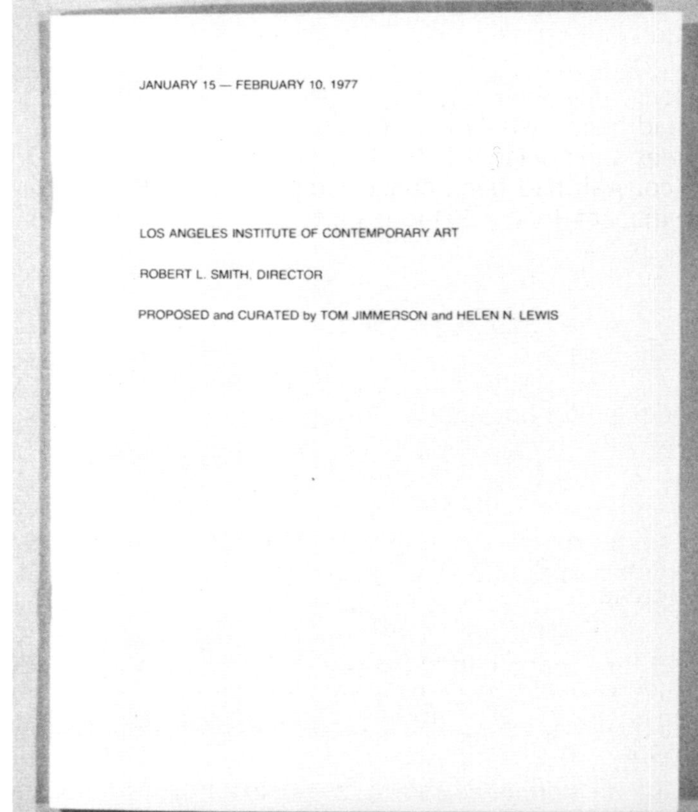

JANUARY 15 — FEBRUARY 10. 1977

LOS ANGELES INSTITUTE OF CONTEMPORARY ART

ROBERT L. SMITH. DIRECTOR

PROPOSED and CURATED by TOM JIMMERSON and HELEN N. LEWIS

Exterior view of the Los Angeles Institute of Contemporary Art
located at the ground floor of the ABC Entertainment Center,
Century City, California. Photograph by Michael Asher.

Catalogue cover design by Michael Asher.

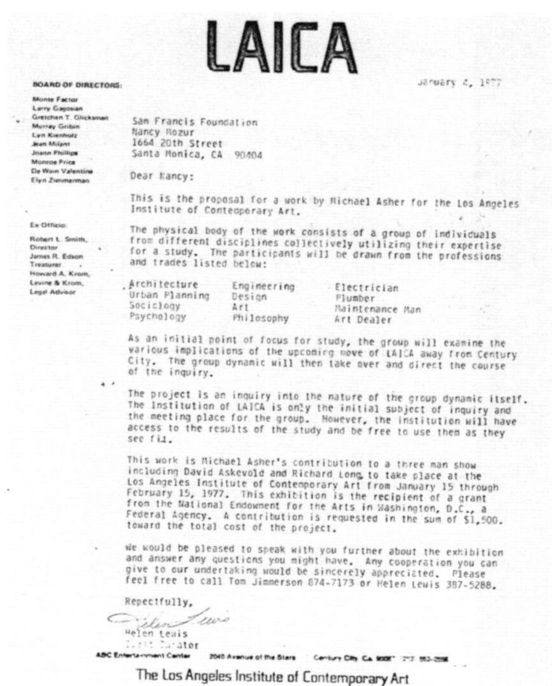

LAICA

January 4, 1977

BOARD OF DIRECTORS:

Monte Factor
Larry Gagosian
Gretchen T. Glicksman
Murray Gribin
Lyn Kienholz
Jean Milant
Joann Phillips
Monroe Price
De Wain Valentine
Elyn Zimmerman

Ex-Officio:

Robert L. Smith,
Director
James R. Edson
Treasurer
Howard A. Krom,
Levine & Krom,
Legal Advisor

Sam Francis Foundation
Nancy Mozur
1664 20th Street
Santa Monica, CA 90404

Dear Nancy:

This is the proposal for a work by Michael Asher for the Los Angeles Institute of Contemporary Art.

The physical body of the work consists of a group of individuals from different disciplines collectively utilizing their expertise for a study. The participants will be drawn from the professions and trades listed below:

Architecture	Engineering	Electrician
Urban Planning	Design	Plumber
Sociology	Art	Maintenance Man
Psychology	Philosophy	Art Dealer

As an initial point of focus for study, the group will examine the various implications of the upcoming move of LAICA away from Century City. The group dynamic will then take over and direct the course of the inquiry.

The project is an inquiry into the nature of the group dynamic itself. The Institution of LAICA is only the initial subject of inquiry and the meeting place for the group. However, the institution will have access to the results of the study and be free to use them as they see fit.

This work is Michael Asher's contribution to a three man show including David Askevold and Richard Long to take place at the Los Angeles Institute of Contemporary Art from January 15 through February 15, 1977. This exhibition is the recipient of a grant from the National Endowment for the Arts in Washington, D.C., a Federal Agency. A contribution is requested in the sum of $1,500. toward the total cost of the project.

We would be pleased to speak with you further about the exhibition and answer any questions you might have. Any cooperation you can give to our undertaking would be sincerely appreciated. Please feel free to call Tom Jimmerson 874-7173 or Helen Lewis 387-5288.

Repectfully,

Helen Lewis
Guest Curator

ABC Entertainment Center   2040 Avenue of the Stars   Century City, Ca. 90067   213 553-2598

The Los Angeles Institute of Contemporary Art

Facsimile of support letter.

Tom Jimmerson and Helen Lewis were appointed by Robert Smith, director of the Los Angeles Institute of Contemporary Art (LAICA), to act as guest curators for an exhibition by myself, David Askevold, and Richard Long. A grant for this alternative space exhibition project was provided by the National Endowment for the Arts.

At the time of the exhibition, LAICA was located on the ground floor of the ABC Entertainment Center, 2040 Avenue of the Stars, in Century City, California, an urban area on the west side of Los Angeles. The LAICA space was 113 feet long, 15 feet wide, with a ceiling height of 14 feet 8 inches. The walls, ceiling, and floor of the space were similar to those in unfinished warehouses. LAICA had installed a partition wall covering 87 feet of the north wall and a 77-foot partition wall located 17 feet 6 inches from the south glass curtain wall. Three more partition walls, one 24 feet long, one 26 feet long, and the third 20 feet long, had been installed on a north-south axis at right angles and adjacent to the long walls. In addition, a 20-foot wall had been constructed on an east-west axis adjacent to the 20-foot partition wall. All partition walls were 12 feet high. These partition walls were not build especially for the exhibition. Two of them had been relocated from their positions in previous exhibitions.

Curators Jimmerson and Lewis hoped to combine works from Europe and different parts of North America with regional works, in a formula that could serve as a model for similar exhibitions in the future at other institutions in the Los Angeles area. Their goal was to familiarize the Los Angeles public with lesser known contemporary works by artists from both the area and abroad.

The exhibition, which had originally been planned for the second half of the year, was suddenly rescheduled to begin on January 15. In the three weeks prior to opening, I submitted several proposals for possible works.

My original proposal for the exhibition had been to initiate a goal-oriented study focusing on the implications and consequences of the planned relocation of LAICA from its then current location to 2020 South Robertson Boulevard. This study would have served as a point of departure for subsequent investigations to be undertaken by three different groups of people.

The first group would have been made up of specialists in various fields related to this particular situation and community activities in general. This group would have operated continuously throughout the exhibition from one studio and would have included the following professional individuals: architect, urban planner, sociologist, psychologist, engineer, designer, artist, philosopher, electrician, plumber, maintenance person, and art dealer. A second group would have consisted of consultants who could be contacted when necessary to provide assistance and additional information to the continuously operating research group. A third group would have been made up of visitors potentially interested in the research project.

This proposal was not feasible, however, since compensating the individuals involved would have exceeded the available funding. Attempts to obtain additional funding from private and public sources (e.g., the Sam Francis Foundation) were not successful.

After several subsequent proposals, the following project was accepted: I would use the $1300 allocated to me from the budget to employ three or four persons as participants for the duration of the exhibition. These participants would be present six hours a day during the hours that LAICA was open to the public, and would receive a wage of four dollars an hour. These participants were asked to place themselves in the space that had been set aside for my work.

At the front door and desk, leaflets were available acquainting the visitor with the exhibition and the individual artists and their work. The leaflet text was written by the director of LAICA.

The works of David Askevold and Richard Long were located north of the 77-foot partition wall, whereas my work was assigned to the area south of this wall. The total area allocated to my work was a space 97 feet by 17 feet 6 inches. This area was adjacent to the LAICA bookshop and the open office area visible at the east end of the exhibition space. The area was equipped with only a few chairs, a couch, and a table, as well as a coffeemaker and whatever else would be needed by the paid participants so that they would be comfortable for their six hour daily stint. The chairs and tables were placed so as to be easily seen by visitors from the entry on the north-east side.

In principle, the paid participants were expected to be present for the full six hours, but they did have the option to leave or interrupt their stay at any time during the day. A time sheet recording the hours that they actually spent in the work was kept by the secretary. The paid participants were free to pursue their day-to-day activities as usual in as much as the context of the situation would allow them to do so. Five participants did such things as read and write, and one of them edited a film. Nothing was required of the participants other than their presence within the actual installation area or within the confines of the LAICA exhibition space. Presence was temporarily defined by arrival or departure in the building. The definition of presence was flexible enough, however, to encompass relocation of the couch for one afternoon to a place outside the glass curtain wall, facing Olympic Boulevard, in a position corresponding exactly to its previous placement inside the building.

The definition of presence also hinged on the paid participants' perceptual and cognitive response to the work, as well as their interaction among themselves and with visitors to the exhibition. I chose participants mostly by telephone, from a list I had drawn up from suggestions, made by friends, acquaintances and other people according to categories of professional activity. The activities ranged from housewife and student, to a very small number of professionals, such as artist, manufacturer of architectural models, architect, art critic, and art dealer. Among the actual participants who finally agreed to cooperate were two artists, several students, an art critic, an alternative-space curator, two housewives, an arts-and-crafts instructor, and a photographer. The number of actual participants in-

creased through word of mouth, or by visitors' direct response to the work as the exhibition proceeded. The composition of each group differed from day to day and generated a different dynamic and understanding within the group and inside the work. It sometimes happened that the group remained the same since new participants were unavailable. It also happened that all of the participants were unknown to each other. On other occasions, some participants already knew one another, or all of the participants had previously met outside the context of the work.

I did not attend the work daily nor did I necessarily stay for the full six hours when I visited the exhibition. Just as the participants were under no obligation, so were the visitors free to either acknowledge the presence of the participants by talking to them, or even joining them, or they could ignore them altogether. The desks of the staff were approximately 16 feet away from my work area, and both the staff and the participants could overhear and view each others' activities throughout the day. Thus an exchange of observations and experiences between salaried employees, working in the institution, and paid participants, working in the installation of my work, occurred intermittently throughout the day. Unlike the paid employees and the paid participants, the visitors—the third group capable of interaction in this situation— did not receive pecuniary compensation for their presence in the work.

It was suggested that all of the paid participants and the artist meet at the conclusion of the exhibition to describe collectively their experiences in the work. As indicative as this proposal might have been of a sustained interest in the work, it seemed totally contrary to its spirit, since it implied that the work was dependent on my mediation and presence, rather than independent of it. This obviously did not prevent my speaking with individual participants during and after the installation about how they perceived the work, and how they defined themselves in relation to it.

It was hoped that this installation would serve as a model for a locus outside of academic, commercial,

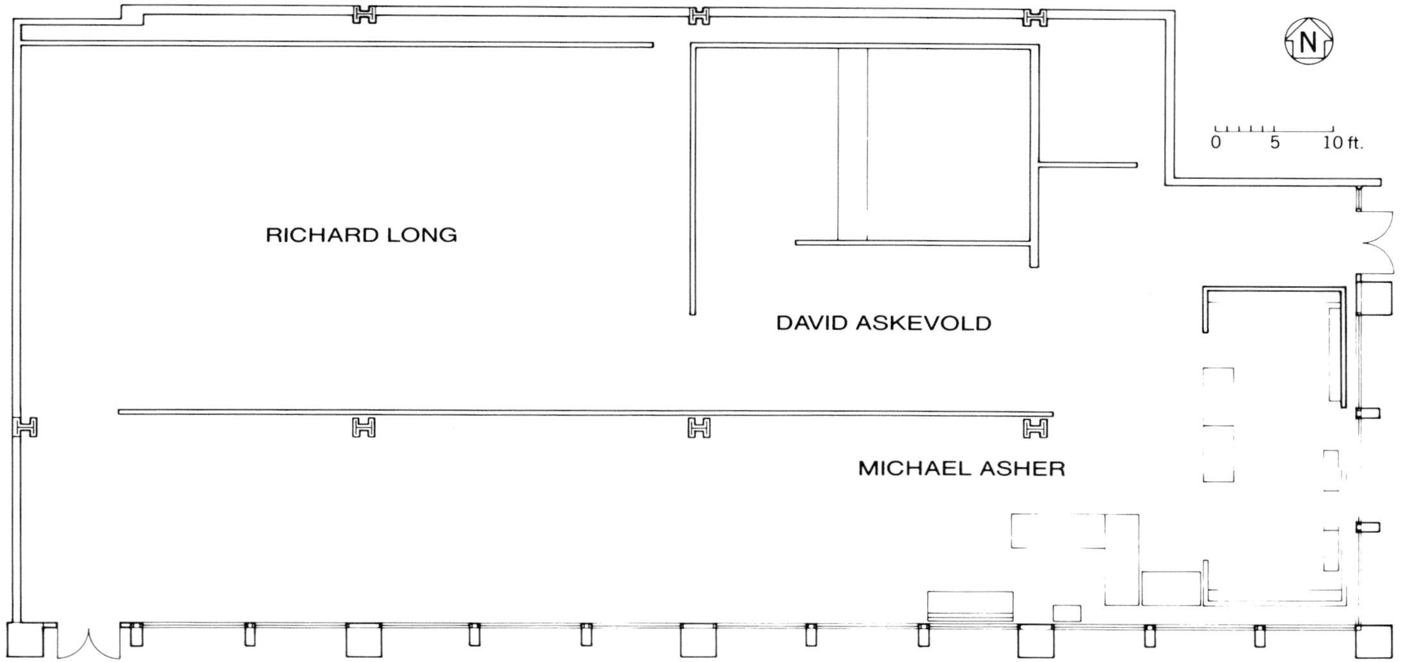

or private social situations, where discussion and study could take place. This seemed a particularly pressing need at the time for individuals who were either practicing artists or directly concerned with the question of contemporary art practice, but who—in the vast urban sprawl of contemporary Los Angeles—were fairly isolated in spite of their common interests.

The structure of the work was not a collaboration between an artist and paid participants, but the creation of the artist alone. If there was any collaboration within the work, it was among the paid participants. On the other hand, the *function* of the work was determined by both the artist and the participants; while performing their function within the defined structure, participants acted as individuals or as a group in collaboration, modifying their function according to their needs or the situation. For example, one participant questioned the limits of the work, and whether they extended into his day-to-day existence in as much as the compensation for the work enabled him to pay for his food and housing. Another participant described his understanding of the collaborative effort as follows:

I don't really wish to 'evaluate' the work, since doing so would tend to fix it, conceptually; to render it static. A good deal of aesthetic production seems intentionally amenable to formal analysis, but the application of that approach to work which is, by nature, process rather than object, seems ludicrous.

Nevertheless, a good deal of formal analysis is objectionable primarily for its positivistic restriction to *what is*—whereas we *can* develop formal models of negative facts, as well. What follows, then, is a model of a 'progressive' art, with which Michael Asher's piece may be compared, contrasted, and, in some sense, evaluated. As against the escapism, manipulation, and outright stupidity of mass culture; in opposition to the elitism and superficiality of so much high culture, we might hold out for an art which (a) contains a moment of liberation, in which the sensuous aspects of human nature are developed (especially as concerns human *relationships*);

(b) contains a teleological moment, in which the moment of liberation is, through the attainment of a critical distance, contrasted with the sterility and inhumanity of bourgeois exchange relations and their cultural reverberations; and (c) socially *organizes* the mediations (forms) in such a way that the attendant aesthetic experience is co-determined by all participants, as a way of moving towards obliteration of the distinction between (i.e., synthesizing) producer and consumer. (*Why* this is progressive is another exegesis which, unfortunately, space doesn't permit.)

Does Asher's work satisfy any of these requirements? Whatever his intentions (which I won't presume to intuit), I believe that it does move in that direction. I've empirical evidence for the first point: the occasions on which I was present were marked by highly enjoyable discussion and debate, and though our relations, as participants, remained mediated, the individuals and not the mediations seemed to predominate. We confronted one another as people, not as instruments. Second, the work was rife with moments of "critical distance." (One might say that this was due to the people, not the piece, but the selection of participants was an *aspect* of the piece.) The third criterion is more difficult to meet, and it is perhaps here where the work's concessions to the status-quo become more apparent. Although we could determine the nature of our participation *within* the piece, its limits and definition were fundamentally under Asher's control. Further, it will be *seen* (appropriated?) as "Michael Asher's piece at LAICA," not as a collaborative endeavor —and so forth. Nevertheless, these conclusions are the result of an analysis nurtured by the work itself, and the fact that one is able to become critical of, and question, the basis of that work just might (in its impetus toward eventual transcendence of the given form) be its most progressive aspect.

Frederick Dolan
Los Angeles Institute of Contemporary Art,
January 15—February 10, 1977.

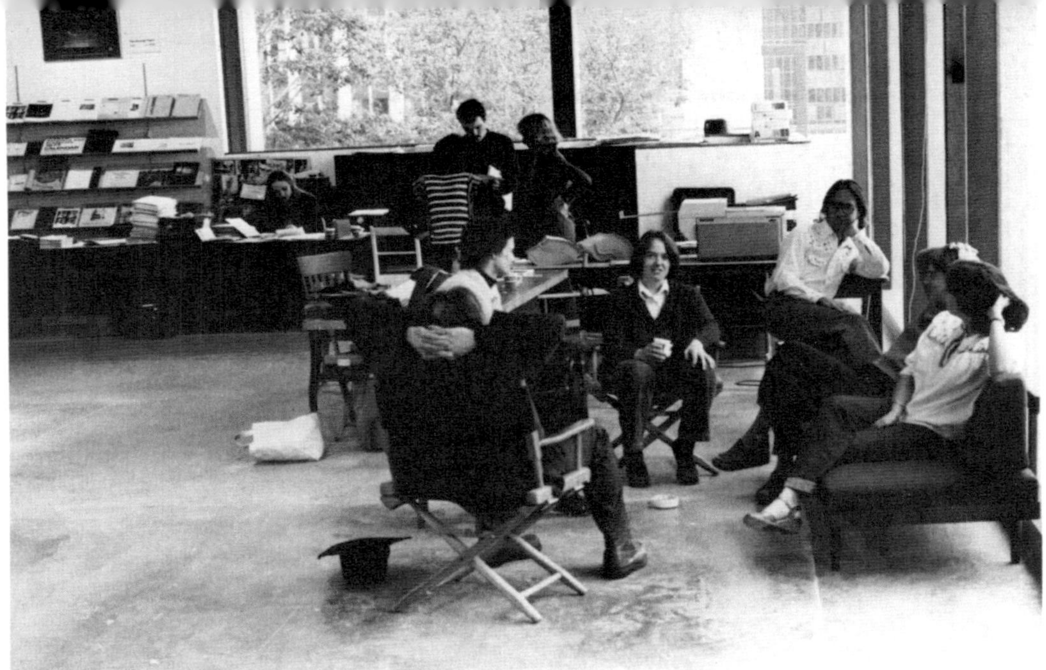

Viewing east in installation, showing group of paid participants and visitors
in exhibition area and secretary at work in office/bookstore area.

A third participant who withdrew after having collaborated for a short period of time, gave her reasons in the following letter:

January 23, 1977

Dear Michael:

After spending approximately seven and a half hours under your employment (in conjunction with the National Endowment for the Arts) and after serious thought about that situation, I find it necessary, on several grounds, to terminate my participation in your show at LAICA.

Knowing your penchant for documentation and my inability to communicate concisely on a verbal level, I thought it best that I state my position in writing.

Other participants have indicated that payment was problematic. I find that aspect of the work most intriguing; money is as valid a basis for transaction as any structure facilitating social intercourse. Under these circumstances, such a financial arrangement seems to act as a lubricating agent—between the audience/viewer, the administration, yourself as artist/employer and the other participants. To some degree a simple contractual agreement (time in exchange for wages hourly) assuages any guilt or other emotional complication that might arise from a more conditional exchange i.e. friendship or volunteerism. Such a situation also tends to minimize role conflicts that might occur between, let us say, students, other artists, tradesmen, administrators, etc. and better pinpoints the implicit relationship between the audience and attendents.

In the case of the LAICA show, however, the politics are much more complicated. Just what do we have? My presumption is that you were invited to show new work by two co-curators, working with LAICA who were working with the National Endowment of the Arts, who funded the event. I think about your earlier work and wonder if the dynamics of the above situation might have been adequate fertile grounds for work; you have rejected that possiblity for whatever reason.

"Social interaction," you say: big concept—encompassing at the least. As a concept, social interaction is inherently pointless within, shall we say, a pointed structure. As a physical actualization, in this case, such interaction seemed aggressive in a convoluted kind of way.

Perhaps my response to this aggression is the crux of my disturbed reaction to this work. (I might interject here that I am fully cognizant of the fact that I am not *out* of this piece at this point—equally as disarming.) Being present at LAICA, I was aware that I was someone else contextually; that I was helplessly, hopelessly arting. I was arting my lunch and arting my coffee. The fact that nearly all discourse (limited as it was) taking place was art-referential was blackly humorous but not particularly relevant. Social interaction = art discourse. Largest common denominator. I'd rather be pointing somewhere else.

I regret that I am unable to take these various thoughts and synthesize them adequately. Perhaps that is unnecessary.

With fond regards,
Sally

In modernist aesthetic practice, the idea of collaboration seems to compromise individuation, one of the essential aesthetic principles held within this practice up to now. This work insists upon the individual artist's autonomy as much as it insists upon the necessity of collaboration within social production as a functional means and necessary condition for producing a work of art. In traditional modernist practice, aesthetic production must evidence itself as having been individually conceived and realized so that the spectacle of supposed primary invention can be read. This work, however, resisted the traditional reading of artistic practice by increasing the visitors' awareness of the contradiction between the author's presence in the definition of the work and the participant's/viewer's

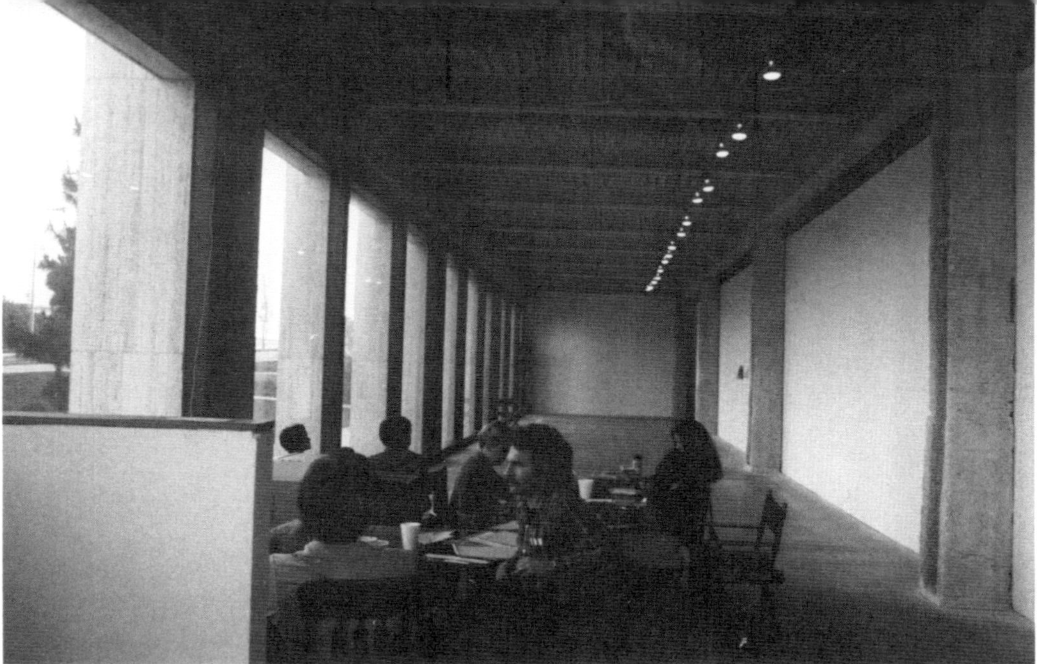

Viewing west from secretary's desk into installation area
toward west wall. Photographs by Bob Smith.

social interaction in the realization of the work. The idea of individuation operates within artistic practice as a model reflecting socio-economic practice which, as it seems, out of its own necessity, determines a division of social functions and thereby categorizes, stratifies, and isolates individuals in social production. The division of these functions is visibly embodied in the work's construction of separate yet integrated elements, ranging from the author's practice to the participant's practice and from the presence of the visitors to the presence of the administration. Furthermore, this division of functions was clearly exemplified and incorporated in my concept for the design of the catalogue cover and contents page, which distinguished institution, administrator, and organizers of the exhibition (on the cover) from the producers of the works in the exhibition (on the contents page).

By integrating these separate functions (author, visitor, participant, administrator) within the work, the work remained free of the economic stratification inherent in the division of these functions.

Traditionally, art constructs such as painting and sculpture have addressed the viewer through a process of objectification. Even works constructed in film and video confront the viewer with objects of mediation, and performance activities appear either to be objectified in theatricality or mediated through their sculptural objectifications. The viewer may perceive a work of art as embodying authorship through an objectified mediating device, so that the artist is considered inseparable from the work, As long as the viewer can identify the work with the author, a comfortable distance obtains between the viewer and the work. If the viewer perceives the author within the object, the object is necessarily anthropomorphized. Yet, personification and objectification prevent the viewer from recognizing the work's contingent relationship to a wider historical and social discourse. The integration of the artist with the object makes it possible to differentiate the roles of author, viewer and mediator. In this way, individuals responsible for delivery, mediation, and reception can be easily identified and maintained within a subject-object relationship.

The LAICA installation, however, distanced work and artist by appearing to relieve me of my responsibility as author. Since the paid participants as subjects mediated the work to the viewers and to themselves, viewers were unable to personify or objectify them in the work, nor could they distance themselves from the work by means of these viewing conventions. But if the viewers were to personify/objectify the paid participants in the work, it would probably involve transforming them into either a reified theatrical spectacle or a reified aesthetic experience. This would instantly alienate the viewers from their presence as individuals. In confronting this moment of alienation, the viewers realize that in the conventional response to works of art this process of reification is deferred either to the object or to the author. If the viewers realize that their aesthetic expectation and response is intrinsically linked to this process of reification, they would also suspect that this work requires a transformation of their experience. This leaves them with the responsibility which, in traditional aesthetic practice and perception, was deferred to either author or object.

Viewers would, therefore, realize that ultimately the paid participants, the institutional staff, the artist, the curators, and they themselves were operating inextricably within a collaborative effort. In a collaborative work that seems to negate individuation, and in which the focus is redirected both from the artist and the object to the viewer as *subject*, the primacy of *invention*, as a concept traditionally necessary to aesthetic production, becomes disfunctional. The desire for a unique aesthetic experience through artistic invention is analogous to the desire to acquire individuality in a product/commodity. Artistic invention traditionally deflected the viewers' desire from individual and social realities because it seemed to promise a unique experience that was synonymous with the myth of individuality, originality, and innovation. In this way the concept of invention prevented the viewers from reflecting their own individual and social realities back upon themselves.

The fulfillment of these aesthetic expectations seems to result in the neglect of the viewers' actual individual and social reality. Through loss of individuality, the viewers attempt to invest each aesthetic construct with the invention that seems to allow them to reacquire that individuality.

Some viewers might have felt that the work reduced their experience to a positivist affirmation of their given momentary reality. This reduction of experience in the work would imply a deprivation of artistic and sensual pleasure, aesthetic anticipation, speculative transgression, and a denial of critical analysis. Such a reading of the work was to be expected from viewers who approached the work with those traditional aesthetic expectations. By negating their own presence and insisting instead upon the presence of aesthetic objects, these viewers would have denied their own perception of the work. Whether the work was viewed as a denial of aesthetic experience, or misperceived as a sculptural installation, it was a falsely attributed object status that suggested reification of both the specific work of the paid participants and the author. If this semblance of reification alienated the viewer from the work, it did so only in order to allow the viewer to recognize the mechanisms of reification.

Modernist aesthetic tradition required that the work of art be essentially without purpose, that is, free of any utilitarian function. And it had to convey at the same time a sense of the highest facility and craftsmanship; yet, paradoxically, it had to conceal that skill in order to appear as if it had been accomplished without effort.

The work reveals paid, alienated labor within a structure that is expected to embody a model of unalienated labor. The work is therefore consistent in its denial of the traditional expectations brought by the viewer to the work of art. The work abandons its aesthetic promise of unalienated labor and loses its commodity status, once considered to be the work's last guarantee of independence. It seems to reaffirm the condition of alienation and reification within the aesthetic structure itself. But, in fact, it exposes the totality of reification that determines the conditions of aesthetic production and distribution.

By mimetically incorporating the presence of the paid participants as the framing support of the work, and their labor as the subject of the work, a nonhierarchical situation was created which revealed the conditions of material reproduction that traditional aesthetic structures had promised to conceal.

Viewing west into adjacent exhibition area.

Viewing east from west wall of installation area toward paid participants' table. Photographs by Bob Smith.

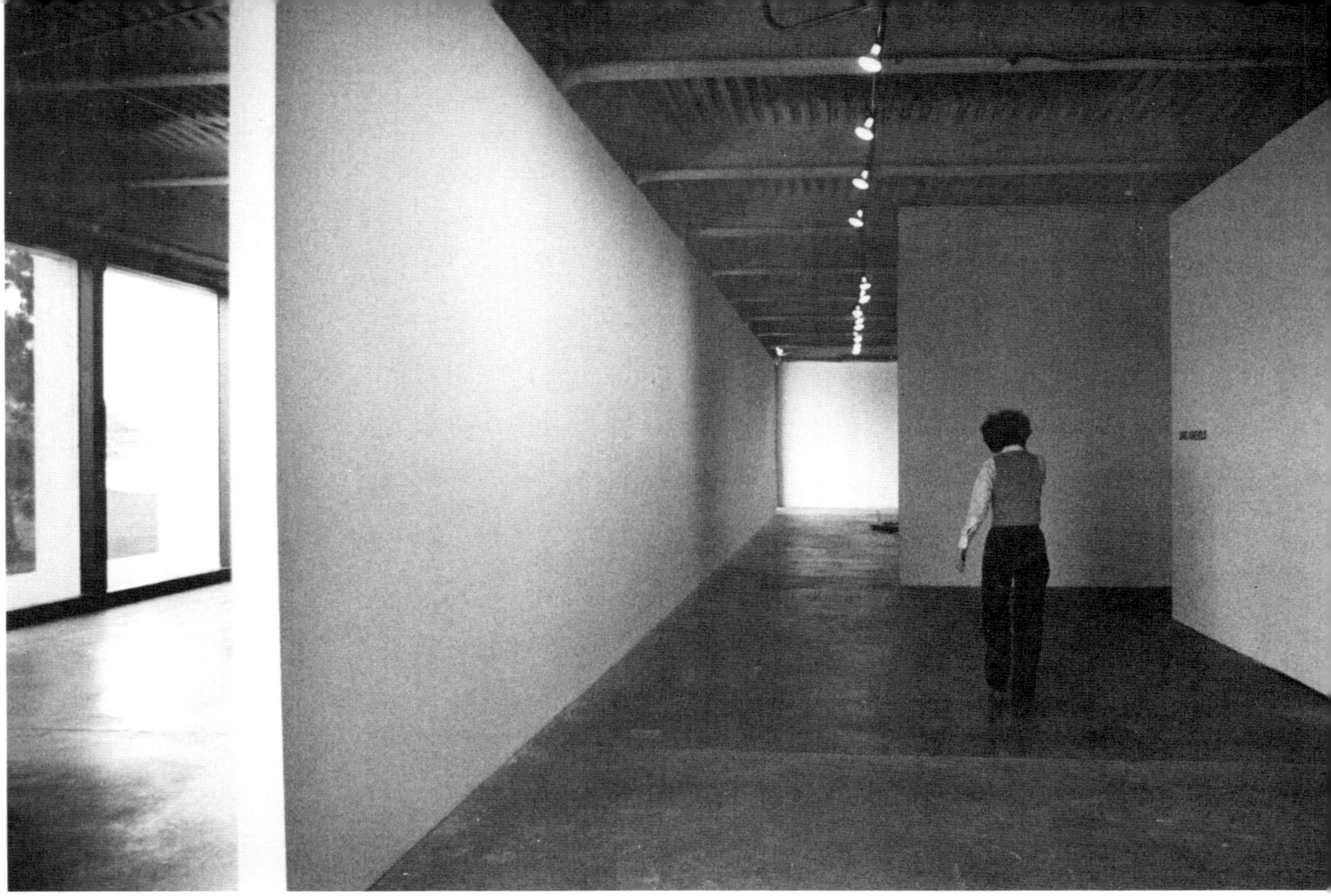

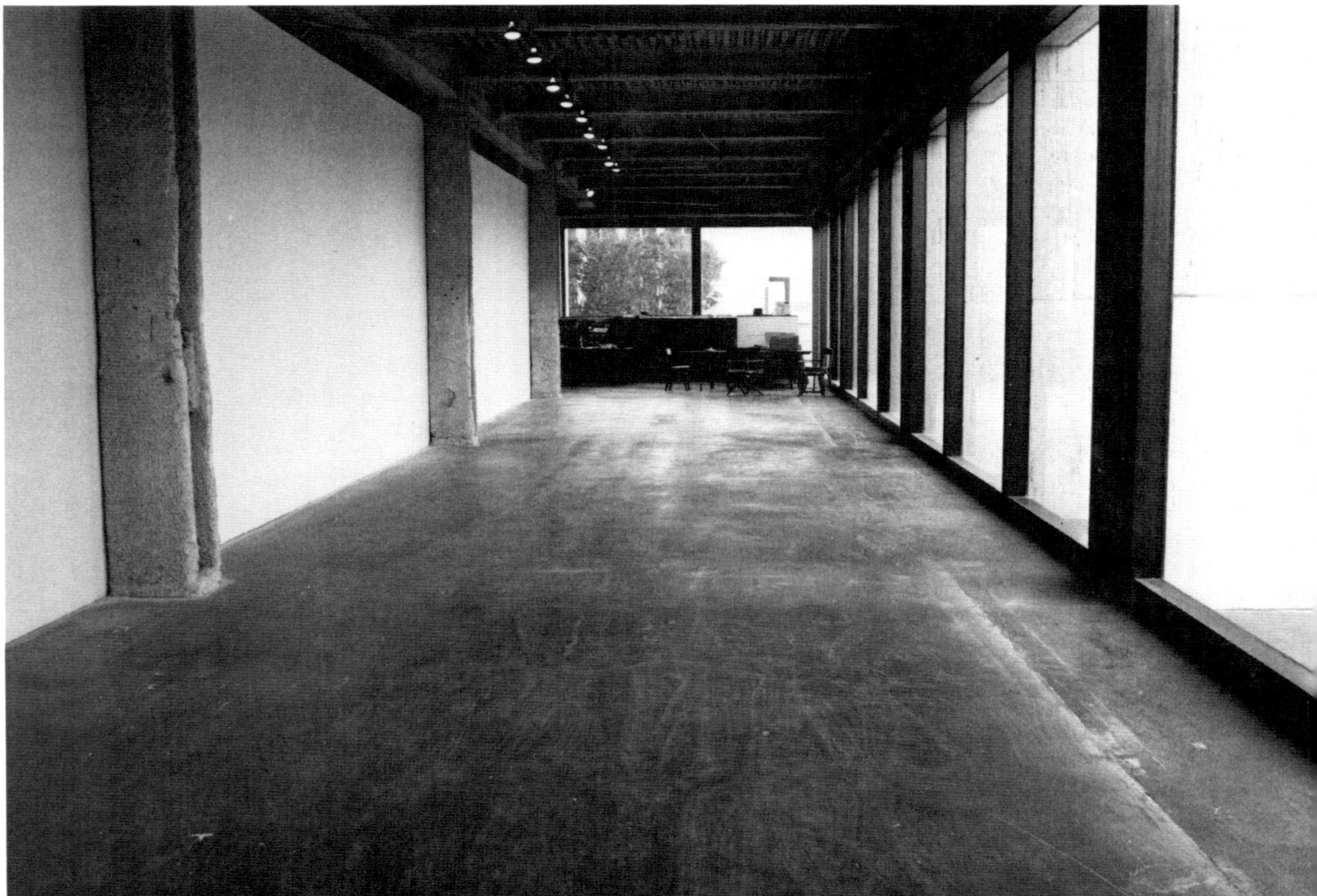

February 8–26, 1977
Morgan Thomas at Claire Copley Gallery Inc.
Claire Copley Gallery Inc. at Morgan Thomas
918 North La Cienega Boulevard, Los Angeles, California
2919 Santa Monica Boulevard, Santa Monica, California

MORGAN THOMAS AT 918 NORTH LA CIENEGA, LOS ANGELES, CALIFORNIA

FEBRUARY 1977

INSTALLATIONS

S	M	T	W	T	F	S
		1	2	3	4	5
6	7	8	9	10	11	12
			RAUL GUERRERO AND DOUG METZLER			
13	14	15	16	17	18	19
			PETER ALEXANDER AND DAVID BUNGAY			
20	21	22	23	24	25	26
			JAMES HAYWARD AND GARY KRUEGER			
27	28					

TUESDAY THROUGH SATURDAY: 12-5 PM AND BY APPT. 652-0900

**Michael Asher
February 8, through 26, 1977,
Morgan Thomas at Claire
Copley Gallery Inc. 918 North
La Cienega Boulevard, Los
Angeles, California 90069,
telephone 652-0900**

FEBRUARY 8 THROUGH FEBRUARY 12:   DANIEL BUREN
                                   peintures sur toile

FEBRUARY 15 THROUGH FEBRUARY 19:   ON KAWARA
                                   postcards

FEBRUARY 22 THROUGH FEBRUARY 26:   WILLIAM LEAVITT
                                   photographs

**Michael Asher
February 8, through 26, 1977,
Claire Copley Gallery Inc. at
Morgan Thomas, 2919 Santa
Monica Boulevard, Santa
Monica, California 90404,
telephone 828-4676**

Announcement of the Morgan Thomas Gallery exhibitions on
display at the Claire Copley Gallery during the installation of
Michael Asher's work in February 1977.

Announcement of the Claire Copley Gallery exhibitions on
display at the Morgan Thomas Gallery during the installation
of Michael Asher in February 1977.

Joint announcement of the Claire Copley/Morgan Thomas
Gallery for the Michael Asher installation. Front and back.

This work opened two days before the installation at the Los Angeles Institute of Contemporary Art concluded. Some time in early November, I was asked, almost simultaneously by two Los Angeles gallery owners, to have an exhibition. Claire Copley, with whom I had already exhibited in 1974 (s. page 95), asked me to do a second exhibition at the same location. Morgan Thomas, who owned a gallery on Santa Monica Boulevard, invited me to show for the first time in her space. The Claire Copley Gallery was situated at street level on La Cienega Boulevard, an area where most of the Los Angeles galleries were located, and received a steady flow of gallery visitors. Morgan Thomas was located in Santa Monica some twenty-five minutes' drive away, on the far west side of Los Angeles, on the second floor of a building on Santa Monica Boulevard. This area of Santa Monica was mainly a small business district, and had only a few isolated art galleries and therefore comparably fewer gallery visitors. Claire Copley's gallery had been a commercial storefront space, now transformed into a gallery with a square footage of approximately three times the size of the Morgan Thomas space which was a former apartment, transformed into a relatively small exhibition space. There were two signs identifying the Claire Copley Gallery, one painted on the front window and another larger sign mounted on the front of the building; the Morgan Thomas space was announced to the public by a small inscription on the door of the building. The works on exhibition at the Claire Copley Gallery could be seen from the storefront window; the Morgan Thomas space had three small windows on the second floor that had been drywalled over to allow for more exhibition wall surface. The Claire Copley Gallery showed East-Coast and European artists as frequently as it showed West-Coast artists, and most of the work was historically associated with post-Minimal and Conceptual art. Morgan Thomas exhibited predominantly local West-Coast works by artists who were primarily painters and sculptors. It was generally believed at the time that the Claire Copley Gallery was a place that would take risks and that it was exhibiting the most progressive work; the Morgan Thomas Gallery on the other hand was a gallery where young and lesser known local artists were given an opportunity to exhibit for the first time. The Claire Copley Gallery regularly advertised its exhibitions in a major art journal; the Morgan Thomas Gallery hardly ever advertised. In spite of these differences, a substantial number of people within the community who were actively interested in the arts regularly visited and supported both galleries, and the art communtiy's adherence to the two galleries was generally equal. Also, both gallery owners mutually supported each other's activities and programs.

Taking all of these differences into account as well as the galleries' shared interest in my work, I suggested to Claire Copley and Morgan Thomas that they jointly and simultaneously install one of my works. I further posed that they exchange their gallery spaces for a regular exhibition period. The proposal stipulated that all regular day-to-day functions of both galleries, including the installation of works of artists whom they represented, would have to be carried out in the other's space. The proposal also stipulated that the artists and works to be shown simultaneously were to be selected by the gallery owners and I did not have to be informed of their choice. It was agreed as well that the artists exhibiting during this time would be informed about my installation. All objects necessary for the continuation of regular gallery business (i.e., typewriter, files, photographs, library, desks, and chairs) would remain in place unless either part did not agree to the use of the other's equipment during the exhibition. Furthermore, telephone calls would be either forwarded by a telephone exchange service or, during gallery hours, be directly forwarded by the gallery owners or their secretaries. Obviously all other secretarial activities would also be carried out in the other gallery's space.

On November 20, 1976, I asked Claire Copley whether she would be willing to consider the proposal for her gallery. At first, she was reluctant to accept on the grounds that her integrity as a dealer would not allow her to exhibit artists' work in a space other than

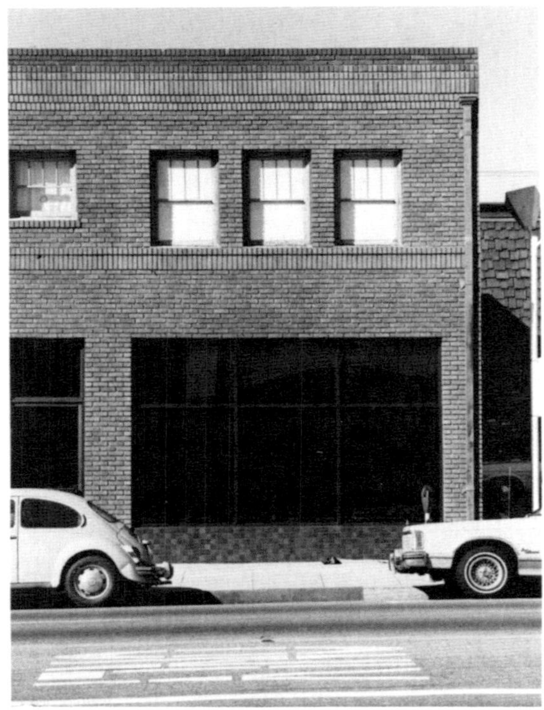

Building on 2919 Santa Monica Blvd., Santa Monica, CA., where the Morgan Thomas Gallery was located on the second floor. Photograph by Gary Krueger.

the one they had previously approved and been involved with. By November 24, Claire Copley had accepted the proposal, however. On November 27, 1976, I submitted the same proposal to Morgan Thomas, informing her of Claire Copley's agreement to the exhibition project. Morgan Thomas accepted the proposition immediately, contingent on her being able to synchronize her exhibition schedule with the Copley Gallery's. Subsequently I met with both gallery owners to clarify the project, its implications, and our mutual responsibilities. All stipulations of the proposal were agreed to. A mutually acceptable exhibition period of three weeks was chosen. A press release was formulated, and a joint announcement, to be designed by myself, was accepted.

The announcement card was placed on the bulletin board at Morgan Thomas and on the Main desk at Claire Copley to announce the exhibition to visitors. The galleries also agreed to mail out announcement cards for exhibitions by other artists occurring during my installation.

Both gallery owners, when actually exchanging galleries on the Sunday and Monday prior to the exhibition, did not consider it necessry to accept my offer of assistance since, ultimately, only a few objects had to be moved.

Morgan Thomas opened an exhibition of Paul Guerrero and Doug Metzler on the same day my work began. The second week she showed an exhibition by Peter Alexander and David Bungay, and the third week an exhibition by James Hayward and Gary Kruger. Claire Copley, during the same period, showed several works by Daniel Buren the first week, postcards by On Kawara the second week, and photographs by William Leavitt the third week. I was assured that all artists had agreed to show simultaneously with my exhibition.

During the exhibition each gallery had three different groups of visitors: First, those who, having seen the announcement of my exhibition, came to see the galleries in their new setting; second, those who were unaware of my work, but were acquainted with the galleries and their owners and had simply come in to see an exhibition; and third, those who were visiting either gallery for the first time, and were therefore intitially unaware of the exchange.

Once the two gallery owners had actually moved, they had to spend some time trying to adapt to their new situations and their slightly altered day-to-day operations. Each of them was confronted with the problem of installing an exhibition in a space with which she had no previous experience.

Claire Copley adapted successfully in a practical sense to the new gallery space. She took great care to have each of the three exhibitions installed in order to establish a continuity of exhibition content and presentation that was consistent with her own gallery. Yet personally, as she mentioned on several occasions, she did not adapt as successfully since, for several reasons she felt uncomfortable in the new location. First, because of its relative isolation from the visiting public; second, because of the substantially reduced gallery space; and, third, because she felt awkward about exhibiting artists' works in a location different from the one she had anticipated for them.

Morgan Thomas, on the other hand, seemed to be more excited about being in the new gallery environment and she also seemed to particularly enjoy the increased communication with the larger number of visitors at the La Cienega Boulevard location. She created a casual atmosphere in the gallery by moving the office chairs into the exhibition area so that visitors could sit down and view the exhibition in a relaxed setting. She installed the exhibitions in the new gallery space in a way that was similar to her usual style of presenting art, and she seemed·to have no problem adapting this style to the new environment.

Having been asked by two galleries at approximately the same time to do an exhibition I was confronted with the problem of the traditional art-market strategy of exhibiting one artist in two or more commercial institutions at the same time. Normally, two galleries implement a joint presentation to create the illusion of a certain degree of objective, historical necessity of one author's work. In this way, a gallery at-

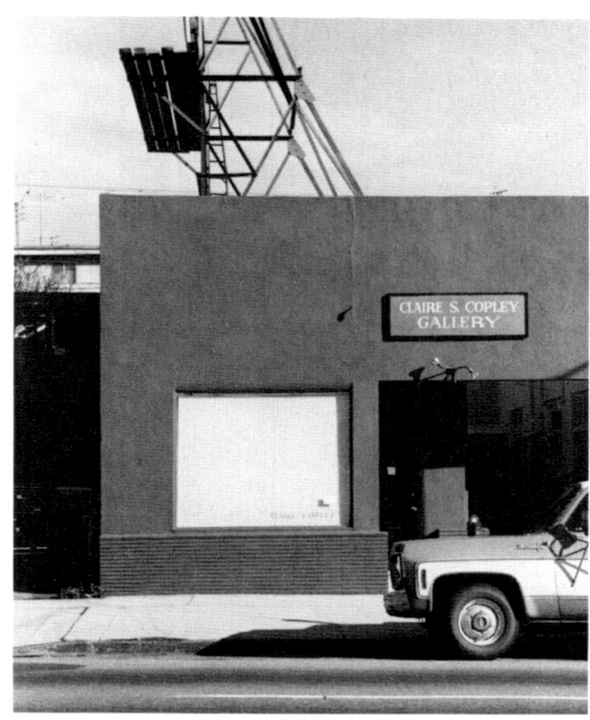

Facade of the Claire Copley Gallery on 918 North La Cienega Blvd., Los Angeles, CA. Photograph by Gary Krueger.

tempts to increase a work's impact on the market. It was usually understood that a double-gallery presentation could not be shared with any other artist since that would automatically decrease the presence and impact of the work. In this instance, however, the situation was different since both gallery owners had initially been unaware of the other's invitation to exhibit my work individually. I therefore decided to return their invitation and invite them myself to collaborate on this particular exhibition project.

In contradistinction to the usual isolation that follows increased presence and impact in double-gallery presentations, this simultaneous installation of my work did not prohibit other artists from showing in both galleries at the same time as my exhibition. The structure of this work did not, therefore, materially or formally, in any way whatsoever, impose on or interfere with the work of the other artists exhibiting concurrently with me. In a reverse sense, the work of the other artists sharing the exhibition time and space (whatever its materials or presentation format) could not impose upon or interfere with the structure of my work.

However, since my work caused both a temporal and spatial dislocation of the works in the exhibition (in its disjunction of the galleries from their usual spatial and operative frame), my work functioned as a framing device. Paradoxically, this put both the other exhibitions in the two galleries and my single installation, which exchanged and synthesized those two galleries, into context.

Ultimately, all elements had to operate in relation to each other in order to activate this work: the individual work, the gallery as a functioning exhibition institution, the gallery owners' collaboration, and the individual artists' participation in the exhibition. At the same time, the work asked for nothing more than what every artist would usually ask to have realized in the installation of a work for exhibition. The exhibition by the other artists, juxtaposed in the framework of the gallery spaces, were left intact, as conventional exhibitions by the framing device of my installation.

The two gallery exhibitions displayed works de-fined traditionally as commodities, with my work which programmatically negated that status. By referring the two gallery institutions back upon themselves and mediating their function—which normally was to mediate the object/commodity—this work intervened in the dominant distribution form of the work of art. Therefore, in this installation, the two galleries, as mediators of objects, became the object of the work itself. Through the device of disjunction and juxtaposition, the work—as much as it was intrinsically a part of the actual physical location and the commercial context in which these two galleries operated —achieved a dimension of structural autonomy that was intricately connected at all points with the determinant factors of its framework. The situational aspect of this work, however, was not primarily embodied in the actual material elements of the context within which the work interfered. But, since it interfered directly with the ideological convention of commercial exhibition practice, it had to abandon any material manipulation whatsoever, in favor of a practice that ultimately had to be perceived as social practice.

Inasmuch as any attempt at social practice within aesthetic practice seems to reject or ignore the specificity of formal and plastic concerns, this installation was inescapably reclaimed by the determining framework of its cultural conventions, such as the isolation of the work in individual autonomy and its subsequent appropriation by and relegation to the aesthetic discourse. These conventions alone, along with the rigidly formalized organization of the daily activities in the commercial institutions within which the work operated, already guaranteed the work's formal characteristics.

Commercial gallery exhibition practice is involved in the construction of individual identities at various levels which appear to be separate but are essentially interwoven. The individual identity of artists and the identity of their works as products are as integral to the gallery practice as the individual identity of the gallery owners and the identity of their artistic programs which specify and differentiate the various institutional activities from and against each other. These are paradoxically, as individual identities, subjected to the abstracting forces of the market as the ultimate institution.

Since contemporary practice confronts these cultural conditions and has to inscribe itself within them, the situational function of my work excluded any particularization or individuality as essentially contradictory to the intentions of the work. Therefore, the work could be exhibited by potentially anyone who desired to do so.

In spite of the fact that this work operated on a different level of physical materiality (that of the actual cultural institution and its functions rather that the concrete material embodiment of those functions in individual material objects), it took as its point of departure the very specific difference of the institutions' concrete existence: the actual locations of the two galleries.

This shift from concrete physical particularity to the abstract generality of the social institution, necessitated a new method of addressing the material givens of a situation. Comparing it, for example, with my earlier installation at the Claire Copley Gallery, this work addressed a larger scale of physical givens and a wider scope of social and cultural conditions by enlisting two galleries in their totality of functions as sociocultural institutions.

The work's scope ranged from the most minute detail of exhibition practice (the announcement card functioning as the sign of the exhibition) to the totality of gallery functions in order to insist on the institutional nature of artistic production, distribution, and reception.

My labor, as author, to define the work consisted of the organization and administration of the gallery exchange. This work, therefore, suspended its own further administrative handling and commodification. I administered a work which could not be subjected to any other administration but which contained in its totality all administrative labor performed by the gallery owners upon works of art (possibly including my own) by other artists subjected to their administration.

The question arises as to whether my administrative labor could be considered as material production, or, whether it remained a simple declaration in the manner of the readymade within the discourse of aesthetic practice alone.

The material transformation of social practice—as a condition of production—was generated by this work when the galleries actually exchanged location and property. As much as the structures of each gallery were subjected simultaneously to both administrative declaration and material dislocation, they nevertheless remained—as dislocated and disjuncted elements —operative in their functions.

On the one hand, in its administrative definition, the work inscribed itself as aesthetic practice into the ideological discourse of the prevailing institutional character of cultural production. On the other hand, the work operated as an actual material transformation of the production-distribution chain within contemporary social practice.

The collaboration in this work between the author and the other artists as well as the gallery owners and the visitors is seemingly comparable to the collaborative venture of the work at the Los Angeles Institute of Contemporary Art (see p146). It was the group of paid participants and not the director and staff who played the prominent role in the LAICA work; whereas in this work, the gallery owners were of primary importance. In the LAICA work I employed paid participants; in this work I was employed as an artist. Here the gallery owners, even though dislocated as a result of my intervention, found their own preexisting structure and out of sheer necessity, had to maintain the limited program of daily institutional functions. In the LAICA work, the participants, even though employed and paid, could operate without limitations according to their own needs.

As this installation focused on institutional conventions, it qualified as a situational work. Since this installation functioned within a totality of common conventions which are universally shared by commercial

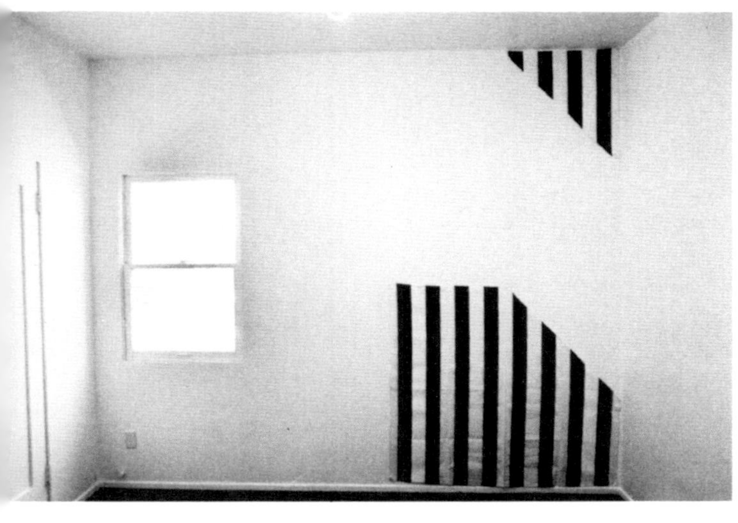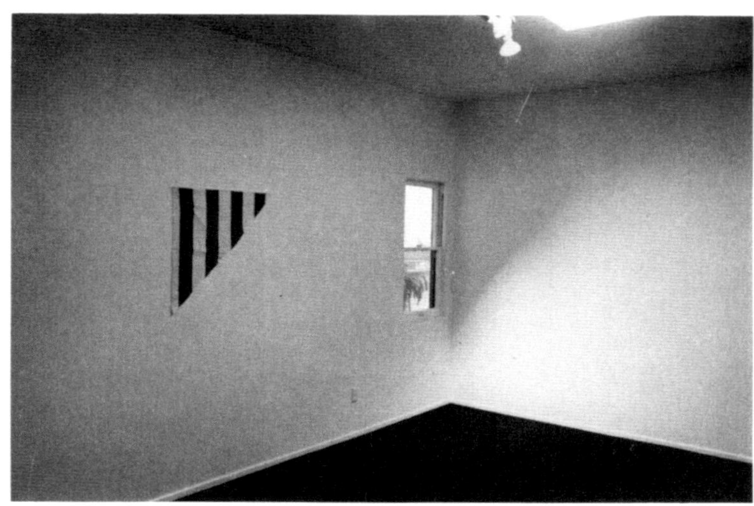

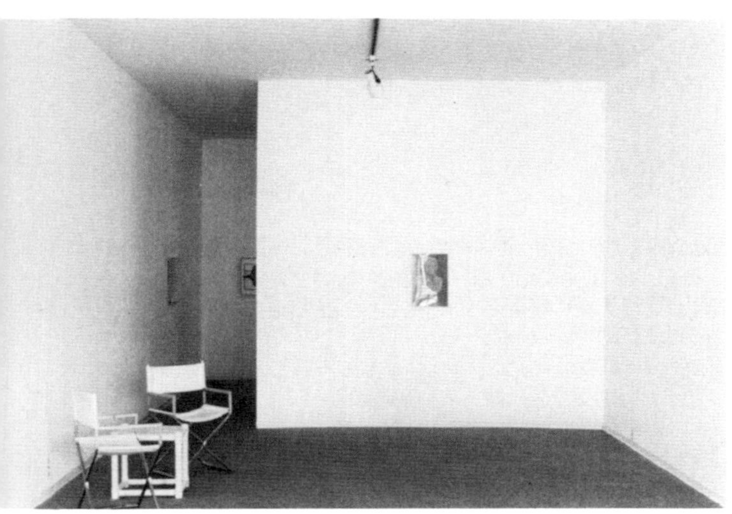

galleries, it is conceivable that this work could potentially operate with any two galleries in a similar situation.

As historical conditions change, it becomes questionable whether situational aesthetics can still be successfully applied and remain operative. A situational analysis of the concrete embodiment of the conditions framing aesthetic practice, either manifested in specific elements (e.g., constructed or movable gallery walls), or in situations (e.g., exhibition themes or institutional particularities), is no longer capable of adequately addressing the universal conditions of abstraction within which the work of art has to exist. Those conditions, even though they had been addressed concretely in past situational work that had seemed tending toward social practice, in fact were often ignored, the degree to which a work remained within the formal determinations of modernist high art remained obscure. Situational aesthetics also often reproduced the abstractions of the modernist tradition, including that of the commodity status of the work which, by necessity, disconnects itself from any situational context other than the market.

This work's concrete presence forced the universal abstraction out into the open reality of the market and seemed to strip the two gallery owners of the system of identity references which had been theirs within their gallery shell.

By opening the work's structure and assimilating it to the dimensions of universal abstraction, the work's material definition and formal manifestation had to be reduced to the administrative act of an announcement card design.

Very much to my surprise, several months after the conclusion of this exhibition, both Claire Copley and Morgan Thomas decided to collaborate on a non-profit project in Los Angeles which they called "Foundation for Art Resources." This foundation initially declared as its goal the raising and providing of funds for contemporary artistic practice independent of a fixed exhibition space and schedule.

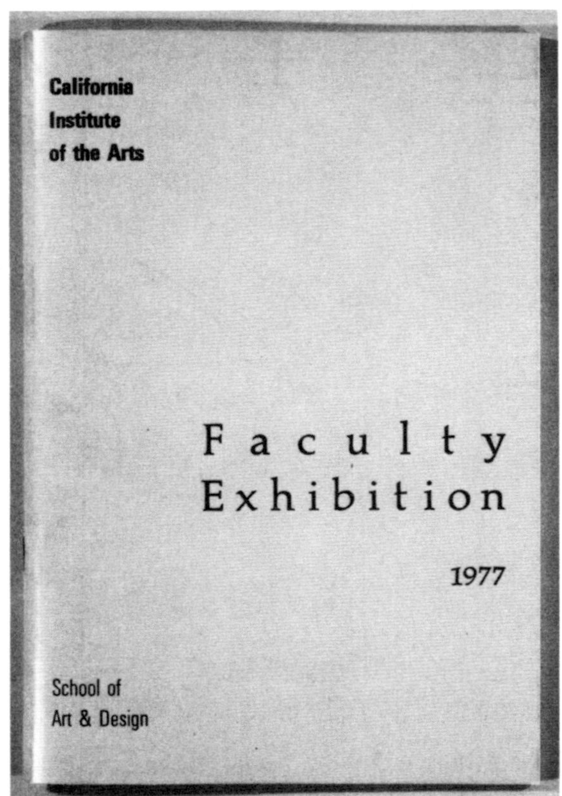

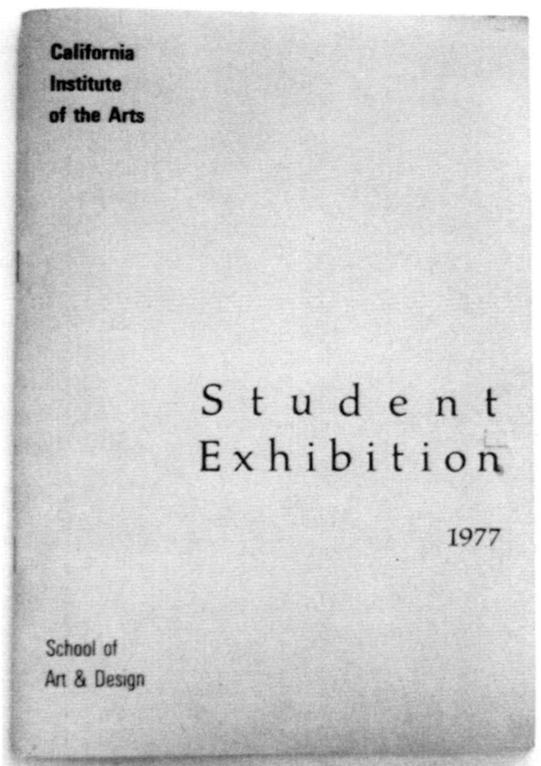

Faculty Exhibition and Student Exhibition catalogues.

Ground plan of the Main Gallery at the California Institute of the Arts. Drawing by Michael Asher. A reproduction of this ground plan functioned as an exhibition handout during the installation.

As an instructor at the California Institute of the Arts, I was invited to contribute a work to a faculty/student exhibition in 1977. The two exhibitions were installed in the largest open area of the Institute, which contains the main gallery and the mezzanine.

The main gallery measures 112 feet on the north-south axis and 56 feet 6 inches on the east-west axis. The mezzanine follows the perimeter of the main gallery at a height of 14 feet 8½ inches above the main gallery floor. It extends 33 feet on its north-south axis and 14 feet 6 inches on its east-west axis as a box construction forming the floor of the mezzanine and the ceiling of the overhang into the gallery. It is 14 feet 6 inches from the ceiling of the main gallery. Main gallery and mezzanine form an atrium space 99 feet long on the north-south axis and 31 feet 8 inches wide on the east-west axis, with a height of 19 feet 2½ inches. Main gallery and mezzanine are connected by a stairwell extending 19 feet within both spaces. The front plane covering the mezzanine box construction facing the atrium is built of dry wall and painted white. It begins 11 feet above the main gallery floor and is 44½ inches high. This plane continues around the entire perimeter of the atrium.

The student exhibition was installed in the main gallery and contained works by all B.F.A. and M.F.A. students graduating in 1977. A faculty exhibition was installed simultaneously on the mezzanine level of the main gallery, containing works by all instructors of the School of Art and Design at the Institute. Although student exhibitions occurred regularly during the school year in both the main gallery and the mezzanine, this was the only faculty exhibition to my knowledge at the Institute within recent years.

Students and faculty agreed there should be a division between the two exhibitions; and the main gallery, a more traditional exhibition space, was allocated to the students for easier access by visitors during the graduation ceremonies.

For this exhibition I had one hole ¼ inch in diameter drilled into each of the four front planes of the mezzanine construction. Each one of these holes was

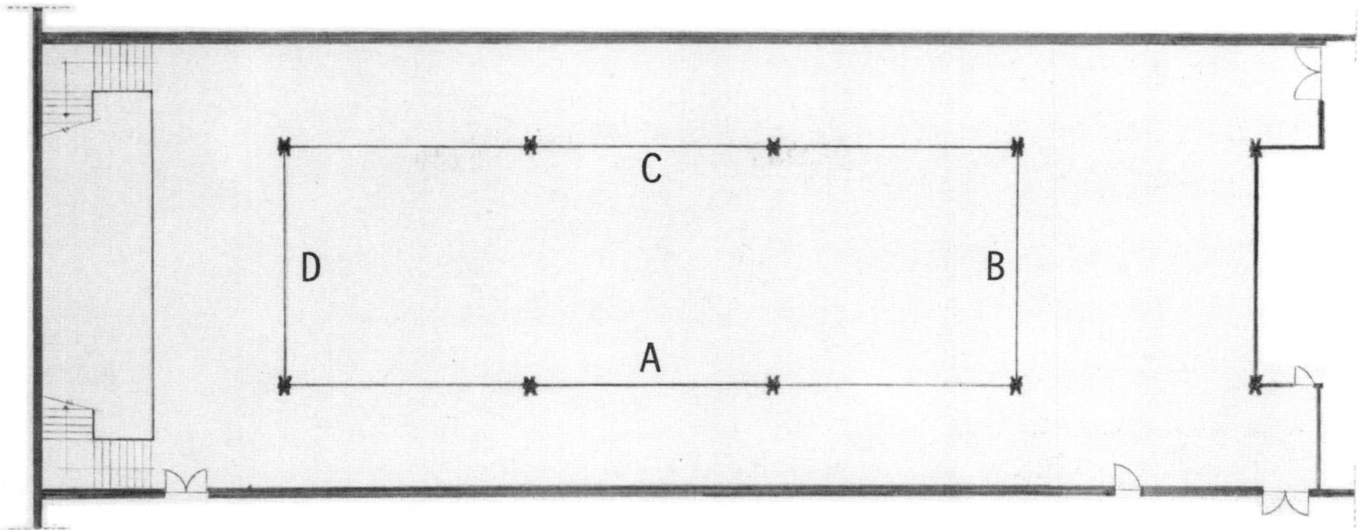

Michael Asher   A hole through the center of each horizontal wall areas (A, B, C, D) between the mezzanine and the main gallery

located at the horizontal and vertical center of the plane. The diameter of the holes was determined by visibility from the furthest possible viewpoint in the gallery, from the south-east corner diagonally to the north side (approximately 130 feet). Using different size paper dots as models, I chose the size that was at the threshold of my sight. Once I had decided on the size, I drilled the holes carefully through the dry wall facing.

A second element of my installation, located in the Faculty Exhibition on the mezzanine, was an 8½-inch-by-6-inch pad of paper which was congruent with the format of the catalogue and showed the viewer a diagram description and identification of the work. The pad was placed on a pedestal, approximately 4 feet high, next to the wall near the stairwell and when all the sheets had been torn off, a new pad was put in its place.

The work was either the smallest in the exhibition, since the four holes put together could have been contained in a 1 inch surface mark; or the largest, if the four holes were viewed as extending across the entire gallery within a space 99 feet by 31 feet 8 inches.

In spite of their being drilled relatively deeply into the mezzanine plane, the holes could have easily appeared to be painted black dots and only on close inspection could the viewers identify them as actually penetrating the plane's surface. The minute holes drilled into the frame of the main exhibition gallery might have been lost to the viewer without the accompanying description, yet, due to that contradiction between architectural size frame and minute pictorial mark, they could, once discovered, be perceived as predominant elements. In fact, the holes appeared to be particularly conspicuous since they were not only placed as focal points within an architectural perspective but met the viewer's eye along the main lines of the foot-traffic in the gallery. The work functioned like graffiti in the sense that by marking an instant and abstract sign it pointed to overlooked space and staked out its own territory.

Two separate but similar catalogues were printed, one for the student and one for the faculty exhibition, containing photographic reproductions of most of the work. Since I wanted my work to be installed only the night before the opening and the catalogue had been printed by then, a space in the catalogue, allocated for information about my work, contained the following notice:

Michael Asher's installation is not reproducible for a contribution to the catalogue.

The boxed-in structure below the mezzanine floor functioned as a frame separating the faculty and student exhibitions. Having spent the school year working with both students and faculty, I decided to use this structure as a framing device between the two exhibitions. So that my work would reflect my activity at the school I wanted it to be located within the context of both exhibitions.

Art instructors should have their work effectively presented and received outside of the academic institution. A work that has been developed inside the institution and is employed as a teaching device will, to my understanding, stand to loose its essential dialectical relation with reality and therefore eventually suppresses student motivation. For this reason I had originally considered not participating in the faculty exhibition, but ultimately I decided to contribute in order to prove or disprove to myself the validity of these observations.

After seeing the entire exhibition and the place my work had in it, my work seemed to remain operative; but only within the limits of the exhibition's specific conditions, that is, as a statement about the relationship between students and instructors in an institutionalized art context.

West view of installation. Detail.

North view.

South view.

East view.

West view. Photographs by Gines Guillen.

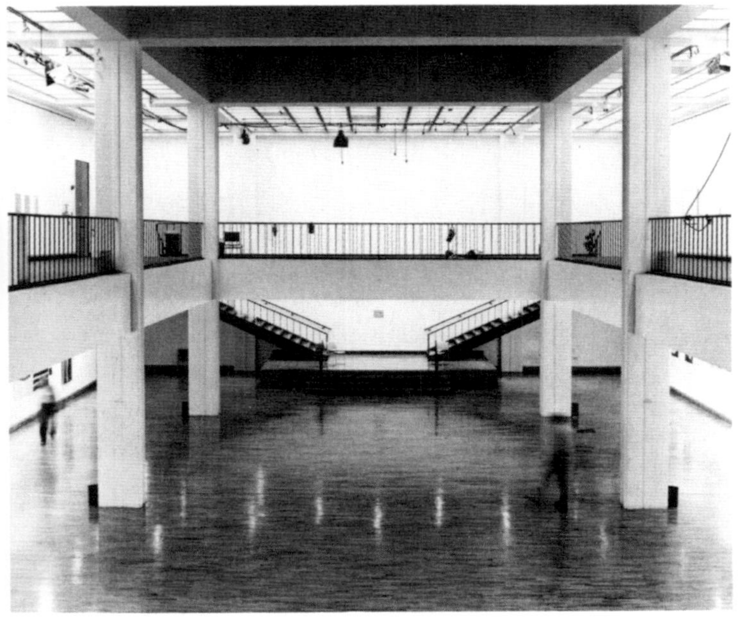

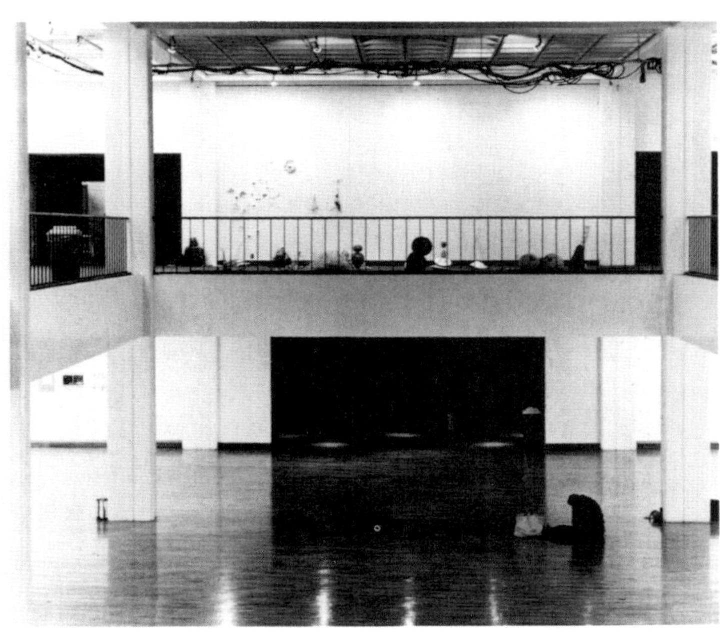

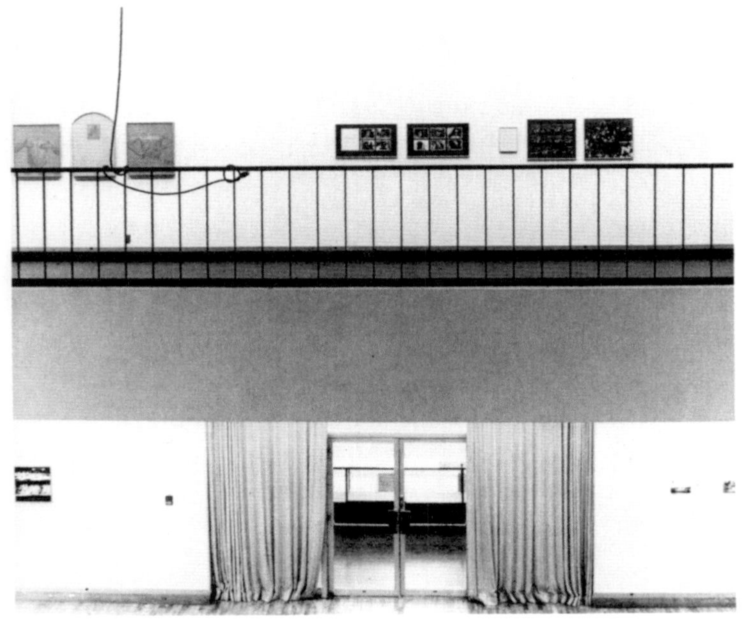

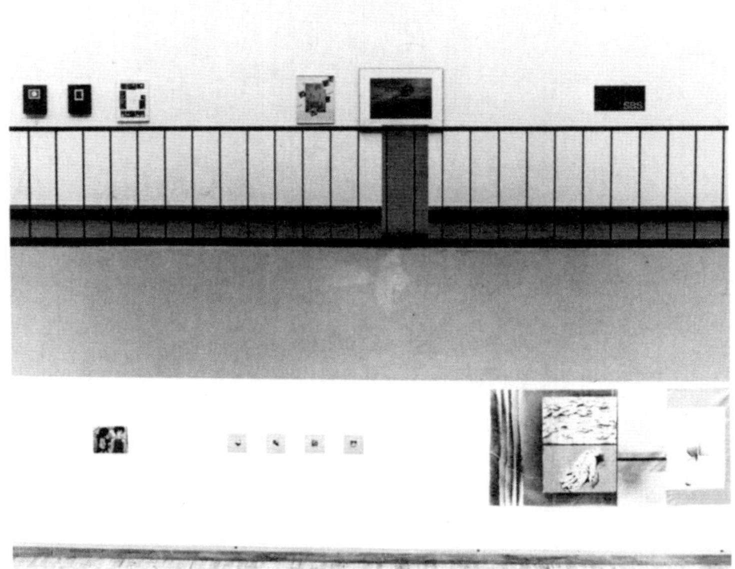

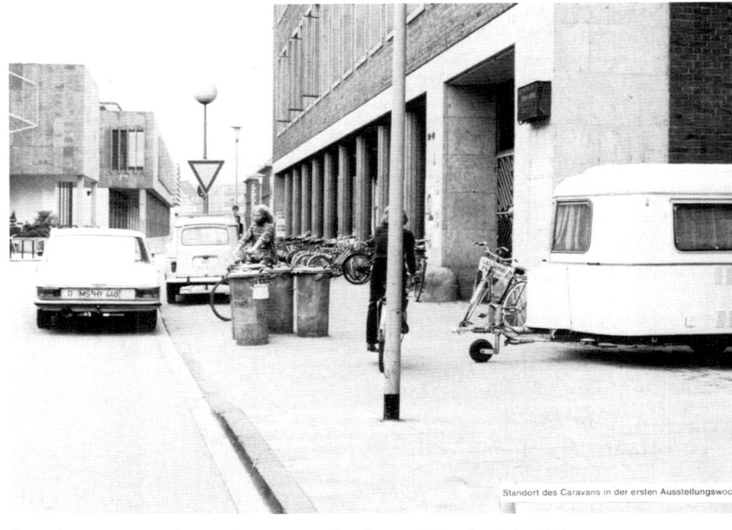

Catalogue page from the second volume (Projects) of the
exhibition catalogue *Skulptur*, Münster 1977, showing
the first position of the trailer on the right and the entrance of
the museum with a sculpture by Josef Albers on the left.

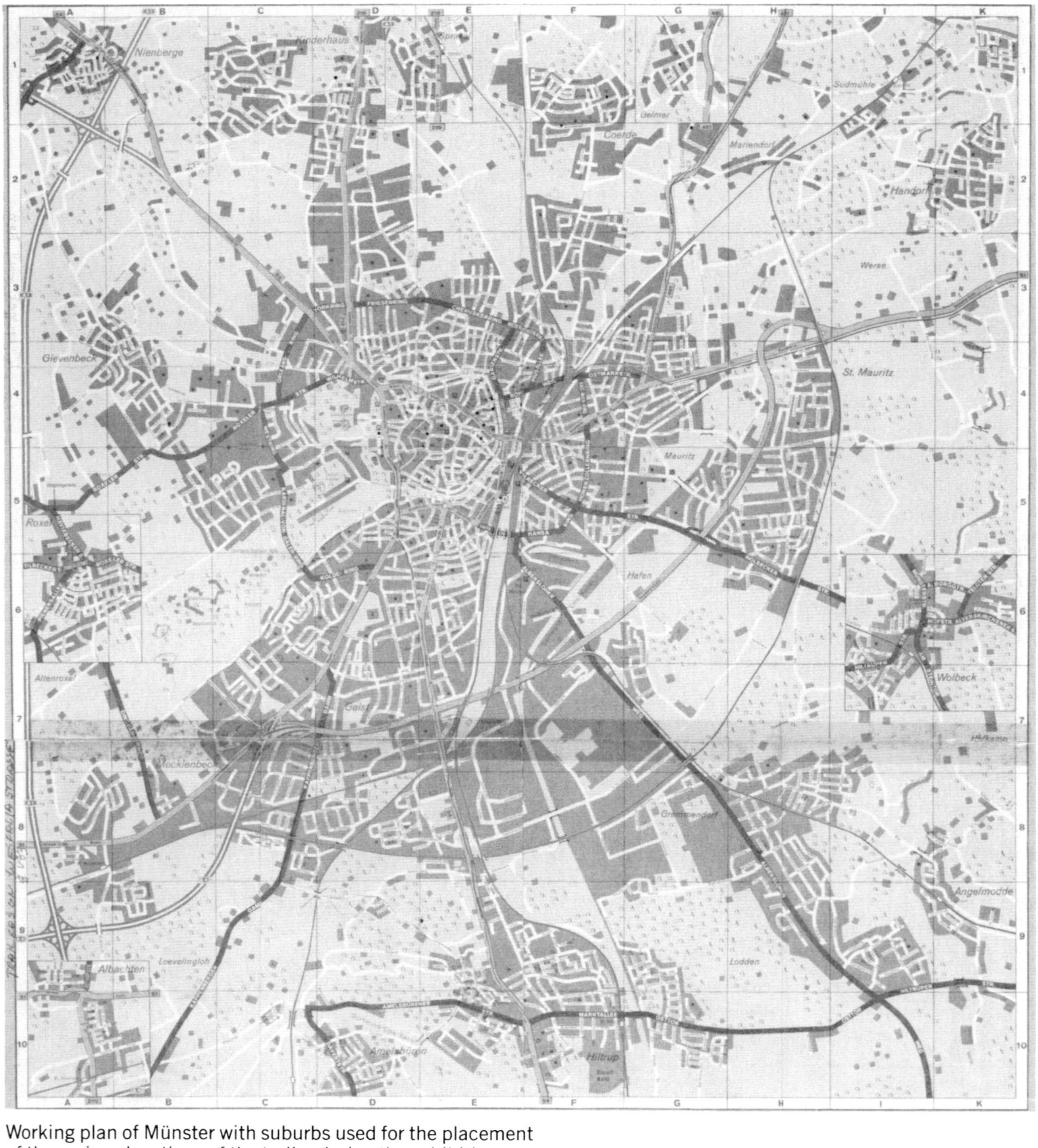

164 Working plan of Münster with suburbs used for the placement
of the various locations of the trailer during the exhibition.

Skulptur
Ausstellung in Münster 1977
3. Juli bis 13. November

Projektbereich

Michael Asher
1943 in Los Angeles geboren
lebt in Venice, Kalifornien

„Installation Münster"
Standort:
19 verschiedene Plätze in und um Münster
Durchführung:
Dauer der Ausstellung

Vorhaben in Münster

Es handelt sich hierbei um das Aufstellen eines
Caravans in und um Münster für die Dauer dieser
Ausstellung, die sich über 19 Wochen erstreckt.
Der Caravan (annähernd 4 m lang) wird jeden
Montag in der Nähe von Gebäuden oder Grünan-
lagen neu plaziert, wobei insgesamt 19 verschiedene Standorte gewäht werden. Der Hinweis auf
den Standort des Caravans und die Zeit, während
er dort zu finden ist, ist im Foyer des Museums zu
erhalten.

> Parksituation der ersten Woche 3. bis 11. Juli
> Siegelkammer und Pferdegasse

Skulptur
Ausstellung in Münster 1977
3. Juli bis 13. November

Projektbereich

Michael Asher
1943 in Los Angeles geboren
lebt in Venice, Kalifornien

„Installation Münster"
Standort:
19 verschiedene Plätze in und um Münster
Durchführung:
Dauer der Ausstellung

Vorhaben in Münster

Es handelt sich hierbei um das Aufstellen eines
Caravans in und um Münster für die Dauer dieser
Ausstellung, die sich über 19 Wochen erstreckt.
Der Caravan (annähernd 4 m lang) wird jeden
Montag in der Nähe von Gebäuden oder Grünan-
lagen neu plaziert, wobei insgesamt 19 verschiedene Standorte gewählt werden. Der Hinweis auf
den Standort des Caravans und die Zeit, während
er dort zu finden ist, ist im Foyer des Museums zu
erhalten.

> Parkposition der zweiten Woche 11. bis 18. Juli
> Parkhaus Geisbergweg, unterhalb des Reg.-
> Präsidenten 1-3. Entweder Platz 62 o. Platz 5

Skulptur
Ausstellung in Münster 1977
3. Juli bis 13. November

Projektbereich

Michael Asher
1943 in Los Angeles geboren
lebt in Venice, Kalifornien

„Installation Münster"
Standort:
19 verschiedene Plätze in und um Münster
Durchführung:
Dauer der Ausstellung

Vorhaben in Münster

Es handelt sich hierbei um das Aufstellen eines
Caravans in und um Münster für die Dauer dieser
Ausstellung, die sich über 19 Wochen erstreckt.
Der Caravan (annähernd 4 m lang) wird jeden
Montag in der Nähe von Gebäuden oder Grünan-
lagen neu plaziert, wobei insgesamt 19 verschiedene Standorte gewählt werden. Der Hinweis auf
den Standort des Caravans und die Zeit, während
er dort zu finden ist, ist im Foyer des Museums zu
erhalten.

> Parkposition der dritten Woche 18. bis 25. Juli
> Alter Steinweg - Parkplatz der Fa. Hill

Skulptur
Ausstellung in Münster 1977
3. Juli bis 13. November

Projektbereich

Michael Asher
1943 in Los Angeles geboren
lebt in Venice, Kalifornien

„Installation Münster"
Standort:
19 verschiedene Plätze in und um Münster
Durchführung:
Dauer der Ausstellung

Vorhaben in Münster

Es handelt sich hierbei um das Aufstellen eines
Caravans in und um Münster für die Dauer dieser
Ausstellung, die sich über 19 Wochen erstreckt.
Der Caravan (annähernd 4 m lang) wird jeden
Montag in der Nähe von Gebäuden oder Grünan-
lagen neu plaziert, wobei insgesamt 19 verschiedene Standorte gewählt werden. Der Hinweis auf
den Standort des Caravans und die Zeit, während
er dort zu finden ist, ist im Foyer des Museums zu
erhalten.

> Parkposition der vierten Woche 25. 7. bis 1. 8.
> Kiffe-Pavillon, vor der Parkuhr Nr. 1063

Set of the first four exhibition handouts which were available at the front
desk of the museum for each of the nineteen weeks of the exhibition.

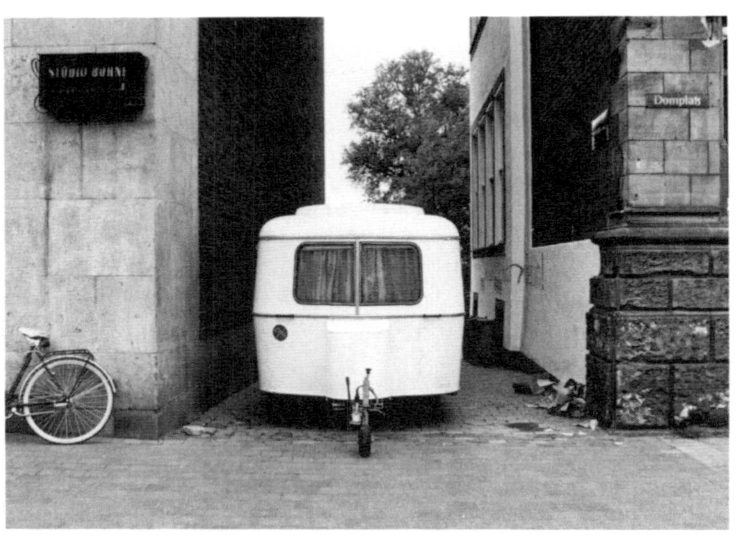

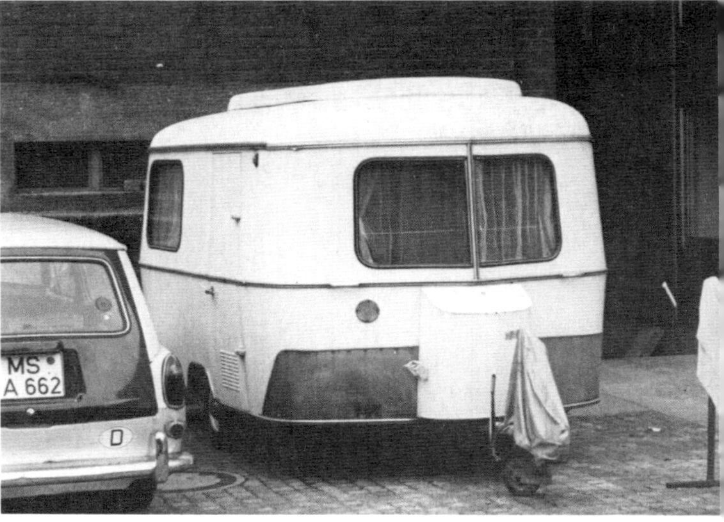

1

2

The "Skulptur" exhibition, sponsored by the West-fälisches Landesmuseum, Münster, West Germany, was divided in two parts. The first part, curated by Klaus Bussmann, functioned as a retrospective which "feature[d] important stages in the development of modern sculpture."[1] The second part of the exhibition, which was called "Project Section," was conceived and organized by Kasper Koenig. The following artists, in addition to myself, participated: Carl Andre, Joseph Beuys, Donald Judd, Richard Long, Walter de Maria, Bruce Nauman, Claes Oldenburg, Ulrich Rueckriem, and Richard Serra. It was proposed to the artists to either work with specific outdoor sites to which the museum had access, or to suggest sites that could possibly be used for the installation of outdoor sculpture.

Substantial funding for the exhibition was allocated by the museum, the local city government, and the provincial government. In addition to these sources, funds were also available for acquisition of outdoor sculptural projects. These funds derived from a law by which the government was required to spend 2 percent of the construction costs in the construction of all public buildings on visual art projects. Therefore, it was hoped that each outdoor installation of the sculptures in the exhibition would also be of interest to the city authorities in regard to future acquisition of those works.[1]

In the summer of 1976, I was invited to consider participating in the "Project Section" of the "Skulptur" exhibition. In order to visit and inspect the exhibition grounds, I traveled to Münster where I stayed from July 27 to 31, 1976. On September 1, 1976, I confirmed my participation in the exhibition in a letter to Kasper Koenig and I started working on several proposals for this project.

The setting of the exhibition was a landscaped park area in Münster, an early medieval city which had preserved many of its original planning features and historical architectural details. The city itself was nearby a lake and was surrounded by smaller villages, farmland, and forests.

During the subsequent period of approximately eleven months I submitted and discussed fourteen proposals for possible contributions to the "Skulptur" exhibition. All of them were either discarded for technical and financial reasons or turned out to be otherwise unfeasible. In late June 1977, I returned to Münster still assuming that I could bring a work to fruition. At this time I submitted three more proposals, one of which was finally accepted. The proposal was to have an ordinary trailer relocated weekly in and around the city of Münster. I decided upon nineteen various locations since the exhibition lasted for nineteen weeks. Since the museum/exhibition was closed on Mondays, on that day each week the trailer would be moved to its new location. Each week a pad of differently colored leaflet announcements was placed at the front desk of the museum which notified visitors to the exhibition where they could find the trailer in its current location. I selected locations for the trailer in both urban and suburban architectural and natural settings, in existing parking spaces, or just off the road. The locations were in all four directions (north, south, east, and west) from the center of the city but were not consistently in any one direction or particular pattern, since it was important to find locations where the trailer would be seen in context. The trailer was placed in what appeared to be perfectly obvious locations, in places where it might have appeared to be slightly out of context, and in locations where it would have been unlikely to appear altogether.

The method of placement was intended to create the impression that the trailer was an integral part of its surroundings, rather than an entity in or of itself. I used areas that were zoned for commercial and industrial purposes as well as parks, densely populated areas, and areas with isolated individual family residences. The trailer was located for the first week of the exhibition across the street from the front entrance of the museum in an alley leading to the university. The trailer's final and last location during the last week of the exhibition was also next to the university, but closer to the museum. After the first week the trailer was located on the north side of the cathedral in a parking lot adjacent to an open mall, then in a parking place

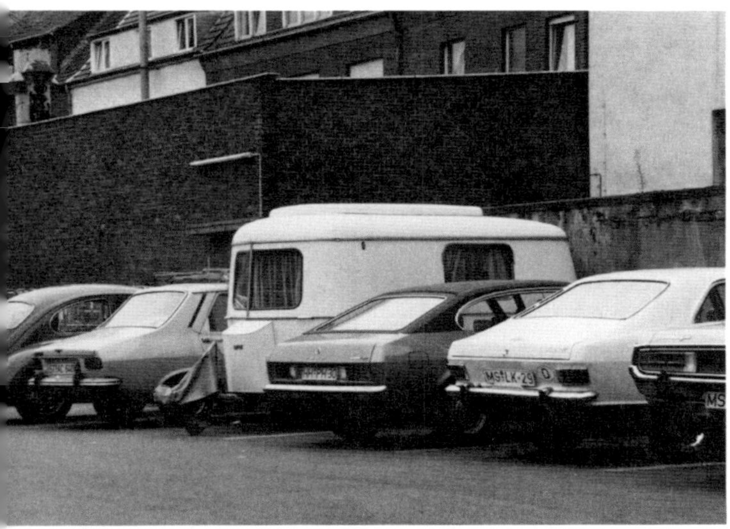

3

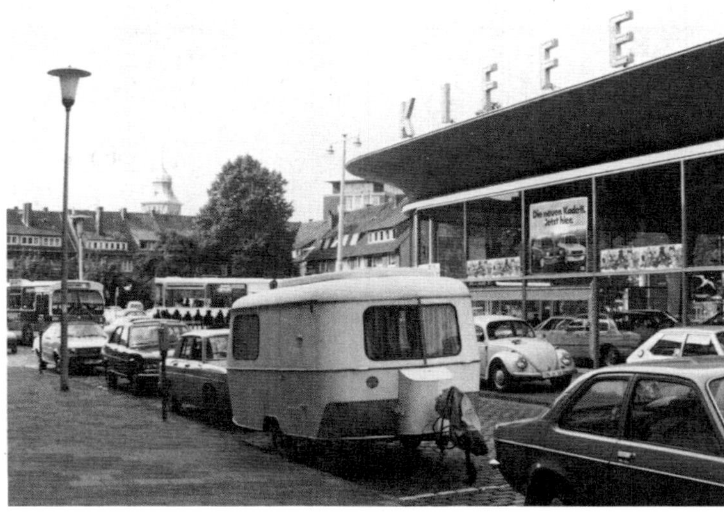

4

in front of a car dealer, in a wealthy residential area; next to parks, then in an industrial complex, then next to a canal, to a high-rise apartment building, and a school; at the end of a dead-end street; next to an urban shopping mall in a parking lot, a church, a store, and a torn-down building opposite a number of residences; in an empty lot, in a forest, in a large open parking lot in the city, in a parking lot in front of the train station, and, second to last, in front of a bar.

In order to find a trailer that would fulfill all the requirements of this particular installation, I bought a catalogue containing most of the currently manufactured trailers available in West Germany. The trailer that I eventually selected was not so large that it would dominate its location. It was compact, its design well-suited to its function, and recognizable as a West German product rather than unusual or foreign-looking.

The trailer was 4.56-meters long, and was rented from a trailer agency in Münster for the duration of the exhibition. When the trailer was moved to the above locations, the window curtains were closed and the door was locked. The locations branched out from the center of town (across the street from the museum) to 4.5 kilometers northwest of the city, approximately 5 kilometers to the northeast, and 2.5 kilometers to the west, 0.75 kilometers to the east, and 4.5 kilometers to the south.

Complete sequential viewing of all locations was possible, but not a necessary requirement for the viewer's understanding of the work. I was informed subsequent to the completion of the exhibition that people did in fact use the information sheet that I had provided at the museum counter, as a source of information to direct them to the actual location of the trailer at that moment. I have no knowledge of whether anybody viewed the work in all its sequential placements. I also do not know how many people, if any at all, might have discovered the trailer at a particular location and would have questioned its placement or perceived it as a work of art.

The sequential occurrence of one work by one artist provided an extended time frame for both viewer and work as opposed to the exhibition, where several works by various artists could be viewed in a condensed time frame. As the work was relocated each week it demanded from the potential viewer the added effort of traveling across town to see it. In opposition to the other outdoor sculptural installations, however, which could not relate travel distance to the specific interaction of the viewer's presence, the object, and the location, this work, by changing locations within a wide range of specific urban landscapes, set up a situational relationship with the viewer, rather than being simply specifically situated. The work therefore claimed to be situational, not only in terms of its concept and location but also in the way it expected to be addressed by the viewer. By multiplying context as opposed to maintaining any specific, singular context, the work increased its situational specificity.

This work responded to the concept of the exhibition and the inherently static tradition of public outdoor sculpture that it conveyed. Once set in place public outdoor sculpture cannot participate in the perpetually changing makeup of its surroundings. Unlike the dominant practice of public outdoor sculpture, this installation—due to its temporal specificity—did not remain identical to itself, nor did it repeat itself in a series of identical objects arbitrarily placed in various spatial contexts.

In earlier process sculpture the viewer was confronted with a finalized work, even if its production procedure became transparent. The viewer remained, therefore, in an abstract and static relationship with the concrete material and procedural change of the work.

Unlike earlier process-oriented sculpture, this work derived its temporal specificity from the structure and context of its location rather than from the constituent elements of its materials and production process.

The trailer as a functional object extended from reality and, partially suspended in function, evaded the abstraction implied in a process work. This object had, however, a double referent: to the context of the exhibition as a work of outdoor sculpture and to the real spatial and temporal context of its sequence of

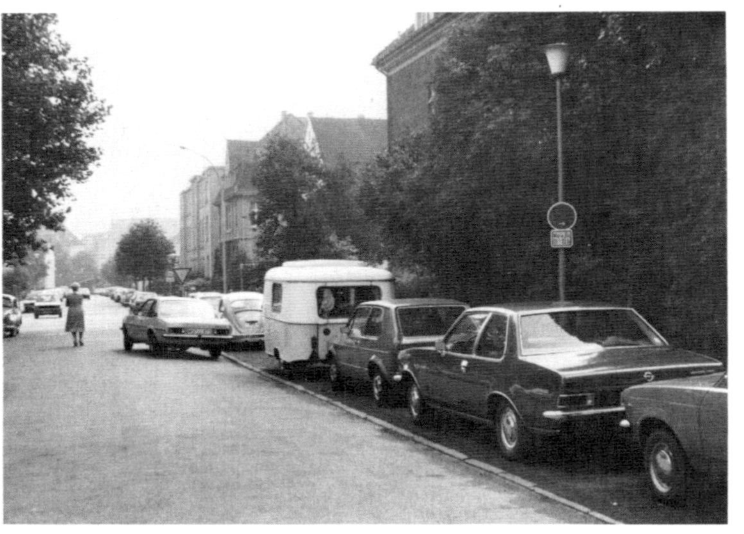

5

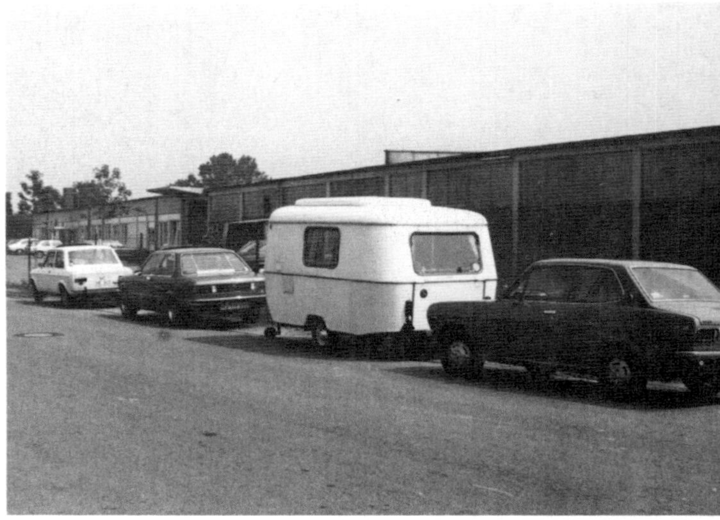

6

placements outside the exhibition. Both contexts were potentially experienced by the viewer in real time and space parallel to the exhibition framework. The viewer was linked by actual temporal and spatial displacement to the temporality and spatiality of the work.

Traditionally, public sculptural installations were legitimized by the inherent features of the category (outdoor sculpture) and those specific requirements of the commission. Public sculpture could therefore neither reflect upon its very mode of existence nor on its actual spatial placement. These traditions were so much taken for granted, that even the outdoor installations in this exhibition maintained the prior principles of public sculpture. The placement and context for these sculptural installations were arbitrarily derived from criteria which are essentially those that applied to the installation of indoor sculpture. By interconnecting the category (public outdoor sculpture) with the context (exhibition-subject) and the placement (the literal interaction between object and architectural framework), this work found its legitimation in its context and placement rather than in its category or commission. The temporal and spatial mobility specified the work's function and the viewer's perception of it as an installation that operated in an outdoor context determined by that funciton. It could not be reversed—unlike most other outdoor installations in this exhibition—back into the institutional exhibition framework. As a result of its function, the work as sculptural object could not become a separate satellite of the exhibition, but referred consistently to and depended upon the subject of the exhibition. By adding a dimension of temporal specificity to the specific placement of the work, the abstract and often arbitrary notion of place inherent in Minimal sculpture —whether installed indoors or outdoors—clearly became insufficient. My work while not being necessarily specific to a particular place, it actively breaks down into a variety of contextual relationships rather than particularizing itself as a static structure, which eventually prohibits contextualization.

Inevitably an outdoor work must be on a larger scale than sculptural works found in galleries or museums in order to identify itself in opposition to its architectural or natural setting, such as a plaza, mall, or landscape, and to specify itself as an artistic production. If the small-scale objects of sculpture seem to be protected within their discourse because they are contained within the institution, outdoor sculptural objects seem to contain the institution in their scale to authorize their presence in public space.

In addition to the strategy of scale, other forms of abstraction are necessary to validate outdoor objects as high art; for example abstracting the object by locating it within a spectacular culture-nature polarization. Public outdoor sculpture must abstract itself from the discourse of high cultural objects in the institution as it must also distance itself from the discourse of low cultural objects in everyday reality.

In my work at Münster the trailer as object was extracted from the "low cultural" context of everyday reality and common experience. By framing this object within the exhibition theme it was declared a sculptural object of high art. Through this transformation into sculpture the work maintained the function and sign of a trailer, thereby allowing it to refer to its different settings within the landscape and the cityscape.

The trailer's declaration as a contribution to an exhibition of contemporary outdoor sculpture could be identified as possibly deriving from the tradition of the readymade. But by being only partly suspended and/or dislocated from its usual function and placement, this installation did not fulfill the traditional criteria for a readymade. Lacking the necessary contextual transformation for that strategy, its presence afforded both a purely functional understanding of it as a recreational vehicle, and as the sculptural work of an individual author.

The trailer as the object of this installation remained functional as was evidenced by its mobility during the period of the exhibition. Its function as a recreational vehicle is generally defined in opposition to its function as a city dwelling by a temporally restricted usage. It is therefore often vacant over ex-

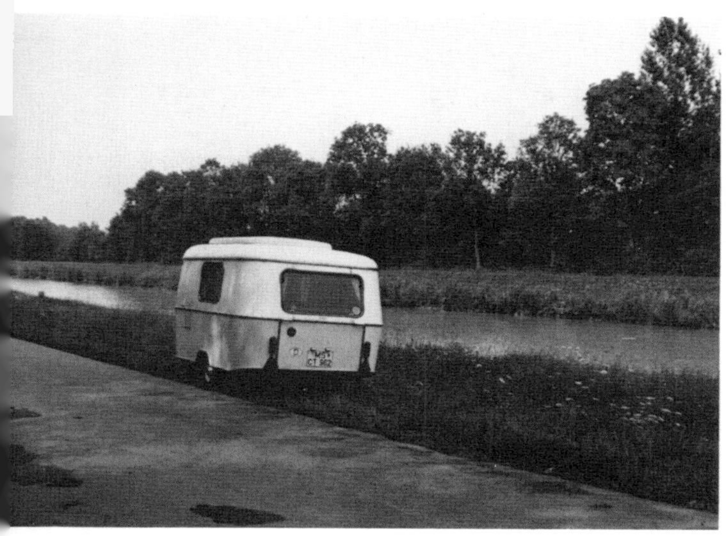

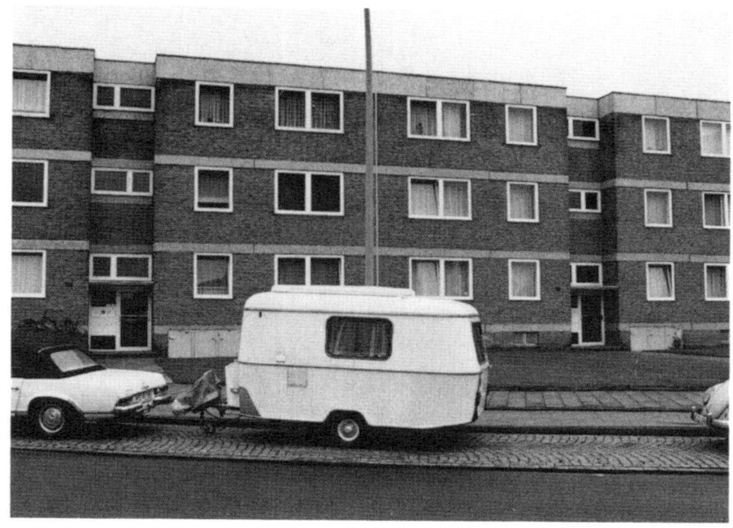

tended periods of time and parked on side streets or stored in city dwellings. Furthermore, it remained functional in terms of its spatial context, since it was placed in locations where it could very easily be set in opposition to the readymade, whose spatial rupture and unexpected presence fixed in the museum frame is essential to its operation. The functional character of this object was further evidenced by the fact that as a piece of equipment bound by rental agreement it was destined to return into its original functional circulation at the conclusion of the exhibition. At the same time, to appropriate a mechanically produced object of common usage and to insert it into an exhibition context seems to be congruent with the readymade's method of appropriating an object and suspending its original function.

Due to the extreme limitations placed on the work's operation within the problematic context of public outdoor sculpture, or, even more precisely, in this unique and particular exhibition, the work took on a functional dimension which distinguished it from the readymade's universal and timeless existence.

The trailer installation might also have appeared as the result of a readymade strategy because of the rupture that it introduced into the stylistic conventions of post-Minimal outdoor sculpture in general and even more so because of its unexpected presence in the context of this exhibition in particular. The trailer as a specific object of common use was essentially neither out of context nor was its function abstracted when perceived by the viewer. The trailer as a declared *sculptural* object interrupted the existing viewing conventions of outdoor post-Minimal sculpture in the context of this exhibition in a manner similar to the readymade. However, as it inserted itself into the discourse (of this specific exhibition and the phenomenon of outdoor sculpture) and interfered only within the signification of the discourse, it did not—quite unlike the readymade—take on aesthetic object status and did not continue to exist as a sculptural object (it ceased to exist with the exhibition's closure).

The installation of this work was dismantled after the exhibition and the work's residual elements (i.e. photographic reproductions) could be enlisted for the documentation and mediation of the work. The trailer as object was again used outside of the exhibition context. This differed from both the continued existence of the appropriated object as a work of art as well as from documentation which assumes object status. This work was not individually fabricated or manufactured to remain in existence, and it could not therefore achieve commodity status. For this temporally and spatially contextualized and limited activity within the discourse of high art, I received an honorarium as compensation.

This work was conceived and realized for an exhibition of contemporary outdoor *sculpture*. Therefore it seems useful to recall some of the typical conventions and functions of the category of public sculpture. These range—most generally—from addressing, commemorating, and celebrating individuals to mirroring collective experience. For these purposes individual icons, symbols, and architectural elements were once created from a stock of individual, regional, and national cultural and stylistic conventions for a patron class of aristocrats and their governments, and subsequently, in the late eighteenth and nineteenth centuries, for the newly instated representatives of the bourgeoisie.

Contemporary public outdoor sculpture is commissioned by government agencies as well as private and corporate enterprise. In general it draws on the highly particularized stylistic and procedural conventions of modernist sculpture and in particular on the characteristic features of the work of an individual artist.

It displays the economic achievements of governmental or local institutions or of corporations as a cultural signal to the community, and it functions within the community as a mark of identity and differentiation. Contemporary outdoor sculpture testifies to its own particular historical moment of production in order to arrest or to embody that moment. As *contemporary* sculpture it testifies to the future orientation of its

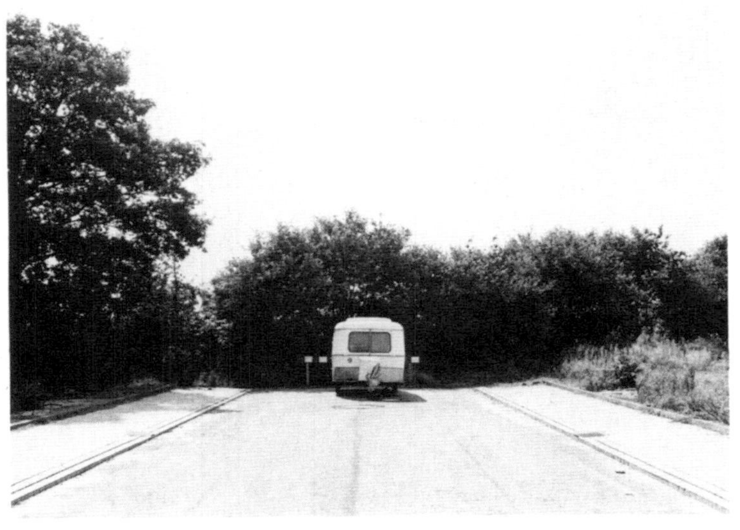

9

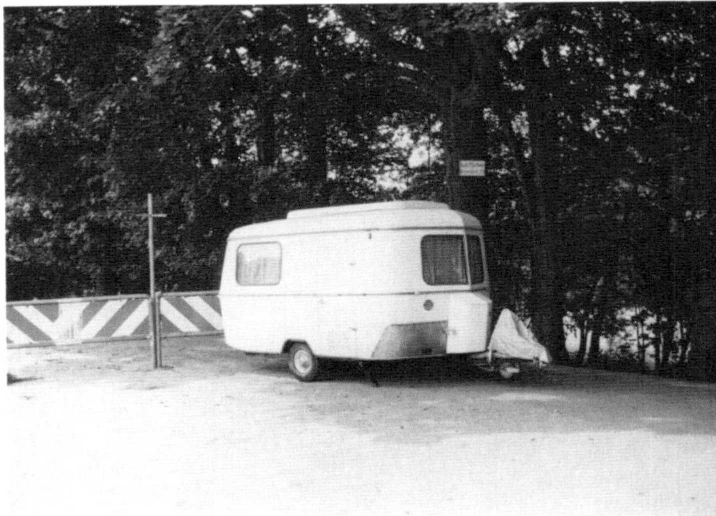

10

patrons and their affirmation of a technologically oriented notion of progress. Furthermore, it adds to the landmarks of an urban center and assists visitors and tourists in these urban centers to orient themselves in the cityscape. In the gentrification of urban areas, the presence of public sculpture as a sign of cultural (governmental or corporate) commitment to a particular area within a community may attract real-estate speculation and enhance the property values of that area. It presents a concretized and monumentalized form of ideology to the public. It is almost always located in centralized plazas or parks where the individual can be addressed by ideology as public individual. Public monumental sculpture is hardly ever found in residential neighborhoods.

Architecturally individualized artists' homes promising cultural improvement in slum neighborhoods, as well as privately installed museums for individual contemporary artists in gentrified neighborhoods function in a manner analogous to that of public monumental sculpture; yet their speculative economic character is more evident.

More recently, with the advent of postmodernism, architecture itself can assume the function of public sculptural sign systems. It no longer draws from the modernist tradition and no longer employs its sculptural conventions, but it treats these conventions as available historical stock to create an architectural rather than sculptural spectacle.

As a monumental public example of pure and particularized unalienated labor, the results of this sculptural practice are effectively legitimizing the universal conditions of alienated labor. It diverts the viewer's attention from the division of labor and offers a retreat of unalienated creativity to the public. As a unique individual production it actually confronts public space —the space of the collective participation in the social production process—with its own individuated space. As a result of this confrontation the public does not only perceive itself as practicing alienated labor and being (systematically) prevented from access to unalienated labor, but it understands the imposition of individuated space onto the space of collective production.

Public sculpture, once installed in its definitive outdoor setting, assumes the features of spatial stability and temporal perpetuity. Abstracted from both its original place within the discourse of sculpture— its material location—as well as the time of its conception and realization, it becomes an arbitrary, but monumental structure without explicit references or dedications. Its social and ideological function therefore is to disperse an abstract notion of monumentality. Anchored into the ground of public space, that notion functions as its pedestal.

The installation at Münster was intended to function as a negation of contemporary public sculpture. The trailer as a mass-produced object (in contradistinction to an industrially produced unique sculpture) denied invention, special fabrication, and the unique existence that establish the spectacle of individual unalienated labor in public sculptural works. As an industrially produced recreational vehicle it embodied the split and unity between alienated labor and alienated leisure time.

By changing the object of this sculptural installation regularly to different locations throughout the exhibition period, this work resisted public sculpture's traditional claim to static perpetuity and its ideological implications.

This installation used the temporal and contextual body of an exhibition of outdoor sculpture as its materially specific and temporally limited pedestal. The work addressed those social spaces which public sculpture refuses or neglects to address or those which it wants to conceal. Instead of abstracting the viewers' experience of reality through an ideological address in public cultural spaces, the work suggested a concrete analysis of individual alienation where it is most solidly authored, in the urban and suburban homes, the factories and urban businesses and shopping centers. By drawing the viewers' attention to those placements in social space an imposition through cultural presence was avoided.

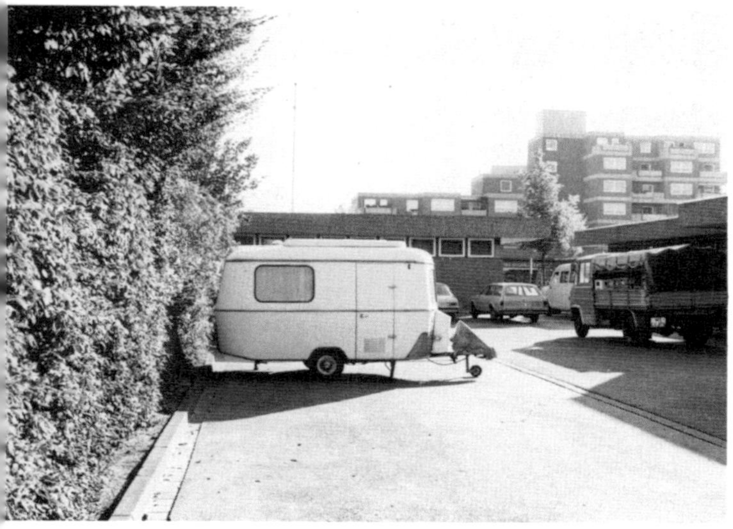

11

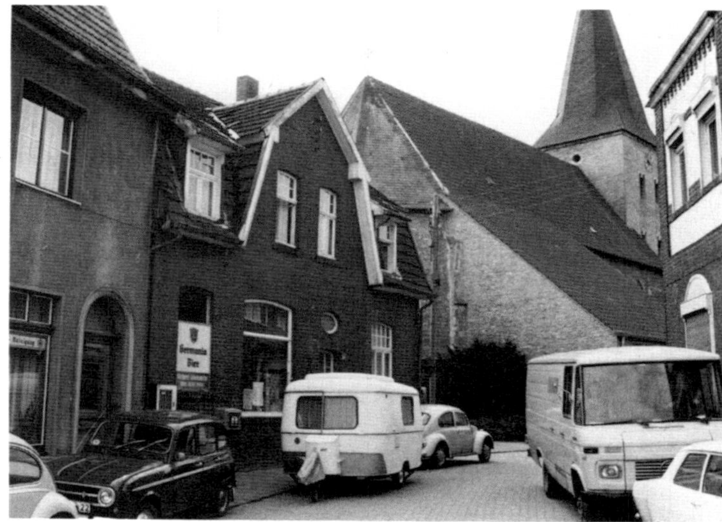

12

The work actively opposed the implications inherent in the economic structure of public outdoor sculpture by illuminating the extraordinary material and economic investment necessary for its construction and installation, which goes far beyond the production costs of any other sculptural manifestation. The cost to install this work as a temporary public outdoor sculpture at Münster amounted to a very modest monthly rental charge. Since the work did not imbue its surroundings with the presence of cultural and economic achievement, and since it did not allow for any aesthetic abstraction from its context, this installation also did not function as a cultural endorsement for potential real-estate speculation.

This work did not participate in the shift from gallery commodity to government or corporate commission, which was deemed necessary for the production of public outdoor sculpture. Such a shift had occurred in the mid to late seventies when Minimal and post-Minimal sculpture, for example, which had originally been conceived and developed for gallery and museum spaces, had saturated the market for private collectors and museum institutions.

An expansion into public commissions seemed, therefore, to be a logical step. It could be speculated that the museum/exhibition of contemporary outdoor sculpture functioned as a showcase/mediation agency for local and regional governmental and corporate commissions. Due to its temporal and spatial specificity and its appearance as an industrially produced readymade, my work at Münster did not participate in this shift, nor was it available to the exhibition as showcase/mediator for public acquisition. Several works from the exhibition were, in fact, as intended, acquired and installed permanently by the city government.

When seen at its various locations by viewers who were unaware of the exhibition context, the trailer could be read as an architectural structure, standing for itself, not representing anything but itself. Perceived within the exhibition context, however, the trailer became an indexical sign in the tradition of the readymade, while simultaneously referring symbolically to both the discourse of sculpture and architecture. The indexical reading of the object prevented the viewer from reducing it to a sculptural or architectural entity alone, whereas the symbolic reading prevented the viewer from reducing it totally to a mute object. The object as both index and symbol was complemented by the object as both sculptural object and architectural structure. Being neither pure sculpture nor pure architecture, both levels of discourse constantly interacted with one another within the exhibition context of sculpture/architecture. In this way the object with all the features of architecture (a functionalized, human-scale shell suitable for dwelling) and all the attributes of sculpture (a three-dimensional voluminous container, to be seen in the round, attached to the ground by its own mass) attempted to cross-reference, superimpose, or place its separate institutionalized discourses upon one another. Inserted into the precise limits of the exhibition context, yet denied object status as either architecture or sculpture, this work—unlike certain examples of postmodernist architecture—did not attempt a false, total synthesis of sculptural and architectural signifiers.

As a concrete object the trailer could have been seen as a sculptural, architectural hybrid. In the exhibition context, however, its declarative method negated, in the manner of an allegorical statement, the validity of both discourses—sculpture and architecture. A double negation, this work required that reified high-cultural notions (public sculpture) be reintegrated into the basic, underlying social practice (architecture), and that the reification within social practice be confronted with the perspective of high art individuation. By bracketing both, the work tried to dismantle the notions of a separate existence of ''high'' and ''low'' cultural practice. Therefore, the work questioned the historical legitimization of contemporary sculpture which pretends to be disconnected from social practice, as it also questioned the legitimization of architecture which, by assembling past stylistic conventions, attempts to recuperate its failure as social practice.

---

[1] Statement quoted from the agreement submitted by the museum to participating artists on March 15, 1977.

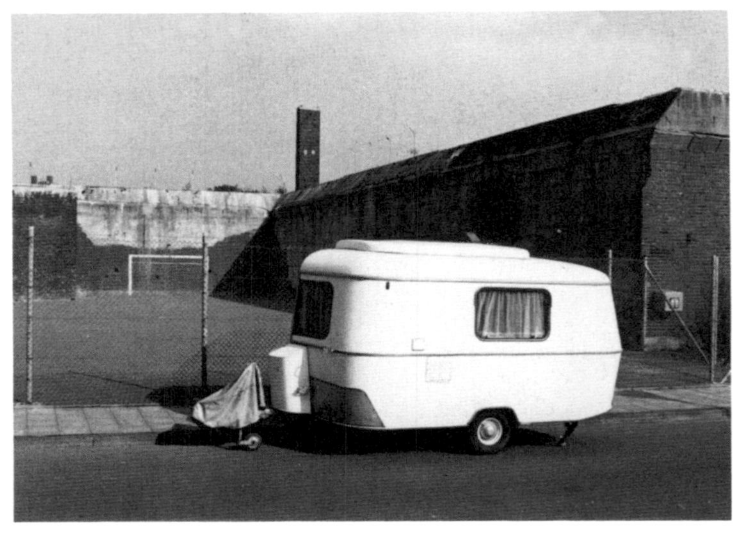 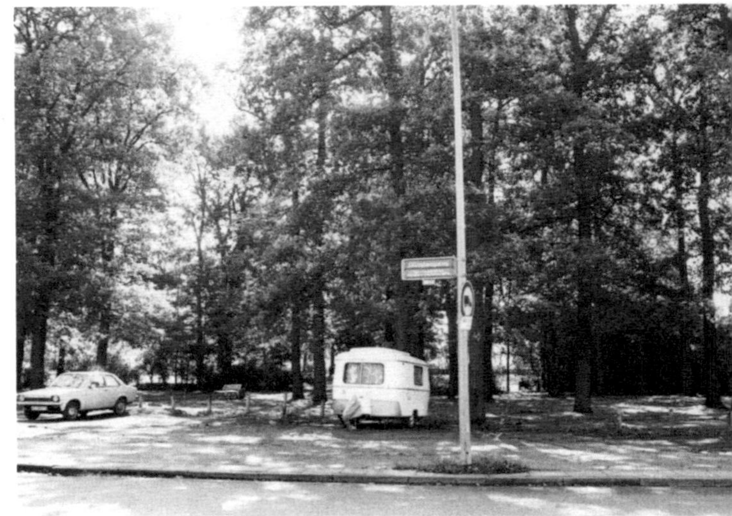

13 14

3. 7.–11. 7.1977	1	Spiegelkammer und Pferdegasse
11. 7.–18. 7.1977	2	Parkhaus Geisbergweg, unterhalb des Regierungspräsidenten 1-3. Entweder Platz 62 oder Platz 5
18. 7.–25. 7.1977	3	Alter Steinweg-Parkplatz, vor der Ziegelmauer mit dem Zeichen 'Stricker'
25. 7.– 1. 8.1977	4	Kiffe-Pavillon, vor der Parkuhr Nr.275 oder Nr.274
1. 8.– 8. 8.1977	5	Hörster-Friedhof – Piusallee. Parken auf der Hörsterstraße zwischen dem Park und der Piusallee
8. 8.–15. 8.1977	6	Kleimann-Brücke Nr. 17. Parken auf der gegenüberliegenden Straßenseite vor dem Zaun des Verlages.
15. 8.–22. 8.1977	7	Dortmund-Ems-Kanal, ca. 300 m nördlich der Königsberger Straße am Rügen-Ufer
22. 8.–29. 8.1977	8	Königsberger Straße 133-135, zu parken vor dem Hochhaus
29. 8.– 5. 9.1977	9	In der Nähe des Bröderichweg 36 oder am Ende der Sackgasse der Sparkassenschule
5. 9.–12. 9.1977	10	Am Ende der Sackgasse Idenbrockweg in Kinderhaus in der Nähe des Friedhofs
12. 9.–19. 9.1977	11	Vorplatz Coerde-Markt neben der Parkuhr vor der Konditorei
19. 9.–26. 9.1977	12	Vor dem Lebensmittelgeschäft auf dem Kirchplatz in Nienberge östlich der Altenberger Straße
26. 9.– 3.10.1977	13	An der Ecke Möllmannsweg – Hollandstraße zwischen Münster und Gievenbeck
3.10.–10.10.1977	14	Kappenbergerdamm – Düsbergweg, Parkplatz an der Südost-Ecke
10.10.–17.10.1977	15	Neben dem Wald am Jesuiterbruck in der Nähe von Hühnenburg oder nördlich der Hühnenburgstraße
17.10.–24.10.1977	16	Gerichtsstraße – Hindenburgplatz auf dem großen Parkplatz unter den Bäumen der Westseite
24.10.–31.10.1977	17	Hauptbahnhof, auf dem Parkplatz vor der Parkuhr Nr.351
31.10.– 7.11.1977	18	Sonnenstraße, nähe Ritterstraße, halb auf dem Bürgersteig und halb auf der Straße
7.11.–14.11.1977	19	Germanistisches Institut, auf dem Parkplatz unter den Bäumen und so nah wie möglich auf der Johannisstraße und vor dem Parkplatz Spiegelkammer

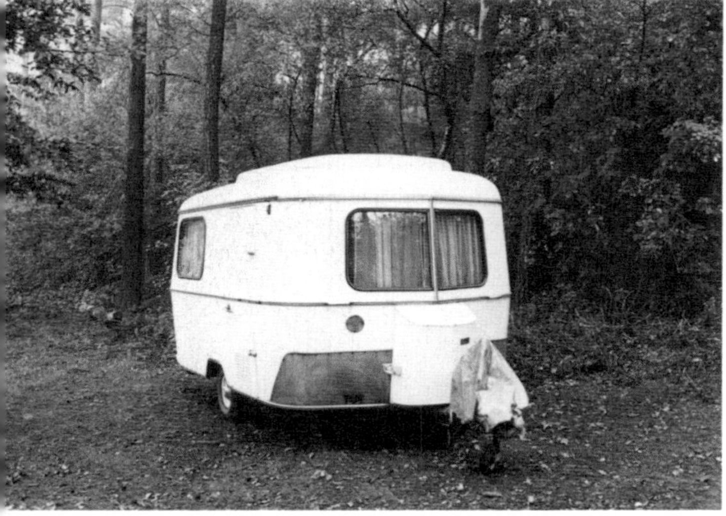

15

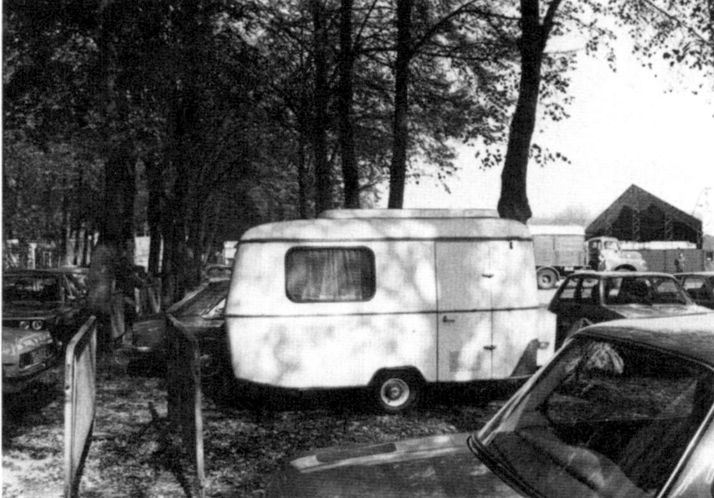

16

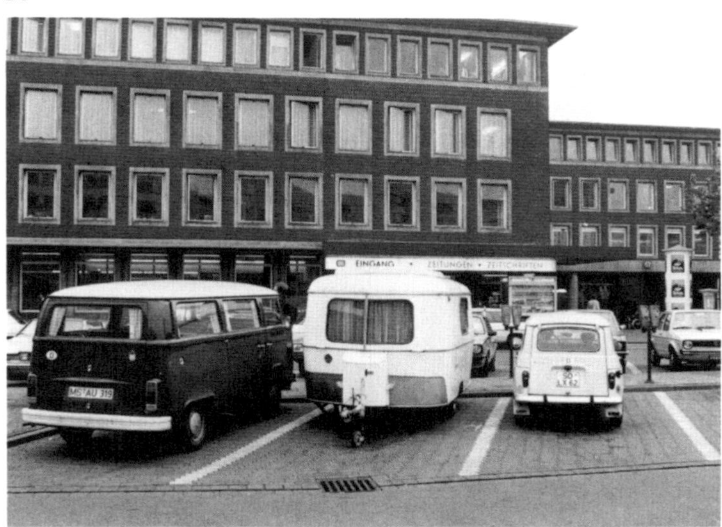

17

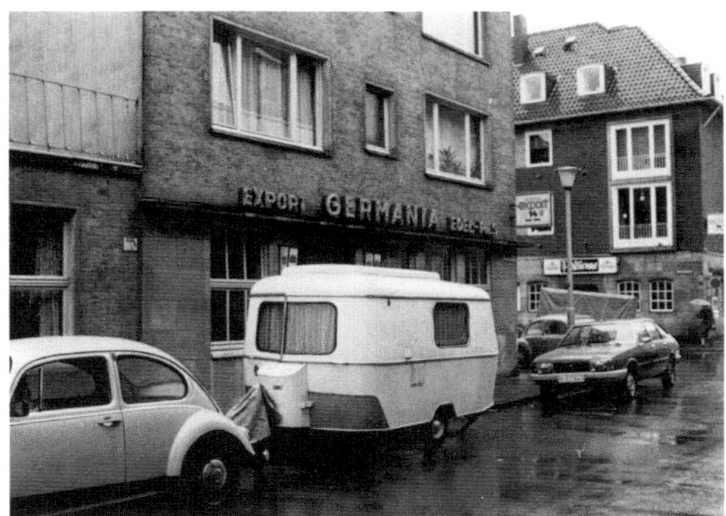

18

19

Dates and locations of trailer in Münster during the exhibition
"Skulptur." Photographs by Rudolf Wakonigg.

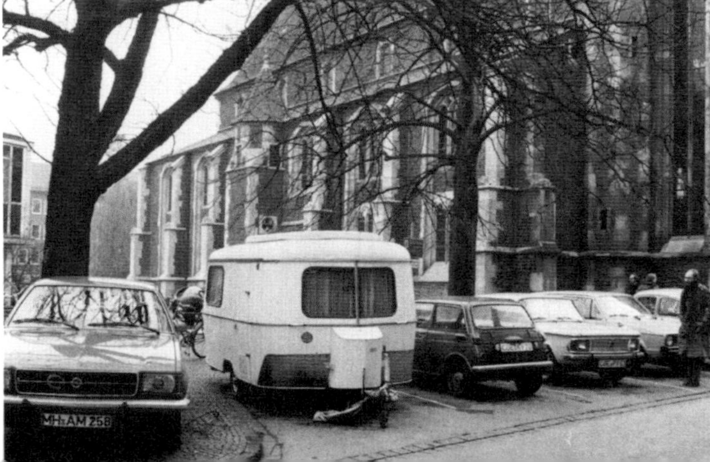

August 3–August 29, 1977
Stedelijk Van Abbemuseum
Eindhoven, Netherlands

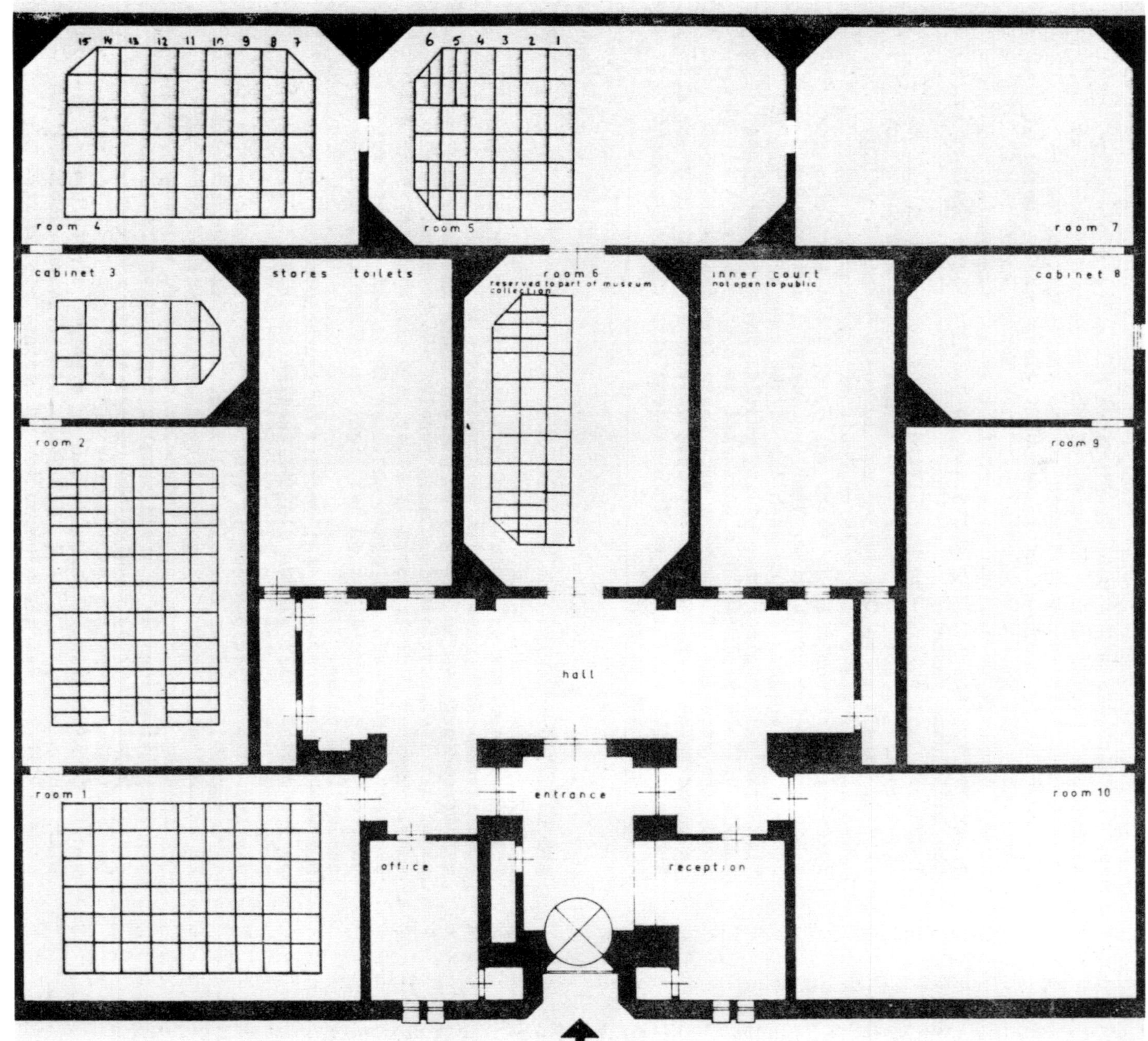

Ground plan of the Stedelijk Van Abbe Museum used as an exhibition handout during the exhibition indicating the areas where the panels were removed for the installation. The front page gives a description of the work. Courtesy: Stedelijk Van Abbe Museum.

MICHAEL ASHER
VAN ABBEMUSEUM EINDHOVEN
03.08.1977

DESCRIPTION

The Van Abbemuseum has been constructed following a formally symmetrical ground plan. The part of the structure which I am most immediately interested with is the glass ceiling below the roof. It is composed of translucent glass panels installed throughout the museum approximately five meters above the floor level. Since it is covered by a roof it is not exposed to the exterior, but the ceiling functions to diffuse light throughout the individual rooms.
I propose that before the exhibition opens on August 3, all the glass ceiling panels in rooms 1, 2, 3 and 4 plus all the glass ceiling panels up to the center row in rooms 5 and 6 – which means all the glass panels in one half of the museum – shall be removed; which would leave rooms 10, 9, 8, 7 and part of rooms 5 and 6 open for exhibition. Starting August 3 and working 4 hours every morning during each day of the work week, an exhibition crew will replace the ceiling panels. The original glass panels will be replaced on a northeast to southwest axis for 15 rows. The sequence of covering will begin from the center row in rooms 5 and 6 and end at the west wall of rooms 1, 2, 3 and 4. The end of the exhibition will correspond with the replacement of the last row in room 1.

BESCHRIJVING

Het Van Abbemuseum is gebouwd volgens een strakke geometrische plattegrond. Het gedeelte van de constructie waarin ik het meest geïnteresseerd ben is het glazen plafond onder het dak. Het bestaat uit lichtdoorlatende glazen panelen die over het gehele museum, ongeveer 5 meter boven de vloer zijn aangebracht. Daar dit overdekt is door een dak staat het niet in direkt contact met buiten; het plafond dient om het licht te verspreiden door de afzonderlijke zalen.
Het werk bestaat daaruit dat voordat de tentoonstelling opengaat op 3 augustus, alle glazen plafond panelen in zalen 1, 2, 3 en 4 plus alle panelen tot aan de middenrij in zalen 5 en 6 – dat wil zeggen, alle glazen panelen in een helft van het museum – verwijderd worden; waardoor de zalen 10, 9, 8, 7 en een gedeelte van de zalen 5 en 6 voor tentoonstellingen beschikbaar blijven. Te beginnen op 3 augustus, en 4 uren elke ochtend op werkdagen, zal een inrichtingsteam de plafond panelen terugleggen. De originele glazen panelen worden teruggelegd op een as van noordoost naar zuidwest over 15 rijen. De volgorde van het leggen zal beginnen vanuit de middenrij in zalen 5 en 6 en eindigen bij de westelijke muur van zalen 1, 2, 3 en 4. Het einde van de tentoonstelling zal samenvallen met het terugleggen van de laatste rij in zaal 1.

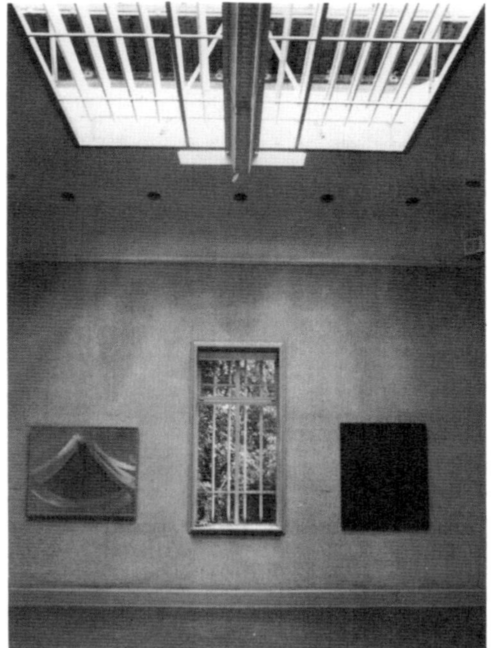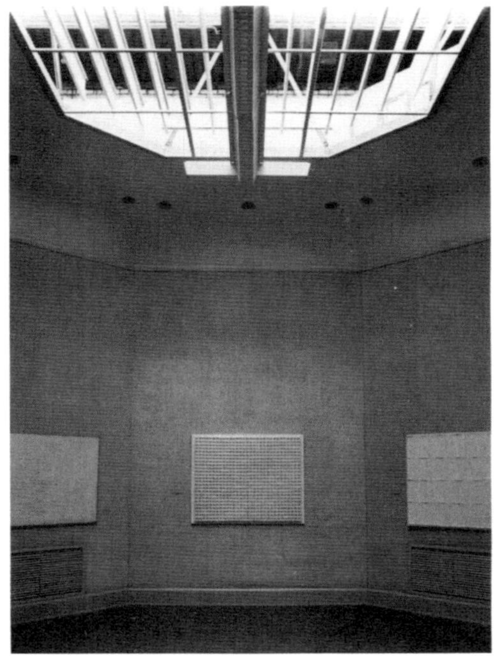

Study photographs taken one year before the actual installation. Photographs by Michael Asher.

On July 24, 1975, I received a letter from Rudi Fuchs, the director of the Van Abbemuseum, inviting me to participate in an exhibition scheduled for the spring of 1977. I agreed in principle to do a work for the exhibition in my reply of September 8 of that year, with final commitment contingent on viewing the actual exhibition space. In the meantime I asked that ground plans and photographs be sent to me so that I could get some idea of what the pre-existing area would be. From July 23, 1976 to July 26, 1976, I visited Eindhoven, saw the museum, and committed myself to making a proposal for the exhibition, which by then had been more precisely scheduled for May/June of 1977. (Since it had been overlooked in the original planning stage that the museum's work crew would be on vacation at that time; the installation had to be rescheduled for the month of August.)

Since Rudi Fuchs had only seen one of my works (Documenta V, 1972), my other work was described to him by several fellow artists.

I had some knowledge through periodicals and various sources of the museum's contemporary exhibition history, particularly exhibitions of Minimal art which the museum had organized in the late sixties. The museum appeared to be the one major art institution in Eindhoven, a city which has an active art community beyond the museum itself. And due to the excellence of the collection and the museum's exhibition program, it attracts a large number of visitors from the surrounding community, the major cities in Holland as well as from the bordering countries Belgium and Germany.

After visiting the museum it became clear to me that one of the museum's most prominent architectural features, its symmetrical ground plan—one side a mirror image of the opposite side—would be the basis of my proposal for the exhibition and that it would incorporate preexisting architectural elements of the building.

Interior dimensions of the museum building were 39.42 meters on the north-west/south-east axis, approximately 7.20 meters from the floor to the peak of the roof, and 5 meters from the floor to a glass ceiling functioning as a light diffuser suspended from the roof. The roof contained skylights and just above the glass diffusers was a louvre construction which directed light from the skylights through the ceiling into the galleries. The louvres could be operated mechanically from the inside of each of the rooms, and set at a different pitch throughout the day, although they seemed to be generally left in one position.

Between the translucent ceiling diffusers and the roof was an attic which not only contained the louvres, but also air ducting, mechanical equipment (electrical wiring, alarm systems, etc.), and structural elements of the building. The ducting and electrical systems were set back far enough around the perimeter of the glass ceiling to make room for a maintenance pathway. The glass ceiling in seven exhibition rooms contained fifty-six glass panels each, whereas in two of the exhibition rooms the ceiling held eighteen panels only and in one room it contained seventy-two glass panels. Altogether there were thirty rows of glass panels in the ceiling along the north/west-south/east axes. The average diffuser panel was approximately 86 centimeters by 86 centimeters. The panels rested on a metal frame construction and they could be removed for cleaning and maintenance purposes. The ceiling's light-diffusing system augmented the architecture's classical symmetry by directing the visitors' patterns of circulation.

The symmetrical layout of the museum was such that four exhibition areas on the east side corresponded to four areas of equal size on the west side, with two separate exhibition areas on the central axis of the building. On the east and west side there were three exhibition rooms which measured 8 by 12 meters each and one exhibition room which measured 6 by 8 meters. The entrance and hallway as well as the service areas were also laid out symmetrically. Wall surfaces were covered with beige jute cloth and the floor was covered with dull gray linoleum. Each room was separate and self-contained yet laid out so that there was a specific viewing order. The architectural condi-

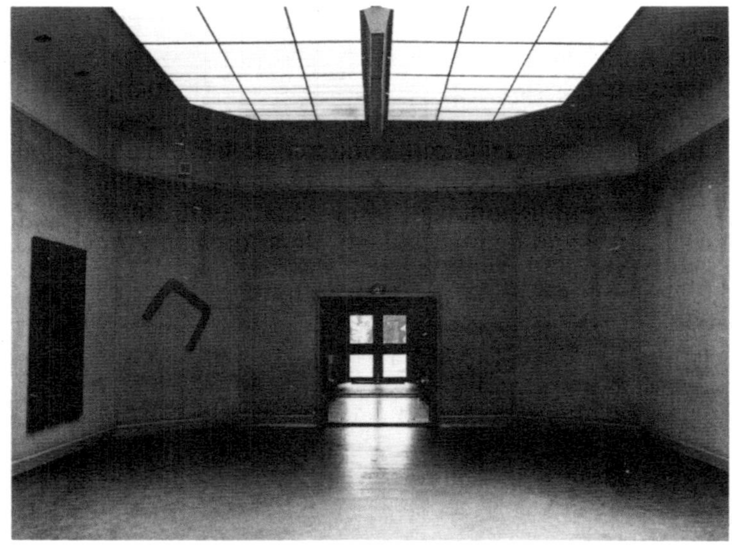

Room 6, viewing south during exhibition with paintings by Richard Tuttle and Alan Charlton.

Room 4, viewing east during exhibition.

Room 5, viewing west during exhibition with remnants of a former installation by Daniel Buren. Photographs by Hans Biezen.

tions that I encountered are best described by Rudi Fuchs, the museum's director, in his brief history and description of the museum:

> The situation encountered by Michael Asher in Eindhoven, in the late spring of 1976, was that of a museum. In terms of European cultural history, the Van Abbemuseum is rather young. It was founded in 1936, following a substantial gift from a local industrialist, Henri van Abbe, which paid for the building. The operating costs of the museum were to be carried by the municipality. At first the city council, which was and still is the museum's final authority, hardly knew what to do with the institution. The notion of a public cultural service was, at that time, rather strange to the exclusively industrial city of Eindhoven. Only after the war a long-term program was developed: the museum should show and collect works of modern and contemporary art, that is art produced after 1900, nationally as well as internationally.
>
> The architect of the building, selected by Mr. van Abbe himself, was someone noted for his Roman-Catholic churches in a severe, neo-Romanesque style, Kropholler. And indeed, the museum he designed, set upon an artificial mount, certainly looks like a sanctuary: high, closed walls; a tower above the entrance; heavy, bronze doors; stairs leading towards the entrance, flanked by sculptures of rearing horses, done in a fitting medievalist mode by the architect's friend, John Raedecker.
>
> The symmetry of these horses introduces the symmetry of the lay-out of the rooms inside. Symmetry is the absence of spatial tension; inside, therefore, the museum is at complete rest. The gallery is quiet and peaceful, an invitation to contemplation. The outside world is shut out. Two narrow, barred windows only, on either side, enable the visitor to look outside. The light comes through a glass ceiling underneath a glass roof. Thus, upon entering the museum, the outside world becomes a memory.
> The museum is an idealistic receptacle: a sanctu-

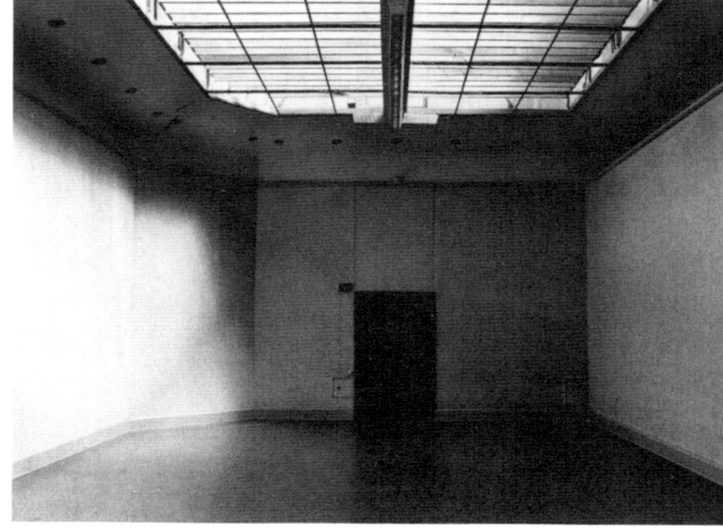

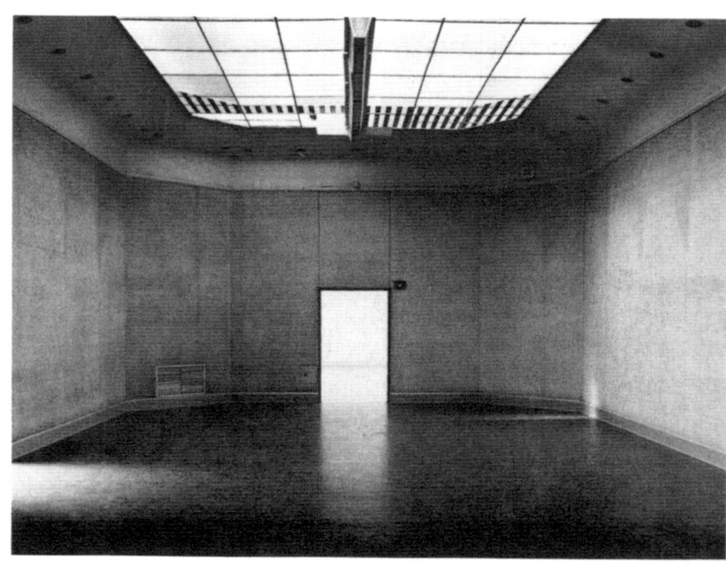

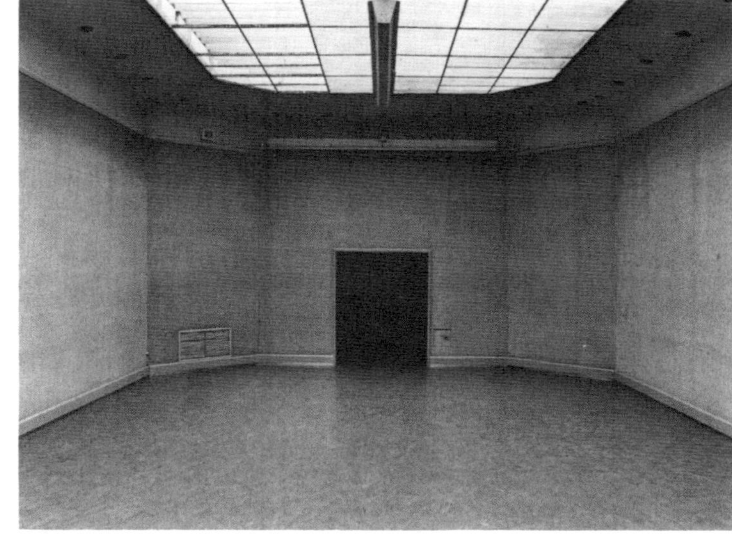

Room 6, viewing work, during exhibition. Photograph by Hans Biezen.

Room 4, viewing west during exhibition. Photograph by Hans Biezen.

Room 5, viewing east. Photograph by Michael Asher.

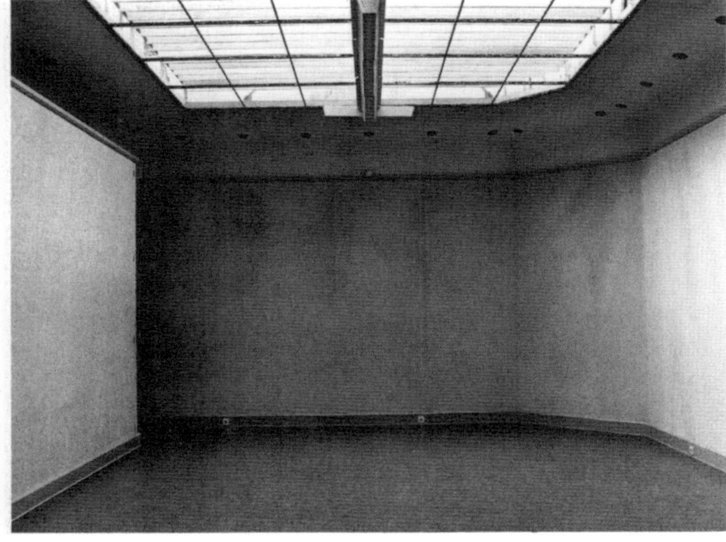

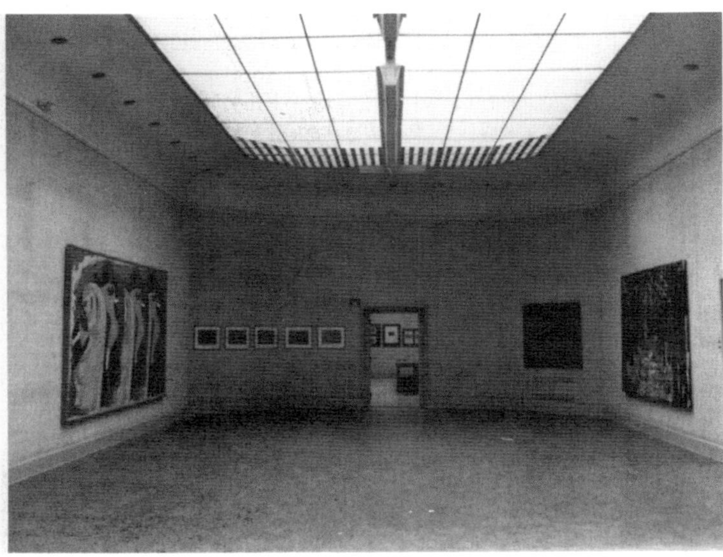

ary for the artistic endeavours of man which, through the supreme act of imagination, reach beyond this world and lead mankind to a better, more imaginative existence. This understanding of the function and meaning of art as the *other* world, is quietly emphasized if one enters the museum and goes through the galleries. Coming from the small parking-lot in front, which used to be a formal garden, one goes up the steps, past the stone horses, looking upwards to the central entrance. Inside one finds oneself first in a small vestibule, vaulted in red brick, and then in a larger hall of severe architecture, dimly lit through the vaulted ceiling and fittingly adorned with terracotta emblems, symbolizing Day and Night and the Eternity of Art. From the twilight of the hall one then passes into brightly illuminated gallery rooms, white walls and dull, grey floors. Entering the museum is the passage from the world into the detached realm of mind and imagination.[1]

I had to take into account in my proposal an addition to the original building which was at that time in the planning stage since I did not want my installation to interfere in any way with construction work once it began.

Several proposals, all of them dealing with the symmetrical layout of the building, were submitted. The final proposal was accepted since it responded to the museum's architectural conditions and was in line with the museum's administrative policy. It was printed on a letter-size sheet of paper and distributed in the museum's information brochures. Illustrated with a ground plan, it read as follows:

The Van Abbemuseum has been constructed following a formally symmetrical ground plan. The part of the structure which I am most immediately interested in is the glass ceiling below the roof. It is composed of translucent glass panels installed throughout the museum approximately five meters above the floor level. Since it is covered by a roof it is not exposed to the exterior, but the ceiling functions to diffuse light throughout the individual rooms.

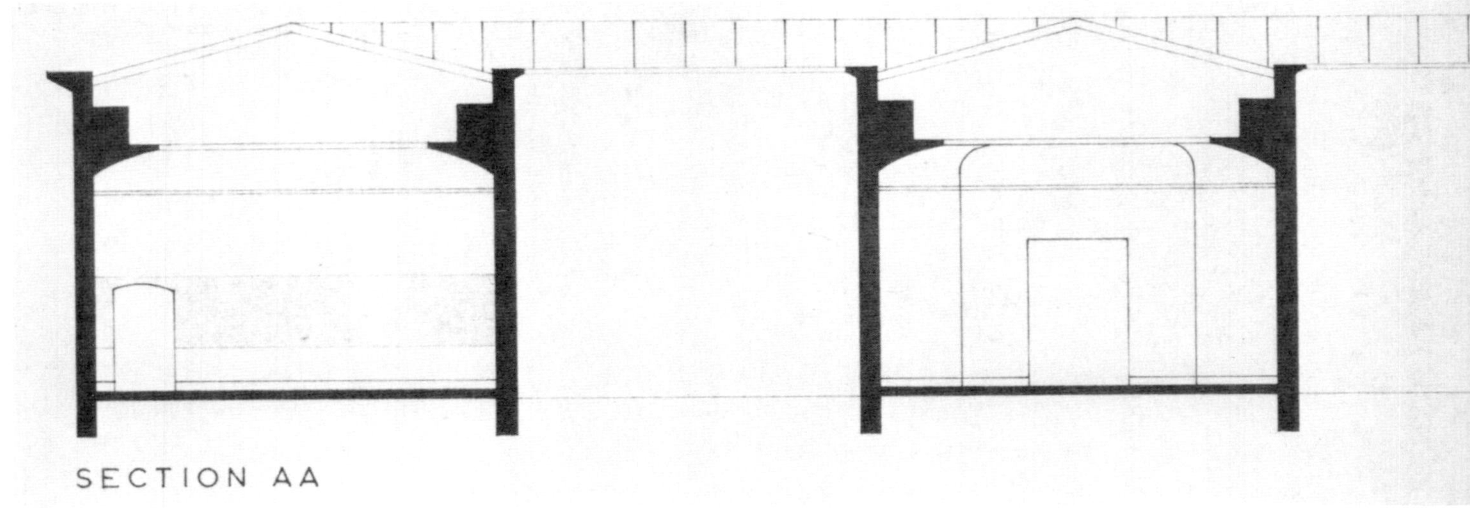

I propose that before the exhibition opens on August 3, all the glass ceiling panels in rooms 1, 2, 3 and 4 plus all the glass ceiling panels up to the center row in rooms 5 and 6—which means all the glass panels in one half of the museum—shall be removed which would leave rooms 10, 9, 8, 7 and part of rooms 5 and 6 open for exhibition. Starting August 3 and working 4 hours every morning during each day of the work week, an exhibition crew will replace the ceiling panels. The original glass panels will be replaced on a northeast to southwest axis for 15 rows. The sequence of covering will begin from the center row in rooms 5 and 6 and end at the west wall of rooms 1, 2, 3 and 4. The end of the exhibition will correspond with the replacement of the last row in room 1.[2]

Given the symmetrically divided arrangement of the exhibition rooms and museum policy stipulating that only one half of the available exhibition space could generally be used for one artist's exhibition at a time, I decided that dividing the space into two equal but opposite parts would be the structuring device for my work. Complementing the spatial division was a temporal division requiring that only the first half (four hours) of the museum work crew's eight-hour working day (five days a week) be spent on the installation of my work. Also, for the duration of my exhibition, the other half of the museum space would contain an installation of work from the museum's permanent collection, selected by the museum director who was also the curator of my exhibition. By clearly distinguishing and specifically presenting the different participants (work crew, curator, artist) that make an exhibition possible at such an institution, I wanted to show how these necessary but separate functions are equally essential for the constitution of a work.

Half of the actual installation work was never seen by the public because the panels had to be removed during hours when the museum was closed to the public before the exhibition opened. The dismantled diffuser panels were stored in the attic between ceiling and roof where they were stacked to be subsequently reassembled in the second stage of the installation. The other half of the installation, however, could be viewed during the exhibition the day the work crew began to reinstall all the panels that had been previously removed. The reinstallation of the glass panels signaled to the viewer during the actual exhibition time not only the preparatory work necessary for an exhibition but the labor necessary for deinstallation and renovation subsequent to an exhibition which is normally concealed from public view.

The renovation that was a result of setting up the work and that was necessary for setting up the subsequent exhibition, became the exhibition's own subject. If exhibition preparation generally results in a completed installation to be revealed at its opening, in this case the completed "installation" (the total removal of the ceiling diffusers) was already incomplete, since the exhibition itself implied the reinstallation of the removed ceiling elements. In general exhibition practice, the opening marks the shift from preparation to maintenance. Preparation and maintenance of an exhibition are part of an institutional practice that is generally not supposed to be seen by the public, they are considered to be separate from the work in the exhibition. The process of exhibition preparation performed before the opening, resulted—as indeed in any exhibition—in a first stage in which its own display elements (the institutional and architectural exhibition functions) were dismantled. Normal institutional exhibition preparation aims to conceal itself in order to foreground the work of art, consisting of such operations as finishing walls, adding display elements, installing lighting fixtures, and positioning displays for optimum effect.

As the preparation is involved with its own concealment, so is the work crew effecting the preparation who remain out of public view once the exhibition has opened.

This installation focused on one of the key elements in presentation practice—the lighting of installation areas. In reverting presentation practice back to its own key elements (before the opening of the

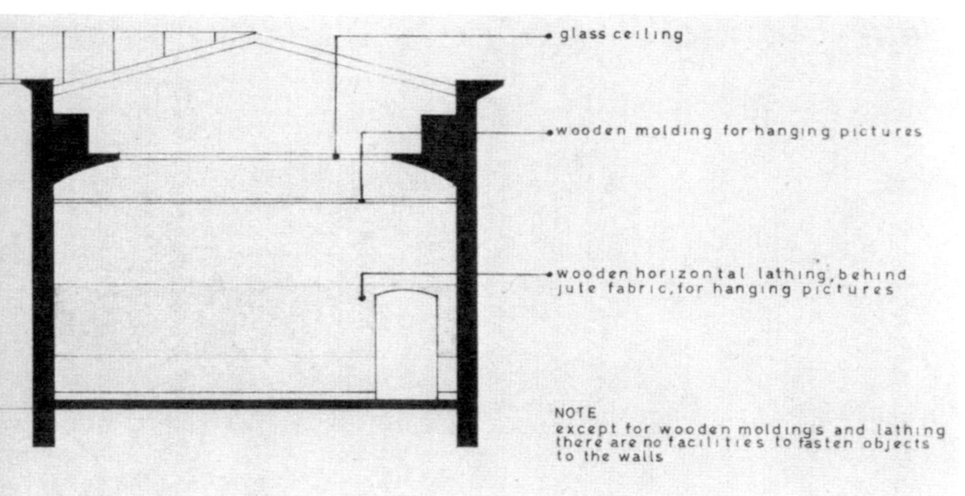

Section of the Stedelijk Van Abbe Museum.
Courtesy: Stedelijk Van Abbe Museum.

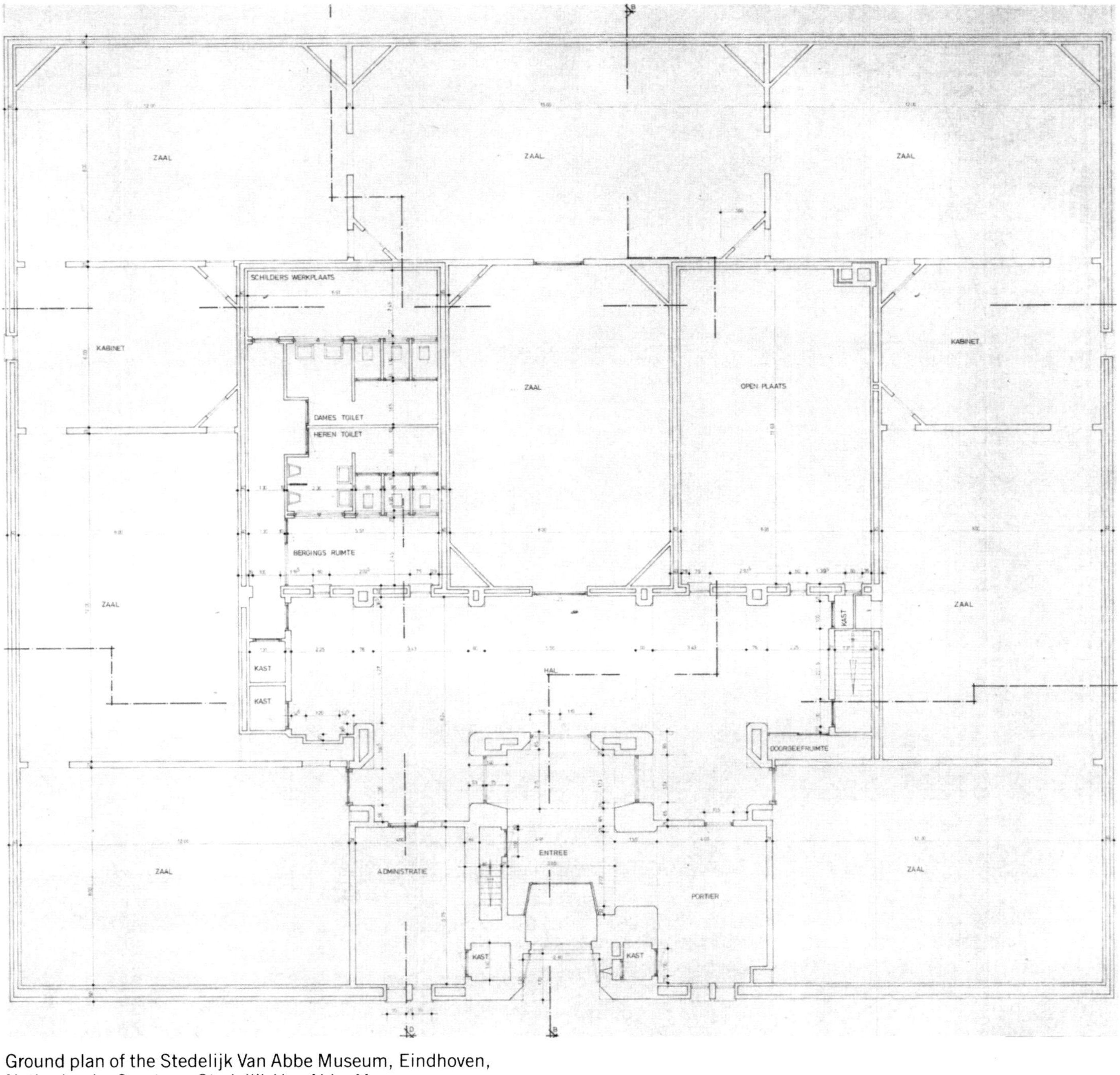

Ground plan of the Stedelijk Van Abbe Museum, Eindhoven,
Netherlands. Courtesy: Stedelijk Van Abbe Museum.

exhibition), the installation negated the need for a completed presentation in favor of a process displaying the function of preparation. At the same time, the director was asked to use the preparation period to present an exhibition in the other half of the museum based on traditional display techniques for works from the permanent collection. Both parallel, juxtaposed preparation processes were opened to the public at the same time.

The second stage of the installation began when the exhibition was opened to the public and consisted of the replacement of the diffuser panels to their original position in the ceiling grid. If the exhibition began by removing elements determined by the architecture and their institutional function, the second stage of the installation opened with the replacement of those architectural elements. The replacement process that would conceal the prior dismantling revealed how the work had been fabricated. Also, the work crew and the labor they expended effecting this reconstruction were visibly present during half of the daily exhibition hours and were integral to the installation.

Visitors to the museum on the morning of the day of the opening could have witnessed the beginning of the reconstruction work, but the visitors actually attending the preliminary ceremonies could only know from the descriptive information sheets that the reconstruction was already in progress. The first row of diffusers, nearest to the center of the museum, had been partially recovered by the time of the official exhibition opening later in the afternoon. This reconstruction process lasted for twenty-six days and its completion determined the actual closure of the exhibition. As the diffusers were progressively replaced from one workday to the next, the installation of the work—and therefore the exhibition itself—was in a continual state of change in clear distinction to the exhibition in the other half of the museum which remained a static display.

The materials that were necessary to construct the work and the materials that were necessary to exhibit the work became congruent in the same way the

Viewing detail of ceiling construction and wall during exhibition. Photograph by Michael Asher.

process of constructing the work and the process of exhibiting the work were superimposed on each other to become identical. Necessarily, therefore, on a temporal axis, the work's time of material construction as well as its time of existence coincided with its actual exhibition time and all three were terminated simultaneously. Since this installation at its conclusion reintegrated itself totally into the existing architectural structure and ceased to exist materially and visually without leaving behind any residual elements of the processes of construction and exhibition, it reverted to exactly the same material state of the architectural structure whose prior deconstruction had generated the work's material existence.

The installation was present to the viewer in a palpably material way as well as in a purely conceptual strategy. The work's radical interference with given architectural elements to produce a sculptural presence of various materials makes it superficially comparable to the sculptural appearance of certain process works; this applies as well to its alteration of light and ambient sound conditions, its opening up of the exhibition container, its disassembling of elements in a grid structure and their subsequent distribution within the visual range of the installation. The affinity with process works was further reflected in the progress of the work crew's daily alterations leading to final closure. On the other hand, the work appeared as a purely conceptual strategy since all of its material sculptural elements eventually merged with the original architectural functions of the museum structure.

Upon entering the rooms of the installation visitors were aware of a noticeable increase in lighting intensity compared to light conditions in the other half of the museum's exhibition rooms. The viewers were also aware of a marked difference in the quality of sound. In those areas where the ceiling had been removed acoustics were more active and resonant. Since those rooms were separated from the outside by only one layer of glass roofing, outside noise entered more easily and mixed with inside ambient noise. In the other half of the museum the acoustics were far more

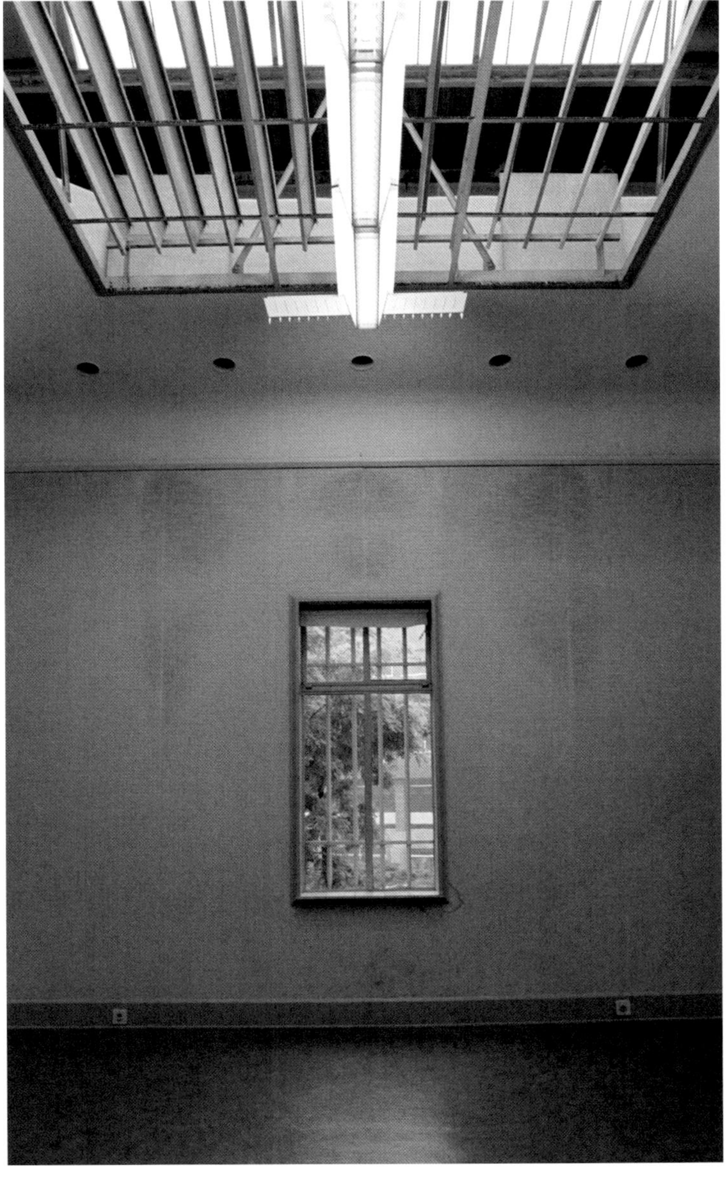

Cabinet 3, viewing west during exhibition. Photograph by Michael Asher.

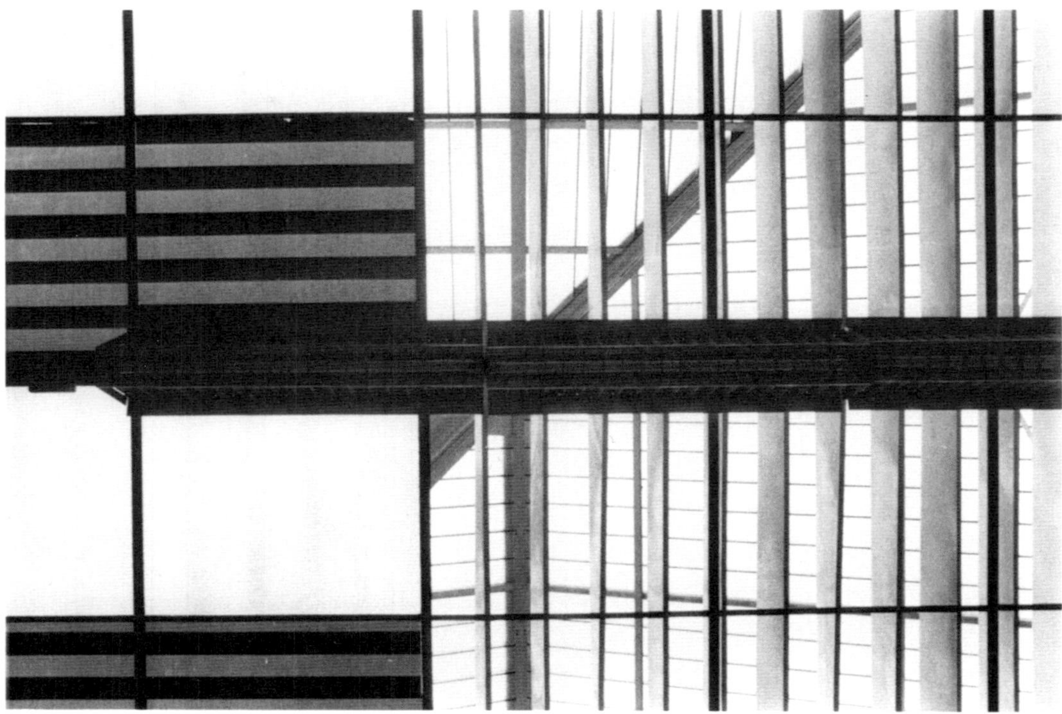

compact and the viewers felt more like they were in an isolated closed spatial container. In this work the light louvres for each exhibition area were set perpendicular to the floor which gave the strongest overhead light as well as the most direct visual exposure of the attic area above the ceiling.

Opening up the ceiling in one half of the museum drew the visitor's attention to a spatial area normally concealed from view, but essential to the museum's function. On a horizontal axis therefore, the viewer might have been aware of a spatial demarcation similar to the vertical division of the museum's ground plan. Similar to the perceived difference in sound and light in the two opposing halves of the museum, the visitor was confronted with the opposition between a horizontally open spatial container emptied of all objects yet giving visual access to its vertical extension and the mechanical functions it contained, and a sealed container precluding visual access to function as a stage for its contents.

It was possible to observe the installation's operation at any time during the exhibition in both temporal halves of the work, both with and without the presence of the work crew. While the work crew actually operated the installation, nonoperational features of the installation were also apparent. The most conspicuous aspect of the installation then became the presence of the workers—the sounds they generated replacing the diffusers and talking with each other. Their physical movements were analogous in their function to viewers' movements in the exhibition area. The workers could be perceived by the viewers as actually fabricating the work. Yet they were obviously not the authors of the work, nor could they be perceived as objects since they had their own working procedure within the confines of the work.

Normally, all exhibitions, and installation works in particular, conceal alienated labor. The more spectacular the display and the more successful the creation of illusion, the more these works have to conceal the alienated labor that entered into their production and exhibition. Therefore they institute on the level of display and exhibition practice an essentially aesthetic claim, that the work of art excludes from itself and negates the necessity of alienation. This work incorporated alienated labor into its process of fabrication and exhibition which was publicly manifest to the viewer. By introducing alienated labor into the framework of a supposedly unalienated aesthetic production, the production procedures as well as the display procedures that constitute the work's exhibition value were, in this case, no longer disconnected from each other and were materially and visually accessible. The question arises whether the need to introduce the viewer to the presence of alienation in the work's display does not result in a false aestheticization of alienated labor and whether it does not objectify the workers performing their task. The question is whether alienated labor exposed as a special task within a work of art does not imply aestheticized alienation.

Appropriation of a function necessary to the museum's daily existence and exhibition practice would have implied in fact an aestheticization of alienated labor. However, a task both invented and referring back upon itself as *function* without actually performing that function (to display an object aesthetically) could not truly be aestheticized but only reveal the actual degree of hidden alienation within exhibition practice.

---

[1] R.H. Fuchs, *Michael Asher, Exhibitions in Europe 1972-1977*, Eindhoven, Van Abbemuseum, 1980.

[2] Text of handout available during the exhibition.

Detail of ceiling construction during exhibition. Photograph by
Michael Asher.

Room 6, viewing south toward entry/exit, during preparation of
installation at the Stedelijk Van Abbe Museum. Photograph by
Hans Biezen.

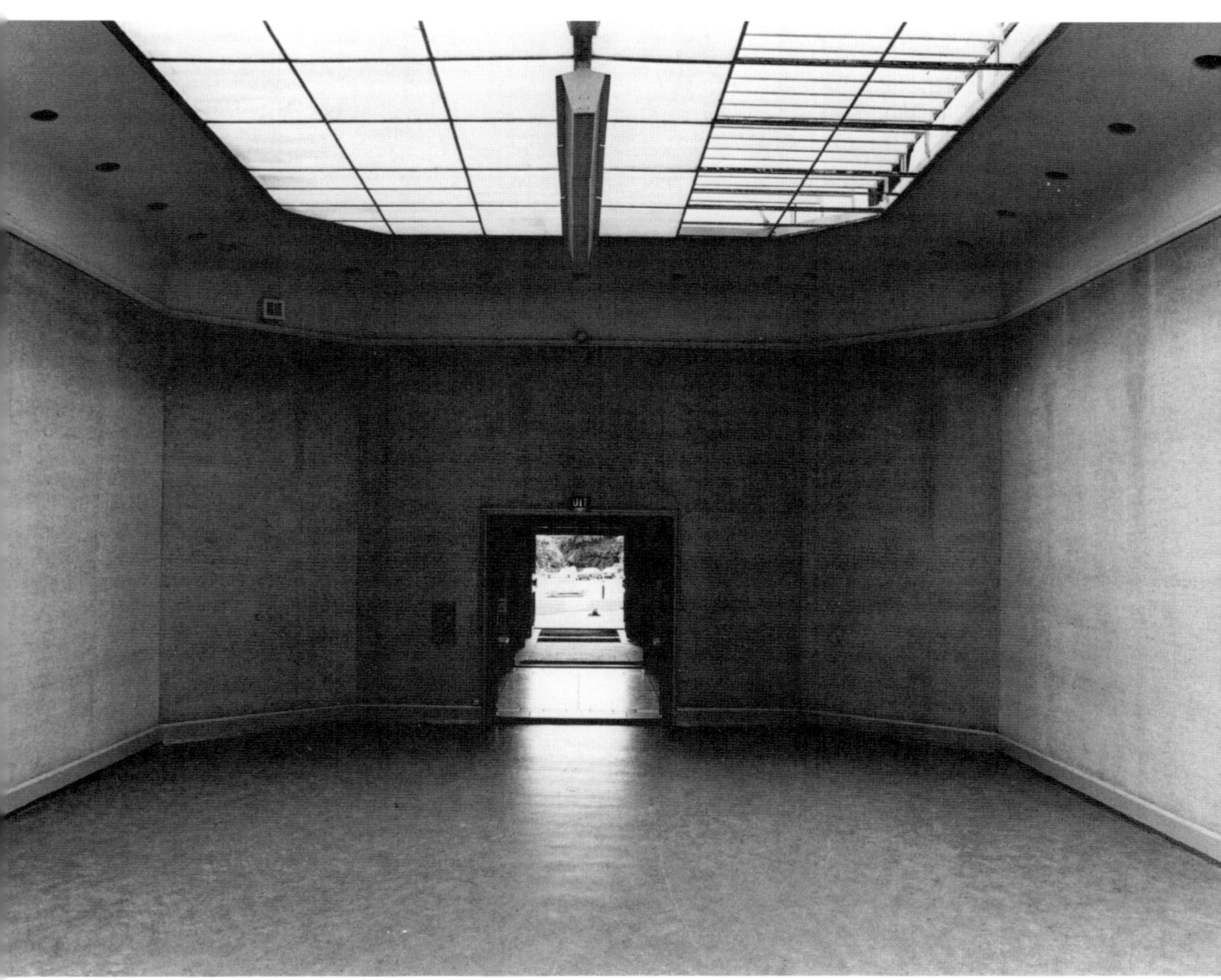

In the late spring of 1977, Marge Goldwater, curator of the Fort Worth Art Museum, visited me in Los Angeles to discuss the possibility of my participating in an exhibition, entitled "Los Angeles in the Seventies." In a letter dated June 14, 1977, I was officially invited to contribute a work to this exhibition which included works by Michael Brewster, Guy de Cointet, Judy Fiskin, Lloyd Hamrol, Loren Madsen, Michael McMillen, Eric Orr, and Roland Reiss. Conceived as a traveling exhibition of the work of Southern California artists, it was subsequently installed at the Joslyn Art Museum in Omaha, Nebraska, from March 1 to April 15, 1979. (see page 190) In the summer of 1977, I visited the Fort Worth Art Museum and started working on a proposal for the exhibition.

Soon thereafter, I submitted a proposal which was provisionally accepted by the museum, contingent on the approval of the other parties involved in the project. In addition to the sponsoring institution, the Fort Worth Art Museum, my proposal asked for the participation of two other museum institutions located in Fort Worth. These were the Kimbell Art Museum and the Amon Carter Museum of Western Art. Both museums were located within the immediate neighborhood of the Fort Worth Art Museum and were within several minutes' walking distance.

The Fort Worth Art Museum is dedicated to the collection and exhibition of twentieth-century and contemporary art. The Kimbell Art Museum houses a substantial collection of European painting and sculpture prior to the twentieth century as well as American art of that period. The Amon Carter Museum of Western Art houses a collection of early nineteenth- and twentieth-century American art.

The Fort Worth Art Museum was originally designed by Herbert Bayer. An addition to the original building was designed by Richard Oneslager. A second addition was constructed by the regional architectural group Ford, Powell, and Carson in 1973. The Kimbell Art Museum was designed and constructed by Louis L. Kahn and opened in 1972. The Amon Carter Museum of Western Art was designed by Philip Johnson and opened in 1961.

Because their collections and the architectural structures which house them differ so markedly, each museum is perceived in the community as having a separate identity. Due however to its impressive collection and its architectural merit, the Kimbell Art Museum is the major recipient of the community's interest if not its revenue. The Amon Carter Museum with its recognized collection of Western art of the United States and its architectural design by one of the better known American architects, is considered in the community as being of almost equal importance. The building and the contemporary collection of the Fort Worth Art Museum, on the other hand, has generally been considered to be of a more modest standing within the community.

Yet all three museum institutions clearly shared certain functions, such as the maintenance and storage of the collections, the mounting and dismantling of exhibitions, shipping and receiving of loans for exhibitions, and so on. These constants were reflected materially in the activities of the service vehicles in each museum's parking area. They were also manifested in the daily presence during working hours of private vehicles in those same parking areas belonging to administration and staff members who carried out similar functions in each institution. The three museums are located near a major intersection, approximately five minutes driving time from downtown Fort Worth.

All three institutions had separate parking areas for their visitors as well as specific parking zones for service and staff vehicles which were located behind each museum. It was partly these most obvious conditions that determined the structure of my proposal.

My proposal for this exhibition suggested that from November 14 to November 20, the last week of the exhibition, all three museums would share a parking lot for all their service and staff vehicles. This parking lot, which was in the vicinity but independent of all three museums' service parking areas, was central to the main entrances of all three museums and within a

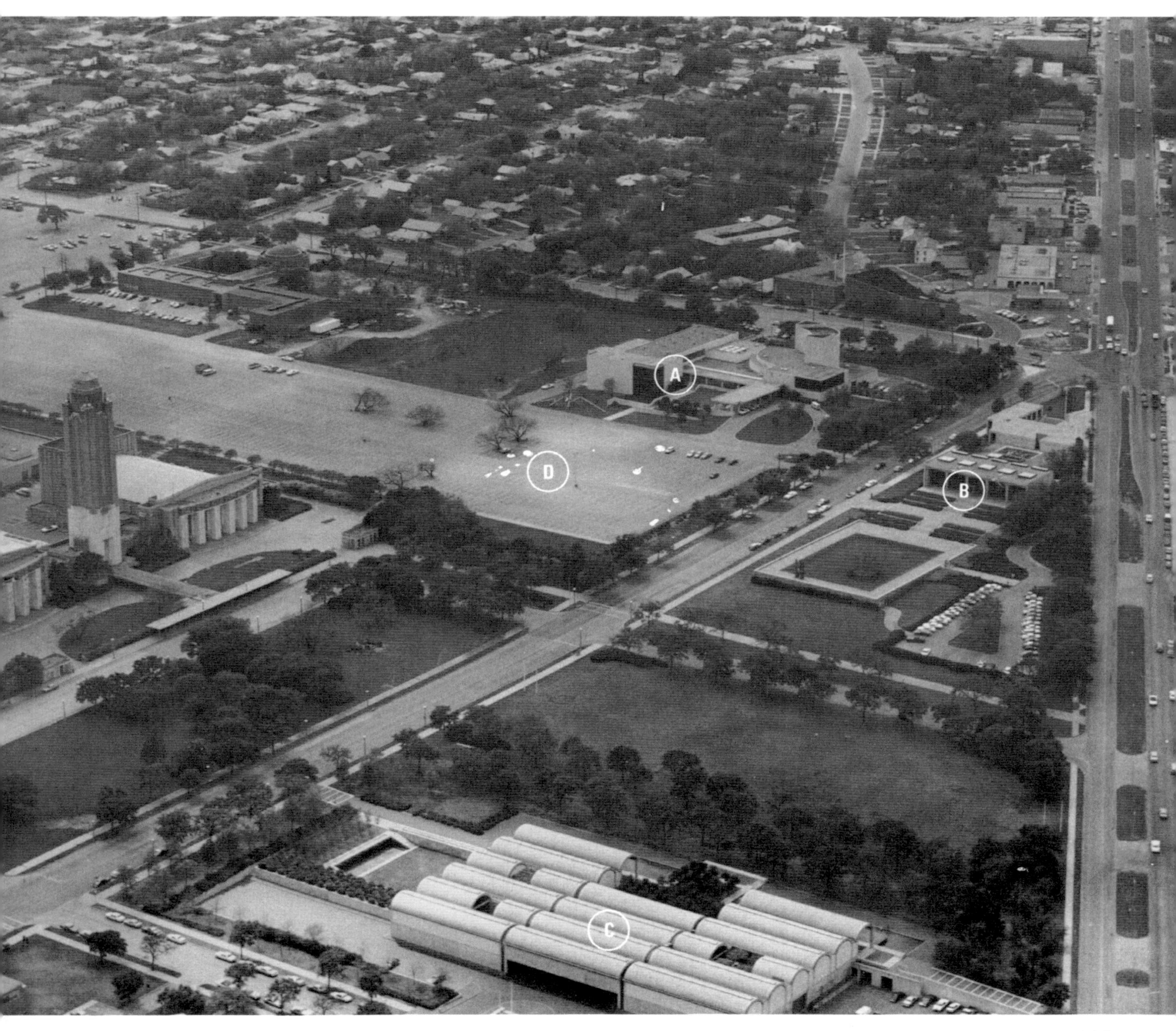

Aerial view. Courtesy: Fort Worth Art Museum, Fort Worth, Texas.
a. Location of service area of the Fort Worth Art Museum.
b. Location of service area of the Amon Carter Museum.
c. Location of service area of the Kimbell Art Museum.
d. Central parking lot area used for the installation.

Fort Worth Art Museum. Delivery area and service entrance.
Courtesy: Fort Worth Art Museum.

Kimbell Art Museum. Delivery area and service entrance.
Courtesy: Fort Worth Art Museum.

Amon Carter Museum. Delivery area and service entrance.
Courtesy: Fort Worth Art Museum.

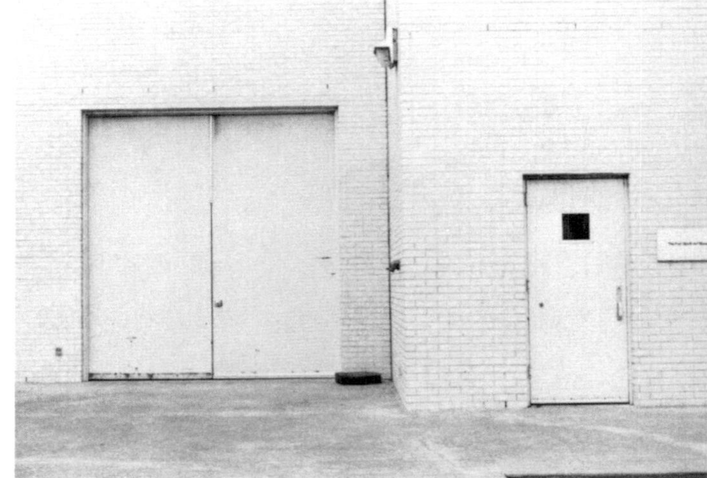

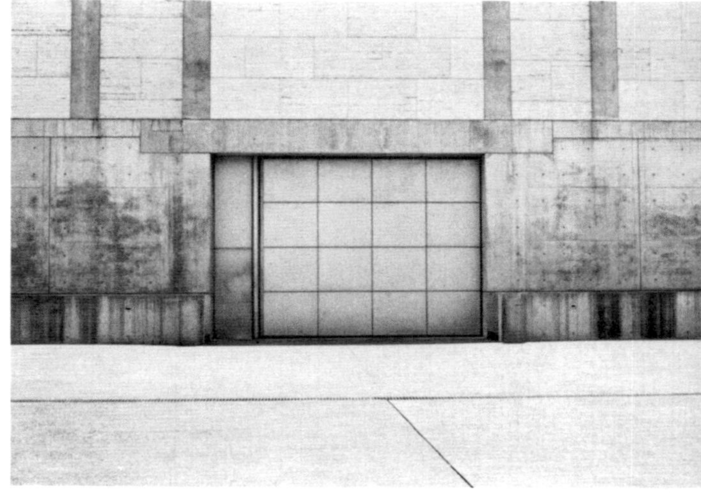

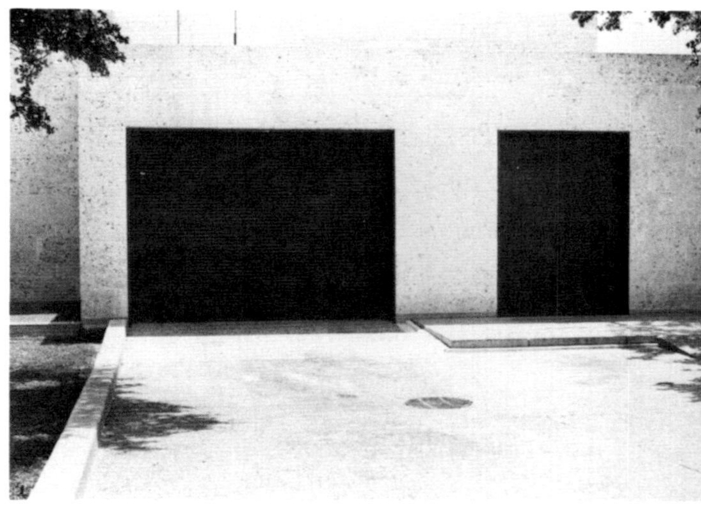

few minutes walking distance. It was understood that the regular service activities such as loading and unloading would be carried out by the service vehicles as usual in the respective service areas of each museum after which the vehicles would be parked in the temporarily defined common parking zone. A description of the work was available to visitors at the bookstores of the three museums.

This proposal, which I submitted in written form, was first accepted by the staff and administration of the Fort Worth Art Museum. All staff members at the Fort Worth Art Museum volunteered to participate in the work for the duration of one week. I made a verbal presentation of the same proposal at the lecture theater of the Kimbell Art Museum to inform the staff and administrators of the museum of my intentions and ideas and to invite them to participate. The comments that were made in the discussion after the presentation further revealed the lack of any social interaction between the staff members of the three institutions and questioned whether this proposal could possibly effect a change in the situation. There were questions about the spatial and temporal limits of the work; for example, one person asked whether on leaving the parking lot in his car he was still participating in the work. The museum photographer felt the idea should not be imposed on the staff but that the staff should itself shape the proposal and decide whether it was pertinent to them and whether their participation was reasonable or desirable. The general response to this presentation was positive, and I subsequently received a letter from Richard Brown, director of the Kimbell Art Museum, affirming the museum's support and collaboration with my project.

I approached a number of staff members and administrators at the Fort Worth Art Museum and discussed the proposal individually with them. In a communication to the curator of the Fort Worth Art Museum they confirmed their general participation in the project after they had learned about the Kimbell Art Museum's participation.

As of November 14, the work began with most of

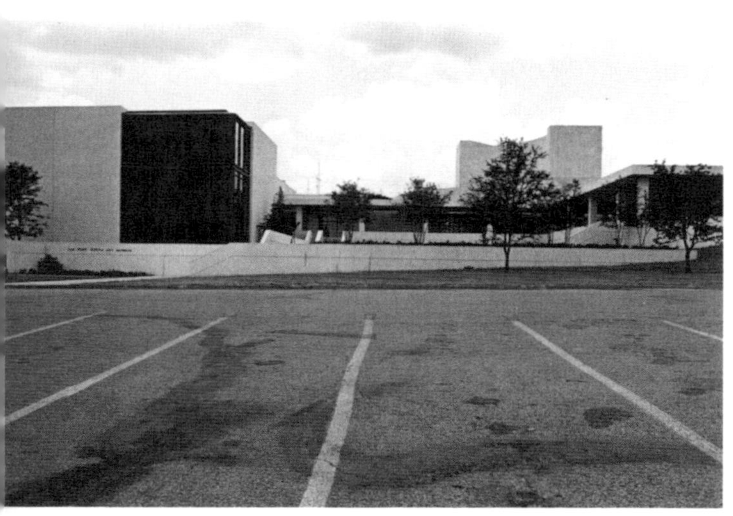

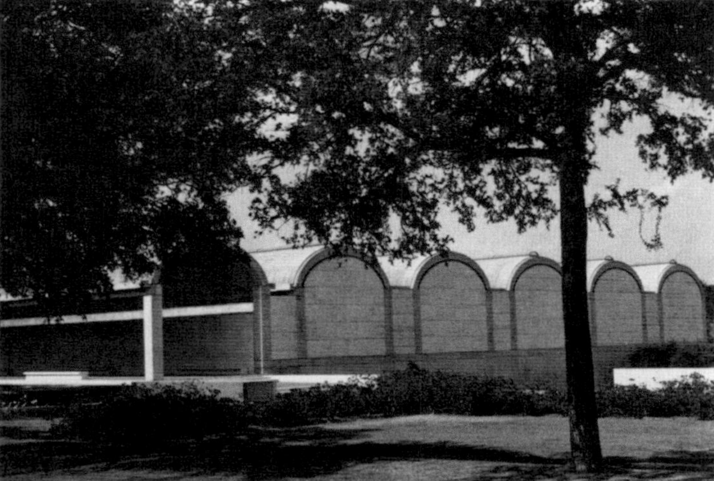

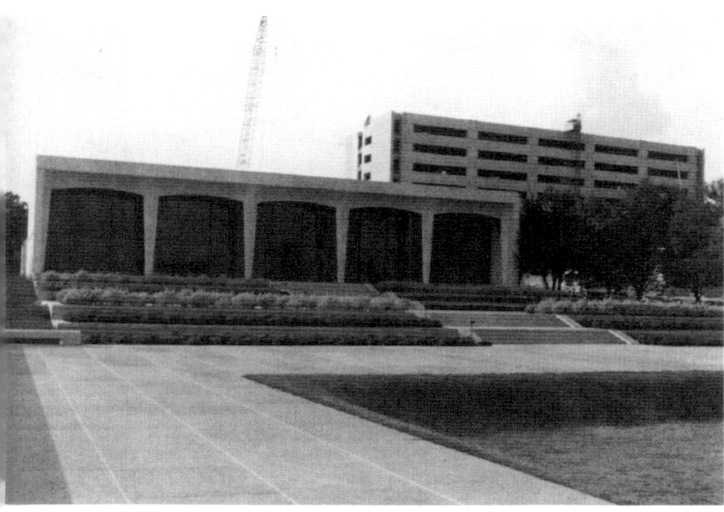

Side view of the Fort Worth Art Museum. Photograph by Michael Asher.

Frontal view of the Kimbell Art Museum. Photograph by Michael Asher.

West view of the facade of the Amon Carter Museum. Photograph by Michael Asher.

the service and staff vehicles parking in the northeast corner of the parking lot between the Will Rogers Coliseum and the Forth Worth Art Museum which had been assigned as the common parking zone. This involved an additional two- or three-minute walk to and from the parking lot for staff members to reach their respective workplace. This meant that staff had to alot at most an additional three minutes particularly in the morning, in order to arrive on time. The staff members of the three institutions did not necessarily arrive or depart at exactly the same time, as their lunch-hour habits differed individually. Yet it frequently happened that staff members and administrators of the three institutions encountered each other while parking their cars in the morning on arrival or when departing from the parking lot after working hours. Some members of the different institutions actually met and talked to each other in the parking lot. The service vehicles of the three institutions arrived and departed from the parking lot at various times during the day or were parked for periods of time in this lot while not in service.

I had decided to stay in Fort Worth for at least the first two days of the work's operation to be available for any questions or suggestions coming from the participants. During this period it seemed to me that almost all members of the staff and administration of the three museum institutions had decided to actually follow up on their commitment to participate. Some of the staff members informed me that they had changed their habit of entering or leaving the building only through the service entry/exit and that by using the main entrance they found they were paying more attention to the presence of the collection in the museum. One curator, for example, told me that she normally entered the exhibition area only on those occasions when she had curated the exhibition herself, whereas now she passed through the exhibition area regularly before entering her office. Some of the staff members also said that they had hardly ever taken the time to notice what the main entrance of the museum looked like.

I realized on the second day of the installation that staff members were clustering their cars together on the parking lot, whereas on the first day it seemed they had parked their cars in a completely random order. It seemed that many staff members knew their colleague's cars through make and model, and by identifying the cars parked on the lot they seemed to learn about their colleagues' participation in the work. Furthermore, they tended to become acquainted with other colleagues first through recognition of their cars' make and model in the temporarily defined parking lot.

The installation was completed on November 20, when the staff members returned to their habit of entering their museum building through the staff entrance and parking their vehicles in each museum's service areas.

In this work I tried to deal with the notion of collaboration. Normally museum staff members facilitate the staging of exhibitions by performing their various functions and specific responsibilities which remain hidden from the viewer and are unrecorded in any documentation that may exist; their activities are obliterated by the work itself and are therefore not perceived as essential to the work's production, presentation, and reception. Yet by suggesting a slight, nondisruptive alteration to the daily pattern of the staff's arrival and departure to and from the museum, the work did not claim to be a participatory work or a group performance. Participation would have meant that their daily work activities be transformed into a "performance" or become part of an exhibition spectacle. By focusing on the employee's transportation vehicle and its arrival and departure, the work directed viewers' attention to an essential object in which alienated labor was materialized. It also pointed out the function of transportation to and from work that that object actually performed, whereas actual labor could not be perceived in the work itself. Demonstrating the actual labor performance by which the employees contributed to the maintenance of the institution and its continued exhibition activities would have meant aestheticizing alienated labor. Subject-

ing their labor to aesthetic appropriation would have alienated their work a second time. In this regard, the work was essentially different from the installation at Eindhoven where alienated labor had been integrated in the fabrication of the work.

This work was defined by the construction of a single meeting point which abolished temporarily the instrumental separation between the three museum institutions and their employees' arrival and departure at those institutions. The work generated the following questions: Did the fact that employees of the three different institutions complied with the work's proposal to temporarily abandon their normal affiliation with one institution (inasmuch as it was embodied in their daily pattern of choosing the separate parking lot) deprive them of their daily experience of secured identity? Or, was their sense of identity increased by the fact that this work made them realize that the instrumental separation of their individual institutions had alienated them from other individuals working in similar positions in similar institutions?

The viewer could perceive this work through the description and definition of the work that existed for the viewer as a handout in the bookstore/information areas of all three museums; or as a material procedure occurring in a location outside of the three museums. The material elements visible in this location, however, were not necessarily part of the work's procedure but existed also as separate entities outside the confines of the work's definition.

Both of these elements of the work were mutually dependent upon each other for readability and visibility. The definition of the work functioned as an intervention/operation within a support structure that consisted of the behavioral everyday patterns of each institution. This operation was integrated within the support structure to such a degree that it coalesced with it and lost its own separate visibility and identity as a construction of visual meaning. Therefore, instead of foregrounding or extrapolating elements from a given support structure and integrating them into an aesthetic structure, the work introduced procedural change within the existing support structure itself.

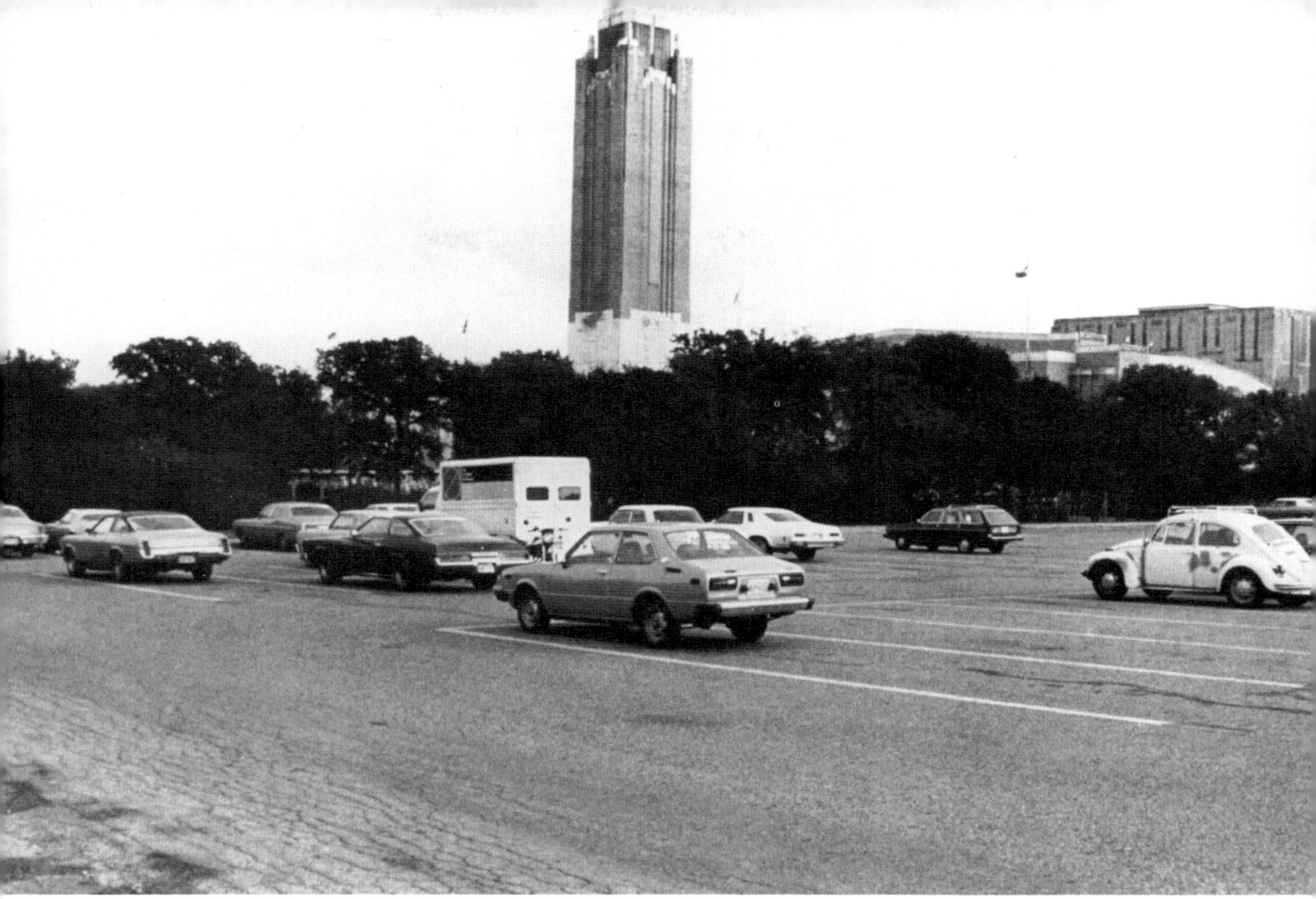

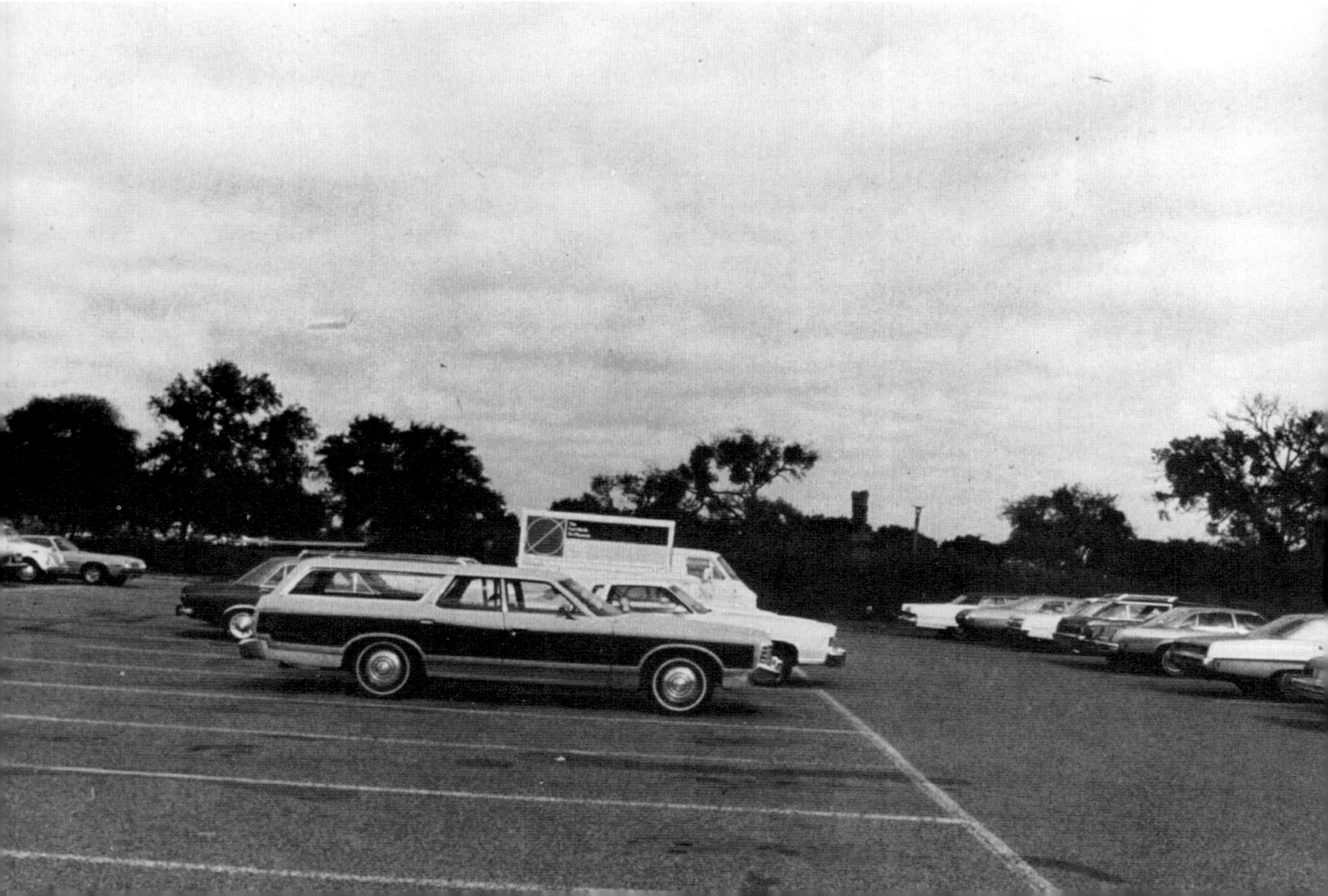

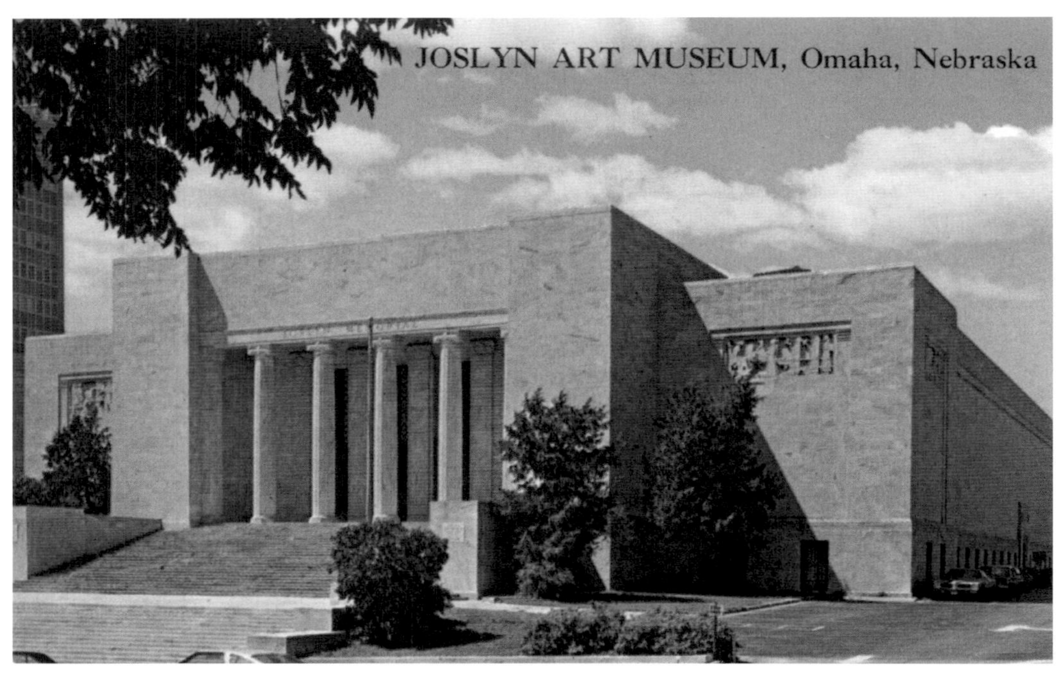
JOSLYN ART MUSEUM, Omaha, Nebraska

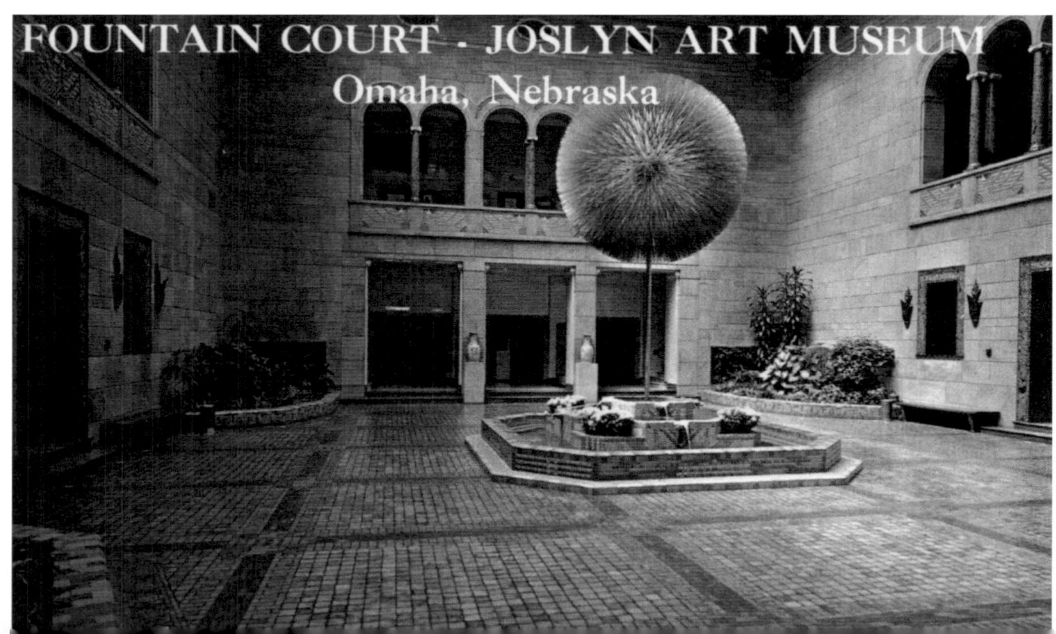
FOUNTAIN COURT · JOSLYN ART MUSEUM
Omaha, Nebraska

Postcard of the Joslyn Art Museum, Omaha, Nebraska. West view of the facade.

Postcard of the Fountain Court of the Joslyn Art Museum. West view.

In late June 1978 I visited the Joslyn Art Museum in Omaha, Nebraska, in order to prepare my contribution to the second installation of the traveling exhibition "Los Angeles in the Seventies." The Joslyn Art museum was designed and constructed by the Omaha architects John and Alan McDonald from 1928 to 1931, a late twenties synthesis of neoclassical style and Art Deco architectural ornamentation. The ground plan of the main floor of the museum is symmetrical along its east-west axis, but asymmetrical along its shorter north-south axis. The plan shows a core of five areas that are connected but that do not function as the main exhibition space. These are from east to west: the east entrance and lobby, the fountain court which functions as a rest area for visitors, and the foyer, all of which are approximately the same size; the large concert hall, almost the same size as the first three areas combined, and, finally, a smaller room, used as a members room and not accessible to the general public. On the north and south side along this core there are five actual gallery spaces. Their east-west spatial divisions, dimensions, and sequence are identical in both the north and south wing. Two identical hallways that are also used for exhibition purposes separate the exhibition gallery on the north and the south side from the east entrance, the fountain court, and the foyer. The design of these hallways reappears behind the concert hall in the form of two small vestibule areas which give access to the Joslyn Members Room and are used as exhibition areas for the decorative arts. The north wing is used for temporary exhibitions, while the south wing houses the museum's permanent collection of art that spans the fifteenth to the twentieth century.

The "Los Angeles in the Seventies" exhibition was planned for the north galleries on the main floor. My proposal was to create a zone from the south wall of the north galleries to the middle of the core museum spaces, extending the full length of the museum, thus bisecting the core area into two zones of equal size. It so happened that the two zones of the core space were each approximately equal in width to the

exhibition galleries on the north and south sides. From the northern zone all movable objects were removed, such as paintings and sculpture, benches, ashtrays, display cases, stands, bases, and flags. Only those objects that were permanently installed or part of the interior remained, such as built-in planters and plants, heating elements, and lighting fixtures. The objects that were removed were put into storage for the duration of the exhibition and the zone remained empty and unaltered according to my instructions. My proposal did not affect the galleries on the ground floor or those on the second floor, but only those on the main floor where the actual installation of the exhibition "Los Angeles in the Seventies" was visible.

A description/definition of my installation and a ground plan showing the location of my work within the museum was available to the viewer at the main-floor front desk in the east-entrance lobby and the ground-floor bookstore.

Upon entering viewers found themselves in the east-entrance lobby from which no objects had been removed. As viewers moved on into the next room of the core zone, they entered the fountain court. On the west side of the fountain court a pair of ancient Chinese Ming vases was normally displayed on solid stone pedestals, and a pair of ancient Chinese sculptures representing mythical animals was installed on identical pedestals on the east side of the fountain court. There were also two benches and two ashtrays, each symmetrically placed on the north and south side of the court. One of each of these symmetrically displayed elements in the fountain court was removed from the north side according to my proposal. In the next room of the core zone, the foyer, there were two glass display cases, symmetrically placed north and south, containing small-scale ancient artifacts. The one on the north side, including its contents, was removed and placed in storage. The systematic removal of all these elements from the north side of the three core areas established a viewing perspective that connected all areas on an east-west axis that had been depleted of movable objects. The areas on the south side were

JOSLYN ART MUSEUM

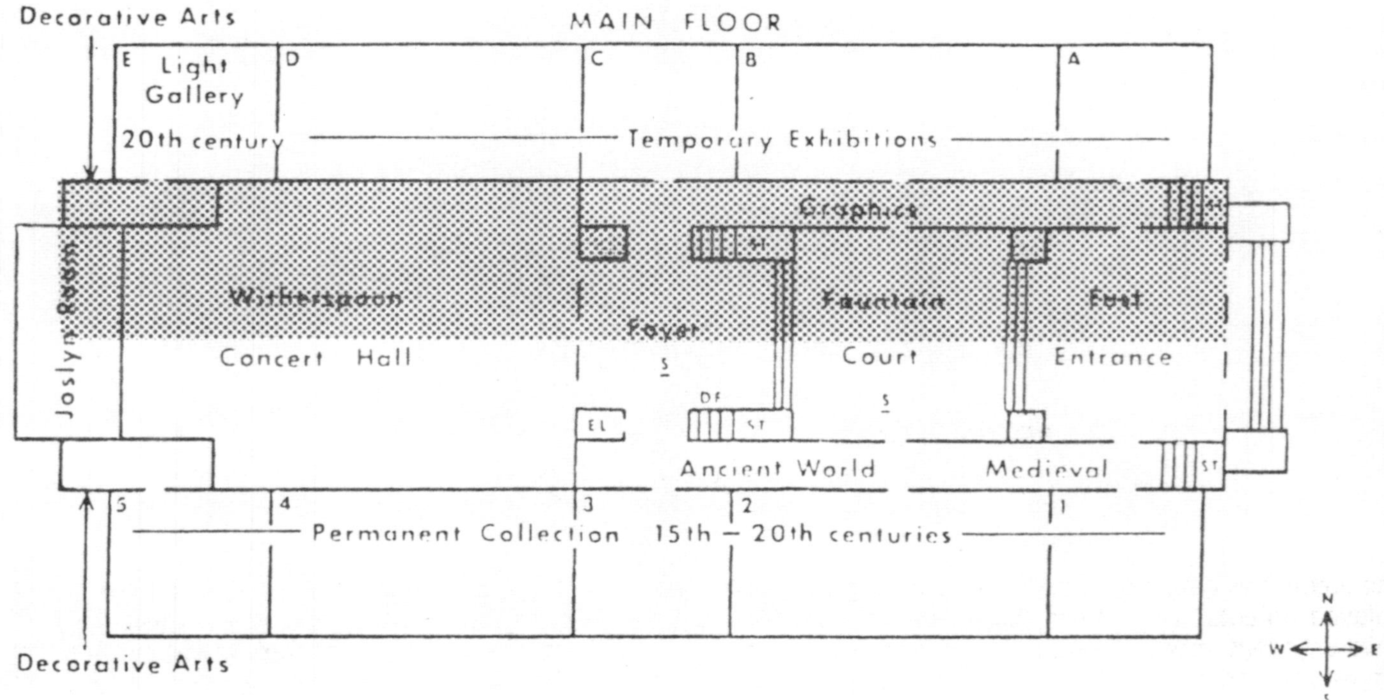

Michael Asher

"The Joslyn Art Museum was constructed following a symmetrical ground plan so that the north and south sides mirror one another in interior size, shape, and detail. At the same time, the perimeter galleries were constructed with a common centerline to mirror each other from their furthest extents from east to west. Contained in the middle is the main entrance, fountain court, foyer, concert hall, and Joslyn room which together form an assymetrical core from the east to the west walls of the museum. I am particularly interested in the formal layout of the museum and its attention to ornamentation and construction detail.

"Generally, the southern galleries are used for the permanent collection. From March 1 to April 15, the northern galleries will contain the exhibition "Los Angeles in the Seventies". It is this exhibition I am a part of. Yet my contribution to this exhibition is not in the northern galleries, but adjacent to them. For the exhibition, I am creating a zone by framing an area from the northern wall of the north hallway to the centerline of the museum and extending it from floor to ceiling. Everything which is movable from this area has been put in storage. This includes all artifacts or works of art, ornamentation, benches, cases, stands, ashtrays, vases, and flags."

MICHAEL ASHER

connected by the presence of those symmetrically displayed objects. The viewer could therefore perceive two adjacent zones throughout the core area of the museum, one filled with objects, the other emptied of objects, within a biaxial, symmetrical, neoclassical architectural framework.

All graphics, prints, and flags displayed in the north hallway were removed, with only the permanently attached display paneling left in place. The south hallway, however—like the southern half of the core areas—remained untouched and continued to contain its usual quantity of display elements, art objects and medieval artifacts. Decorative art objects were also removed from the north vestibule, whereas similar objects in the south vestibule remained in place. As a result of this bisection the northern zone of the museum core areas was subjected to the same operations that were normally performed in the northern galleries for temporary exhibitions, such as dismantling and removal, and reinstallation of art objects and presentation devices. Whereas the southern zone of the core area remained static, as did the permanent collection in the adjacent southern galleries.

This was the first of my installations to subject other works of art and their nonarchitectural presentational devices to a material operation, in this instance removal or withdrawal. In previous works the process of removal had focused on the material architectural elements of presentation within the gallery/museum context (for example, the works at the Toselli Gallery, the Logsdail Gallery, and the Eindhoven Museum). Yet, the installations at the Stedelijk van Abbemuseum Eindhoven and at the Claire Copley/Morgan Thomas Galleries did have, in fact, implicit consequences for the installation and display of other works of art. Focusing on an institution's actual art objects rather than on its presentational strategies seemed necessary in my work in order to avoid its being understood as a formal aesthetic, perceptive operation within a purely architectural context.

This work responds to the architectural display system that alienates works of art by manipulating their sense of origin, to the extent that they are perceived as being materially out of context. The abstraction and rigidity of the architectural display system is further revealed by the fact that objects of everyday use, with no apparent cultural value, such as benches and ashtrays, are subjected to the same ordering system of symmetrical display within the museum structure.

Rather than interfering with the actual objects, this work intervenes within the institutional conventions that contain and display cultural objects and objects of everyday use interchangeably, revealing in what way they are dispersed, displayed, and codified.

The work questions therefore whether the perception of the viewer within an institutional situation is determined more by the modes of object display and their dependence on the architectural conditions of a given structure, or by the discourse of abstracted and alienated cultural objects themselves.

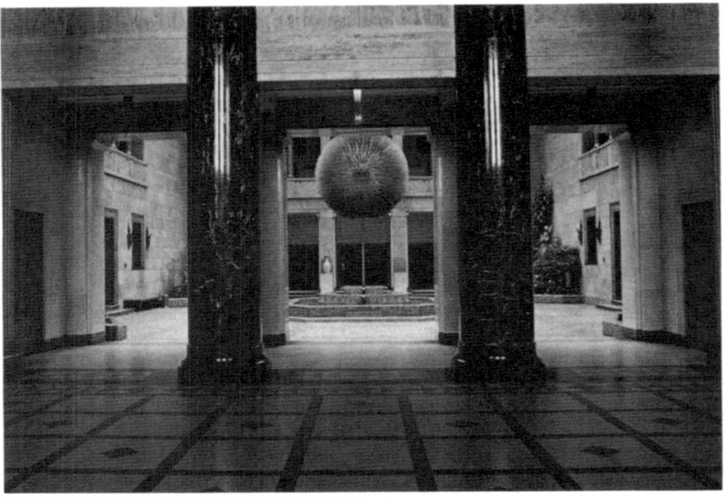

Viewing west from entry/exit toward Witherspoon foyer.

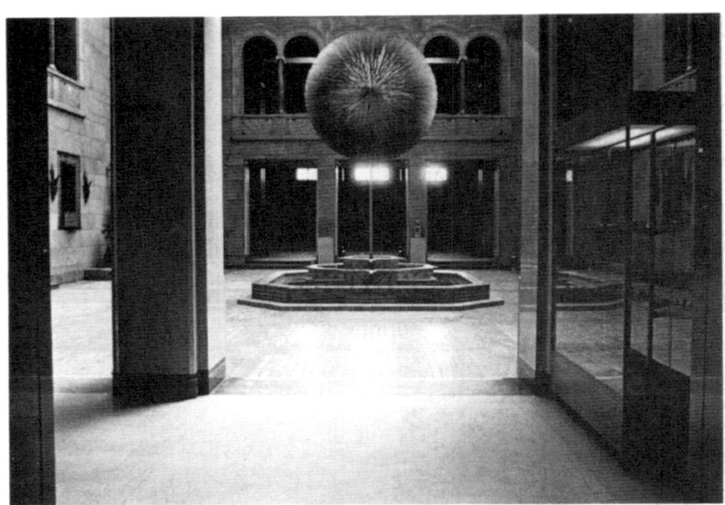

East view from Witherspoon foyer toward entry/exit.

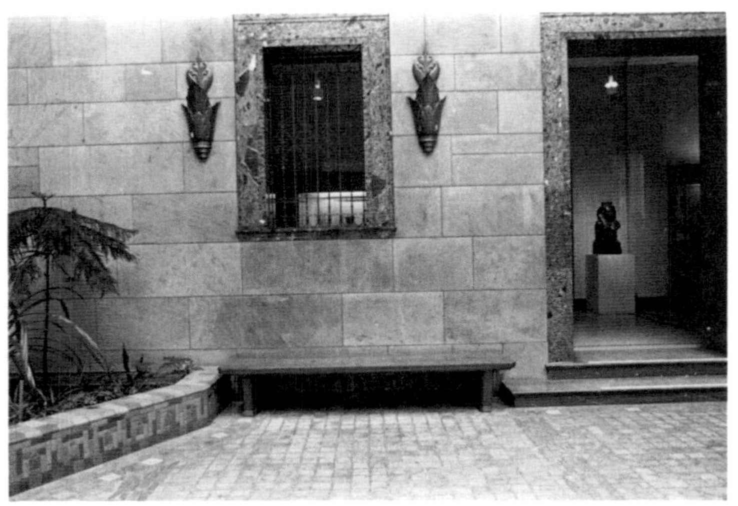

Fountain Court. South view.

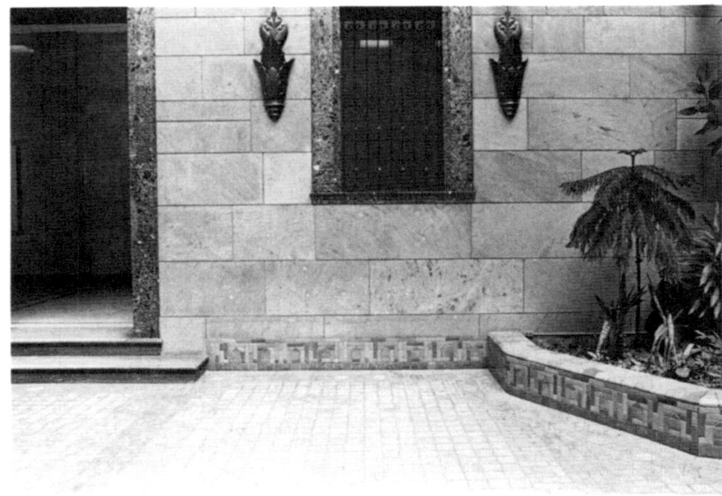

Fountain Court. North view.

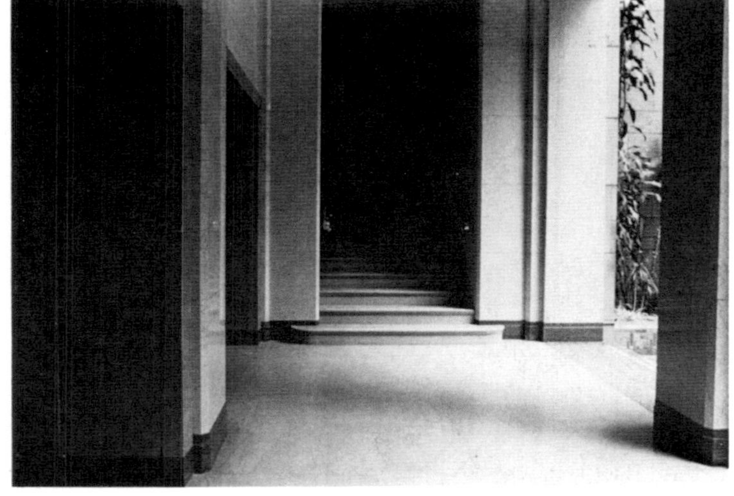

Viewing north in Witherspoon foyer.

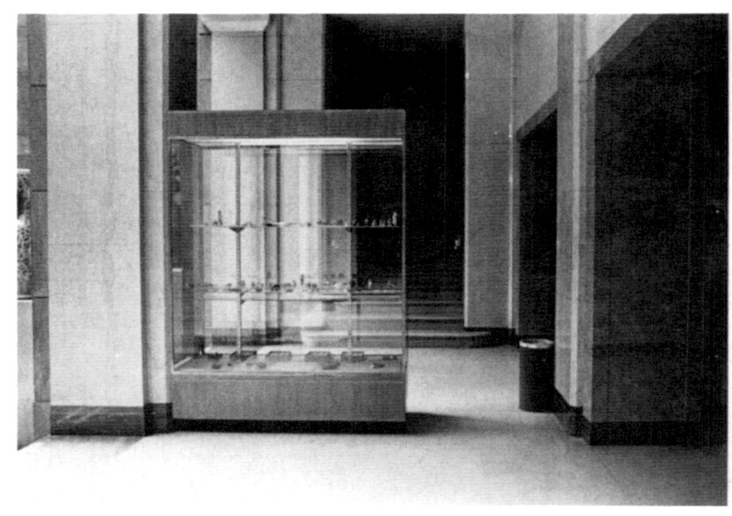

Viewing south in Witherspoon foyer.

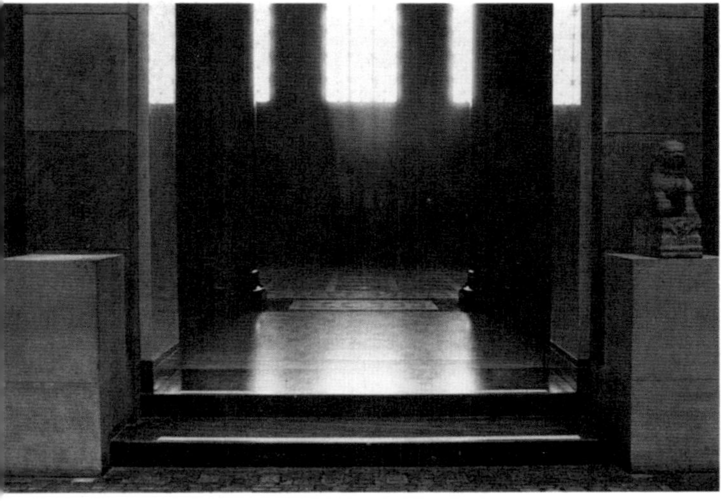

Viewing east toward entry/exit from fountain court.

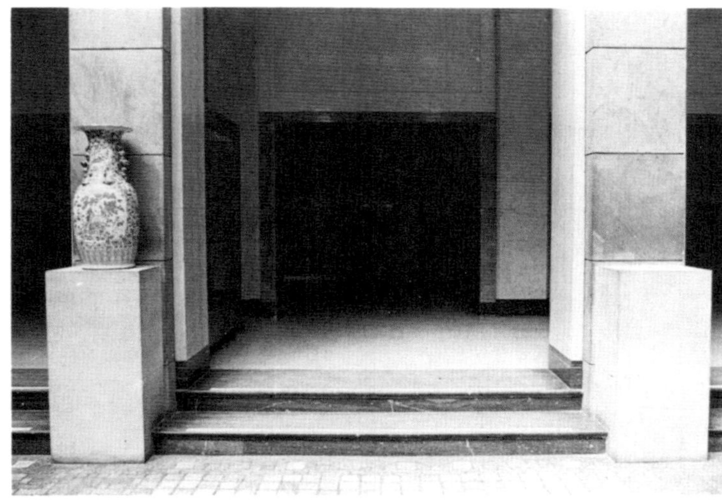

Viewing west from Fountain Court to Witherspoon foyer.

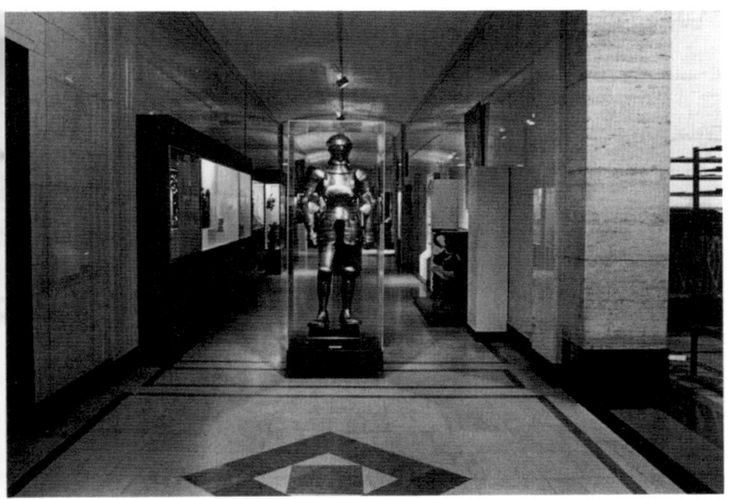

South hallway (Ancient World and Medieval), viewing west.

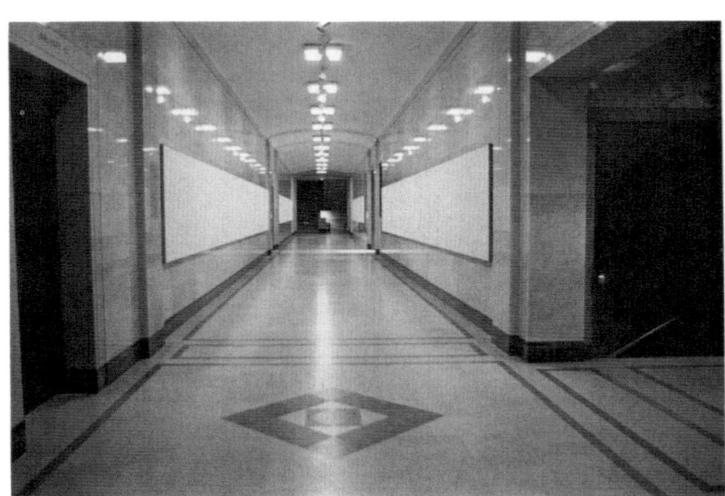

North hallway (graphics), viewing east.

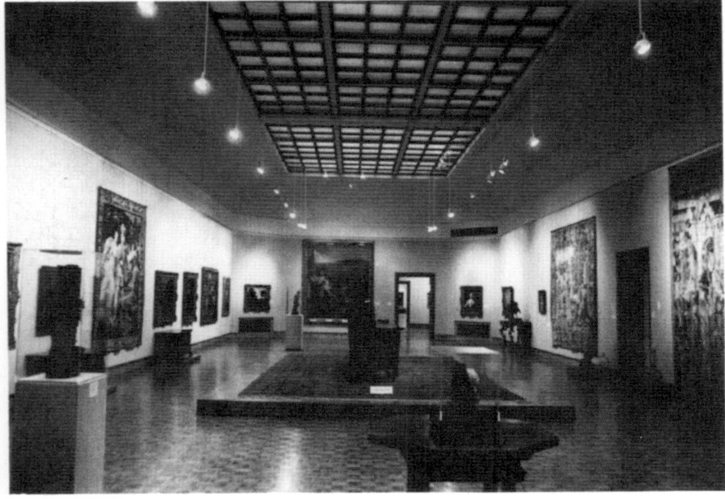

Permanent collection. Viewing west.

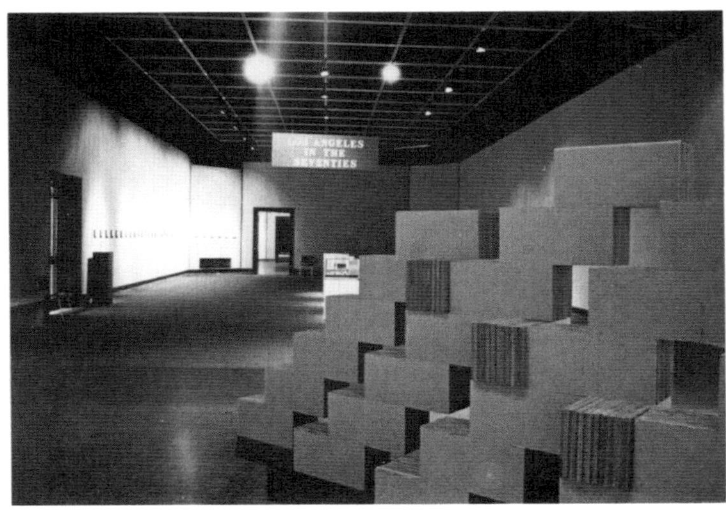

Temporary exhibitions area, viewing west.

In July 1978, I visited the Museum of Contemporary Art in Chicago at the invitation of Judith Kirshner, its curator, to discuss plans for a forthcoming exhibition. The museum was in the very early stages of being entirely remodelled, so that it was difficult to visualize what its future spatial and architectural dimensions would be. I therefore requested the architectural plans to augment photographs I had taken of the existing museum structure and the area surrounding it.

I then developed my concept for an installation based on the design of Booth, Nagle, and Hartray, the architectural firm that had been commissioned to redesign the museum. The plans called for an annex to be built on the museum's west side and a glassed-in promenade-gallery, which would bridge the new annex to the east side of the museum. The glassed-in structure, named the Bergman Gallery, would function as a showcase, so that the art presented inside the gallery would be visible from the street. It would be constructed at second-story level, above and in front of the already existing building, to create the appearance of a larger architectural structure. My plans for an installation were based on this new gallery structure, which was completed before the installation of my work.

The Bergman Gallery is 75½ feet long, 13 feet wide, and 19 feet from floor to ceiling. The plans included an entirely new design for the facade which was based on a 5½ foot square-grid pattern, idiomatic of the International Style. The same grid pattern, constructed of glass and aluminum framing, was applied to the facade of the Bergman Gallery, with aluminum panel cladding used to cover the existing museum facade on either side. The aluminum panels appear to wrap around the entire building, but, much like a prop in a Hollywood movie set, terminate approximately 15 feet beyond the corner. This appearance of being unfinished conveys the notion of future growth and an interest in expanded museum activities, and lays the groundwork for the future stages of construction included in the original design.

The aluminum cladding and architectural detail-ing are derivative of what we may call the history of the interrelationship of modernist architecture and art. For example, the diagonal webbing and glass seen in relation to the perpendicular cladding constitute a reference to elements of Constructivism, which had been absorbed and translated into formal abstractions by International Style architecture. The aluminum cladding refers to International Style architectural elements, but, even more so, to the subsequent integration of Constructivist and Bauhaus elements in the idiom of Minimal sculpture. This is reflected in the square-grid pattern as well as in the flat, square metal panels and their textured anodized finish. Therefore the outer shell of the new facade billboards itself not only as architecture but also as contemporary sculpture. By juxtaposing elements of these two different disciplines, it deprives both disciplines of their specific meaning and function, and creates an ideological language that conveys a message of a cultural notion of technocratic progress.

For my installation I proposed that the two horizontal rows of aluminum panels on either side of and on the same level as the Bergman Gallery windows should be removed from the facade and placed on an interior wall of the gallery for the duration of the exhibition. The ten panels from the east side of the building and the eight panels from the west side were to be arranged inside in the same formation and sequence, but in a position which was not identical to what their exterior placement had been.

The east tower of the museum had four panels on the street side of the facade and six more panels wrapped around the alley side of the tower. These ten panels were extended around in a sideways projection and placed sequentially as a flat plane on the interior wall. The last two aluminum panels in each row were only 38 inches wide, due to the depth of the new construction. These two panels lined up with the vertical window mullion of the east side of the gallery and the rest of the panels extended 22 feet along the wall, from the east toward the center of the gallery wall.

The west tower had eight panels on the street

Facade of the Museum of Contemporary Art, Chicago with panels in place and work in public storage. Photograph courtesy The Museum of Contemporary Art, Chicago.

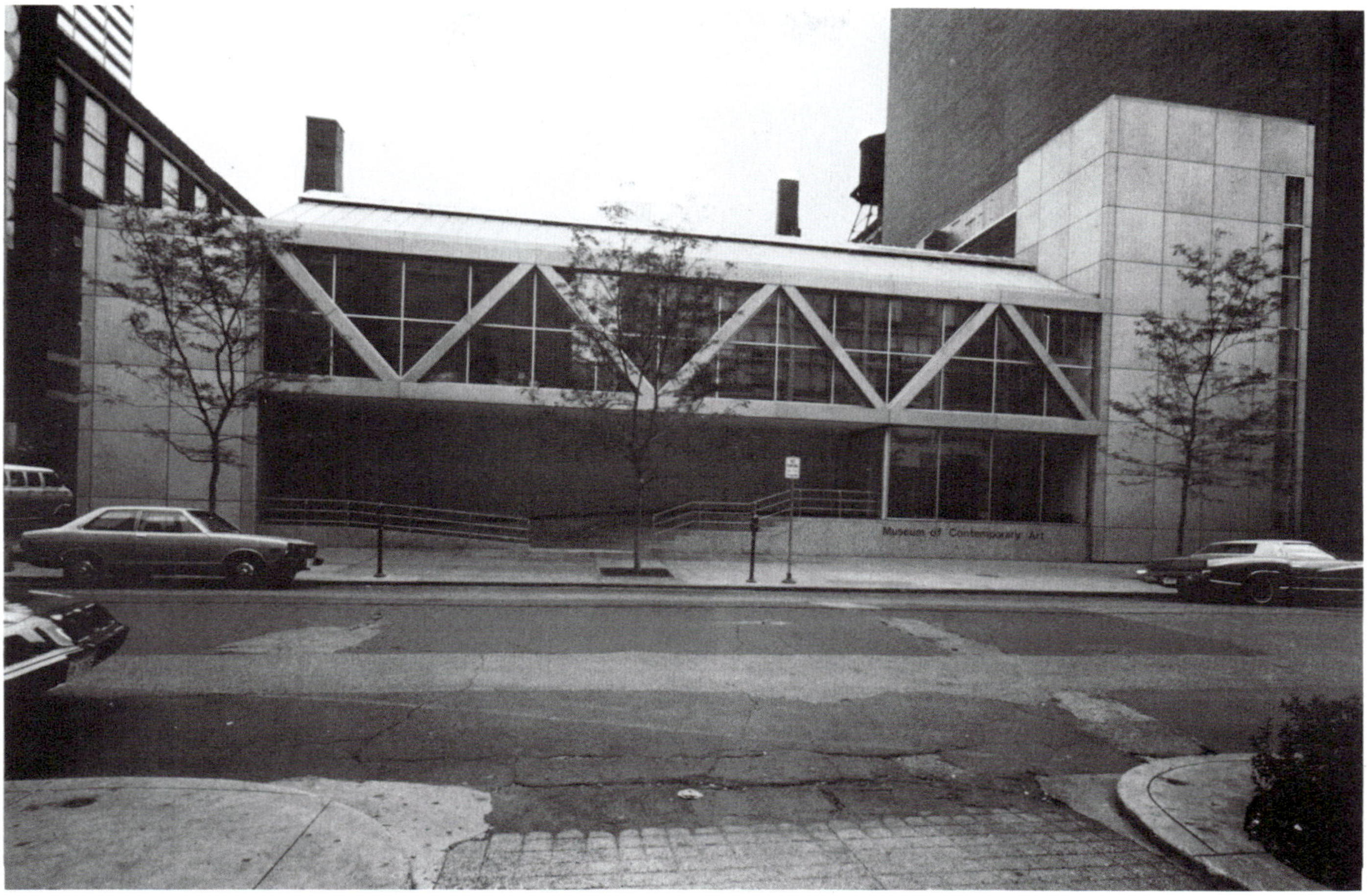

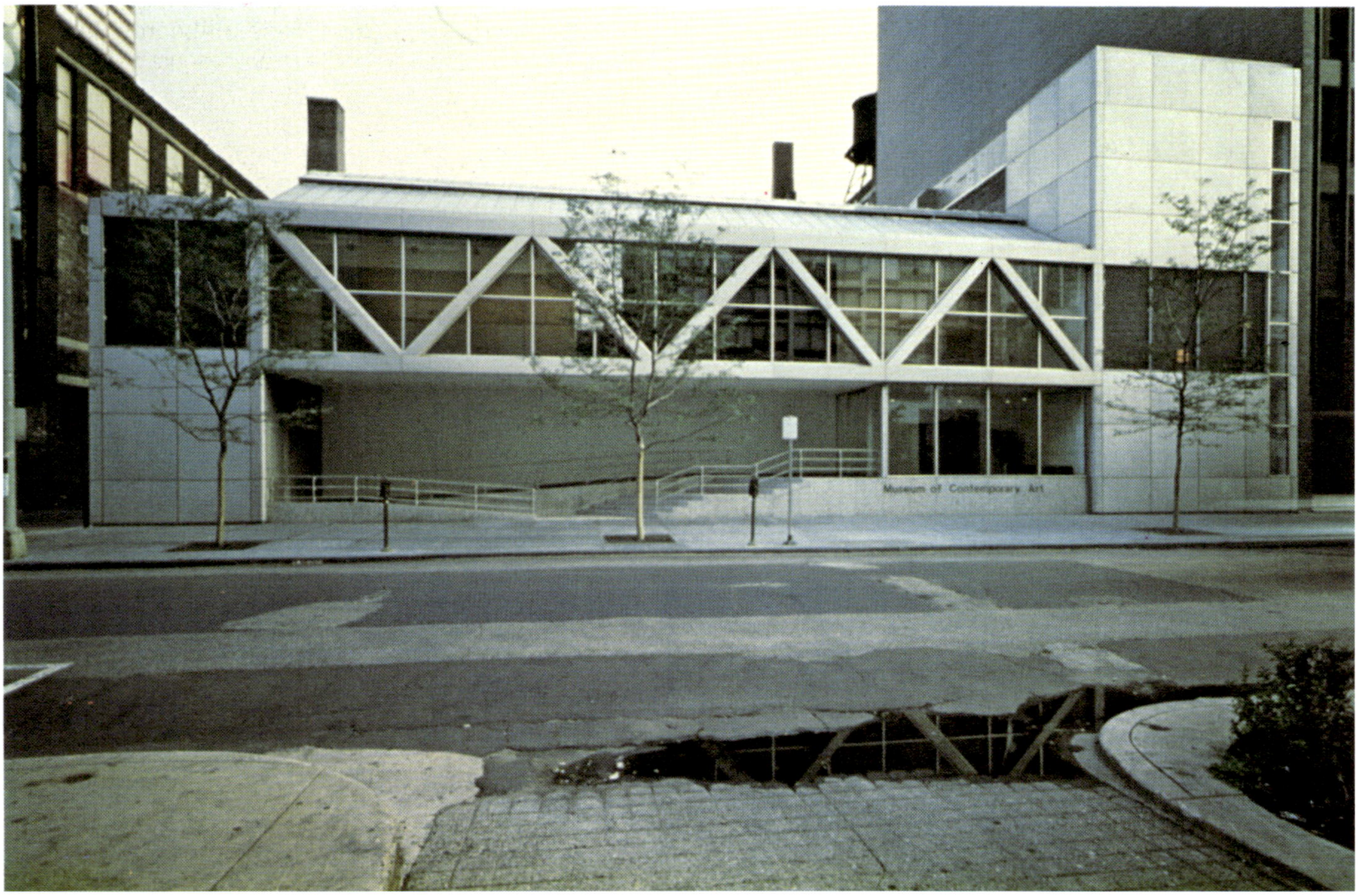

Facade of the Museum of Contemporary Art during exhibition. Photograph courtesy The Museum of Contemporary Art, Chicago. Photographs by Tom Van Eynde.

side, the last two of which measured only 30 inches in width in order to make room for a window construction running vertically along the facade. These eight panels were also projected sideways and placed on the gallery wall, beginning at a point 30 inches east of the vertical window mullion, to take into account the absence of panel cladding on this part of the exterior facade, extending 24 feet 9 inches towards the center of the wall, leaving 30 feet of unused wall space in between. Besides lining up with the outer margin at the first window mullion on an east-west axis, the installation was also placed at the same height as the windows; so that the bottom lined up with the bottom of the window-frame and the top lined up with its top, leaving 8 feet of empty wall space above the panels.

In their new interior position, the panels were located the same distance from the wall ($2\frac{1}{4}$ inches) as they had been in their original outdoor relief. For the purposes of this installation, the channels holding the cladding to the exterior walls had to be modified in order to allow for the removal and replacement of the panels. Identical channels were made and attached to the gallery wall in order to accept the cladding. The entire work, both its exterior and interior elements, could be viewed from the street. The removal of the cladding from the exterior revealed the painted cement block of the building. It became apparent that the aluminum cladding functioned as a skin of ornamentation for the exterior.

Once these plates were placed on the walls within the interior of the museum and were showcased behind glass, they became subject to the perceptual conditions that permit and determine an artwork's existence. Here the installation of the cladding panels assured features that were idiomatic of Minimalist aesthetics; in particular, the modular grid systems and the prefabricated industrial material elements. Although the aluminum panels in the museum were identical to those on the exterior, they were no longer perceived as a symbolic expression of the museum's expansion and future growth. Rather, they were perceived as an autonomous sculptural phenomenon within the modernist tradition.

Because of the assumption, within the modernist tradition, that applied art is different from autonomous art, the panels showcased in the museum appeared to have greater importance than the identical panels on the exterior wall, where the aluminum cladding functioned only as a decorative element of architecture.

The display wall of the Bergman Gallery was constructed primarily as a neutral backdrop for large-scale modernist painting. In order to preserve its formalist discourse, Minimal sculpture also used the supposedly neutral architectural container as one of its constituent parts. Another crucial concept at the origins of Minimalist aesthetics was the idea of the relief as a transition from two-dimensional to three-dimensional objects. In the work at the Museum of Contemporary Art these formal and material elements of Minimal aesthetics were utilized and were then returned, for the purpose of observation, to the interior architectural support structure from which they had originated.

The work at the Museum of Contemporary Art points to the conditions in which architecture and art, as practices, have become irreconcilable. Stylistic similarities may be the only manner in which these two practices seem to cross-reference.

Because the historical differences between the two practices had to be clarified, in this installation, I attempted to literally deconstruct the elements of the facade, thereby changing their meaning by negating both their architectural and sculptural readings, which the building had originally attempted to fuse. I contextualized the sculpture to display the architecture and the architecture to display the problems of sculpture.

Sculpture can be only momentarily effective if it allows its inherent contradictions and ambiguities to become visible within the present institutional and cultural conditions. Although the possibility always exists that architecture could be influenced by art, its integrity is not based upon these influences but on its own capacity to function and to fulfill needs.

Five months prior to the actual installation, the Museum of Contemporary Art in Chicago agreed to purchase the work for their permanent collection. The museum's goal of increasing its permanent collection, which finds its expression in the placement of the aluminum cladding as exterior ornament, was addressed by the installation of that cladding in the interior and by the work's integration into the permanent collection. This installation was meant to operate only until the next phase of the museum's construction.The museum's staff will decide when the installation of the work will be repeated. Each time it will be installed for two months or the length of a temporary exhibition.

The first installation of this work took place from June 8 through August 12, 1979. After August 12, 1979, the aluminum panels were reinstalled on the exterior of the building. Each time the aluminum panels are replaced to their original exterior position, they are being stored in full public view or, in other words, in open storage, while the rest of the museum's permanent collection remains inside and generally inaccessible to public view.

During the first installation, Sol Lewitt chose to do a wall drawing on the 30 feet of unused center wall space between the east and west cluster of installed panels.

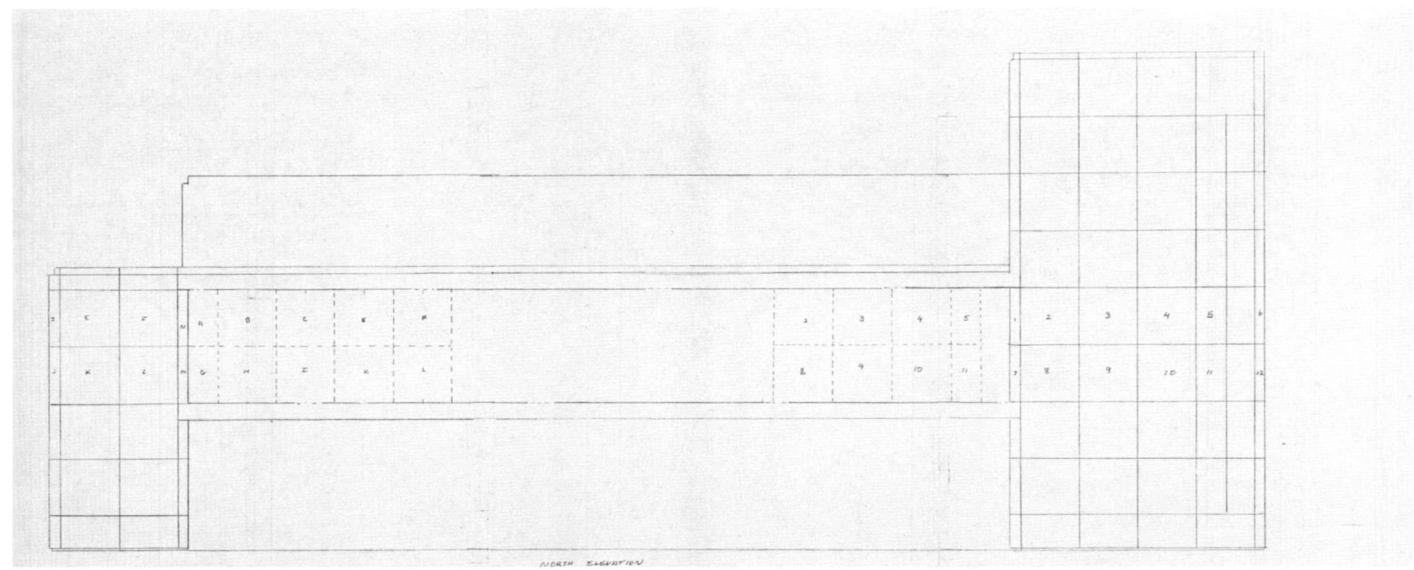

North elevation (facade of the Museum of Contemporary Art)
designating panels to be removed. Drawing by Michael Asher.

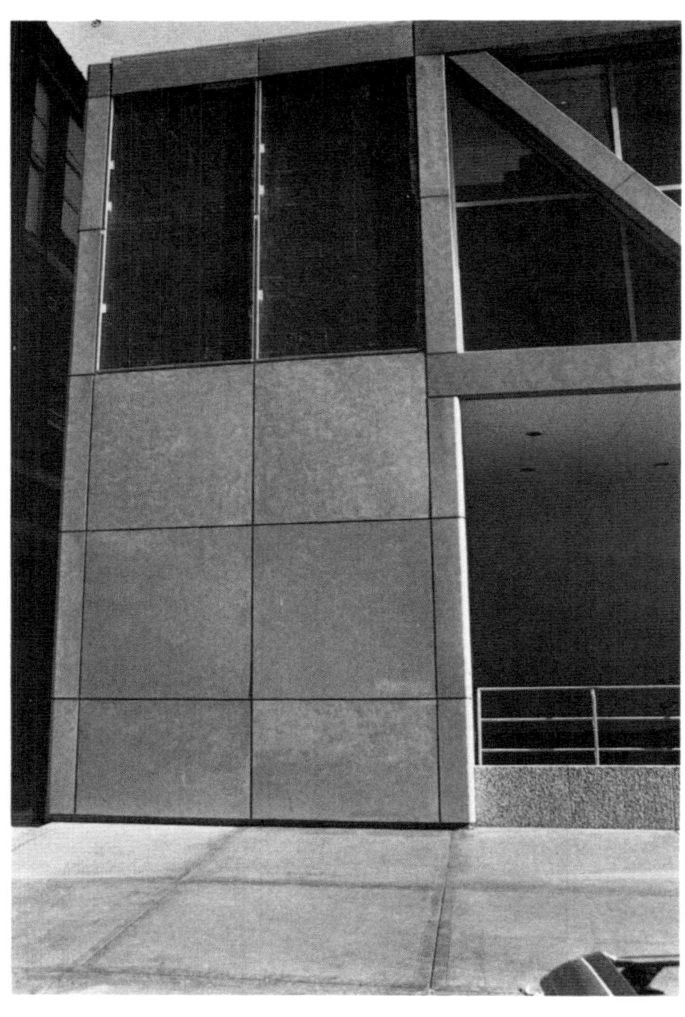

East tower of museum during exhibition.

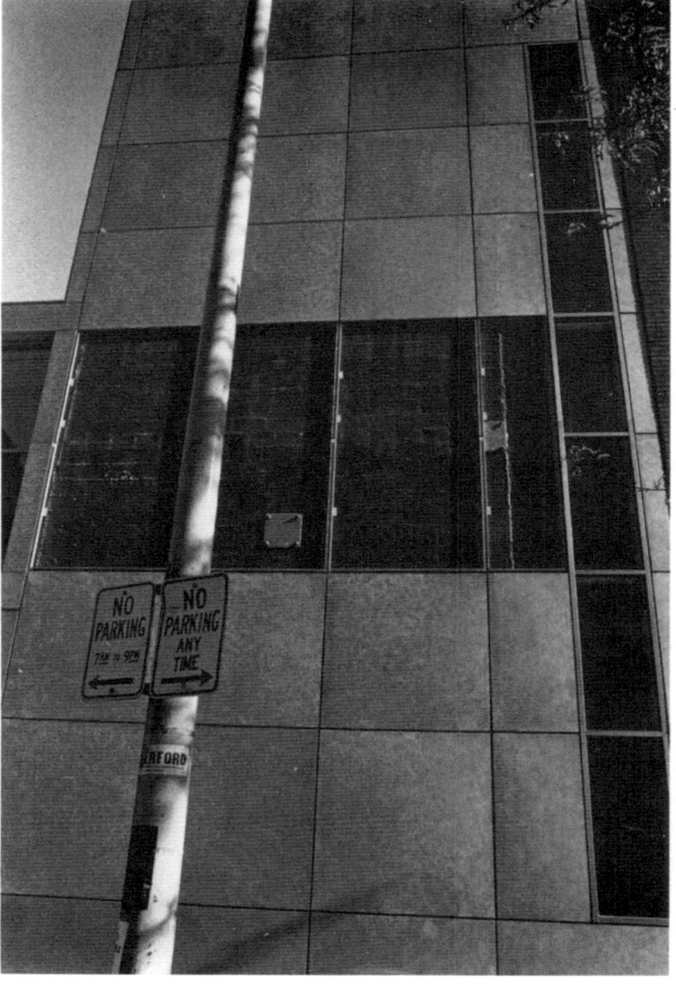

West tower of museum during exhibition.
Photographs by Michael Asher.

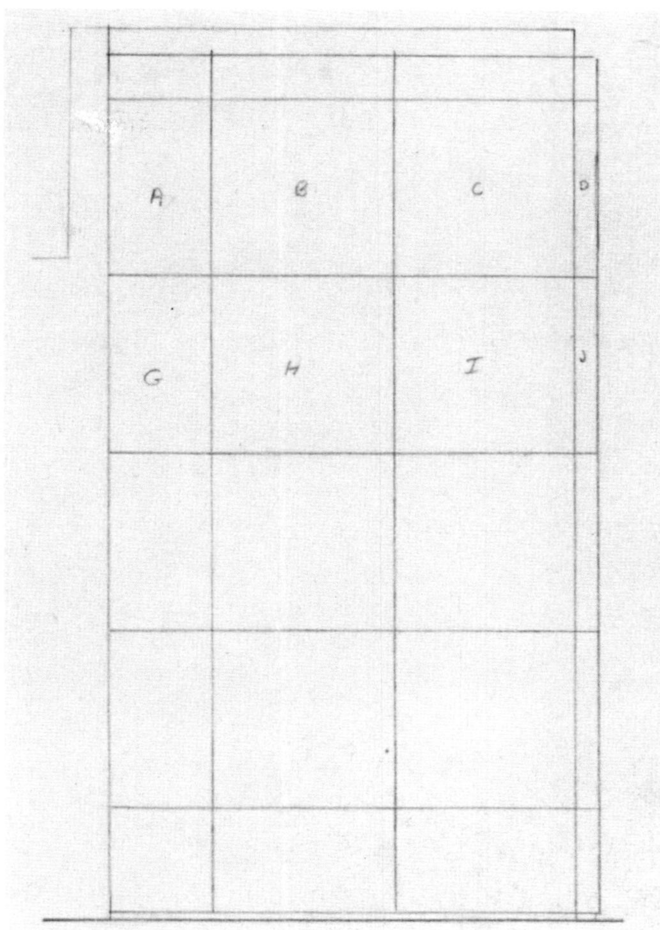

East elevation. Drawing by Michael Asher.

North elevation of facade. Drawing by Booth, Nagle and Hartray.
Courtesy: The Museum of Contemporary Art, Chicago.

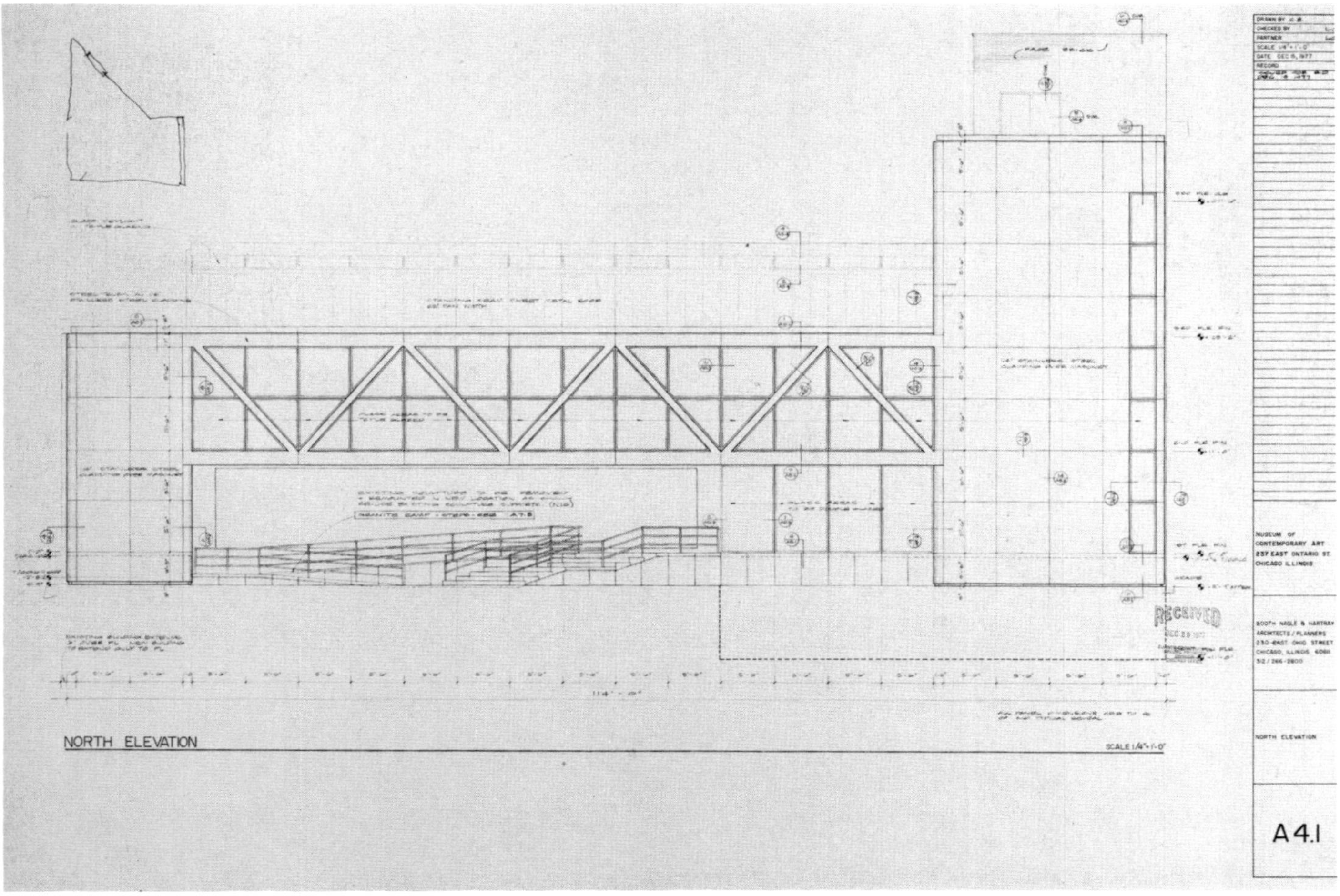

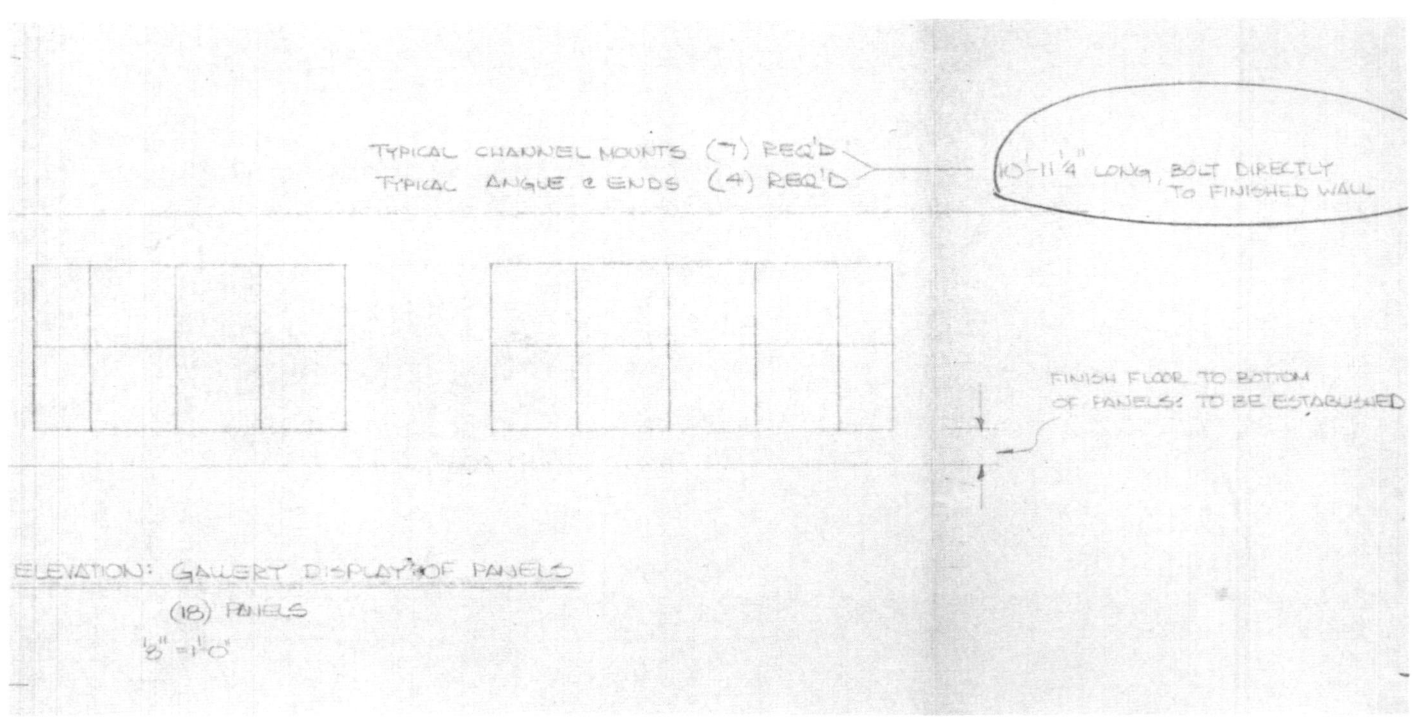

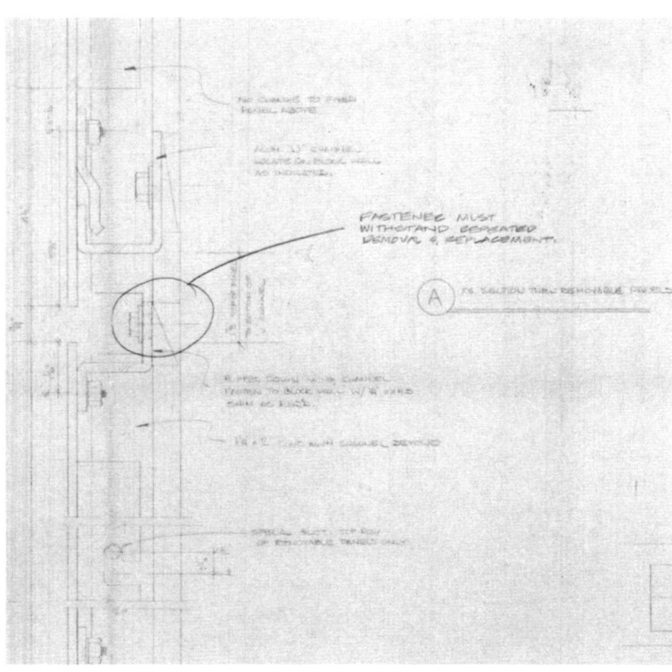

Gallery display panels. Elevation. Drawing by Booth, Nagle and Hartray. Courtesy: The Museum of Contemporary Art, Chicago.

Section through removable panels. Drawing by Booth, Nagle and Hartray. Courtesy: The Museum of Contemporary Art, Chicago.

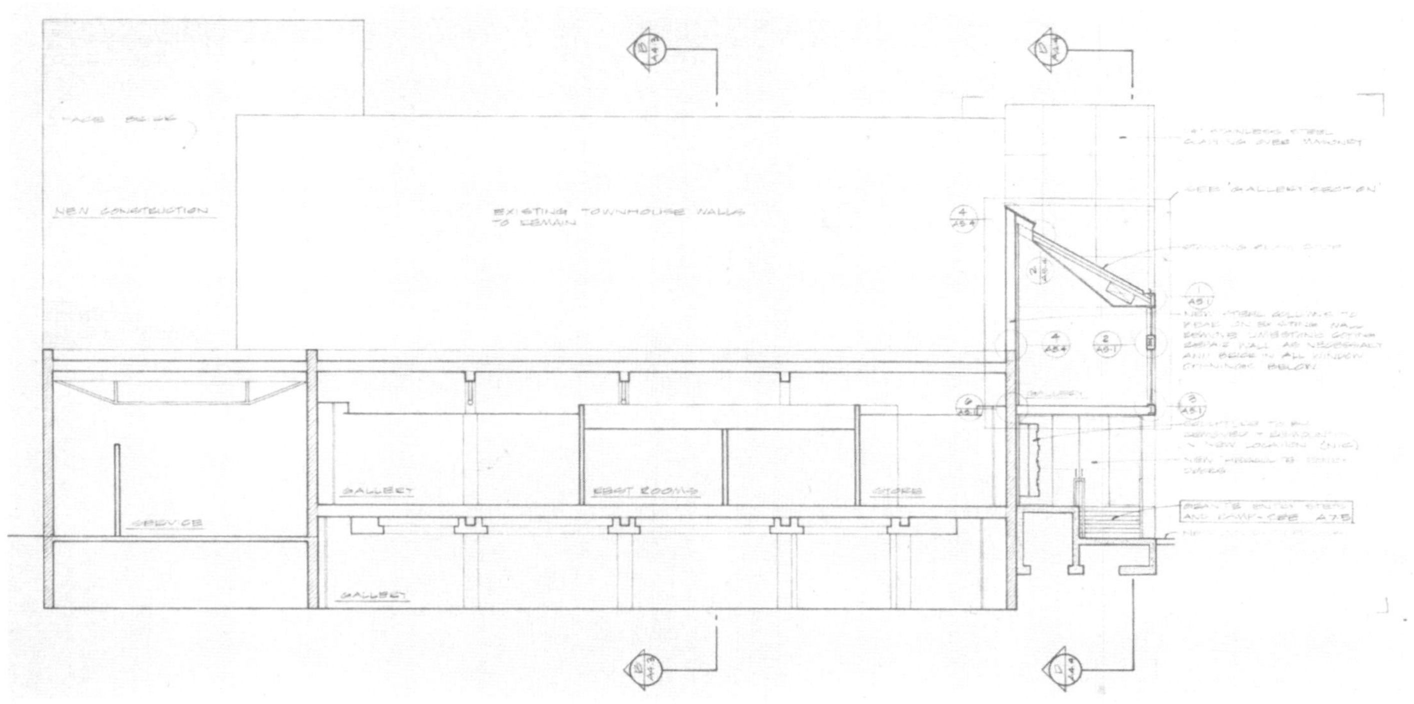

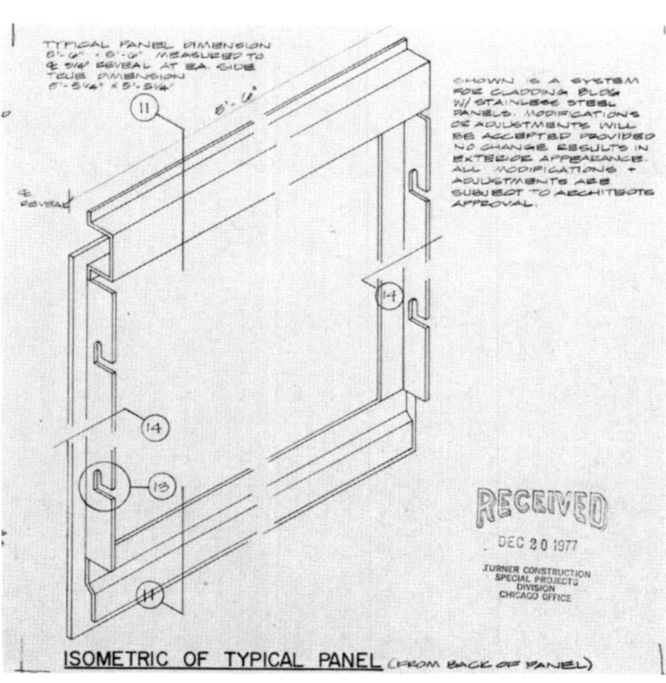

Section of second floor (Bergman Gallery). Drawing by Booth, Nagle and Hartray. Courtesy: The Museum of Contemporary Art, Chicago.

Isometric of typical panel. Drawing by Booth, Nagle and Hartray. Courtesy: The Museum of Contemporary Art, Chicago.

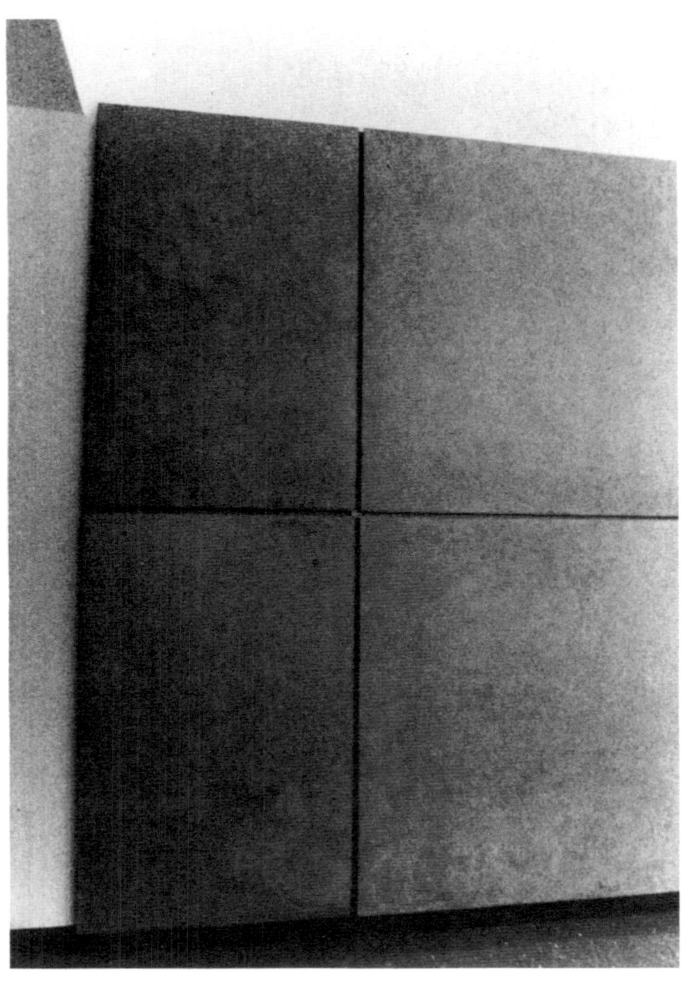

Detail of installation. End of panels displayed on the east side
of Bergman Gallery. Photograph by Tom Van Eynde.

General view during exhibition, viewing west. Photograph by
Michael Asher.

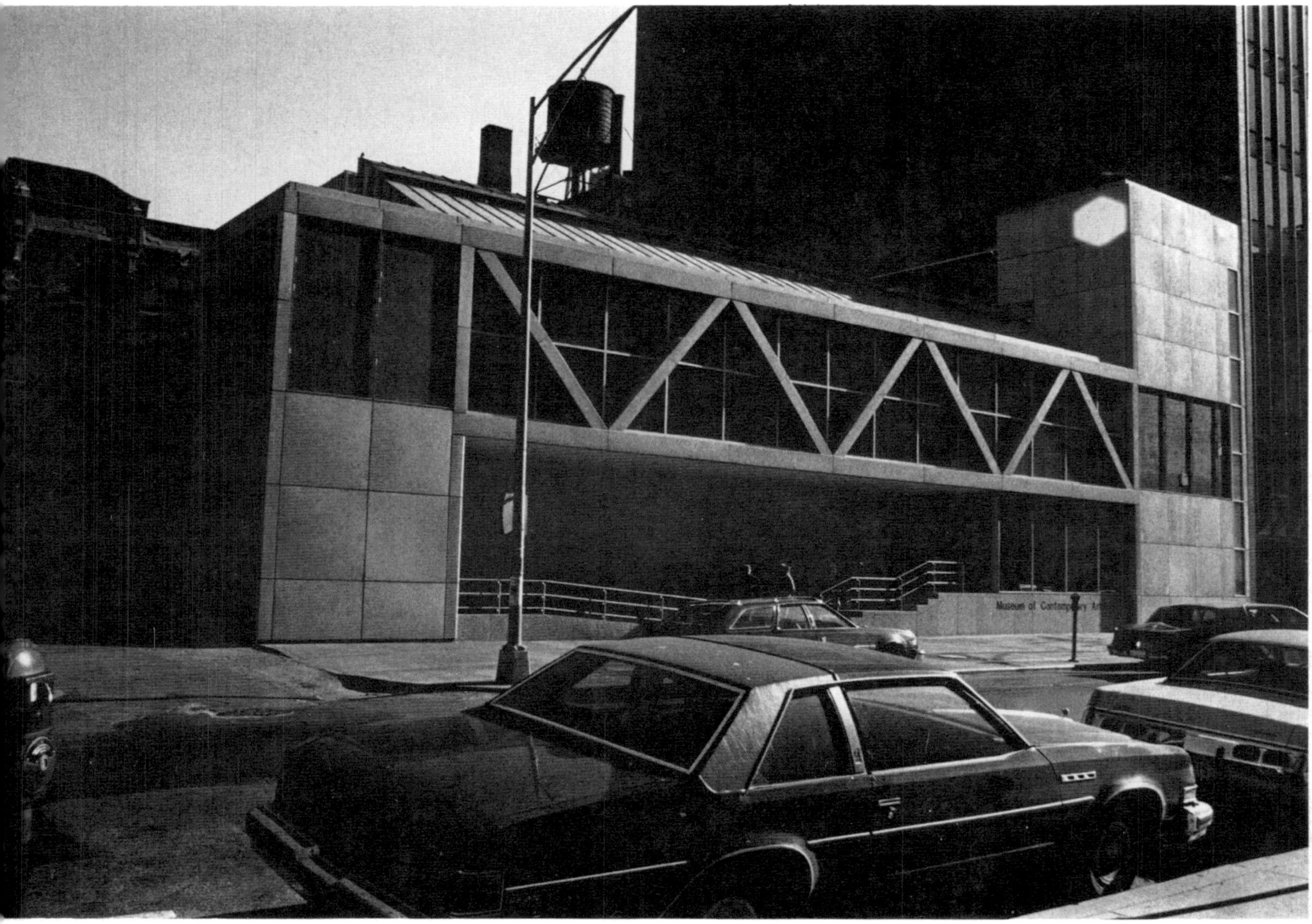

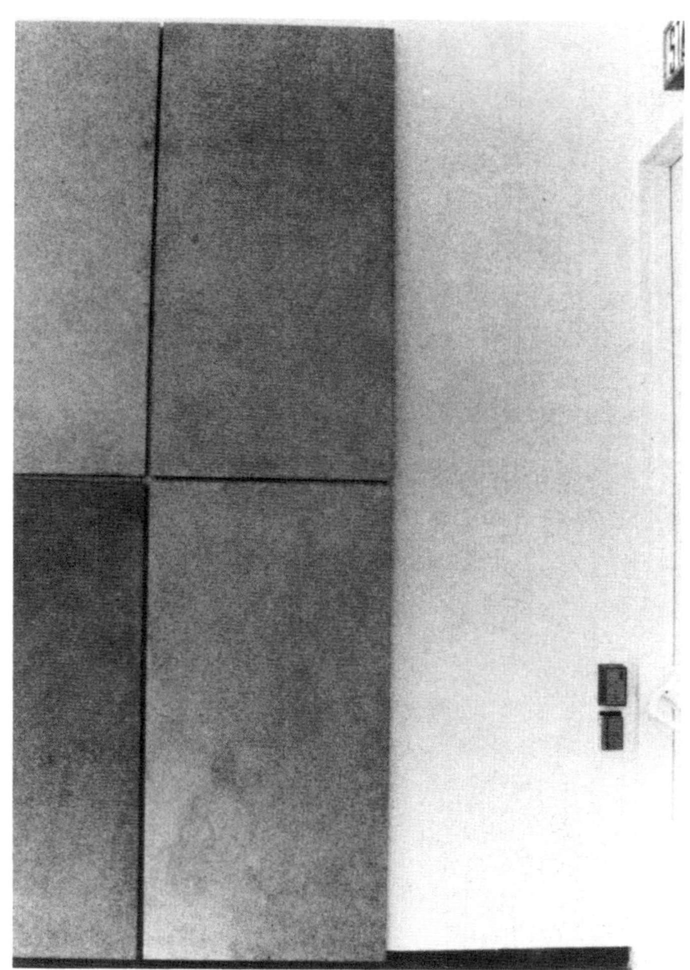

Detail of installation. End of panels displayed on the west side of Bergman Gallery. Photograph by Tom Van Eynde.

General view of installation at the Museum of Contemporary Art, viewing east. Photograph by Michael Asher.

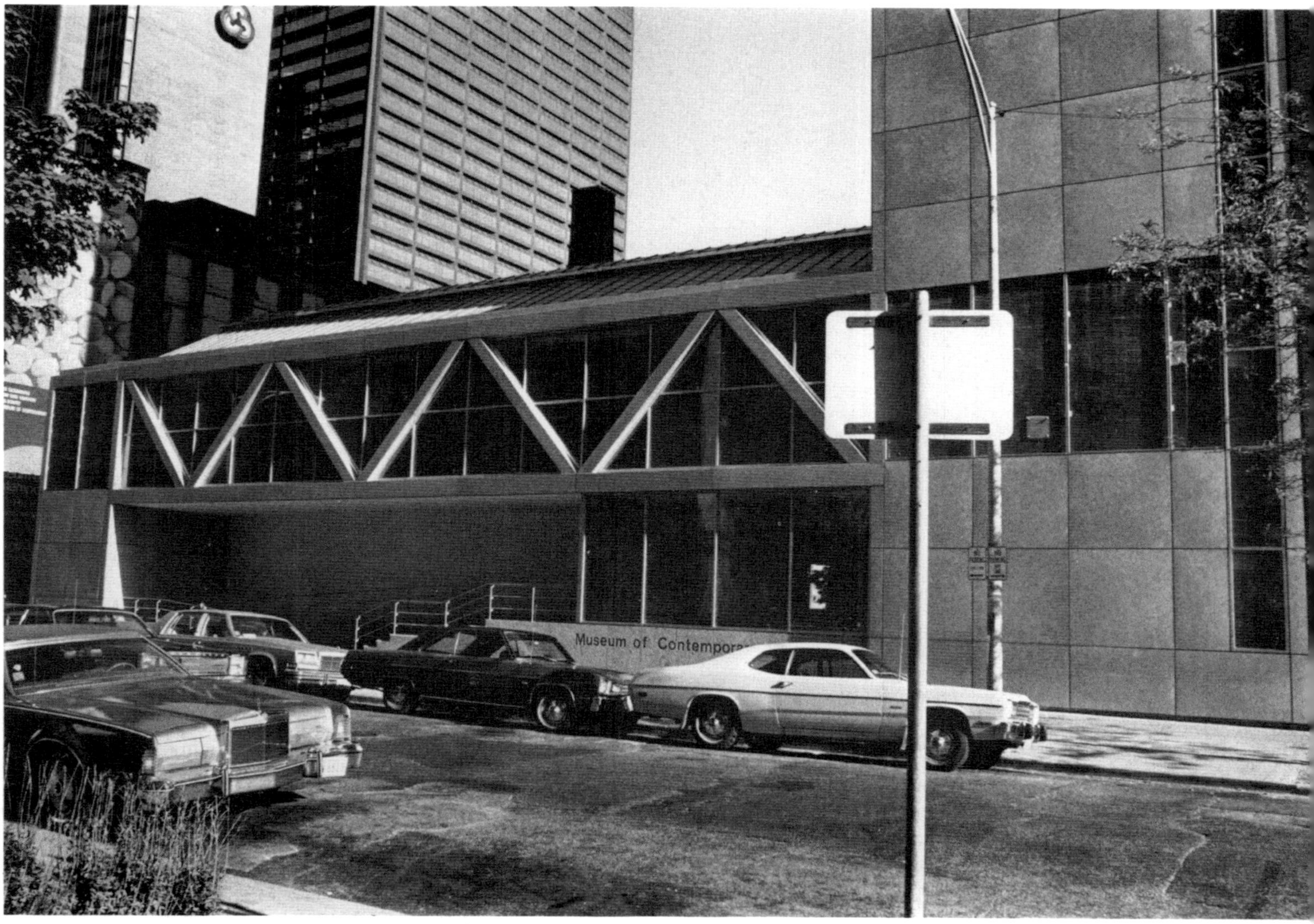

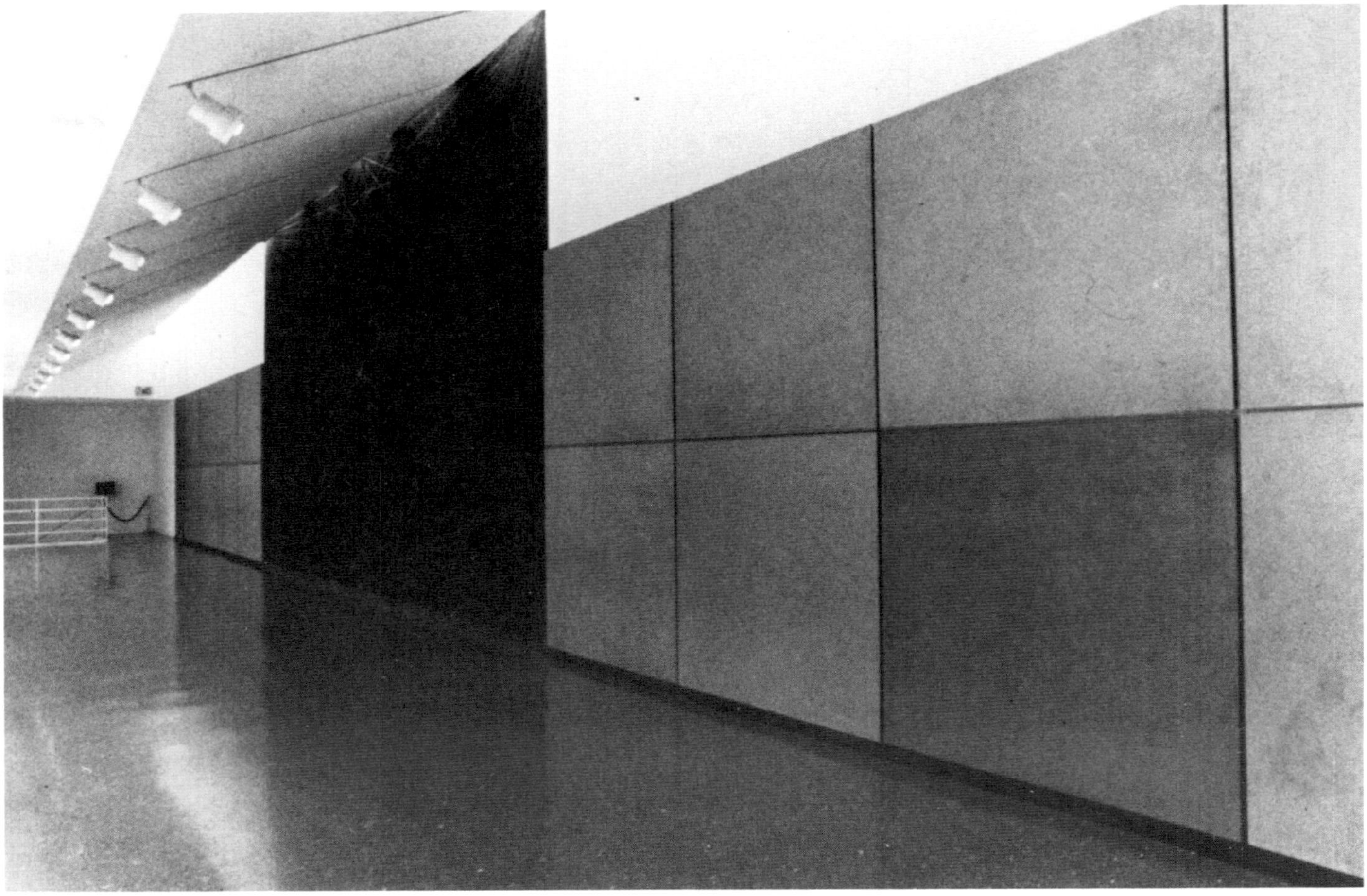

Viewing east in Bergman Gallery during exhibition.

Viewing west in Bergman Gallery during exhibition.
Photographs by Tom Van Eynde.

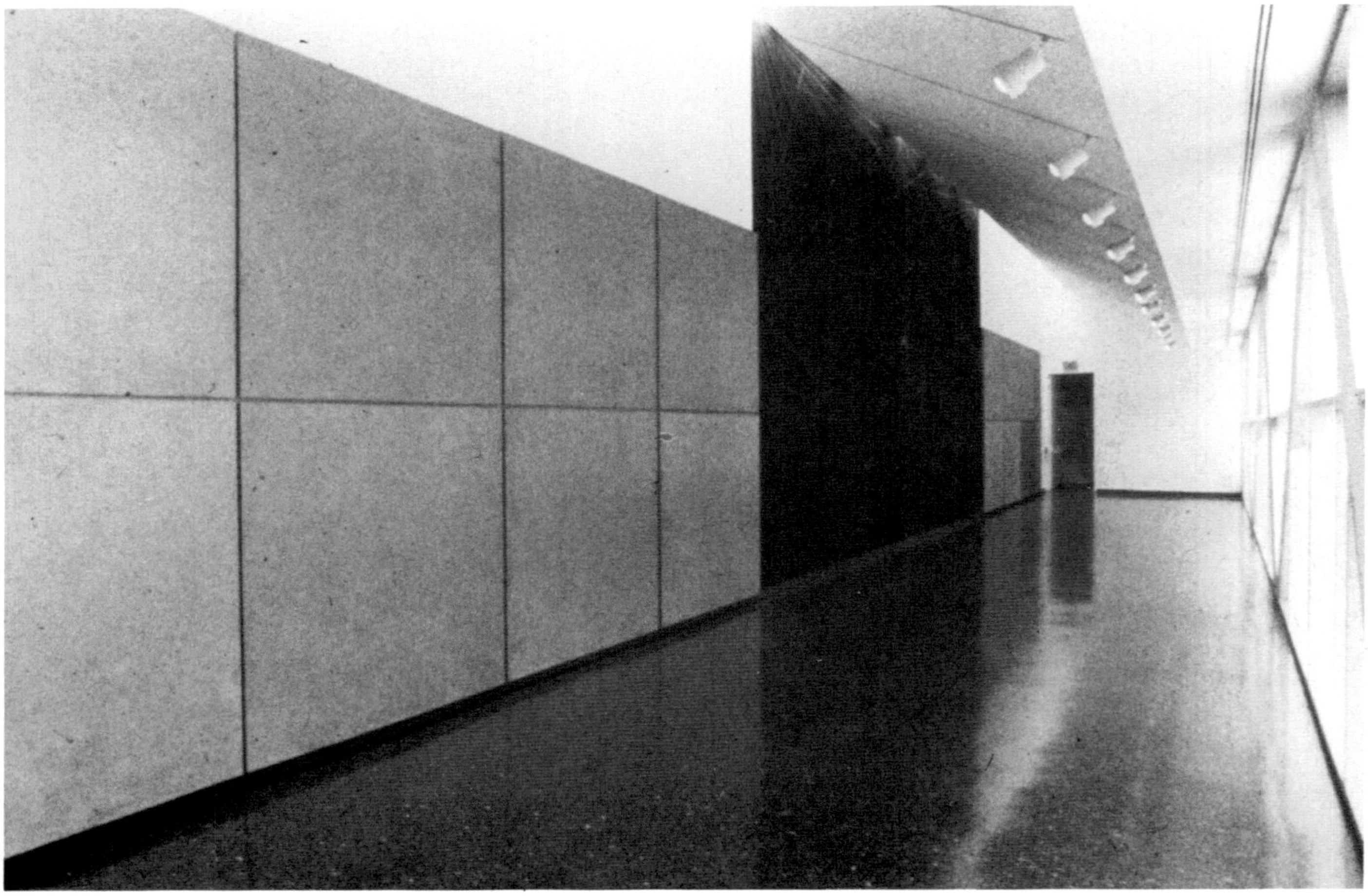

June 9–August 5, 1979
73rd American Exhibition
The Art Institute of Chicago
Chicago, Illinois

The exhibition at the Art Institute of Chicago was organized by A. James Speyer, Curator, and Anne Rorimer, Associate Curator, both in the department of 20th Century Painting and Sculpture. This was a group exhibition with the following participants: Robert Barry, Dan Graham, Michael Heizer, On Kawara, Sol LeWitt, Agnes Martin, Bruce Nauman, Maria Nordman, Allen Ruppersberg, Edward Ruscha, Robert Ryman, Fred Sandback, Richard Serra, Frank Stella, and Lawrence Weiner.

After an initial visit to the Art Institute in December 1978, to discuss my participation in the exhibition, I submitted three proposals. The first two could not be realized for "practical and logistical reasons" (Anne Rorimer, preface to the Catalogue, 73rd American Exhibition, The Art Institute of Chicago, Chicago, 1979, p. 13). The third proposal was for a sculptural work that normally stood in front of the Art Institute's Allerton Building, whose main entrance is located on Michigan Avenue. The work is by the French artist Jean-Antoine Houdon, and is a life-size representation of George Washington. Houdon traveled to the United States in 1785 to study his subject and, after returning to France, he made the original marble sculpture in 1788. The work, which is now at the Capitol in Richmond, Virginia, was intended to be a sculptural representation of the historical subject. The version purchased by the Art Institute is a bronze replica which was cast and acquired in 1917 and installed in 1925 at the Michigan Avenue entrance. The sculpture is placed on a black granite pedestal which is 4 feet 9 inches high and 34 inches wide. The ground-floor level of the Michigan Avenue facade is constructed with five evenly spaced arches. An arcade between two blind arched openings leads to the main entrance/exit doors placed on either side of the arcade. The sculpture by

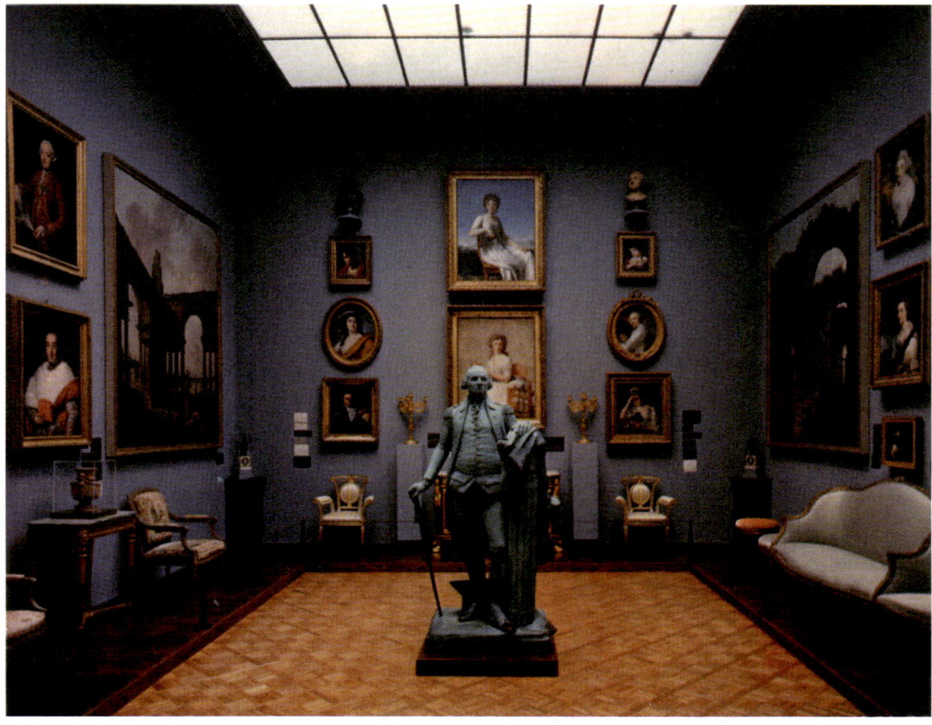

Color postcard of the installation in Gallery 219 published by the Art Institute of Chicago after the 73rd American Exhibition. Photograph by Rusty Culp. Courtesy of The Art Institute of Chicago.

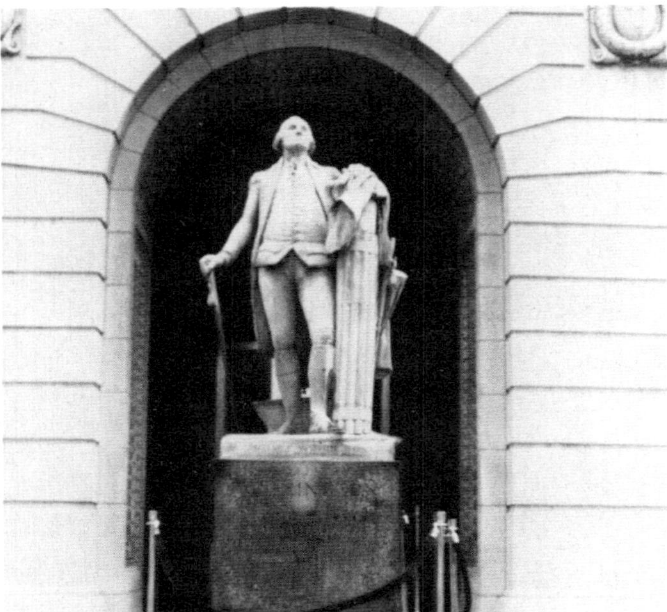

Frontal view of Michigan Avenue main entrance with statue in original location.

Jean-Antoine Houdon was originally located on the center axis of the center arch. A few years later, the sculpture was moved straight forward, out from under the arch, so that it would stand at the top of the steps approaching the Art Institute.[1] The late eighteenth-century sculpture has little or no stylistic reference to the neo-Renaissance facade, yet its placement at the top of the steps clearly breaks up the classical order of the facade, which in turn reinforces the sculpture's decorative function. It functions therefore as a monument, conveying a sense of national heritage in historical and aesthetic terms.

I proposed removing the sculpture from its pedestal and placing it in its original historical context in an eighteenth-century period room, Gallery 219, with paintings and decorative arts. The granite pedestal was dismantled and put into storage. The sculpture was placed in the center of Gallery 219, on a wooden base which was identical in height and color to the other wooden bases in the gallery.

The European period galleries on the second floor of the museum are arranged in chronological order. Gallery 219 contained works from 1786 to 1795 (see drawings a, b, c, and d). The gallery is 15 feet high, 22 feet wide, and 26 feet 6 inches long; it has a glass ceiling to diffuse light and a parquet floor. Its walls were painted a gray-blue-green. The paintings in the gallery were hung in the manner of an eighteenth century salon. Objects of the decorative arts, such as furniture and silver, were placed around the perimeter of the gallery. Once the sculpture of George Washington was installed, it became apparent that the patina, resulting from the sculpture's having been outdoors for many years, almost matched the colors of the walls. The weathered outdoor look of the sculpture made it appear out of place in a gallery of well-maintained indoor artifacts from the same period.

As a decorative object disrupting the museum's exterior architectural continuity, the sculpture had undergone changes to its own surface. Once it was reintroduced into its original period context, however, it disrupted the continuity of the interior: in its outdoor context the sculpture by Jean-Antoine Houdon seemed to have had a different use or function and had acquired material features which now conflicted with its setting as an object of high art in a well-guarded museum interior. In the interior, the sculpture of Houdon no longer had the appearance of being a public monument, which it possessed while installed on its granite pedestal outside the museum. Stripped of its monumentality, it could be compared stylistically to other artifacts in Gallery 219 and could be observed almost exclusively in aesthetic and art-historical terms. But at the same time, it was hardly possible to forget that, iconographically, the sculpture of George Washington was a representation of an American hero, displayed within a context of eighteenth-century European art. In light of its former monumentality and its iconography, the work now questioned the viewer's perception of history within the abstraction of an art-historical container. Was the sculpture, once it had been placed in its historical setting, abstracted in a manner similar to that of its former monumental setting? Can we say that it was more adequately read, once it was observed almost exclusively in stylistic and aesthetic terms, within a fictitious assembly of historical artifacts?

On the north wall next to the entrance, a Plexiglass box contained information sheets identifying the installation as my contribution to the 73rd American Exhibition, and directing viewers to the exhibition in the Morton Wing. Downstairs at the entrance to the exhibition, another box contained information sheets giving an identical definition of the work, except that it directed the visitor upstairs to Gallery 219.

The exhibition area in the Morton Wing was 18 feet high by 49 feet wide by 193 feet long. A long open gallery, it was divided by walls or partitions into separate areas to accommodate the various installations.

The 73rd American Exhibition might best be considered a survey of the specific tendencies in art practice during the late sixties and early seventies. The exhibition was not conceived around a dominant theme, but instead provided a kind of didactic package, a

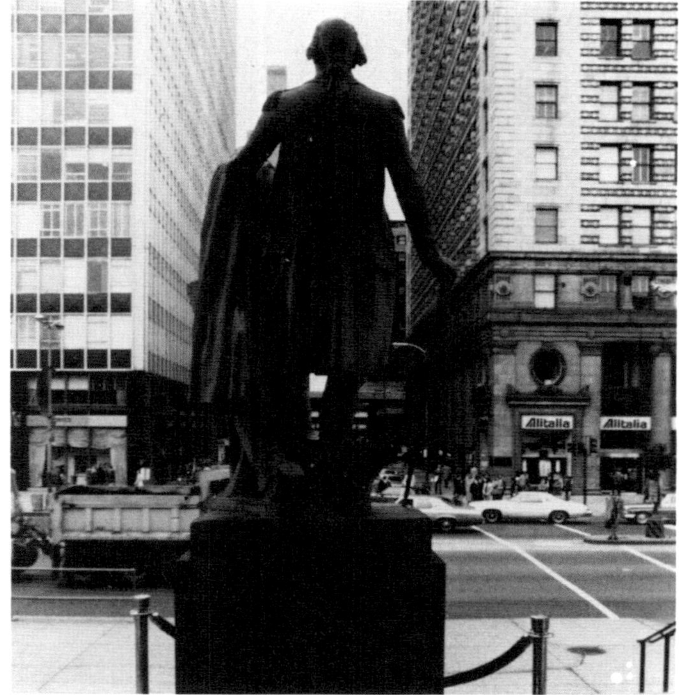

Looking down Adams Street from main entrance with back view of statue. Photographs by Michael Asher.

general overview of the preceding decade.

The most direct route from the downstairs gallery to my installation in Gallery 219, was to walk up a spiral staircase and pass through three chronologically ordered European period galleries. This meant that the walk was a short museum tour, a passage for the visitor, back and forth, between the works in the Morton Wing and my work. It involved a kind of passage through history, in which two different historical periods were connected as well as disconnected. This made it possible to either identify my work with the 73rd American Exhibition, or the 73rd American Exhibition with an archived unit in history.

Historical artworks are usually filed by the museum into an archive, thereby extracting a block of historical time. Simultaneously, contemporary exhibitions have the specific dynamics or presence that prevents them from being read in a historical context. It became evident from my work at the exhibition, however, that contemporary works of art have developed a historical grammar. The exhibition requested a historical reading, while it contradicted the convention of archiving works of art into static blocks of time.

I became interested in iconography in order to see whether elements of the past could be viewed as essential characteristics of the present. The contemporary work in the 73rd American Exhibition is as much of a conditioned iconographic structure as the late eighteenth-century period room. Modernist art would appear to be non-iconographic, but it is actually entrenched in its own perceptual codes. The rejection of each set of past codes is initiated by a generation of artists, who create a new set of iconographic codes. The influence that the rejection of prior iconographic structures exerts on subsequent codes symbolizes aesthetic progress.

Due to the shift from representational to nonrepresentational modes, the modernist code stood for scientific and aesthetic progress, and was a symbol of social progress. My installation in Gallery 219 questioned whether it is possible to use a historic code—in this instance, that of the eighteenth century—to ad-

vance a contemporary aesthetic code.

Aesthetic progress is not in itself an abstract goal, requiring uniqueness or innovation of the work of art, but is concretely bound to an aesthetic production that is capable of revealing within art practice the contradictions in production, exhibition, and distribution, contradictions analogous to those outside the parameters of the production of art.

In my early work, the materials I used were formally assembled to create a cohesive structure. This led to the stage where many of the materials were isolated in order to display their practical function. Finally, as in the installation at the Art Institute and at the Museum of Contemporary Art in Chicago, the work revealed the iconographic significance of the materials. Each stage did not occur in isolation, however, but all three were integrated, with one stage or another predominating at different times.

My decision to use eighteenth-century iconographic elements was partly determined in response to the notion that avant-garde production is essential to every contemporary exhibition. This notion has motivated and limited the traditional idea of aesthetic progress. I was also influenced by the post-modernist inquiry which—rejecting the modernist stance— incorporates different historical styles and elements of iconography into one manifestation (e.g., the International Style). Finally, situational aesthetics, once applied to the 73rd American Exhibition, opened up the possibility of integrating the Houdon sculpture into my work. (Situational aesthetics here being defined as an aesthetic system that juxtaposes predetermined elements occurring within the institutional framework, that are recognizable and identifiable to the public because they are drawn from the institutional context itself.)

In this work I was the author of the *situation*, not of the elements. The given elements remained a part of their specific context and the dynamics of the situation was a function of the integration of the predetermined elements within the institution. By using the given elements directly and displaying them in a model

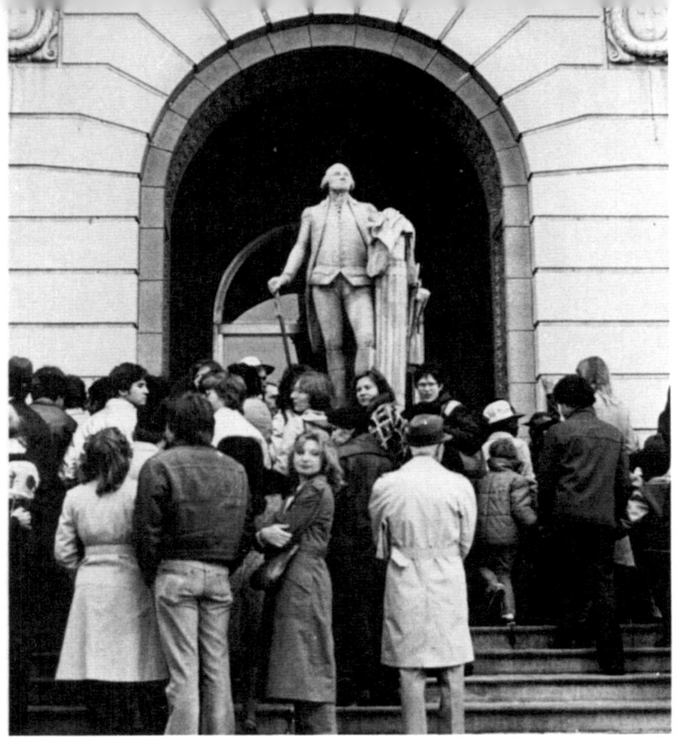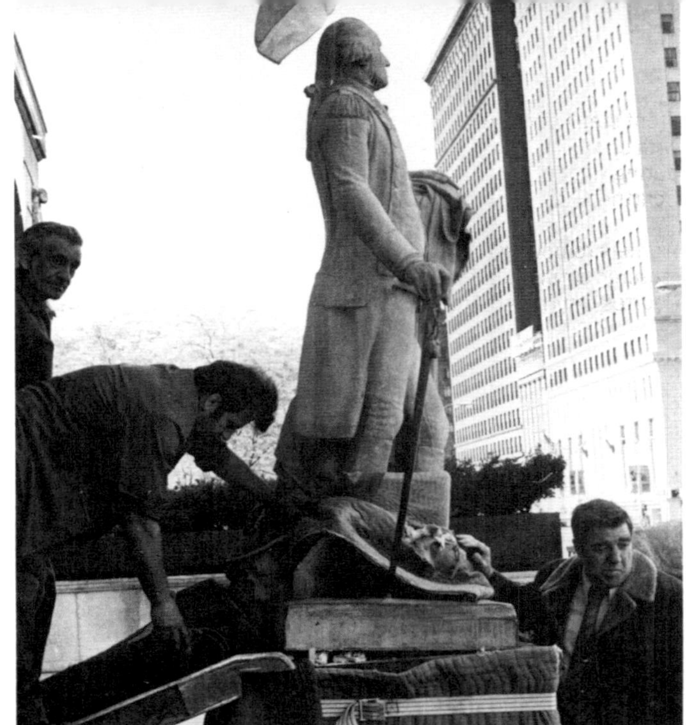

situation, the installation served as a vehicle to question and review the claims of past and existing tendencies in art. The installation questioned whether using historical elements is the only way to analyse and overcome the inherent problems of Modernism, or, whether there are more progressive ways, through practice, to transcend them.

Rather than appropriating historical data in a manner of nostalgic reverence or decoration, post-modernist practice could have appropriated history in the form of an analysis of given facts. The Art Institute installation illustrates the insufficiency of post-modernist analysis, whose method only serves to objectify history.

This work was also a response to some of my former work, done during the late sixties and early seventies, which was produced to fit within the white gallery container. Traditionally it had been modernist painting that the viewer saw within the context of that container, as its proper place of display. A new interrelationship between viewer, sculptural object, and architectural container was created with the advent of abstract Minimal and post-Minimal sculpture which used the modernist backdrops architecturally, similar to the way painting had used the white wall as a two-dimensional plane. Interestingly enough, these tendencies could maintain the characteristics of their genre against this backdrop only as long as they kept to the proportions to which they were confined by the museum/gallery space.

Once this type of sculpture had increased in size and scale to proportions that could only exist and function out of doors, the amount of funding required often exceeded what the individual art collector could afford to pay. The outdoor setting also made it possible to perceive the work without its original modernist backdrop and framework. As they developed, each of these tendencies made the subtle stylistic changes necessary (procedures of production and installation) in order to adapt to the needs and conventions of outdoor monumental sculpture.

Large scale public sculpture could possibly be perceived as an extension of contemporary museum sculpture or simply as a continuation of decorative outdoor sculpture. Or, monumental outdoor sculpture could appear to be an individual production imposed into a public or collective space, displaying itself as a kind of real estate venture, thereby retrieving the ground space from the public's personal space, similar to the way in which a private building appropriates public space.

The Houdon sculpture of Washington, even though appropriated by the museum as a monumental sculpture for outdor decorative use, is not a large-scale sculpture and was not, in its marble original, conceived for outdoor monumental display. My use of the sculpture was not an authorial usage, but one intended to disengage it from its former appropriation. By disengaging a *monument* from its institutional appropriation and placing it in its original historical context as *sculpture*, the work responded to the activity of contemporary monumental sculptural production which had originated in the museum space. Withdrawn from its exterior display, Houdon's sculpture lost its monumental qualities within the public museum space.

Another possible context for the consideration of issues deriving from the late sixties and early seventies and coincidental with the appearance of outdoor monumental sculpture is indoor sculpture developed as a part of architecture. Architects have adapted materials such as chainlink and raw plywood, originally used in sculptural construction, for architectural ornament or decoration, adopting an approach toward materials that is somewhat similar to that of artists working almost ten years earlier (e.g., Bill Bollinger's "Untitled 1968," Raphael Ferrer's "Chain Link," or Bruce Nauman's "Double Steel Cage," 1974). Another example would be the use of the grid system in the facade of the Museum of Contemporary Art in Chicago by Booth, Nagle, and Hartray, which clearly shows the parallels and possible influence of the sculptural practice of Andre, Judd, and LeWitt.

Modernism and the idea of the avant-garde were historically linked. The avant-garde consisted of a segment of artists who seemed to work as separate

Front steps of the Art Institute entrance at Michigan Avenue
with statue of George Washington by Jean-Antoine Houdon
during the 100th anniversary celebration. Photograph by
Courtney Donnell. Courtesy of the Art Institute of Chicago.

Workers removing the statue from the front entrance as
required by installation. Photograph by Courtney Donnell.
Courtesy of The Art Institute of Chicago.

Cleaning up after removal of statue and base at Michigan
Avenue entrance. Photograph by Courtney Donnell. Courtesy
of The Art Institute of Chicago.

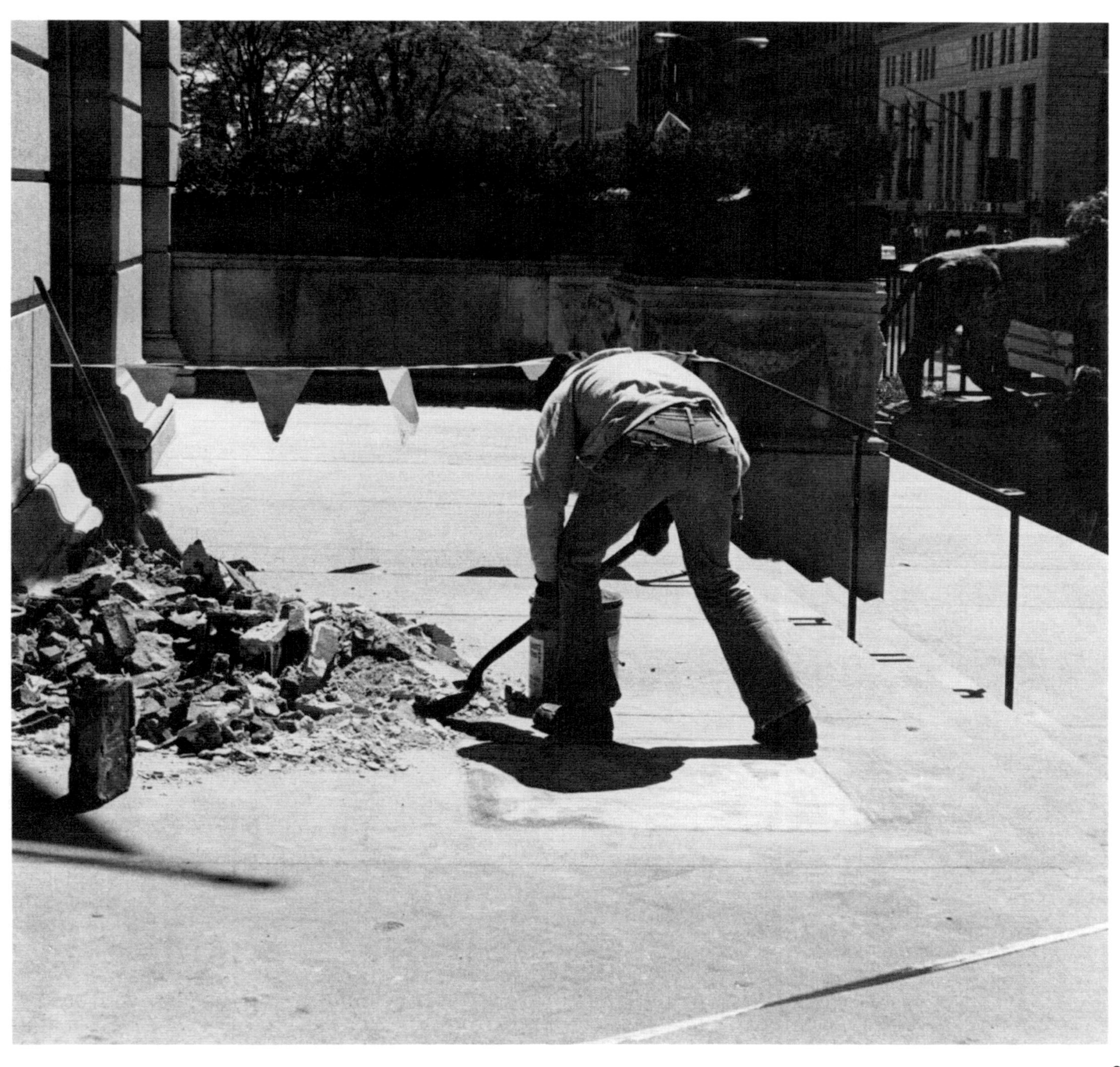

Ground plan for the installation of the 73rd American Exhibition.
Drawing by A. James Speyer. Courtesy: The Art Institute of
Chicago.

Detail of facade design of the Art Institute of Chicago. Original
drawing by Shepley, Rutan and Coolidge. Courtesy: The Ryerson
Library at The Art Institute of Chicago.

Facade of the Art Institute of Chicago at Michigan Ave. and
Adams Street. This photograph was reproduced as Michael
Asher's contribution to the catalogue of the 73rd American
Exhibition, 1979. Photograph by Rusty Culp. Courtesy of The
Art Institute of Chicago.

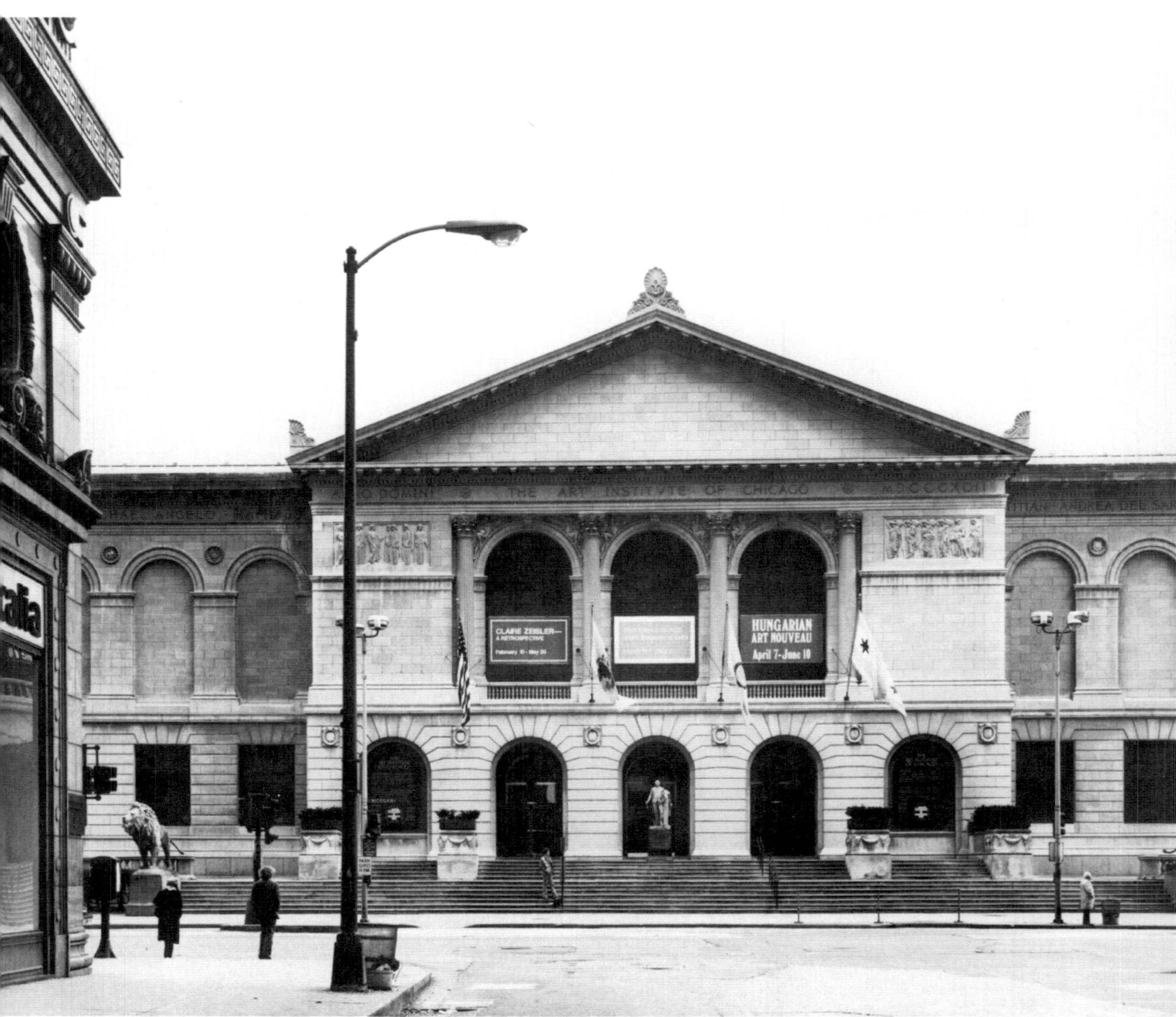

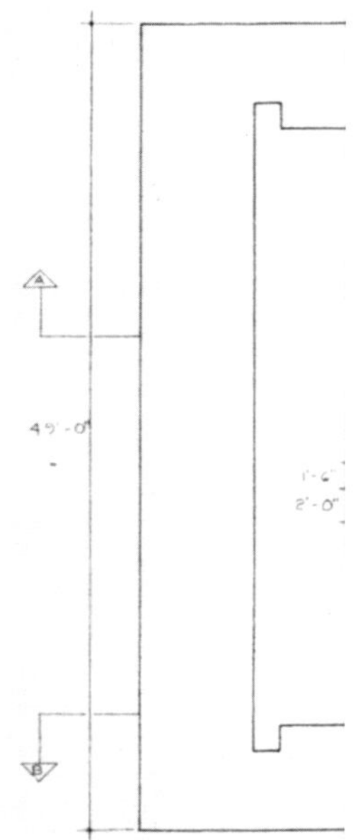

A
49'-0"
1'-6"
2'-0"
B

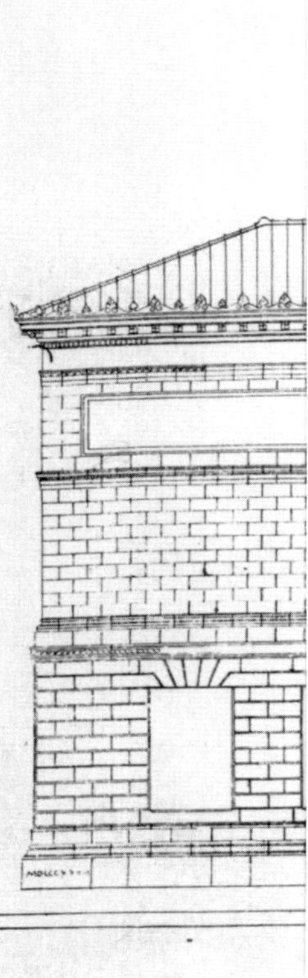

MOLLCI

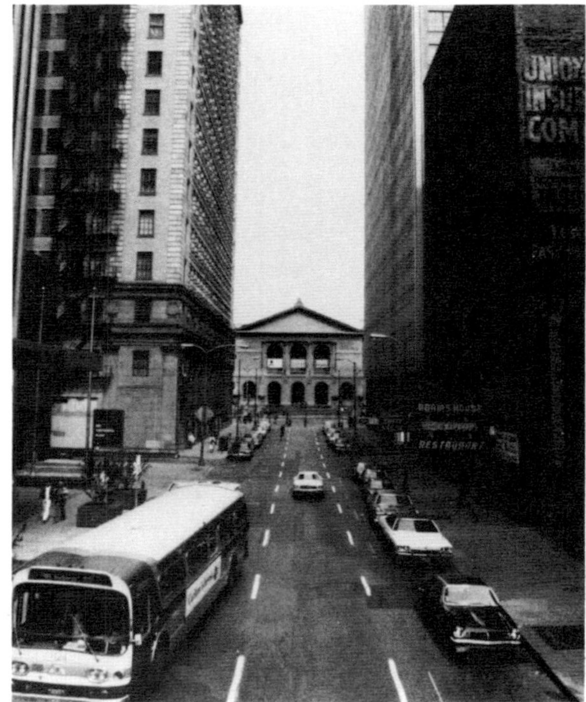

Michigan Avenue facade after removal of statue. Photograph taken from Adams Street.

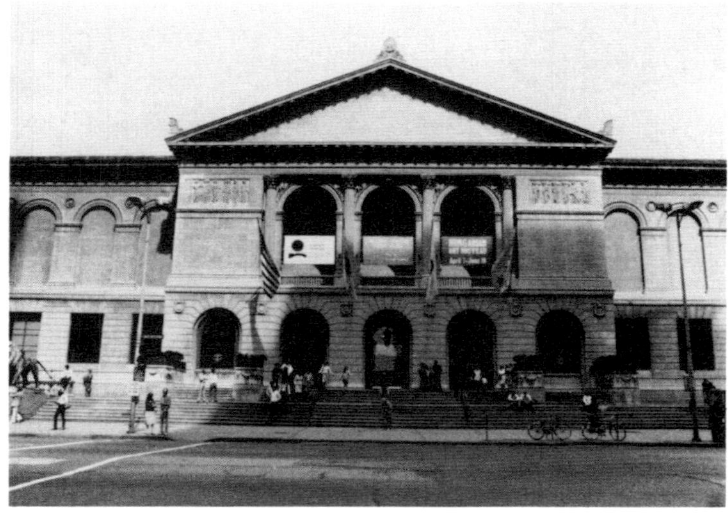

Michigan Avenue facade after removal of statue.

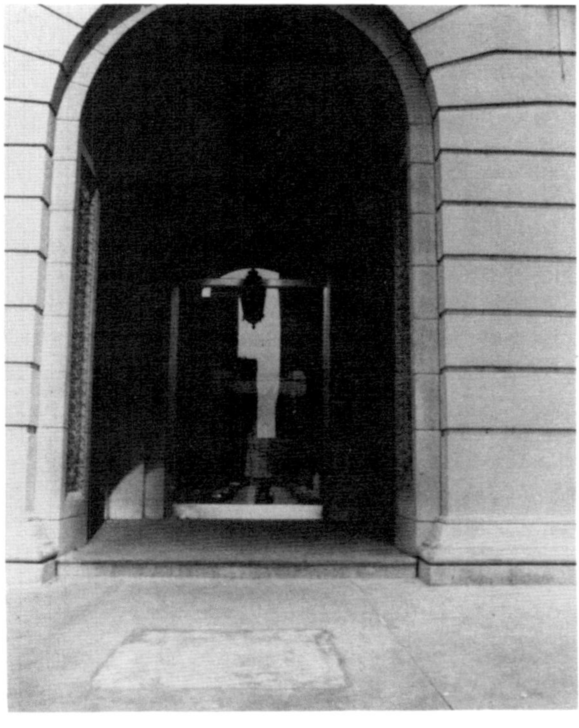

Original location of statue. Patch of concrete indicates former placement of base.

Installation of statue in Gallery 219. Photographs by Michael Asher.

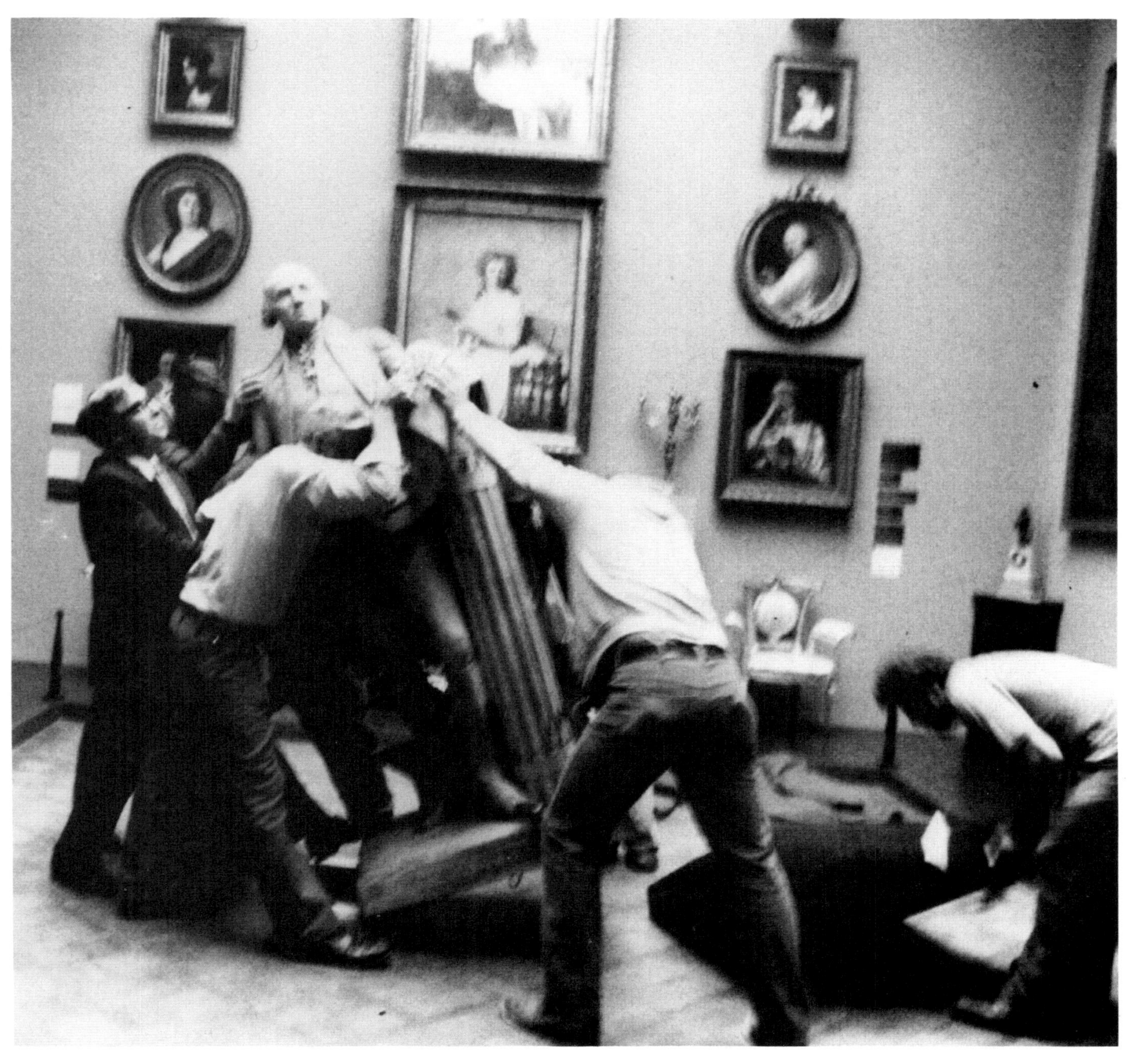

a) Gallery 219. North elevation. Drawing by Eric Chatlain.

b) Gallery 219. East elevation. Drawing by Eric Chatlain.

c) Gallery 219. South elevation. Drawing by Eric Chatlain.

d) Gallery 219. West elevation. Drawing by Eric Chatlain.

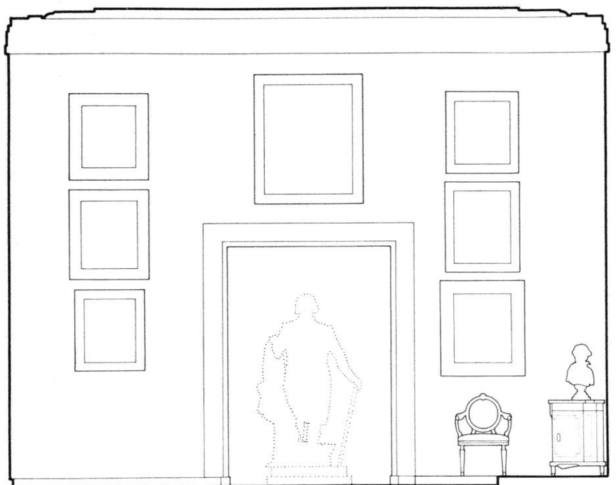

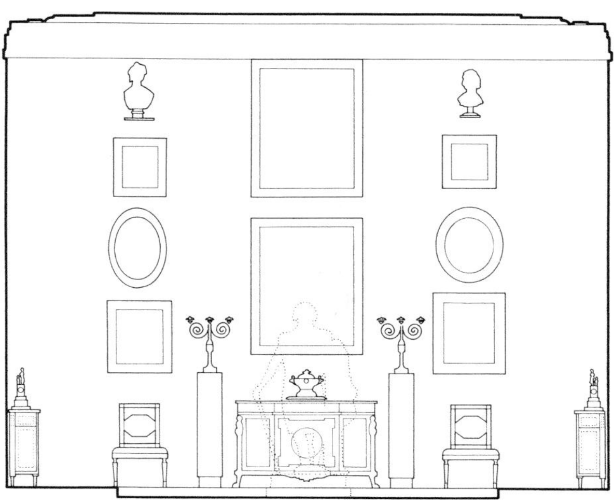

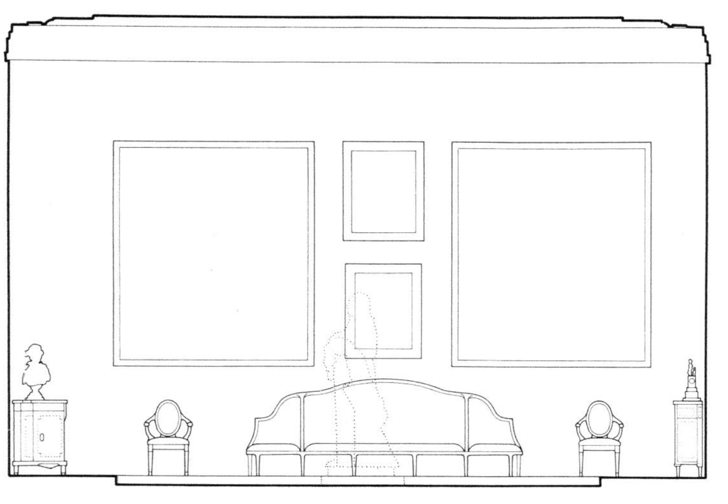

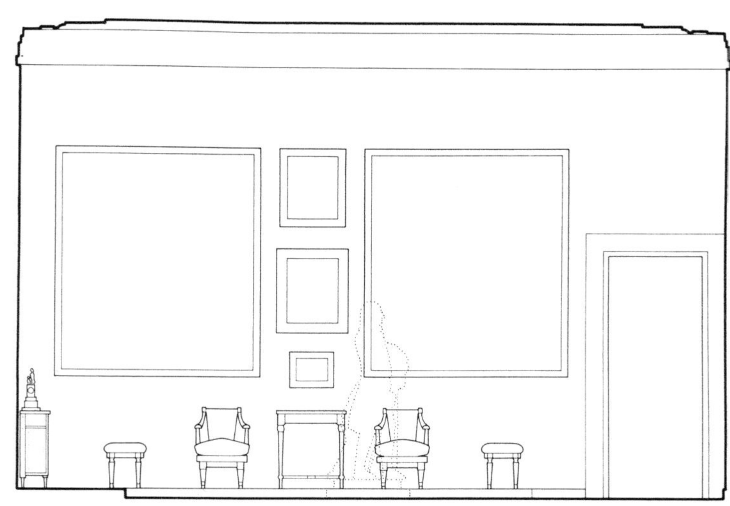

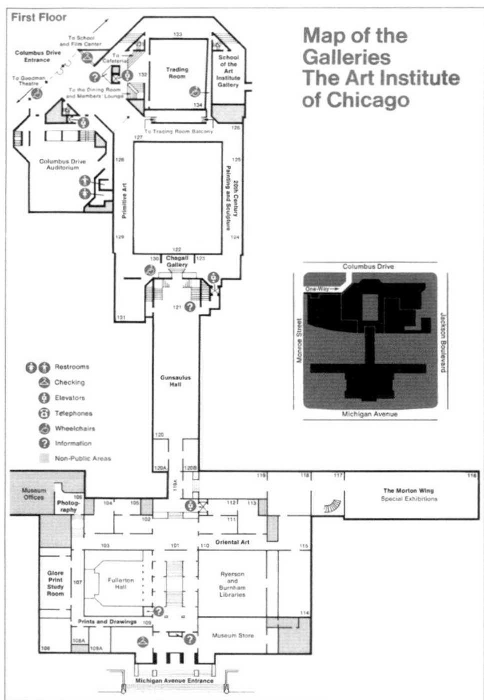

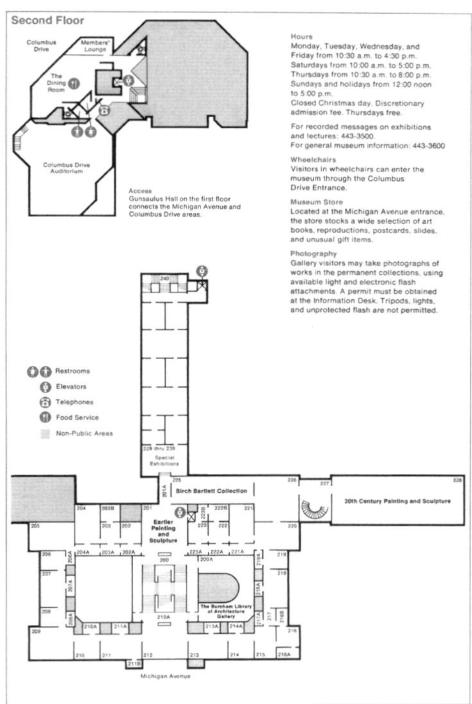

individuals, and who believed they were historically autonomous, and who therefore thought of their production in singular and independent terms. The avant-garde seemed to manifest itself in what was thought to be the ultimate advanced production. My work responded to this tradition by creating a model in which the physical installation was detached from the viewer's notion of contemporary aesthetics, while in fact the installation was an entity within a contemporary exhibition. Therefore it questioned whether the features of avant-garde production are a necessary prerequisite for an institution to invite an artist to participate in a contemporary exhibition. If this is possible, then what is the aesthetic and cultural impact of this type of inverted juxtaposition? A restorative position in art-making always results from the artist's distortion of history through aesthetic terms. This distortion is a manipulation of history by means of aesthetic elements. This kind of artwork in fact uses history indirectly, without acknowledging its sources, but it incorporates them, covertly creating a pretense to history. The indirect use of history is accomplished as a formal synthesis, without understanding the motivation for using it. This aesthetic manipulation of history also responded to the viewer's given inclination and longing for historical experience. If history is thereby falsified, it does not only mean that a denial of history is operating, for it also complements and continues the ahistorical position of modernism.

My installation at the Art Institute of Chicago did not only return the sculpture to its historical boundaries but equally so to its cultural boundaries, both historical and contemporary.

Comparative notes on the two installations in Chicago

Each of the installations was primarily determined by the respective institution's public orientation and goals within the community. The Art Institute is committed to the conservation and exhibition of historic and contemporary artworks; whereas the Museum of Contemporary Art focuses exclusively on the collection and exhibition of contemporary art. The structures of the installations in both institutions resulted from a similar methodological approach: both were dependent upon historic and iconographic references which were derived from each institution. The complementary structural elements in the two exhibitions were installed simultaneously and both used preexisting ornamentation and decoration withdrawn from the exterior of the building and inserted into the interior. Each installation generated three situations: the first was constituted by the disclosure of exterior parts of the architecture once the respective elements had been withdrawn. The second situation was constituted by the addition of these elements to a given interior. The third situation referred to the works' own historic realities: in the one case an exhibition-contribution and in the other a collection-contribution. Therefore both historic realities did not exist in any way, except within the institutional structures of an exhibition and a collection. In both installations, the exterior decorative elements assumed the position of aesthetic elements in their interior placement. However, in each situation the elements introduced into the interior contradicted, if not falsified, the specific features of their former exterior use. While it seemed they would fit perfectly into the interior context, once installed there they conspicuously denied the false harmonization of the particular contradictions which they generated.

Both structures can be analysed as separate entities, whereas they also generate a comparative analysis. The two installations are defined by sculptural and architectural components in order to create a mode which is not categorized by any singular aesthetic discipline.

One of the similarities and, simultaneously, one of the essential differences, between the two works was the fact that the structures of the installations extracted historical elements which were separate from the time-frames of the works themselves. Yet the actual elements were derived from time-frames 200 years apart in history. The iconographic references at the

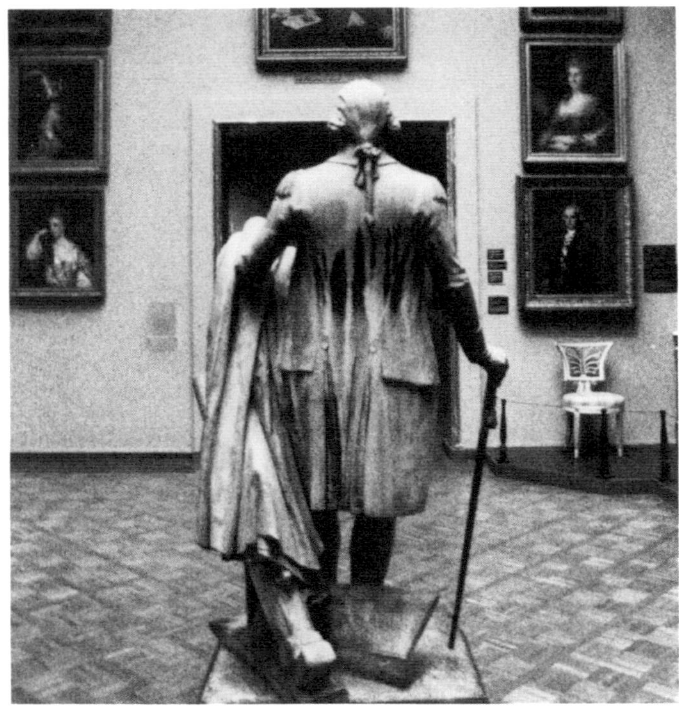

Gallery 219. Installation of the statue by Jean-Antoine Houdon in 18th-century period room. Back view. Photograph by Michael Asher.

Art Institute installation were determined by my selecting an eighteenth century time-frame. Whereas at the Museum of Contemporary Art, my selection of a sixties modernist time-frame determined a nonrepresentational iconography. The bronze cast at the Art Institute, a copy of an 18th century marble sculpture which was used as architectural decoration, was designed by a sculptor, while the decorative aluminium cladding at the Museum of Contemporary Art was designed by an architect, yet was possibly derived from sculptural design. The actual manifestations situate themselves between the works' conceptual decisions and material elements which constitute the installation, disallowing either of them to function independently within the analytical model.

With the advent of the works at the Art Institute and the Museum of Contemporary Art in Chicago, a shift in the way I structured elements became clear. It resulted in the use of elements for their iconic and iconographic references. It also meant a shift from more formally determined elements (issues developed in the late sixties) toward more site-specific context-oriented elements. During the early seventies these elements began to be used in order to emphasize or reveal objects, functions, or activities within exhibition situations. In the later seventies, my work integrated the properties resulting from these preceding shifts with institutionally determined elements and functions which were clearly recognizable as having been extracted from the institution.

In functioning as models, these works operate as fictions. The possibility that the work in the future would physically operate outside the given time and institutional site-structure is, in principle, excluded. If it should happen that this approach becomes formalized and ineffective, another method would have to be adopted.

<hr>

[1] Anne Rorimer, "Michael Asher: Recent Work," *Artforum*, Vol. XVIII, No. 8, p. 46.

Installation view of Gallery 219 with statue by Houdon after removal from Michigan Avenue entrance. Photograph by Rusty Culp. Courtesy of The Art Institute of Chicago.

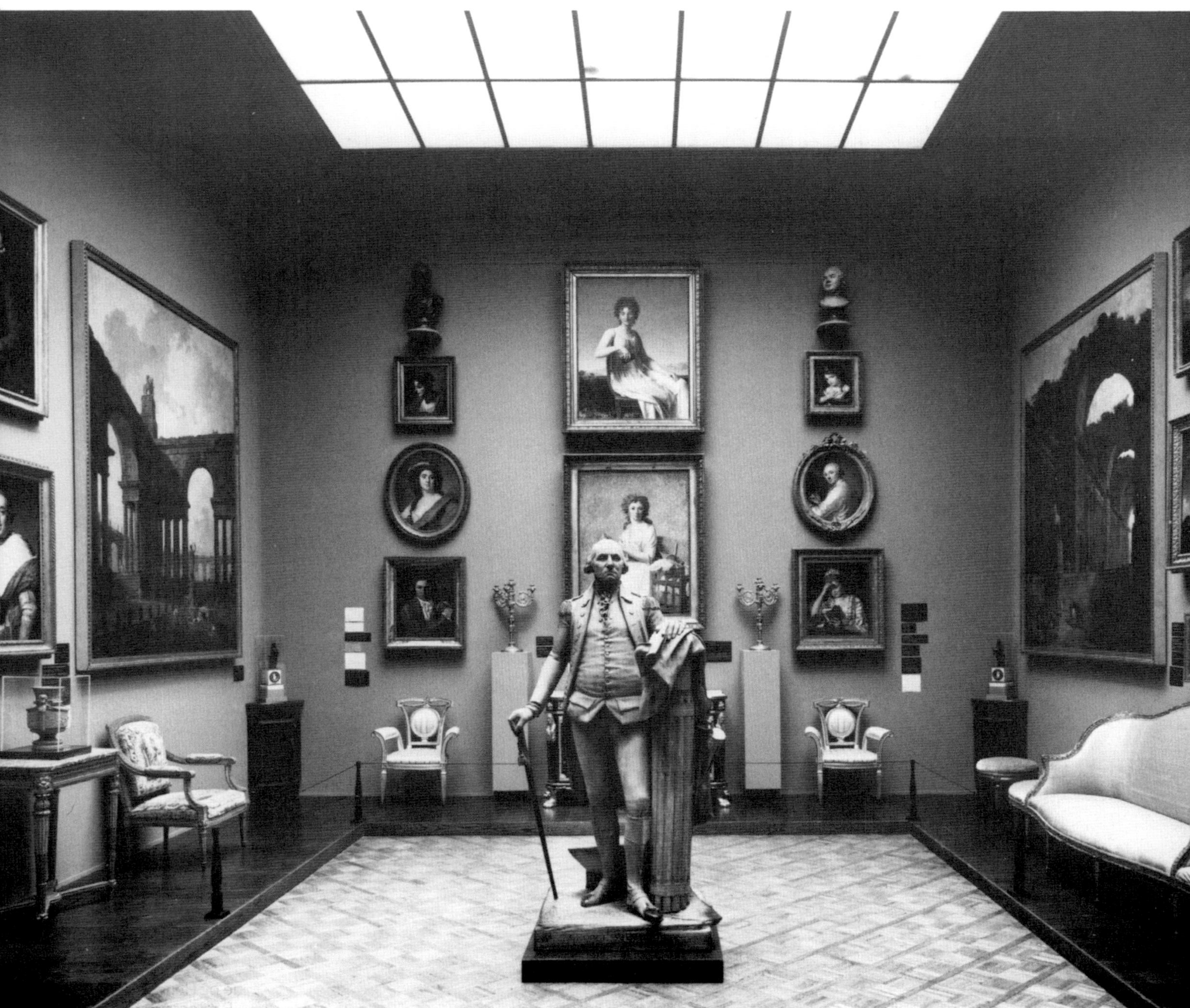

Exhibitions

Individual Exhibitions

1969 La Jolla Museum of Art
La Jolla California
November 7-December 31

1970 Gladys K. Montgomery Art Center at Pomona College
Claremont, California
February 13-March 8

1972 Market Street Program
Venice, California
March 22-April 16

1973 Gallery A 402
California Institute of the Arts
Valencia, California
January 8-11

Project, Inc.
Boston, Massachusetts
August 18

Lisson Gallery
London, England
August 24-September 16

Heiner Friedrich Galerie
Köln, West Germany
September 4-September 28

Galleria Toselli
Milan, Italy
September 13-October 8

1974 Claire S. Copley Gallery Inc.
Los Angeles, California
September 21-October 12

1974 Anna Leonowens Gallery
Nova Scotia College of Art and Design,
Halifax, Nova Scotia
October 7-October 10

1975 Otis Art Institute Gallery
Los Angeles, California
February 24-March 9

1976 The Clocktower
New York, New York
March 20-April 10

The Floating Museum
San Francisco, California
May 1-May 22

1977 Claire Copley Gallery Inc.
Los Angeles, Ca.
and Morgan Thomas Gallery,
Santa Monica, Ca.
February 8-February 26

Stedelijk Van Abbemuseum
Eindhoven, Netherlands
August 3-August 29

1979 The Museum of Contemporary Art
Chicago, Illinois
June 8-August 12

Corps de Garde
Groningen, Netherlands
August 30

Installation of work in the collection of Stanley and
 Elyse Grinstein
Los Angeles, Ca.

1982 Museum Haus Lange
Krefeld, West Germany
May 16-July 14

1983 The Museum of Contemporary Art
Los Angeles, Ca.
November 18-December 20

Group Exhibitions

1967   Los Angeles County Museum of Art
       Los Angeles, California
       "I am Alive"

1968   Lytton Gallery of Visual Arts
       Los Angeles, California
       "Mini-Things"
       January-February

       Art Gallery
       University of California, San Diego
       "New Work/Southern California"
       January 9-February 4

       Portland Art Museum
       Portland, Oregon
       "West Coast Now"
       February 9-March 6

1969   San Francisco Art Institute
       San Francisco, California
       "18'6" × 6'9" × 11'2½" × 47' × 11³⁄₁₆" ×
          29'8½" × 31'9³⁄₁₆""
       April 11-May 3

       Newport Harbor Art Museum
       Newport Beach, California
       "The Appearing/Disappearing Image/Object"
       Mary 11-June 28

       Whitney Museum of American Art,
       New York, New York
       "Anti-Illusion: Procedures/Materials"
       May 19-July 6

       Pavilion of the Seattle Art Museum
       Seattle, Washington
       "557087"
       September 4-October 5

       Kunsthalle Bern
       Bern, Switzerland
       "Pläne und Projekte als Kunst/Plans and Projects
          as Art"

       November 8-December 7, 1969
       Traveled to Aktionsraum I, München, West-
          Germany (November 19-December 11, 1969),
          and as "Künstler machen Pläne, andere auch" to
          Kunsthaus Hamburg, West-Germany, February
          14-March 15, 1970

       Museum of Modern Art
       New York, New York
       "Spaces"
       December 30, 1969-March 1, 1970

1970   Allen Art Museum
       Oberlin College, Oberlin, Ohio
       "Art in the Mind"
       April 17-May 12

1971   Los Angeles County Museum of Art
       Los Angeles, California
       "24 Young Los Angeles Artists"
       May 11-July 4

1972   Documenta V
       Kassel, West-Germany
       June 30-October 8

       Los Angeles County Museum of Art
       Los Angeles, California
       "Ten Years of Contemporary Art Council
          Acquisitions"
       December 19, 1972-March 4, 1973

1973   New York Cultural Center
       New York, New York
       "3D into 2D: Drawings for Sculpture"
       January 19-March 11

       Pasadena Museum of Modern Art
       Pasadena, California
       "The Betty and Monte Factor Family Collection"
       April 24-June 3

       Gallery 167, University of California
       Irvine, California
       "Recent Works"
       May 14-18

1975   La Jolla Museum of Contemporary Art
       La Jolla, California
       "University of California, Irvine, 1965-75"
       November 7-December 14

1976   Portland Center for the Visual Arts
       Portland, Oregon
       "Via Los Angeles"
       January 8-February 8

       San Francisco Museum of Modern Art
       San Francisco, California
       "Painting and Sculpture in California: The Modern
         Era"
       September 3-November 21

       La Biennale di Venezia
       Venice, Italy
       "Ambiente Arte"
       July 18-October 16

1977   Los Angeles Institute of Contemporary Art
       Los Angeles, California
       "Michael Asher, David Askevold, Richard Long"
       January 15-February 10

       California Institute of the Arts
       Valencia, California
       "Faculty Exhibition"
       April 19-May 22

       Westfälisches Landesmuseum für Kunst und
         Kulturgeschichte
       Münster, West-Germany
       "Skulptur"
       July 3-November 13

       The Fort Worth Art Museum
       Forth Worth, Texas
       "Los Angeles in the Seventies"
       October 9-November 20

1979   Joslyn Art Museum
       Omaha, Nebraska
       "Los Angeles in the Seventies"
       March 1-April 15

The Art Institute of Chicago
Chicago, Illinois
"73rd American Exhibition"
June 9-August 5

1980   Parachute
       Montréal, Québec
       "Performance: Arts Plastiques, théatre, danse,
         musique, cinéma d'aujourd 'hui"
       Université du Québec à Montréal
       October 9-11

1981   Westkunst
       Köln, West-Germany
       "Heute"
       May 29-August 16

       Los Angeles County Museum of Art
       Los Angeles, California
       "Seventeen Artists in the Sixties—The Museum
         as Site: Sixteen Projects"
       July 16-October 4

       The Banff Centre for the Arts
       Banff, Canada
       "Vocation/Vacation"
       December 3-December 13

1982   Documenta 7,
       Kassel, West-Germany
       June 19-September 28

       The Art Institute of Chicago
       Chicago, Illinois
       "74th American Exhibition"
       June 8-August 1

1983   The Banff Centre for the Arts
       Banff, Canada
       "Audio by Artists"
       January 13-February 6

       À Pierre et Marie (Part II),
       Rue d'Ulm, Paris, France, Summer 1983

Bibliography

Individual Exhibition Catalogues:

Michael Asher: Exhibitions in Europe 1972–1977: edited by R.H. Fuchs, Stedelijk van Abbe Museum, Eindhoven, 1980.

Michel Asher and Daniel Buren, edited by Gerhard Storck, Museum Haus Lange, Krefeld, 1982.

Exhibition Catalogues and Publications containing references to the work of Michael Asher or reproductions:

Ambiente Arte: Dal Futurismo alla Body Art, edited by Germano Celant, La Biennale di Venezia, Venice 1977.

Anti-Illusion: Procedures—Materials, edited by James Monte and Marcia Tucker, The Whitney Museum of American Art, New York, 1969, p. 11.

Art in Los Angeles: The Museum as Site, edited by Stephanie Barron and Maurice Tuchman, The Los Angeles County Museum of Art, Los Angeles, 1981.

Art in the Mind, edited by Athena Tacha, Oberlin College, Oberlin, 1970.

Dan Graham: Video, Architecture, Television, edited by Benjamin H.D. Buchloh, The Press of the Nova Scotia College of Art and Design, Halifax, 1979.

Documenta V, edited by Jean-Christophe Ammann and Harald Szeemann, Kassel 1972, pp. 17.85–86.

Documenta VII, Vol. I & II, edited by Saskia Bos, Kassel 1982, Vol. I, pp. 237–238, Vol. II, pp. 22–23.

Faculty Exhibition, California Institute of the Arts, School of Art and Design, Valencia, Ca., 1977.

557.087—Seattle Art Center, edited by Lucy Lippard, Seattle, 1969.

I am Alive, Los Angeles County Museum of Art, Los Angeles, 1967.

Künstler machen Pläne—andere auch, Kunsthaus Hamburg, Hamburg, 1970.

Los Angeles in the Seventies, edited by Marge Goldwater, The Fort Worth Art Museum, Fort Worth, 1977 and The Joslyn Art Museum, Joslyn, Omaha, 1979.

Michael Asher, David Askevold, Richard Long, edited by Bob Smith with contributions by Dorit Cypis, Frederick Dolan and Tom Jimmerson, Los Angeles Institute of Contemporary Art, Los Angeles, 1977.

Museums by Artists, edited by A. A. Bronson and Peggy Gale, The Art Gallery of Ontario, Toronto, 1983.

Neon-Dekorationen, edited by Rüdiger Schoettle, Munich 1978.

New Work: Southern California, University of California San Diego Art Gallery, San Diego, 1968.

Pläne und Projekte als Kunst/Plans and Projects as Art, Kunsthalle Bern, 1969.

Plans and Projects, Finch College, New York, 1973.

Performance: Textes et Documents, edited by Chantal Pontbriand, Montreal, 1981.

Prospect-Retrospect, edited by B.H.D. Buchloh, Konrad Fischer, R.H. Fuchs and John Matheson, Kunsthalle Düsseldorf, Düsseldorf, 1976.

Six Years: the dematerialization of the artwork, edited by Lucy Lippard, New York, 1973, pp. 198–199.

Skulptur—Project Section, edited by Kasper Koenig and Klaus Bussmann, Catalogue Introduction by Lazlo Glozer, Westphaelisches Landesmuseum für Kunst-und Kulturgeschichte, Münster 1977.

Spaces, edited by Jennifer Licht, The Museum of Modern Art, New York, 1970.

Ten Years of Contemporary Art Council Exhibitions, Los Angeles County Museum of Art, Bulletin Vol. XIX, No. 2, p. 41.

The Appearing/Disappearing Image/Object, Newport Harbor Art Museum, Newport, 1969.

The Betty and Monte Factor Family Collection, Pasadena Museum of Art, Pasadena, 1973.

The 73rd American Exhibition, edited by James A. Speyer and Anne Rorimer, The Art Institute of Chicago, Chicago 1979.

The 74th American Exhibition, edited by James A. Speyer and Anne Rorimer, The Art Institute of Chicago, Chicago, 1982.

3D into 2D: Drawings for Sculpture, The New York Cultural Center, New York, 1973.

24 Young Los Angeles Artists, Los Angeles County Museum of Art, Los Angeles, 1971.

Via Los Angeles, Portland Center for the Visual Arts, Portland, Ore. 1976.

Vocation—Vacation, edited by Brian MacNevin, The Walter Phillips Gallery, The Banff Centre School of the Arts, Banff, Alberta, 1983.

West Coast Now, Portland Art Museum, Portland, Oregon, 1968.

Westkunst-Art since 1939, Vol. II, *Heute*, edited by Kasper Koenig, Wallraf-Richartz Museum, Köln, 1981 n.p.

Essays:

Buchloh, Benjamin H.D., "Context-Function-Use Value," (1978) Exhibition Catalogue *Michael Asher: Exhibitions in Europe 1972–1977*, Stedelijk van Abbe Museum, Eindhoven, 1980.

———, "Michael Asher and the conclusion of Modernist Sculpture." Lecture delivered at The Art Institute of Chicago, November 7, 1979. Published in *Performance*, Exhibition Catalogue, Montreal, 1981, and in

———, The Centennial Lectures of the Art Institute of Chicago, ed. by Susan Rossen, The Art Institute of Chicago, Chicago, 1983, and french version as

———, "Michael Asher et la conclusion de la sculpture moderniste, in: *Penser l'Art contemporain, Rapports et Documents de la Biennale de Paris*, Vol. 3, 1980, pp. 169–190.

———, Allegorical Procedures: Appropriation and Montage in Contemporary Art, *Artforum*, Vol. XXI, No. 1, September 1982.

Celant, Germano, "Arte Ambientale Californiana." *Domus*, Vol. 547, June 1975, p. 52.

———, "Art as the Experience of Experience." *Casabella*, No. 402, 1975, p. 47.

———, "Minimal art, arte ambientale california, arte povera, body arte." Exhibition Catalogue *Ambiente Arte*, La Biennale di Venezia, Venice, 1977.

Fuchs, R.H. "Eindhoven: Michael Asher: 1977." Exhibition Catalogue *Michael Asher: Exhibitions in Europe 1972–1977*, Stedelijk van Abbe Museum, Eindhoven 1980.

Glozer, Laszlo "Skulpturen für eine Stadt." Exhibition Catalogue *Skulptur*, Westphälisches Landesmuseum, Münster, 1977.

Morris, Robert "The Art of Existence: Three Extra-Visual Artists' Works in Progress." *Artforum*, Vol. IX, No. 5, January 1971, pp. 28—33.

Munger, Barbara "Michael Asher: An Environmental Project." *Studio International*, Vol. 180, No. 926, October 1970, pp. 160—162.

Ratcliff, Carter "Adversary Spaces," *Arforum*, Vol. XI, No. 2, October 1972, pp. 40 ff.

Rorimer, Anne "Michael Asher: Recent Work." *Artforum*, Vol. XVIII, No. 8, April 1980, pp. 46—50.

Storck, Gerhard "Michael Asher/Daniel Buren." Exhibition Catalogue, *Michael Asher/Daniel Buren*, Museum Haus Lange, Krefeld, 1982.

Exhibition Reviews and Texts referring to Asher's work:

Antin, David, "It Reaches a Desert in Which Nothing Can Be Perceived But Feeling," *Art News*, Vol. 70, No. 1, March 1971, pp. 38—40, 66—71.

Armstrong, Lois Dickert, "Los Angeles", *Art News*, Vol. 68, No. 4, Summer 1969, p. 74.

Armstrong, Richard, "Heute-Westkunst Cologne," *Artforum*, Vol. XX, No. 1, September 1981, pp. 83—86.

Ashton, Dore, "New York Commentary," *Studio International*, Vol. 179, No. 920, March 1970, p. 118.

Battcock, Gregory, "Politics of Space: Exhibition at the Museum of Modern Art," *Artsmagazine* Vol. 44, No. 4, February 1970, pp. 40—43.

Barron, Stephanie, "The Museum as Site: Sixteen Projects," *Art in Los Angeles*, Exhibition Catalogue, The Los Angeles County Museum of Art, Los Angeles, 1981.

Bruggen, Coosje van, "In the mist things appear larger," Exhibition catalogue *Documenta VII*, Vol. II, pp. ix—xii, Kassel 1982.

Buettner, S., "6 L.A. Artists," *Artweek*, Vol. VII, No. 5, January 31, 1976, p. 16.

Buchloh, Benjamin H.D., "Westkunst-Modernism's Restkunst?," *Art Monthly*, Vol. 50, October 1981, pp. 3—5.

_______, idem in: *Parachute*, Vol. 24 Fall 1981, pp. 17—21.

_______, "Documenta VII: A Dictionary of Received Ideas," *October*, Vol. 22, Fall 1982, pp. 104—126.

Burton, Scott, "Time on their Hands: Summer Exhibitions at the Whitney and the Guggenheim", *Art News*, Vol. 68, No. 4, pp. 40—43.

Crichton, Fenella, "London—Lisson Gallery," *Art International*, Vol. 17, November 1973, p. 46.

Foote, Nancy, "New York Reviews: Michael Asher —The Clocktower, "*Artforum*, Vol. XIV, No. 1., June 1976, p. 64.

Frank, Peter, "New York Reviews:—The Clocktower Gallery", *Art News*, Vol. 75, No. 7, September 1976, p. 122.

Garver, Thomas H. "Los Angeles", *Artforum*, Vol. VIII, No. 5, January 1970, pp. 75—6.

Gianelli, Ida, "Michael Asher: van Abbemuseum Eindhoven," *Saman*, estate 10, 1977.

Glueck, Grace, "Museum Beckoning Space Explorers," *New York Times*, Friday, January 2, 1970.

Graevenitz, A. von, "Eindhoven: van Abbemuseum; Ausstellung: Michael Asher," *Pantheon*, Vol. 35, October 1977, p. 367.

Graham, Dan, "Signs," *Artforum*, Vol. XIX, No. 8, April 1981, pp. 38–43.

———, "Not Post-Modernism," *Artforum*, Vol. XX, No. 4 December 1981, pp. 50–58.

Kibbins, Gary, "The Enduring of the Artsystem," *Parachute*, Vol. XXIX, December 1982, pp. 4–8.

Kirshner, Judith, "The 74th American Exhibition at the Art Institute of Chicago," *Artforum*, Vol. XXI, No. 2, October 1982, pp. 74–76.

Kramer, Hilton, "Participating Esthetics", *New York Times*, Sunday, January 11, 1970.

Leider, Philip, "New York", *Artforum* Vol. VIII, No. 6, February 1970, p. 69

Marioni, Tom, "Out Front," *Vision Magazine*, Vol. I, September 1975, pp. 8–11.

Marmer, Nancy, "Los Angeles: Michael Asher-Claire Copley and Morgan Thomas Galleries," *Artforum*, Vol. XV, No. 9, May 1977, p. 74.

———, "Isms on the Rhine," *Art in America*, Vol. 69, No. 9, November 1981, pp. 112–123.

Plagens, Peter, "Los Angeles: Los Angeles County Museum," *Artforum*, Vol. X, No. 2, October 1971, p. 87.

———, "Maria Nordman," *Artforum* Vol. XII, No. 6, February 1974, pp. 40–1.

———, "Michael Asher: the thing of it is . . . ," *Artforum*, Vol. X, No. 8, pp. 76–78.

———, "Michael Asher: Claire Copley Gallery," *Artforum*,. Vol. XIII, No. 4, December 1974, pp. 83–84.

———, "Site Wars (Site Specific Work at the Los Angeles County Museum)," *Art in America*, Vol. 70, January 1982, pp. 92–93.

Ratcliff, Carter, "New York Letter: Spaces," *Art International*, Vol. 14, No. 2, February 1970, p. 78.

Rorimer, Anne, Introduction, Exhibition Catalogue, *The 74th American Exhibition*, The Art Institute of Chicago, Chicago, 1982.

Sharp, Willoughby, "New Directions in Southern Californian Sculpture," *Artsmagazine*, Vol. 44, No. 8, Summer 1970, pp. 35–38.

Shirey, David L., "Art in Space," *Newsweek*, January 12, 1970.

Singermann, Howard, "Art in Los Angeles-Los Angeles County Museum," *Artforum*, Vol. XX, No. 7, March 1982, pp. 75–77.

Tousley, Nancy, "Last of artist's three part project his most complex," *Calgary Herald*, December 12, 1981.

Townsend-Gault, Charlotte, "Vocation-Vacation," *Vanguard Magazine*, April 1982, pp. 22–25.

Tuyl, Gijs, "Skulptuur: Horen, Zien en Vœlen," *Openbaar Kunstbezit*, Vol. XXIII, No. 3, June 1979, pp. 70–79.

Wallace, Ian, "Revisionism and its discontents;" *Vanguard Magazine*, Volume 10, No. 7, September 1981, pp. 12–19.

Wasserman, Emily, "New York," *Artforum* Vol. VIII, No. 1, September 1969, p. 57.

Wilson, William, "Work of 7 Artists in Newport Display," *Los Angeles Times*, May 1969.

Wortz, Melinda, "Looking Inward: Claire Copley Gallery, Los Angeles," *Art News*, Vol. 73, December 1974, pp. 60–61.

Wortz, Melinda, "Psychological Manipulation: Michael Asher, Morgan Thomas at Claire Copley Gallery, Inc. Claire Copley Gallery Inc. at Morgan Thomas, Los Angeles," *Art News*, Vol. 76, May 1977, p. 105.

THE NOVA SCOTIA SERIES

SOURCE MATERIALS OF THE CONTEMPORARY ARTS

BERNHARD LEITNER
THE ARCHITECTURE OF
LUDWIG WITTGENSTEIN
7¹/₂'' X 11'' 128 PAGES
$30.00 CLOTH

CLAES OLDENBURG
RAW NOTES
7¹/₂ X 11'' 544 PAGES
OUT OF PRINT

YVONNE RAINER
WORK 1961-73
7¹/₂'' X 11'' 364 PAGES
$17.50 PAPER $23.00 CLOTH

SIMONE FORTI
HANDBOOK IN MOTION
6¹/₂'' X 9'' 144 PAGES
$12.00 PAPER

STEVE REICH
WRITINGS ABOUT MUSIC
7¹/₂'' X 9'' 80 PAGES
$9.00 PAPER

DONALD JUDD
COMPLETE WRITINGS 1959-1975
8¹/₂'' X 11'' 240 PAGES
$20.00 PAPER $28.00 CLOTH

HANS HAACKE
FRAMING AND BEING FRAMED
8'' X 10'' 165 PAGES
$12.00 PAPER $20.00 CLOTH

MICHAEL SNOW
COVER TO COVER
7'' X 8'' 360 PAGES
$15.00 PAPER

PAUL-EMILE BORDUAS
ECRITS/WRITINGS 1942-1958
7¹/₂'' X 11'' 160 PAGES
$12.00 PAPER $17.50 CLOTH

DAN GRAHAM
VIDEO-ARCHITECTURE—TELEVISION
7¹/₂'' X 11'' 89 PAGES
$12.00 PAPER $20.00 CLOTH

CARL ANDRE/HOLLIS FRAMPTON
12 DIALOGUES 1962-1963
9'' X 11¹/₂'' 134 PAGES
$20.00 PAPER $30.00 CLOTH

DANIEL BUREN
LES COULEURS: SCULPTURES
LES FORMES: PEINTURES
9'' X 12'' 73 PAGES
$23.00 PAPER (FRENCH OR ENGLISH)

MINING PHOTOGRAPHS AND
OTHER PICTURES 1948-1968
PHOTOGRAPHS BY LESLIE SHEDDEN
ESSAYS BY ALLAN SEKULA AND
DON MACGILLIVRAY
10¹/₂'' X 8¹/₂'' 280 PAGES
$25.00 PAPER

MODERNISM AND MODERNITY
EDITED BY SERGE GUILBAUT
6'' x 9'' 230 PAGES
$15.00 PAPER

NOVA SCOTIA PAMPHLETS

MARTHA ROSLER
3 WORKS
11'' X 8'' 87 PAGES
$12.50 PAPER

JENNY HOLZER
TRUISMS AND ESSAYS
8¹/₂'' X 8¹/₂'' 154 PAGES
$15.00 PAPER

GERHARD RICHTER
128 DETAILS FROM A PICTURE (HALIFAX 1978)
7¹/₂'' X 10¹/₂'' 65 PAGES
$15.00 PAPER

THE PRESS OF THE NOVA SCOTIA COLLEGE OF ART AND DESIGN
5163 DUKE STREET, HALIFAX, NOVA SCOTIA, CANADA, B3J 3J6

Primary Information
155 Freeman Street, Ground Floor
Brooklyn, NY 11222
www.primaryinformation.org

Designer (1983): Michael Asher and Gerald Pryor
Cover Designer (1983): Sarah Pugh
Managing Editor (2021): James Hoff
Managing Designer (2021): Rick Myers

Printed by die Keure

Michael Asher's *Writings 1973–1983 on Works 1969–1979* was originally copublished in 1983 by The Press of the Nova Scotia College of Art and Design and The Museum of Contemporary Art, Los Angeles, and printed in two versions. One version was printed in an edition of 1,500 bearing the sole imprint of The Press of the Nova Scotia College of Art and Design (NSCAD) on its cover. A second version, printed in an edition of 500, bears the imprint of NSCAD and The Museum of Contemporary Art, Los Angeles, (MOCA) on its cover and was further distinguished by the documentation, on the inside of the dust jacket, of a work by Asher for MOCA's *In Context* exhibition series (1983–85). This 2021 book is a facsimile of the second version of the 1983 book with limited corrections to images and captions only. A list of corrections and errata follows.

The Board of Michael Asher Foundation would like to thank Primary Information for its enthusiasm and dedication in bringing this book back into circulation. The Foundation is grateful for the support of the Nova Scotia College of Art and Design and The Museum of Contemporary Art, Los Angeles, and it also wishes to thank all the photographers, draftspersons, and others who contributed materials to the book. The Board further extends its gratitude to Benjamin H. D. Buchloh, Yoko Kanayama, and Dee Williams for sharing their knowledge, and to Christine Steiner for providing invaluable guidance. The Board also wants to acknowledge the extraordinary commitment and conscientious work of Poppy Coles, Karen Dunbar, Roxy Gonzalez, Justin Klasa, and Karin Lanzoni in the realization of this project and offers its deepest appreciation.

Primary Information would like to thank Poppy Coles, Allison Dubinsky, Karen Dunbar, Miriam Kazteff, and Craig Leonard.

This publication is made possible through the generous support of The Graham Foundation for Advanced Studies in the Fine Arts.

Primary Information is a 501(c)(3) nonprofit organization that receives generous support through grants from Michael Asher Foundation, the Greenwich Collection Ltd, the John W. and Clara C. Higgins Foundation, the Willem de Kooning Foundation, the Henry Luce Foundation, the National Endowment for the Arts, the New York City Department of Cultural Affairs in partnership with the City Council, the New York State Council on the Arts with the support of Governor Andrew Cuomo and the New York State Legislature, the Orbit Fund, the Stichting Egress Foundation, Teiger Foundation, VIA Art Fund, The Jacques Louis Vidal Charitable Fund, The Andy Warhol Foundation for the Visual Arts, the Wilhelm Family Foundation, and individuals worldwide. Primary Information is a W.A.G.E. certified organization.

NOTES ON CORRECTIONS, ERRATA, AND NAMES OF INDIVIDUALS

For this publication, Michael Asher Foundation followed the notes and directions for corrections that Asher made in case of a possible future edition, as compiled by the artist's assistant. Since these notes and directions focused on images and captions, all corrections in this publication have been made to the images and captions exclusively and are listed below. No corrections have been made to the front and back matter, contents, entry titles and texts, exhibitions list, and bibliography. Errors in these parts of the 1983 book known to the Foundation at the time of this printing are acknowledged in the lists of errata and names of individuals that follow.

CORRECTIONS TO IMAGES AND CAPTIONS

Factual errors in the image captions, including attributions, have been corrected and are listed below. Spelling errors have been corrected without acknowledgement. Images that were incorrectly oriented have been corrected and are listed below. Images of poor quality or legibility have been improved where possible without acknowledgement.

p. 1	In the caption, "11' 3/16''" has been corrected to "11 3/16"."
p. 2	In the first caption, "Photograph by Michael Asher" has been corrected to "Photographs by Michael Asher."
pp. 14–15	The captions on pages 14 and 15 have been switched.
p. 22	In the bottom caption, "Axonometric drawing" has been corrected to "Ground plan and elevations."
p. 29	In the caption, "Alternate" has been added and "south-west" has been corrected to "northeast."
p. 33	In the caption, "Photographs by Frank Thomas" has been added.
p. 44	In the left-hand caption, "*24 Young Los Angeles Artists*" has been corrected to "'24 Young Los Angeles Artists'" (i.e., italics have been removed and quotation marks added).
p. 52	In the fourth caption from the top, "north-east" has been corrected to "northwest."
p. 67	In the first caption, "north" has been corrected to "southwest."
p. 68	The orientation of the middle photograph has been corrected by flipping it horizontally.
p. 71	The orientation of the top photograph has been corrected by rotating it 90 degrees counterclockwise.
p. 74	In the bottom caption, "Photographs by Paul McMahon" has been added.
p. 76	In the bottom caption, "Photograph by Nicholas Logsdail" has been added.
p. 79	In the bottom caption, "Photographs by Nicholas Logsdail" has been added.
p. 81	In the caption, "Photograph by Nicholas Logsdail" has been added.
p. 106	In the bottom left-hand caption, "Indicated is the placement of the directory board inside the lobby that was used for this exhibition." has been corrected to "The directory board inside the lobby that was used for the exhibition is not indicated on the plan."
p. 109	In the caption, "*Vision Magazine*, Volume 1" has been corrected to "*Vision* magazine, Number 1."
p. 111	In the caption, "Vision Magazine" has been corrected to "*Vision* magazine."
p. 115	In the bottom caption, "Detail of groundplan of master control room showing camera angle during installation/program. Drawing by Michael Asher." has been corrected to "Detail of ground plan of master control room."
p. 116	In the caption, "Photographs by Michael Asher" has been added.
p. 121	In the bottom captions, the attributions "Michael Asher" and "Edmund Shea" have been switched.
p. 122	In the caption, "Plan and elevations" has been corrected to "Elevation."
p. 124	The orientation of the left-hand photograph has been corrected by flipping it horizontally. In the bottom caption, "Photographs by Edmund Shea" has been corrected to "Photograph by Edmund Shea."
p. 125	In the bottom caption, "Photograph by Thomas Struth" has been added.
p. 133	In the captions for the fourteenth floor, the third from the top, "Photograph by John Dent" has been corrected to "Photograph by Helen Winkler." In the fourth from the top, "east" has been corrected to "west." In the captions for the thirteenth floor, the second from the top, "Photograph by Michael Asher" has been corrected to "Photograph by Balthasar Burkhard."
p. 137	In the caption, "Photograph by Balthasar Burkhard" has been corrected to "Photograph by Michael Asher."

p. 146   In the top image caption, "View of installation with passage toward other exhibition areas." has been removed.

p. 157   In the caption, "Photographs by Gary Kruger" has been corrected to "Photograph by Gary Krueger."

p. 160   In the bottom caption, "Faculty Exhibition and Student Exhibition Catalogues." has been corrected to "*Faculty Exhibition* and *Student Exhibition* catalogues."

p. 173   In the caption, "Photographs by Rudolf Wakonigg" has been added.

p. 175   In the caption, "Photograph by Michael Asher" has been corrected to "Photographs by Michael Asher."

p. 183   In the top caption, "Photograph by Gerhard Martini" has been corrected to "Photograph by Michael Asher."

p. 186   The middle and bottom captions have been switched.

p. 193   In the bottom caption, "All photographs by Ruby Hagerbaumer." has been corrected to "Photograph of the permanent collection on page 195 by Michael Asher. All other photographs by Ruby Hagerbaumer."

p. 195   In the middle right-hand caption, "west" has been corrected to "east."

p. 197   In the bottom caption, "Photographs by Tom Van Eynde" has been added.

p. 204   In the top caption, "Photograph by Tom Van Eynde" has been added. In the bottom caption, "Photograph by Michael Asher" has been added.

p. 205   In the top caption, "Photograph by Tom Van Eynde" has been added. In the bottom caption, "Photographs by Michael Asher" has been corrected to "Photograph by Michael Asher."

p. 206   The orientation of the top and bottom images has been corrected by flipping them horizontally. In the bottom caption, "Photographs by Michael Asher" has been corrected to "Photographs by Tom Van Eynde."

ERRATA

The following list indicates errors to the front and back matter, contents, entry titles and texts, exhibitions list, and bibliography in the 1983 book. These errors (with one exception, noted below) were identified by Michael Asher Foundation but not corrected in the 2021 book.

Contents

Contents, pp. 118–37   Note: The entries that start on page 118 and page 125 are out of order chronologically. (The artist also identified this error.)

Entries

p. 42   In the first column, second paragraph, "6 foot-4-inch-by-8-foot-9 inch" should read "6-foot-10-inch-by-8-foot-9-inch."

pp. 43–46   In the first column, fourth paragraph, "north-south" should read "east-west." Throughout the rest of the running text in this entry, the directional information should be corrected by turning the cardinal and intercardinal points 90 degrees counterclockwise. I.e., "west" should read "south"; "south" should read "east"; "east" should read "north"; and "southwest" should read "southeast."

p. 105   In the information transcribed from the exhibition flyer (on page 104), the zip code "99057" should read "90057."

p. 112   In the first paragraph, "January 19, 1976" should read "January 18, 1976." In the last paragraph, "*TV-Review*" should read "*TV PREVUE*."

p. 193   Note: In the first column, third paragraph, "Logsdail Gallery" refers to Lisson Gallery.

Exhibitions and Bibliography

The following list indicates errors to dates and publication issue numbers; misspelled names of individuals are listed in the Names of Individuals section.

p. 224   In the first column, first entry, which begins "Los Angeles County Museum of Art," "1967" should read "1966."

p. 226   In the second column, second entry, which begins "*I am Alive*," "1967" should read "1966."

p. 227   In the first column, first entry, which begins "*Spaces*," "1970" should read "1969," and in the tenth entry, which begins "*Vocation—Vacation*," "1983" should read "1981."

p. 228   In the second column, ninth entry, which begins "Foote, Nancy," "Vol. XIV, No. 1" should read "Vol. XIV, No. 10."

NAMES OF INDIVIDUALS

Misspelled names of individuals have only been corrected in the captions. The correct spelling for all misspelled names that were identified by Michael Asher Foundation in the 1983 book appears below.

1983 Book	*Correct Spelling*	
Jean-Christophe Amman	Jean-Christophe Ammann	p. 57
May Beebe	Mary Beebe	p. 112
Paul-Emile Borduas	Paul-Émile Borduas	Front matter, p. 231
Allan Charlton	Alan Charlton	p. 176
Edward Cornacio	Edward Cornachio	pp. 46, 48
Raphael Ferrer	Rafael Ferrer	p. 210
Lazlo Glozer	Laszlo Glozer	p. 226
Paul Guerrero	Raul Guerrero	p. 156
Than Hyun	Tahn Hyun	p. XI
Louis L. Kahn	Louis I. Kahn	p. 184
Gary Kruger	Gary Krueger	pp. 99, 156, 157
Sol Lewitt	Sol LeWitt	p. 199
Phil Linars	Phil Linhares	p. 4
Walter de Maria	Walter De Maria	p. 166
Alan McKay	Allan McKay	p. 101
Ciacia Nicostro	Ciacia Nicastro	p. 121
James A. Speyer	A. James Speyer	p. 227
Howard Singermann	Howard Singerman	p. 229
Gijs Tuyl	Gijs van Tuyl	p. 229